# The
# Railway
# Interest

# Geoffrey Alderman

Lecturer in the Department of History,
Royal Holloway College, University of London

# The Railway Interest

Leicester University Press
1973

First published in 1973 by
Leicester University Press

Distributed in North America by
Humanities Press Inc., New York

Designed by Arthur Lockwood

Set in 'Monotype' Bulmer
Printed in Great Britain
by W & J Mackay Limited, Chatham
Bound by James Burn (Bookbinders) Ltd, Esher

ISBN 0 7185 1111 5

# Contents

To my parents

# Preface

Industrial growth does not take place in a political vacuum, nor do businessmen refrain from involving themselves in politics. This book attempts to trace the rise and fall of one such business group, the railway interest. It is a study concerned with group politics, with backbench politics, and with aspects of administrative and industrial history. Moreover it tells a story which, I believe, throws new light on the development of political groupings in the United Kingdom.

I have drawn on a wide variety of sources, and owe debts of gratitude to many who have allowed me to consult source material in their possession. In particular I am grateful to the Beaverbrook Library, the University of Birmingham, the Bishopsgate Institute, the British Museum, the British Transport Historical Records Department of the British Railways Board, the Kent Archives Office, Maidstone, the National Trust at

Hughenden Manor, the Public Record Office, and the University of Sheffield. I must also express my thanks to Earl St Aldwyn for permission to consult the papers of Sir Michael Hicks Beach at Williamstrip Park, to Mr Mark Bonham Carter for permission to consult the Asquith MSS. in the Bodleian Library, Oxford, and to Dr J. F. A. Mason, the Librarian at Christ Church, Oxford, for permission to consult the Salisbury Papers.

In all cases where official and private papers were consulted I received much help from the various staffs concerned. My thanks are especially due, and are gratefully given, to the staffs of the Bodleian Library, the British Library of Political and Economic Science at the London School of Economics, the offices of the British Transport Historical Records Department in London, York and Edinburgh, and the National Register of Archives, London. In addition I have derived much benefit from conversations with and suggestions from Dr P. S. Bagwell, Professor T. C. Barker, Mr Peter L. Boulton, Secretary to Leicester University Press, Mr E. H. Fowkes, the Archivist of the British Railways Board, Professor Jack Simmons and Mr K. Tite. Mr A. F. Thompson supervised the research for the University of Oxford doctoral thesis upon which this book is based. His help, encouragement and understanding have proved invaluable.

I am indebted to the following for permission to reproduce copyright material: the University of Birmingham; Mr Mark Bonham Carter; the British Transport Historical Records Department of the British Railways Board; and the Marquess of Salisbury. Transcripts of Crown-copyright records in the Public Record Office appear by permission of the Controller of H.M. Stationery Office.

The knowledge put at my disposal by those whom I have had the good fortune to consult has saved me from many errors. For the errors and imperfections which remain I alone must claim responsibility.

Geoffrey Alderman

# Chapter 1

# Introduction

The study of interest groups, and the examination of British politics in terms of such groups, is a field of research which historians of British political development have largely ignored. In the United States, by contrast, a more 'open' political system, in which the phenomenon of pressure politics has long been known and accepted, has given rise to a substantial body of literature on the subject. In particular, all who study social pressures must acknowledge their debt to the pioneering work of the American journalist Arthur Bentley. It was Bentley who demonstrated the dangers in thinking of pressure groups as being essentially outside the political system, trying to make an impact upon that system. There are very few pressure groups which are not an integral part of that system.[1] Yet though Bentley pointed to this lesson more than 60 years ago, British historians and students of British politics have been slow to learn it. Detailed and documented case studies are all too few; those which examine the work of a pressure group in its political setting are fewer still.[2]

Much effort has however been devoted to the classification of groups. Political scientists, though differing as to details, seem agreed that a pressure group is any group of persons who band together for a common purpose to be achieved through the use, or the threat of the use, of pressures or sanctions, usually directed against the government and its administrative machinery. 'Lobby' is a much wider term covering all promotional groups who try to influence public bodies. The definition of an interest group, especially as applied to nineteenth-century British politics, is more complicated. It may be noted here that an interest group is a special sort of pressure group in two respects: first, the purpose an interest group has in view, or the position it seeks to defend or enhance, is one in which its members have a personal stake, or 'interest'; second, whereas a pressure group need not, of itself, have any political power, an interest group does exercise direct political power.

Hence the impact of interest groups on party politics cannot be over-emphasized. As Bentley himself put it:

> Parties may be found which are best to be described as the special organization for political activity of interest groups, especially of classes, direct. Others are rather the organization in a representative degree of a set of such interest groups.[3]

The implication is clear: a proper understanding of the formation and working of party structures in Great Britain requires an examination of the interest groups out of which these structures have evolved. For the modern period (and with some glances backward to the nineteenth century and earlier) a start has already been made by Professor Beer.[4] Within the field of nineteenth-century British history there have also been case studies of certain pressure groups, such as the Tariff Reformers.[5] But it remains true that no systematic study of the role of the more numerous but less propaganda-minded groups in the nineteenth- and twentieth-century political scene in Great Britain has yet been undertaken. The present work is offered as a contribution towards filling the gap. It is offered, moreover, in the belief that the study of the great emotional issues in politics is not very conducive to the understanding of the day-to-day workings of a political system. The historian who wishes to illuminate the mechanics of party structure in Great Britain must look to the everyday issues, which are a finer testing ground of political loyalties and political cohesion.

This inevitably leads one away from the statesmen in the centre of the political arena, to focus attention instead upon the backbench M.P. In a general way the private M.P. before 1868 has been the subject of socio-logical study and, statistically, of political study.[6] Even for the pre-1868 period, however, the importance of party ties is still in dispute.[7] Except where they were involved in major political controversies, the activities of the 'interested' backbench M.P.s have not hitherto been closely investi-gated. For the period after 1868 the assumption still prevails that the growth of political parties and party discipline robbed the private M.P.s of their independence. Indeed, the Reform Act of 1867 has received praise because it allegedly "helped to restore the clear-cut two party system in the country and in Parliament and ended the dangerous drift towards a system of groups."[8] In fact the influence and dominance of party loyalties after 1867 has been regarded in standard works on the period as all-pervasive. The springs of those loyalties have remained hidden behind the façade of the party system.

One problem in particular has long awaited treatment. It concerns the movement which resulted in a break-up of the Liberal Party and the emergence of a new Conservative Party. In the mid-nineteenth century the Conservative Party was predominantly the party of the land and the Church. The Liberal Party was the party of merchants, traders, indus-trialists. Of course this interpretation should not be pressed too far. Amongst railway director-M.P.s, for instance, a strong Conservative ele-ment was always present; Joseph Pease and George Carr Glyn on the Liberal side were matched by the Denisons, George Hudson and Daniel Gooch on the Conservative side. But certainly by the early twentieth century the Conservative Party had become the party of the 'bosses', the party of big business. Statistics show that the transformation occurred in the late nineteenth century.[9] Yet over-emphasis upon a few major political issues, such as Home Rule and parliamentary reform, as the springs of political loyalty in this period, has led to over-simplification, so that the fundamental causes of this important realignment in British politics have been largely ignored.

Obviously the answer to this problem involves detailed analysis of some fundamental alterations in the basis of mid-Victorian society, and especially within the middle classes of that society. The surface of the problem has hardly been scratched. But the Conservative victories in Lancashire, Westminster and Middlesex in the election of 1868 (which the Liberals won) clearly reflected the rise of Conservatism amongst *nouveaux riches* who had moved away from areas frequented by the poorer classes of society, and thus also from the religious, social and political influence of such areas. Old political cultures were disappearing; suburban Toryism had arrived. By the time of the 1874 election even radicals had to acknowledge that the trend was unmistakable.[10] Moreover, whatever the causes of this trend, it seems certain that the relationship between party interests and business interests occupied a central position in this process. Of those business interests, the railway interest was one of the most dominant.

Professor Finer has defined interest groups as "economic associations which exercise political power; also, they are politically active groups which exercise economic power."[11] In the nineteenth century, however, the term had a somewhat different connotation; it was reserved for commercial, agricultural and religious groups which could exercise some form of political pressure. Of these groups the railway interest was by far the most infamous. This was not simply because of the economic importance of the railway companies, the size of the undertakings, and the consequent importance of the railway directors, but also because of the apparently large representation which the companies could boast in the legislature.[12]

The lobbying of the government by commercial groups in Great Britain has a long history. It grew in importance and developed political overtones in the eighteenth century because the economic and political climates were favourable to it. Moreover it was fostered by the doctrine of political representation then dominant, and championed by Burke, which stressed that it was the duty of an M.P. to represent the interests of the whole community, as well as those of his own constituency and his own electors. Though such a concept ruled out that of the mandate, it acted as a positive encouragement to the right of the legitimate 'interests', that is the social and economic groups, of which the nation was composed, to be represented in Parliament. Thus whilst extra-parliamentary organizations, such as the Yorkshire Association of 1779–80, formed with the avowed aim of putting pressure upon M.P.s, were regarded with suspicion, the political power exercised by such groups as the East India Company and the Bank of England, power based partly upon a bloc of M.P.s and partly upon financial importance, was taken for granted.[13]

The period of political and economic change which followed the accession of George III witnessed a tremendous expansion of the political activities of commercial groups. The West India Interest formed its own Society of West India Merchants to protect the interests of the colonies from the home government.[14] The establishment of the first British chambers of commerce, in New York and Jersey in 1768, was followed by the formation of others within the British Isles, at Glasgow and Belfast in 1783, at Edinburgh in 1785, and at Manchester in 1794. During the

1770s and 1780s important groups of manufacturers, like the Staffordshire potters and the Midland ironmasters, set up trade associations and undertook the organization of interest groups to serve their needs.[15] At this time, too, the expansion of canal-building gave ample opportunity to M.P.s and canal promoters to combine together for their mutual advancement.[16] Nor was it long before employers' organizations sprang up, as at Sheffield in 1814, to resist the demands of trade unions.[17]

Thus by the beginning of the railway age not only was the existence of interest groups taken for granted, but the activities of commercial groups in the political arena were well established. But such activities remained local or regional, without co-ordination. Garbett's General Chamber of Manufacturers, formed in 1785 to oppose Pitt's proposed commercial treaty with Ireland, fell apart the following year over a similar treaty with France. Only when a whole industry was threatened by government action were concerted efforts made to organize counter-measures in and out of Parliament.[18] Local chambers of commerce remained for much of the nineteenth century narrow-minded and inward-looking. Even the formation of the Association of British Chambers of Commerce, in 1860, had little immediate effect. The ineffectiveness of many early farming organizations, such as the Farmers' Club of 1842, led to the formation in 1879 of a far more militant body, the Farmers' Alliance.[19] The British Iron Trade Association was not established till 1876.[20] The shipping interest remained divided even after the formation of the Chamber of Shipping in 1878; the Shipping Federation, organized primarily to fight trade unionism, dated only from 1890, whilst the Shipowners' Parliamentary Committee, whose task it was to look after shipping interests in Parliament, was not formed till 1893.[21] Generally speaking, most industries had to wait until well into the late nineteenth century, when falling profits and higher costs produced a greater sense of urgency, before they obtained national centrally-controlled representative bodies, geared to defend them from political and governmental attack.

To this pattern the railway companies were an exception.[22] Though geographically scattered, many of the large and important companies were based in London whilst some, like the Midland Railway, which were not, still had offices in the metropolis.[23] Moreover they were all the children of Parliament, owing their very existence to private Acts which the promoters of each line had been obliged to steer through the laborious and costly private bill procedure of the two Houses. Initially they required support from individual M.P.s both to smooth the passing of their own Acts and to bar the way to rival schemes. In 1844 Gladstone, then at the Board of

Trade, was responsible for a rule requiring a declaration of disinterested-ness from M.P.s serving on railway bill committees, and in 1855 this declaration was required of members of committees hearing any opposed private bills. There was an old rule of the Commons that the vote of any member with a direct and pecuniary interest might be challenged and, if the House so decided, disallowed. But challenges were few, and only in 1892 were any votes actually disallowed, on an issue involving the votes of three M.P.s who were shareholders in the British East Africa Company, to which the government proposed to give a grant in aid for a preliminary railway survey.[24] In any case, none of these restrictions extended to speaking or proposing motions or amendments. Nor could they interfere with the influence a railway M.P. might choose to exert outside the chamber.

Therefore, as merely the latest in a long line of interest groups in Par-liament, the birth of a railway interest went unquestioned and unnoticed.[25] But as railway companies began to be threatened with general regulatory legislation, the railway interest in Parliament acquired a new importance. The influence which M.P.s could exert nationally and locally made it more than desirable to offer them railway directorships. With the rapid growth of the railway system, and hence of the number of railway M.P.s, in the 1840s, the railway interest came into its own.

Until 1867, however, the railway interest could hardly be called a united body of men. For the railways this was a period of growth and expansion, of bitter rivalries and intense competition. The main parlia-mentary concern of the companies was with their own private bills and the bills of their neighbours and competitors. Parliamentary agents were recruited and parliamentary committees set up by the companies to look after company interests. Outside the railway world companies exerted their influence mainly by diplomacy, bribery, petitions, and through specialized railway journals. Some companies, in a few towns, could exert electoral influence, but such instances were isolated.[26] Where such in-fluence was exerted, a law of diminishing returns applied; by the time of the 1868 election companies were going out of their way to guarantee their employees the "utmost freedom" in casting their votes.[27] Thus though in relation to Parliament and the government the railway companies could undoubtedly have exercised considerable influence, they did not generally do so in spite of the ever-increasing number of director-M.P.s. Permanent joint action was inhibited by company rivalry.

But then joint action was rarely needed. Labour problems were vir-tually non-existent, for the early railwaymen were ruled with an iron discipline and a great deal of paternalism, both of which stifled early attempts to organize trade unions.[28] As for governments, they rarely posed threats to the companies as a whole. This was not because the companies collectively presented no problems to government policy. The reverse was true. The railways were regarded, rightly or wrongly, as monopolistic. In the early days of railway promotion it was thought they would perform much the same service as canals or turnpikes; that is, that the companies would act simply as toll collectors to maintain 'roads' upon which the public would be at liberty to run carriages and wagons, and that competition between the carriers would ensure good standards of service. Developments which accompanied the operation of the first trunk lines, in the 1830s, and which resulted in the railway companies themselves becoming carriers, showed that this had been a mistaken idea. The dangers to public safety, individual favours in the form of lower rates or extra facilities granted to selected traders, but above all the fear of monopoly, forced Whig and Tory governments to grapple with the problems of railway regulation.

But the railway companies, conceived, financed, built and run by private enterprise alone, having their origin in Acts of Parliament obtained, very often, only after costly and protracted struggles, naturally regarded with extreme suspicion any attempt to interfere with their working. Any scheme to increase government control over them they regarded with positive hostility. The private Acts were regarded as sacred agreements, voluntarily come to by Parliament and the companies, which ought not afterwards to be unilaterally abrogated. As one railway director put it:

> the railway companies had obtained their Acts subject to certain conditions which had been well considered with a view to the protection both of public and private interests. The bargain had been made: Parliament had already sealed its conditions, and shareholders had invested their money under them, and it would not now be right to impose additional liabilities upon them.[29]

The companies had the funds, the administrative organization and the legal and technical expertise with which to fight the government. The government, by contrast, had few experts and a Department – the Railway Department of the Board of Trade – which relied more on persuasion than on compulsion, and which did not acquire any real 'teeth' until the very end of the nineteenth century.[30] Thus in the period up to 1868 there were few important Acts of railway regulation; hence, as the companies themselves were content to be left alone, there were few occasions on which they felt the need to act in concert.

The earliest instance of such joint action occurred in May 1838, when railway representatives from 18 companies met at the offices of the London & Birmingham Railway, Euston Square, to consider the proceedings of a Select Committee set up to investigate the carriage of Post Office mails by railway. When the government introduced a bill on the subject, a railway committee managed to obtain some concessions.[31] In 1839, when railway affairs were again under parliamentary scrutiny, a "Railway Society" was set up, ostensibly to promote an interest in railways, but actually to protect the companies from impending legislation. Organized by the legal firm of Messrs Burke and Venables of Parliament Street, Westminster, its leading figure was George Carr Glyn, chairman of the London & Birmingham. The society survived a few months but was then dissolved.[32] But it is interesting to note that the society regarded its main duty as that of keeping a watch "upon all proceedings in Parliament at all likely to affect railway interests", and prided itself that the President of the Board of Trade, Poulett Thompson, "had recognized the Society as the organ through which he should in future seek for any information required on the subject of Railways."[33]

The habit of co-operation survived. There is some evidence that Burke and Venables acted on behalf of the companies in 1840, when a railway regulation bill was before Parliament.[34] In January 1841, threatened with safety legislation which would have given the Board of Trade wide powers over the railways, the companies sent delegates to a conference at Birmingham to consider preventative and remedial action. A commitee set up to watch parliamentary proceedings on this matter was financed by subscriptions from the companies concerned.[35] The following year some companies organized a deputation to the Chancellor of the Exchequer on the subject of the passenger duty.[36]

The first large-scale campaign by the railway interest against the government came in 1844. The occasion was the introduction by Gladstone of a bill which, amongst other things, sought to prescribe the terms by which the railways might eventually have been nationalized.[37] Publication of the bill caused a furore in railway circles. "If it is suffered to pass," one journal predicted, "farewell to all private enterprise in this country. Such an invasion of private rights and vested interests never was . . . before contemplated."[38] Burke and Venables again took a prominent part in marshalling opposition amongst the railway companies. A great meeting of railway representatives in London resolved to send a deputation to Peel.[39] On 1 July 1844 a deputation consisting of representatives of 29 railway companies, the united capitals of which exceeded £50 million, and headed by George Hudson, saw Peel, Gladstone and Lord Granville Somerset. The government refused to postpone the measure.[40] The companies knew they could not influence sufficient votes to defeat the bill, but they determined to make as much fuss as possible.[41] Publicity against the bill was sent to the newspapers. Petitions were presented to Parliament. There was much lobbying of M.P.s. At the same time a fund was opened and subscriptions invited, and obtained, from individual companies towards the expenses of the campaign. *Herapath* warned that Gladstone "may find it easier to carry his bill than to work it."[42]

At the second reading of the bill both Peel and Gladstone expressed amazement and determination, but also anger. Gladstone was inclined to blame the whole agitation upon parliamentary agents and solicitors afraid of proposals to cut the cost of passing railway bills.[43] In reality, though, the government was badly shaken. On 10 July Hudson addressed an open letter to Gladstone in answer to his remarks in the Commons.[44] A week later the two men met to discuss a compromise. The result was that of the original bill's 48 clauses, half were abandoned and others modified; in particular the state purchase clauses were made more favourable to the companies.[45] Whether Peel or Gladstone was behind these concessions, the reason for them is clear. The chances of the bill passing that session would have been remote had not the railway interest been placated. This was a circumstance which cropped up again and again when railway measures were before Parliament. 1844 marked the first real victory for the companies; of all the bill's provisions only those dealing with 'parliamentary trains' for the working classes had any lasting value or effect.[46]

In the late 1840s organization by the railway interest was more sporadic. Meetings of company representatives and railway M.P.s generally took place only with regard to specific legislation. Associations and committees of railway shareholders were also in evidence, for there were widespread complaints both about falling profits and in connection with the chaotic state of railway accounts.[47] But as shareholders were usually in conflict with the directors, none of these movements resulted in a strengthening of the railway interest.

Yet the expectation of increasing rather than diminishing government involvement in railway regulation pointed to the need for organization of a more durable nature. The Railway Clearing House, founded on 2 January 1842, was then the only body representative of all the major railway companies. In the summer of 1851 the Clearing House Committee resolved that "it is expedient to appoint a Parliamentary Agent in London, to watch, at the expense of the associated Companies, any Bills other than Railway

Bills, which may be brought into Parliament, in order that no clause injurious to the interest of Railway Companies may be passed unnoticed."[48] The man chosen was Thomas Coates, a well-known Parliamentary Agent; his salary was fixed at £200 p.a.[49] For a time Coates did useful work, communicating with the companies through the secretary of the Clearing House. But this arrangement had obvious limitations. Moreover Glyn, as chairman of the Clearing House Committee, objected to its being used as a forum for the debate of topics not strictly within its purview.

In 1855 the Committee decided to reduce Coates' fee, and as a result the arrangement came to an end.[50] Already, however, Coates had become involved in an attempt to form a separate and more permanent organization for the protection of railway interests. The occasion was the report of Cardwell's Select Committee of 1852–3 on railway amalgamation, a report which had come out strongly against the principle of amalgamation as applied to railway companies.[51] On 30 March 1854 the representatives of 23 of the principal railway companies met at the King's Arms, Palace Yard, Westminster, to consider the legislative proposals based on the Select Committee's report. A committee of chairmen and deputy chairmen was set up "to take such steps as may be considered necessary for bringing the proposed alteration in the law fully and fairly under the consideration of Parliament." Coates acted as executive officer and funds were provided by a call upon the companies represented. The committee was successful in obtaining changes in what became the Railway and Canal Traffic Act of 1854.[52]

The committee of 1854 survived into the following session and then lapsed. However on 12 December 1855 a meeting of railway representatives at the Clearing House resolved that a permanent committee be appointed to protect railway interests in Parliament. The committee was to consist of all railway directors in either House of Parliament, plus one delegate from each company. Coates acted as secretary. On 12 March 1856 a subcommittee, which included five M.P.s, was appointed to assist Coates. The subcommittee continued in existence till November 1867, when Coates resigned. Its function was to watch proposed legislation concerning railways and to act as a deputation to ministers. Minutes were kept by Coates, though unfortunately they have not survived. The importance of this subcommittee lay in the fact that it was the first body, with any appreciable degree of organization, to undertake the harnessing of whatever power the railway interest possessed.[53]

But the committee over which Coates presided did not enjoy the confidence of all the companies. That this was so is shown by the existence from 1858 to 1861 of a separate body, known formally as the Railway Companies' Association, which held its inaugural meeting at the Euston Hotel, London, on 29 July 1858.[54] It was conceived as a fighting organization, to promote bills as well as to oppose them, and initially enjoyed the support of the largest English companies. Harry S. Thompson, chairman of the North Eastern Railway and soon to become Liberal M.P. for Whitby, presided over its meetings. George Leeman, deputy chairman of the North Eastern, acted as Honorary Secretary.[55] A General Purposes Committee and a Law and Parliamentary Committee were set up. In 1859 a permanent secretary was appointed at £200 p.a.

The unconcealed aim of the association was to increased profits and cut down wasteful competition. Companies were exhorted to settle their differences by arbitration, and the association offered it services for this purpose. In 1859 the association was instrumental in obtaining the passage of the Railway Companies' Arbitration Act. The following year, however, ominous signs of division appeared. A bill to amend the Railway Clauses Consolidation Act of 1845 was withdrawn because the attitude of some companies was "lukewarm" whilst others "were likely to offer active opposition." Though the association hoped to promote legislation, little attempt was made to gain the support of railway M.P.s, who attended only rarely. In 1861 an attempt to amend the law respecting rating of railways was also abandoned. The manifest inability of the association to carry measures against the wishes of the government resulted in a withdrawal of support by member companies. Attendances at meetings fell sharply. On 12 September 1861 the association was dissolved.

The association of 1858–61 died from a combination of over-ambition and divided counsels. The committee over which Coates presided continued in existence.[56] Its great drawback was lack of organization; its great merit, when it functioned, was its intention to work with and through Parliament and the government. Both bodies, however, suffered from the same basic disadvantages. Although in administrative matters, such as the apportioning of receipts on 'through' traffic (which passed over the lines of more than one company) the companies could co-operate successfully— hence the success of the Clearing House – on policy matters, involving continued and consistent co-operation, such a development had to await the end of the great era of railway expansion, and this did not occur till the late 1860s. From then on, with most of the original small companies swallowed up in larger concerns, the companies enjoyed a more settled existence. Until then rivalry and competition outside Parliament were no encouragement to co-operation in Parliament. In spite of the increasing

number of railway M.P.s the power of the companies in Parliament, and
*vis-à-vis* the government, remained weak. The apathy, silence and dis-
unity of these M.P.s was a matter for continual comment in the railway
press. On the occasion of the 1868 election the *Railway Times* observed:

> There were, in the House of Commons during 1868, no less than 158
> directors, few of whom, however, took any great interest in its [the
> railway interest's] general claims for protection or consideration. Many
> were careless, others lukewarm, both retreating under the plea that they
> had not been sent to Parliament as guardians of railway proprietaries.[57]

Already, however, events were taking place which were to transform
this state of affairs. The Royal Commission on Railways, which had sat
from 1865 to 1867, had produced a report in which *laissez-faire* was the
dominant note.[58] As a matter of fact such a doctrine in its purest sense had
never held sway as far as railways were concerned. But certainly up to 1868
railway regulation had largely taken the form of a very general supervision
only. The Board of Trade, for instance, had to inspect and approve all new
lines before they could be opened, but had no powers in respect of lines
once they had been opened. Henceforth railway regulation was to be far
more interventionist in character. In this sense the Royal Commission
marked the end of an era; its advice, that the railways were better left
alone, was brushed aside almost at once.

One subject which the Conservative government in 1868 considered
ripe for legislation was that of railway accounts, whose weaknesses had
been brought out by the financial crisis of 1866, the bankruptcy of the
railway contractor Sir Morton Peto, and the consequent demands, not
least by shareholders, for legislation to establish standardized methods of
railway accounting.[59] Another subject concerned the means of providing
communication between guards and passengers on trains. A private
member's bill to deal with the latter subject had been introduced in 1866
and 1867. In 1867 railway accounts were also the subject of a private
member's bill. In 1868 the government legislated on both subjects.[60] By
then the threat of further intervention in railway affairs had called a new
organization into being.

On 26 June 1867, at the offices of the Midland Railway, 11 Great George
Street, Westminster, there took place the first meeting of the United Railway Companies' Committee, an organization which changed its name to
the Railway Companies' Association in 1870.[61] At the first meeting only
representatives of the Great Northern, Lancashire & Yorkshire, London &
North Western, Midland and North Eastern railways were present. But by

1873 these had been joined by the Great Eastern, London & South Western and Furness companies, and by the principal Scottish lines. Over the next two decades the membership of other companies in England as well as in Wales and Ireland gave the association a truly representative character.

The broad aim of the United Railway Companies' Committee, stated in its first minute, was "to consider questions affecting specially these [the member] Companies or generally the whole railway Interest, and, if practicable, to recommend to their respective boards, some uniform course of action with reference thereto." Each company was to be represented by its chairman, deputy chairman, general manager and solicitor. The committee was to meet monthly during the parliamentary session and quarterly during the remainder of the year, with special meetings called whenever necessary. Until the end of the century it had no permanent offices, but always met in the vicinity of Parliament, sometimes at the Midland Railway offices, sometimes at the London & North Western Railway offices in Parliament Street or the North Eastern Railway offices in Old Palace Yard, and often in one of the lobbies or committee rooms in Parliament itself. Such rendezvous give some idea of the *ad hoc* nature of the United Railway Companies' Committee in its early days.

In other respects, however, the committee acquired all the trappings of a permanent organization. The minutes of each meeting were printed for circulation to the member companies. Income came from calls on the companies, usually at the rate of one or two shillings per £1,000 of the gross revenue of each company in the previous year, and was used for obtaining transcripts of speeches, debates, committee proceedings and sessional papers as well as for incidental expenses and legal fees.[62] The committee was of course a purely voluntary body; each company had only one vote, nor was any member company bound to adhere to any decision once taken.[63] On 5 November 1867, at its fourth meeting, Harry Thompson told the committee that "as between Companies, the Committee could only confine themselves to an expression of opinion."[64] The first appointment of officers took place on 16 January 1868, when Thompson was appointed chairman and his fellow Liberal, J. Brown-Westhead, became deputy chairman.[65]

Since the main aim of the committee was to keep a close watch on current legislation, one of its earliest acts was to set up machinery for co-ordinating its own policy with the action of those M.P.s who were railway directors. In January 1868 a subcommittee was appointed, consisting of the chairman, deputy chairman and five director-M.P.s: Leeman of the North Eastern, W. P. Price of the Midland, J. Barnes of the Lancashire & Yorkshire,

O. Duncombe of the Great Northern, and Sir Daniel Gooch of the Great Western; in all, five Liberals and two Conservatives.[66] At the same time four M.P.s, two from each party – Leeman and Dillwyn for the Liberals, W. H. Hornby of the Lancashire & Yorkshire and J. Bourne of the London & North Western for the Conservatives – were "requested to act on behalf of the Committee in the House of Commons, to represent Railway Companies in matters affecting their interests."[67]

The subcommittee met frequently in 1868. Its duties were akin to those of an executive committee. The following year no separate appointment of M.P.s to represent railway interests in the Commons was made; instead the two bodies were merged into a Parliamentary Subcommittee consisting of the chairman, deputy chairman and six M.P.s.[68] This Parliamentary Subcommittee was enlarged to 13 members in 1870, and to 14 in 1873.[69] In 1874, reflecting the increase both in the number of member companies and in the reliance placed by the association upon parliamentary pressure, membership of the committee was thrown open to all members of the Lords and Commons on the boards of the respective companies, as well as the chairman and deputy chairman of the association.[70]

Much of the work of the association, especially in its early years, devolved upon its parliamentary committee, which was often left to summon full meetings of the association as and when necessary.[71] Though after 1873 the committee was theoretically an extremely large body, in practice, as will be seen, it was not so unmanageable as might have been expected because "only those members of the Committee who were most active in the Railway Interest attended the meetings".[72] Thus constituted, the Railway Companies' Association carried on its activities largely behind closed doors, meeting the challenge from Parliament and the government by drawing on the loyalties of its own members sitting in the legislature. Few even of the opponents of the railway companies seemed to know exactly what it was up to.[73]

Practically the United Railway Companies' Committee had been formed to consider the question of railway accounts, and the legislation of 1868 might have seen the end of its activities. That this was not so, that it quickly superseded and absorbed Coates' committee and, as the Railway Companies' Association, remained in existence until the railways were nationalized in 1948, was a direct result of continued governmental interference and threats of interference; in response the railway interest threw up a permanent organization to meet these dangers.

Already by 1873 Thompson was able to boast that the association had "introduced a more moderate and give & take feeling into the relations between different Companies."[74] The early years of the association's existence were comparatively uneventful, the only measure of note with which it had to deal being an Act of 1871 authorizing formal inquiries into railway accidents and making it obligatory upon companies to furnish returns of accidents to the Board of Trade.[75] In the long list of reforms which Gladstone's government of 1868–74 intended to carry out, railway reform had no place and Chichester Fortescue, who succeeded John Bright at the Board of Trade in 1870, had little enthusiasm to undertake it. But events forced the government to set up a Joint Select Committee of the two Houses of Parliament in 1872; thus did the railway interest and Liberalism experience their first serious encounter. At this time, too, the companies began to feel pressure from another direction, for in 1871 the first permanent railway trade union had been formed. 1873 was to be the first of many years of struggle for the railway companies against increasingly strong opposition from an ever larger number of hostile camps. In the story of this conflict the railway interest played a key role.

The central theme is clear enough. None of the governments between then and the outbreak of war in 1914 had any clear railway policy. Nonetheless during this period Acts which Parliament passed in connection with the railways made them an industry whose regulation was matched only by that of mining. The partnership between the railways and the government was so close that even reluctant commentators thought state ownership inevitable.[76] At the same time labour relations and labour conditions had altered dramatically. The part played by the railway interest in these transformations was as pronounced as the effect which they, no less than political developments, had on the fortunes of the railway interest itself.

# Chapter 2

# The spectre
# of state control

Perhaps it was the mystery surrounding the joint activities of the railway companies which helped build up numerous legends about the size and power of the railway interest. Certainly the parliamentary 'in-fighting' during the classic period of railway growth, the rival schemes, the back-stairs politics, gave to the interest the stamp of a powerful, secretive, unscrupulous body of men. In 1855 Herbert Spencer, the philosopher and former railway engineer, was moved to declare,

> There are eighty-one directors sitting in Parliament; and though many of those take little or no part in the affairs of their respective railways, many of them are the most active members of the boards to which they belong. We have but to look back a few years, and mark the unanimity with which companies adopted the policy of getting themselves rep-

resented in the Legislature, to see that the furtherance of their respective interests – especially in cases of competition – was the incentive. How well this policy is understood among the initiated, may be judged from the fact, that gentlemen are now in some cases elected on boards simply because they are members of Parliament.[1]

Thirty years later, opponents of the railway companies echoed the same sentiments. One writer avowed that the pressure of railway influence on Parliament was "almost overwhelming . . . the members [of Parliament] allied to the railways are so numerous, and their votes so much worth having, that the temptation of all governments is to let the Railway Companies alone as long as possible."[2] Another writer, convinced that the railway interest in Parliament determined the fate of the entire trade and agriculture of the country, suggested that no M.P. be allowed to accept a railway directorship without being compelled to seek re-election by his constituents.[3] As late as 1913 the Liberal M.P. Josiah Wedgwood spoke of the interest being "not so strong in this House as it was twenty years ago, but . . . still firmly entrenched in another place."[4]

Pronouncements like these indicate that the interest was feared as much because of its numbers as because of the personal and actual influence of its members. The men in charge of the railways, however, flatly denied that railway directors in Parliament had any sort of sinister influence on governments, or even that they acted as one body.[5] Clearly any examination of the interest must begin by separating the myth from the reality.

## Outline of the railway interest in Parliament at general elections, 1832–65[6]

HOUSE OF COMMONS

| Year | Whig-Liberal | Tory | Liberal-Conservative | Total | Efficient interest | Bradshaw |
|------|------|------|------|------|------|------|
| 1832 | 4 | 1 | | 5 | | |
| 1835 | 5 | 2 | | 7 | | |
| 1837 | 9 | 2 | | 11 | | |
| 1841 | 6 | 7 | | 13 | | |
| 1847 | 41 | 39 | | 80 | | 86 |
| 1852 | 38 | 37 | 3 | 78 | | |
| 1857 | 62 | 30 | 4 | 96 | 37 | 107 |
| 1859 | 68 | 32 | 9 | 109 | 25 | 112 |
| 1865 | 87 | 55 | 15 | 157 | 41 | 161 |

HOUSE OF LORDS

| Year | Total | Efficient Interest |
|------|-------|--------------------|
| 1852 | 21 | |
| 1857 | 26 | 3 |
| 1859 | 44 | 6 |
| 1865 | 49 | 11 |

In numerical terms the representation of the railways in Parliament increased at every general election between 1832 and 1865. The great influx came in the 1840s, when through the intrigues of the directors and the struggles in the committee rooms, the interest acquired the sinister reputation personified by George Hudson. In its formative period it never belonged directly to any one party. In the railways, as in mines, landownership was often the route to a seat on the board, and therefore in respect of both during the 1840s there were more aristocrats and landed gentry representing them in Parliament than there were other social classes. Thus the railway director-M.P.s divided almost evenly between the two parties.[7] Between the elections of 1847 and 1865 the numbers in the railway interest doubled. At the same time it acquired, in common with other industries represented in the Commons, a distinct Liberal bias.[8]

The general election of 1868 brought about the return to the Commons of 125 railway directors. Except as a crude index of the commercial leanings of the House, the figure has little meaning, for it reveals nothing of the true nature of the 'efficient', as distinct from the 'nominal' railway interest. The effective working strength of the interest can best be assessed on the basis of the companies of which M.P.s were directors, of the sorts of interests that were at stake.

Generally speaking, shareholders can be discounted. The 'star' shareholders, those qualified to be directors, were a mere fraction of the total number. In 1875, of over 20,000 shareholders in one of the large companies, only about one-tenth held a really important stake.[9] There were, of course, many more M.P.s who held railway shares than there were directors. But even if it were possible to compile full lists of shareholder-M.P.s, such lists would be of little value in estimating the strength of the interest.[10] Though occasionally prominent shareholders did defend the railways in Parliament, the interests of shareholders and directors were not always, or even usually, identical. Thus no shareholder-M.P.s have been included in the analyses of the railway interest in Parliament.

The shareholder was concerned only with the size of his dividend; he was only interested in railways as a source of income. Directors were share-holders, but for them the holding of shares was only the formal pre-requisite to a highly valued position of power and responsibility. Many railway directors took office either because they had large family holdings of the company's stock to look after or because the working of a particular railway affected their own businesses.[11] Others, and especially those in Parliament, were approached by the companies, or other interested parties, to join railway boards for specific reasons.[12] Towards the end of the nine-teenth century peers were much in demand. Sometimes, as was the case with the leading members of the railway interest, the power and the respon-sibility developed into a career at least as important and as vocational as that of being in Parliament.

With others, a seat on a railway board was itself a means to a further end, which usually lay in the other business interests of the occupant. This was particularly true of important industrial areas. One of the many complaints of Yorkshire traders against the Lancashire & Yorkshire Rail-way was that it sacrificed their interests to those of Lancashire; this they attributed to the predominance of "Lancashire gentlemen" on the Lan-cashire & Yorkshire board.[13] The North Eastern Railway was even more of a manufacturers' stronghold. Sir Joseph Pease, a man with extensive coal and iron interests in the north, told the Joint Select Committee of 1872: "My interest as a traffic sender is very much larger than my interest as a shareholder or as a director."[14] Large companies, too, liked having mem-bers of Parliament on their boards, partly to assist in the passing of com-pany-promoted legislation and in the defeat of rival schemes, and partly no doubt for reasons of prestige.

Yet for much of the nineteenth century most of the railway directors sitting in Parliament fell into categories other than those discussed above. Those directors who sat on the boards of large companies, or companies of national importance, made up the efficient interest, the group which was prepared to put railways before party politics, to exert pressure in a united fashion on behalf of the independence and well-being of railway property. For the majority of director-M.P.s, railways were well down the list of priorities.[15]

The majority comprised the directors of foreign lines, and of lines in the United Kingdom of purely local importance. The directors of foreign (including colonial) railways were few in number. They had, so far as railways were concerned, no identity at all of interests with their British counterparts. The directors of local lines stood in an entirely different position. They too had no identity of interests with the boards of the large companies. Moreover, many local lines were built in direct competition with the large lines, often because of the allegedly high rates and poor facilities offered by the large companies in a particular area.[16] To include directors of such lines amongst the efficient interest would be as ill-conceived as including directors of competing steamer and tramway companies.

In any case the directors of most local lines sat on their respective boards for local or personal reasons. As a rule (though there are important exceptions) directors who lived "on the line" were not popular, because they "know nothing and want everything."[17] But where small railways were concerned an M.P. on the board of a local branch line was considered a welcome advantage to a struggling company, especially if he also had local ties and influence. Local personalities often wished to be elected on to the boards of local railways to protect their own interests, or because they were prominent in the lists of subscribers to the lines.[18] One of the Presidents of the Board of Trade most unsympathetic to the railways was Sir Michael Hicks Beach, who in 1888 carried the Railway and Canal Traffic Act notwithstanding the fact that he was then chairman of the East Gloucestershire Railway. Lord Henniker, who led the opposition of the traders to the railways in the upper House at that time, was on the board of the Mellis & Eye line. Contemporary critics of the railways, who made much of the supposed over-representation of the railway interest in Parliament, failed, perhaps purposely, to make this point. Though the total number of railway directors in Parliament often ran into three figures, the number of directors actively engaged in the defence and protection of railway interests was much smaller.[19]

Between the general election of 1868 and the fall of Gladstone's Second Ministry, the railway interest in the Commons was still a predominantly but by no means overwhelmingly Liberal body.[20] In round figures the Liberal proportion never rose above 60 per cent and never fell below 47 per cent. In 1871 the Conservative proportion reached a little over 45 per cent, though even on the morrow of Disraeli's victory Conservative director-M.P.s accounted for barely 44 per cent of the total; their numbers suffered heavily as a result of the Liberal landslide of 1880, when they fell to just over 38 per cent. By the end of 1884 the Conservative proportion had reached over 44 per cent; the Liberal proportion had by then dropped from 57 per cent, in 1880, to 50 per cent.

Electoral swings certainly had some influence on these fluctuations in the political spectrum of the interest. In 1868, of the 22 director-M.P.s elected to Parliament for the first time, 14 were Liberal and only 8 Conservative; in 1874, 7 Liberal director-M.P.s sat for the first time, as against 11 Conservatives and 1 Liberal-Conservative; in 1880 the figures were: Liberals 13, Conservatives 5. But the fluctuations in the numbers from year to year suggested that these variations are attributable more to individual circumstances – mainly resignations and deaths – than to the changing features of the political back-cloth.[21] The most significant feature of the new blood coming into the interest each year was the remarkable evenness of its division between the major political groupings.

In the House of Lords during the same period the interest had a slight but unmistakable Conservative flavour, explained largely by the fact of the Tory landowning preponderance in the upper House; of the entire railway interest in the Lords, only nine peerages in the period 1868–79, and only four in 1880–4, were not listed in Bateman.[22] At no time did the Liberal director-peers amount to more than 43 per cent of the total; in 1883 the Conservative directors accounted for as much as 47 per cent. Once again, politics pure and simple played little part in the yearly fluctuations. Between 1868 and 1874 only five railway directors received peerages: the Earl of Feversham, 1868 (Conservative, North Eastern Railway); Lord Robartes, 1869 (Liberal, Cornwall Railway); Lord Brabourne, 1880 (Liberal, South Eastern Railway); Lord Derwent, 1881 (Liberal, North Eastern); and Lord Hothfield, 1881 (Liberal, South Eastern).[23]

Only when the railway interest is broken down into its constituent parts, directors of foreign lines, of local lines, and – the efficient interest – directors of large or nationally important lines, do any well-defined party developments and divisions appear. In the Lords although the number of directors in each group remained, proportionally, fairly steady between 1868 and 1873, the efficient interest hovering between 11 and 12, Conservative and Liberal-Conservative peers of the efficient interest always outnumbered the Liberal total. During 1874–9 the efficient interest gained in numbers slightly at the expense of the local lines. But on balance there was a more even spread between the political groups; in 1879, when the total of the efficient interest was 14, there were as many Liberals as there were Liberal-Conservatives and Conservatives combined. From 1880 to 1884 there were further falls in the number of directors of local lines in the Lords. The efficient interest continued to expand. At the same time the Liberal ascendancy was assured. In 1884 there were almost as many Liberal directors of large railway companies – 15 – in the Lords as there were Conservative directors of local lines – 16.

Since creations of peerages played no major part in such a development, the figures can only mean that during the period 1868–84 the movement of

Liberal peers on to the boards of the larger companies, and simultaneously of Conservative peers on to the boards of smaller, local concerns, was not accidental. Certainly landowning could have had no influence. Only one Liberal peer in the period 1880–4, Lord Auckland (Manchester, Sheffield & Lincolnshire Railway) does not appear in Bateman. It is possible that the movement was the result of deliberate policies, for the landed interests of the Tory aristocracy may have been more local in nature, whilst the Liberal peers, before the schism in their ranks, tended to be more sympathetic towards business. But this can be no more than conjecture.[24]

In the Commons there was a trend in exactly the opposite direction. There, what began as a Liberal ascendancy in the efficient interest had emerged in 1884 as a balanced group. In terms of party, the Conservative directors of large companies increased at the expense of the Liberals. During the Conservative ministry of Disraeli the representation of local lines dropped from 74 directors to 61; that of large lines increased from 40 to 51. Yet whereas the number of Liberal directors of local lines had by 1879 surpassed the number of Conservatives, the distribution of parties within the efficient interest evened out. Gladstone's Second Ministry witnessed the completion of this process. The representation of local lines fell again, from 57 to 53, and that of large lines increased from 34 to 41. Liberal M.P.s maintained their preponderance on the boards of local railways; but amongst the large companies Conservative directors constituted just over half the total number of 41 director-M.P.s by the end of 1884.

Again this cannot be attributed to the election results. In 1874 only four Conservative directors were returned to Parliament for the first time; all the other Conservative directors in that Parliament either held their directorships before re-election, or acquired them afterwards. In 1880 there was only one Conservative member of the efficient interest elected for the first time, Sir Henry Tyler of the Great Eastern. Between then and 1885 only two Conservatives who entered Parliament in 1880 joined the interest: W. L. Jackson in 1883 and W. H. Fellowes in 1884; both were directors of the Great Northern. All the remaining Conservative directors of large companies had been given their directorships before being re-elected to Parliament in 1880. Thus the explanation for the increase in the number of Conservatives in the efficient interest in the Commons would seem to lie rather in company policy and individual preference.

In the Lords, therefore, as the efficient interest grew bigger, from 9 peers in 1868 to 19 in 1884, the Liberal proportion increased. In the Commons in the same period the efficient interest remained fairly constant, rising from 39 M.P.s in 1868 to 51 in 1878 and 1879, but falling to 41 by

1884; but there was an increase in Conservative representation. These railway representatives never constituted a completely homogeneous body. Though subject to various pressures, they were perfectly free to do in Parliament as they chose. Behind the official organization of the Railway Companies' Association there was always a spontaneous interest at liberty to act contrary to the association's authorized policy. Nonetheless it was from such a diverse body of M.P.s, embracing a wide spectrum of political opinion and directing the fortunes of large concerns often in competition with one another, that the parliamentary committee of the association was drawn. It was with this comparatively small body of men that the defence of railway interests in Parliament and against the government of the day, whatever its political complexion, primarily rested.

Yet an examination of the backgrounds of the most prominent director-M.P.s gives an impression not of solidarity as much as of diversity: diversity of social background, of political faith, of commercial interests. The Conservative engineer Gooch had to work closely with the Liberal solicitor Leeman. The Lancashire railway magnate Sir Edward Watkin had to seek the support of the Yorkshire landowner Lord Houghton.[25] For men such as these the Railway Association provided the only common ground for meeting face to face the directors of other railway companies in frank and continuous deliberation on mutual problems. In 1867 memories of the collapse of earlier associations, through company rivalries and sheer lack of interest, were still fresh in the minds of the founders of the new body. As early as the fourth meeting of the United Railway Companies' Committee pleas were made for the companies to sink their differences and refer disputes to the chairmen of the constituent companies.[26]

The Liberal victory of 1868 made a common front all the more necessary, though this was not at first apparent. For two years a Royal Commission had been examining the railway system. It came to the conclusion that the railways were better left to manage their own affairs.[27] The only tangible result of its work was the 1868 Regulation of Railways Act, a harmless piece of legislation feared by the companies only because it endeavoured, on the whole unsuccessfully, to establish a uniform system of railway accounts and permissive government audit.[28] But the period of Gladstone's administration coincided with a hardening of public sentiment towards the railways, partly due to a general shift of opinion in favour of increasing government control of industry when it was a question of the general welfare of the community, and partly because, with this hardening of attitude, governments could place more reliance upon individual M.P.s to support popular measures. As the railway interest quickly discovered, the policies of Liberal and Tory governments towards the railways differed more in degree than in principle; debates on railway affairs in Parliament tended to develop on pro- and anti-railway lines rather than on the lines of a simple Liberal-Conservative dichotomy.

Basically public opinion shifted because the public – the railwaymen, the railway travellers, the traders, the political philosophers – discerned in the early 1870s developments which they regarded as errors both of commission and of omission on the part of the railway companies. Most of the legislative measures taken to deal with the railways after 1870 had their origin in the accidental or deliberate doings of the companies themselves. Generally speaking, defect and remedial legislation went hand in hand. The central problem surrounding the railways, the question whether it was right to impose upon industries created for private profit the duties and obligations of a public utility, was never definitively tackled at all during the nineteenth century.[29] After the deliberations of the Royal Commission of 1865–7, railway legislation took the form simply of *ad hoc* remedies for proven grievances. On the three major railway issues of the 1870s, safety requirements, labour relations and traffic regulations, the impetus towards government control was provided by developments taking place within the railway system. Of these issues the problem of traffic regulation was by far the most contentious. Nor did the circumstances in which it came to the fore make the railway companies any more popular. It provided the Railway Companies' Association with its first test of strength.

At the beginning of the parliamentary session of 1872 a number of amalgamation schemes were put forward which, if sanctioned, would have divided the railways of the country into area monopolies.[30] The schemes deposited included plans for amalgamating the London & North Western with the Lancashire & Yorkshire, the South Eastern with the Great Northern, and the Midland with the Glasgow & South Western; there was also a division of traffic bill promoted by the Great Western and London & South Western companies. The bills were not entirely unexpected, as there had been a steady trickle of such schemes ever since the financial crisis of 1866. In Liverpool the attempted amalgamation of the London & North Western with the Lancashire & Yorkshire aroused great indignation. A joint committee of representatives from Lancashire and Yorkshire was set up, with Sir W. B. Forwood as chairman, to fight the proposals.[31] But the nature and number of all the 1872 proposals were such as to reopen once more the whole question of the railway 'monopoly', and of how the rights of those who used the railways could best be preserved.

From the traders' point of view the opportunity had come none too soon. Between 1869 and 1872 the companies had enjoyed a 20 per cent growth in traffic receipts, due in part to increases in railway rates; rate competition between the companies had virtually ceased.[32] The Railway and Canal Traffic Act of 1854 had been passed with the object of securing facilities for through and other traffic, and equal treatment for all persons and articles.[33] Cardwell's Select Committee of 1853 intended that such questions and disputes should be settled by the Board of Trade. But pressure by the railway companies was able to secure an amendment of the bill, transferring jurisdiction from the Board of Trade to the Court of Common Pleas. This meant costly litigation which the smaller traders could not afford; consequently the trading interest regarded the Act as a dead letter.[34] The effect of the amalgamation proposals in 1872 was thus that, once attention had been focused on the railways, interest and criticism shifted from the amalgamation question to the problem of rate increases and 'undue preference'. The railway companies were faced with the very real prospect that the entire settlement of 1854 would crumble.

Hesitant and unsure of itself, the Railway Association awaited the appointment of a Select Committee. When it became known that the Select Committee was to be appointed to investigate amalgamations generally, the association took a decision which had an adverse effect from its own point of view both on the course the inquiry took and on its report. On 21 February 1872 the companies decided not to have any representation on the Select Committee, on the grounds that the committee's recommendations "would be more likely to command public confidence if no members representing a railway interest were chosen to serve on it."[35]

This decision was naive and unfortunate. It meant that there could be no planning of evidence, that the companies could not rely on their being 'fed' questions by the committee, that replies would have to be spontaneous. The six representatives of the Commons on the committee included the President of the Board of Trade, under considerable pressure from traders on both sides of the House, and the radical J. G. Dodson. With no railway spokesman as a counterbalance the committee was ill-suited to giving the railways a hearing at all sympathetic. It can hardly be supposed that outside the committee-room and in the corridors some consultation between company representatives did not take place. But at no further meeting of the Railway Association or its Parliamentary Subcommittee was there any discussion of the evidence before the Select Committee. The nature of this evidence suggests the reason for such lack of discussion; it also suggests a more plausible explanation for the decision not to have a railway representative on the Select Committee. For though the companies all agreed that further outside control of their affairs was undesirable and deplorable, there was little else that they were agreed on.

The Select Committee took evidence from March to July 1872. With each hearing the reputation of the companies became a little blacker. William Cawkwell, the London & North Western Railway's general manager, declared that competition had "failed altogether" where railways were concerned.[36] James Allport, general manager of the Midland Railway, which stood to suffer considerably by the proposed London & North Western–Lancashire & Yorkshire amalgamation, urged the granting of compulsory running powers.[37] James Grierson, general manager of the Great Western, admitted that competition of accommodation between London and certain west-country towns was really non-existent.[38]

When traders and representatives of chambers of commerce gave evidence, the impression gained ground that whilst rates were high, competition had all but disappeared, though allowances and discounts were given to favoured individuals. Criticisms were levelled at the misuse by railway companies of canals which had fallen into their hands. A plea for more stringent government control came even from smaller railways too weak to stand up to the large trunk lines. The idea was mooted of an independent tribunal "to which . . . matters of dispute as between the railway companies and freighters or the public should be referred", possibly "a mixture of legal and practical men."[39]

Such demands and criticisms the railway interest should have expected. But there was no one to cross-examine witnesses on behalf of the companies. Nor had they prepared a consistent, well-argued case. Conflicting and damaging accounts of the existence and effect of competition on the railways continued to be given when the directors gave their evidence. Watkin, for instance, tried to show how competition between London and Manchester had led to reductions in rates and fares.[40] This piece of self-advertisement received strong criticism from Harry Thompson, who was intent on revealing the beneficial effects of complete absence of competition under the North Eastern Railway, and was completely denied by Cawkwell.[41]

Upon members of the Select Committee the spectacle of two prominent Liberal railway chairmen squabbling in this fashion made a profound impression, profound enough for them to comment upon it in their report.[42] By the time Henry Tyler, then Chief Inspecting Officer of the Railway Department, gave his evidence the recommendation to set up some independent tribunal to put the companies in their place was being taken for granted. Tyler's evidence was crystal-clear: "I think there is only one of two things to do; either let the railways manage the State, or let the State manage the railways."[43] In the public discussion of the question in the coming months these words were often repeated.

The report of the Select Committee condemned not merely the working of the Act of 1854 but the entire notion that competition between railways would ensure a fair deal for the public. It attacked canal-owning railway companies both for manipulating canal rates to force traffic on to the railways, and for allowing canals to become derelict. There was harsh criticism of the "powerful bureaucracy of directors and officers" who ignored the real interests of their shareholders. Though rejecting equal mileage rates and maximum terminal charges, the report urged that traders be given a *locus standi* before railway bill committees, to state their case as to the rates proposed, and that all companies be given powers to make through rates and fares on to the lines of other companies.[44] To act as a court of arbitration and of law for railways and canals, and generally to enforce the provisions of the 1854 Act, the report recommended the setting up of a "Railway and Canal Commission".[45] This novel suggestion, in complete contrast to the philosophy of *laissez-faire* which had permeated the report of the Royal Commission only five years earlier, has rightly been said to have marked "the end of an epoch in the relations of the State to railways."[46]

Trading organizations urged the adoption of the Select Committee's recommendations.[47] Legislation was widely anticipated, and on 10 February 1873 Fortescue brought in the expected bill. The companies, however, did little by way of preparation. There were no preliminary meetings with the Board of Trade, nor was the first reading challenged. Indeed, the only railway director to speak, Charles Gilpin, Liberal M.P. for Northampton and a member of the South Eastern board, whilst warning of the dangers of parliamentary interference with "what was after all private enterprise", nonetheless voiced his acceptance of the need for a tribunal.[48] Yet when the bill was published it confirmed the companies' worst fears.[49] The object of their hostility was not the setting up of the Railway Commission, but the powers proposed to be given to it; these included the power to grant through rates to railway and canal companies applying for them (clause 10), the compulsory sanctioning of arrangements between railways and canals (clause 12), and wide powers to summon witnesses and inspect books and documents (clause 21). Under clause 11 railway companies were to be compelled to keep rate books for public inspection, the books to contain such particulars as the commissioners might, upon application, direct. From the decisions of the commission there was to be no appeal.

These points were discussed at a meeting of the parliamentary committee of the Railway Association on 25 February, when the most prominent Liberal directors were present. Political considerations, quite apart from the fact of public support for the bill, prompted the decision not to oppose its second reading, but to argue detailed amendments with the government.[50] On the following day a large deputation, which included Leeman and Pease of the North Eastern, Price of the Midland, and Gooch and Dillwyn of the Great Western, saw Fortescue but obtained nothing beyond a promise to mention on the second reading that amendments might be necessary in committee.[51] In fact the promise was not kept; if its purpose was to prevent the director-M.P.s from attempting to kill the bill in its infancy, it was a successful ploy. On the second reading the only serious criticism came from backbench Conservatives who, like G. W. P. Bentinck, considered it "only a feeble step in the right direction".[52] The second reading was agreed to without a division.

Such timidity on the part of the railway companies gave rise to warnings in the press, particularly as this timidity contrasted strongly with denunciations of the bill at shareholders' meetings. The *Railway Times*, after attacking the bill as embodying "the maximum of interference with the minimum of responsibility", pointed out:

> With so large a representation of the railway interest in Parliament, we might have at least expected a full discussion of the measure before its principle was assented to . . . The experienced veterans in parliamentary tactics . . . always incline to the belief that you can make better terms pending the second reading of a bill than after that important stage has passed.[53]

The seriousness of the situation began to impress itself on the railway interest at the end of February. It is probable, too, that the difficulties in which the Gladstone administration found itself over the Irish Universities bill played some part in persuading Liberal directors that they might press harder than usual on their own leaders to give way over points in the Railway and Canal Traffic bill, especially in view of their loyalty over the Irish question.[54]

At the end of February the Railway Association's parliamentary committee agreed upon certain amendments which were deposited with the Board of Trade early in March.[55] Whilst attention was centred on the Irish Universities bill and Gladstone's resignation, little could be done. A week later, though, Leeman pressed Fortescue to receive a small deputation.[56] Pressure was now all the more necessary as the Cabinet, with much of its projected legislation for 1873 in ruins, had decided to include the Railway and Canal Traffic bill amongst those measures which might still be carried.[57] Fortescue made concessions on minor points; but the parliamentary committee was far from satisfied. In particular they resented the provision in clause 5, that any decision of the commissioners should be binding "notwithstanding anything in any special Act", and they were anxious that clauses 14–17, relating to the compulsory carriage of mails, should be struck out.

Though there were some members of the interest who wished directly to challenge the government in the Commons, Leeman's view prevailed that gentle pressure constantly applied would be more likely to yield results.[58] As Fortescue appeared anxious to carry his bill this tactic had some success, for when the parliamentary committee came to consider all the proposed amendments to the bill it appeared that the government had accepted many of the committee's proposals.[59] On the points still in dispute, relating mainly to clause 5 and the Post Office clauses, the parliamentary committee decided to appeal to the Commons. A circular was drawn up and sent out with the Votes to all M.P.s on 29 March.[60] Attention then shifted back from the Railway Association and the Board of Trade to the House of Commons.

Fortescue's opening remarks suggested that he had given way on the question of the words of clause 5.[61] But the main opposition with which the interest had to deal did not come from the government; it came from backbench opponents of the railway companies. The committee and report stages in the Commons resolved themselves into a heated duel between the interest and those representatives of the traders who were pressing Fortescue to give the Railway Commission wider powers and stronger teeth.

It was clause 10, relating to through traffic, which gave most trouble. William Rathbone, Liberal M.P. for Liverpool, proposed to extend the prohibition of undue preference to towns and localities, thus paving the way for the legal enforcement of equal mileage rates; he also proposed to add words at the end of the clause to facilitate complaints by corporations and chambers of commerce, even where such bodies were not personally aggrieved. The first of these amendments was negatived and the second withdrawn.[62] The government, however, clearly felt the need to placate the traders. So Fortescue himself moved to add a provision that "Nothing in any special Act contained shall be construed so as to prevent the Commissioners from ordering and apportioning a through rate under this section." This amounted to a reintroduction in clause 10 of the substance of the words he had earlier agreed to omit from clause 5. Under strong pressure from railway directors in the House, led by Leeman, he withdrew the words, though only on the understanding that he would introduce them at a later stage.[63]

Against such determination there was little the Railway Association could do. A meeting of the parliamentary committee on 1 April condemned Fortescue's volte-face over the objectionable words in clause 5, and Rathbone's proposal to give town councils and chambers of commerce a *locus standi* before the commissioners. These resolutions were printed and circulated to all M.P.s "connected with the Companies composing the Association." Circulars to shareholder M.P.s were also sent out by some of the larger companies.[64] But the net effect was small. Leeman's plea to the government that the companies should have some guarantee written into the bill, that they would have an absolute right of appeal from any of the commission's decisions, had no effect.[65] In the closing stages of the committee, Rathbone was able to push through an amended version of his clause providing for complaints to the commissioners by public authorities, whilst G. B. Gregory, a Conservative, carried against the government a clause empowering the commissioners to fix terminal charges.[66] Such radical alterations to the powers of the commissioners were too far-reaching to be ignored. The *Railway Times* took the director-M.P.s to task for having allowed the second reading to slip through without dividing against it; at the same time the journal pointed out that there were members of the House of Lords "who are likely to be influenced by no other consideration than that of justice between the public . . . and the great interest with which it is the main object of the measure to interfere."[67] Fortescue announced the names of the proposed Railway Commissioners on 28 April; the same day the bill passed the Commons and was sent to the upper House.[68]

The possibility of obtaining alterations to the bill in the Lords was a real one. A full meeting of the Railway Association on 1 May decided that the companies could reasonably press the peers to modify clause 10 so as to preserve separate dock and harbour rates, to delete or modify clause 19, which empowered the commissioners to fix terminals, and to insert a compulsory right of appeal.[69] More important was the question of which peers might be asked to put forward these amendments. Although some names were discussed, they were not recorded. But it is reasonable to assume that Lord Houghton, as well as the Duke of Richmond, Lord Cairns and Lord Salisbury, were among them. Salisbury was a former chairman of the Great Eastern Railway, from whose board he had resigned in 1872. Cairns and Richmond, a former Conservative President of the Board of Trade, were not railway directors but could be relied upon, as prominent opposition peers, to take any chance offered of embarrassing Gladstone's government.[70] To add further weight to their views the Railway Association sent a circular to some peers, probably those with railway connections, setting out in detail the views of the companies on the most objectionable clauses.[71] In its tone and content its obvious aim was to present the bill as a wicked attempt to set up an omnipotent tribunal which would minutely regulate on behalf of the government the working of a great and independent industry. The peers dutifully responded by coming down on the side of *laissez-faire*.

Though Richmond did not press his amendment to clause 10, the government reluctantly accepted his amendment to clause 12, to restrict complaints by public authorities to the authorities of those places in which the causes of complaint arose. His attempt to remove clause 19 was defeated by 16 votes. But he was able to amend clause 25 so as to make an appeal compulsory on request.[72] On two vital points, therefore, the railways were able to retrieve something from the position lost in the Commons. With the peers behind them they could now afford to be both firm and magnanimous. M.P.s concerned with the companies composing the Railway Association were circularized to "support the Bill in its present shape."[73]

But this was not quite the end of the struggle. The Lords had made an appeal compulsory in all cases. Fortescue would have conceded this to the extent of allowing a compulsory appeal on questions of law, under those clauses relating to through traffic and the publication of rates; but pressed by Rathbone and R. A. Cross he decided to oppose the Lords' provision in its entirety.[74] With the two Houses at loggerheads the Railway Association decided to make a stand. Richard Moon, the ultra-Tory chairman of the London & North Western, advised the association on 3 July that the companies should petition the Lords "praying to be heard by Counsel that they would insist upon their amendment."[75] Leeman suggested a deputation to Richmond, Salisbury, Cairns and others "with the view of inducing them to support their Amendment." The association decided on both courses.[76] On a division the peers resolved by 79 votes to 63 to insist on their amendment.[77] This prompted Henry Oakley, Honorary Secretary of the Railway Association, to issue on his own initiative a circular to railway M.P.s, requesting their support for the amendment in the Commons.[78] By such means the companies were able to gain much of what they really wanted on the question of appeal. Fortescue's proposal of 23 June was sanctioned by the Commons on 14 July; the bill became law the following week.[79]

The passing of the Railway and Canal Traffic Act of 1873 was regarded by the railway interest as a finality. It proved to be merely the beginning of a new era in the history of the railway rates question. The amalgamation bills to which it owed its origin, and which had been reintroduced in 1873, were killed outright when a special Joint Committee threw out the London & North Western–Lancashire & Yorkshire bill after only an hour's deliberation.[80] The Traffic bill, though, had become law. If it was true, as Lord Houghton predicted it would be, that the companies were able to brush aside the irritating orders of the Railway Commissioners, it was equally true that there had been raised up against the railways a power which directors could not keep on ignoring with impunity, especially as when the commission began functioning early in 1874 it openly advertised for complaints against railways.[81]

The traders naturally never gave up hope of forcing a revision of the settlement of 1873, and in particular of seeing on the statute book a provision allowing private individuals to apply for through rates. The increase in the number of Conservative traders in the Commons as a result of the 1874 election led to a redoubling of their efforts.[82] In 1874 they undertook parliamentary action.[83] When this proved unsuccessful the Associated Chambers of Commerce took up the question, and chambers of commerce pressed their point on the government again in 1875.[84] Though the railway interest was able to persuade the government not to meddle with the settlement of 1873, the powers of the Railway Commissioners were due to expire in 1878, when the whole position was likely to be re-examined. By that time the problem of railway rates had become much more acute.

As there were only two divisions on railway questions in the House of Lords in 1873, that by which the Lords rejected Richmond's attempt to strike out clause 19 of the Traffic bill, and that by which they insisted on their amendment in favour of an absolute right of appeal, little can be said of the loyalty of railway peers at this time. It is noteworthy, however, that in the first division only two peers of the efficient interest voted against the railways, whilst four voted with Richmond: Lord Auckland (Manchester, Sheffield & Lincolnshire Railway); the Earl of Feversham (North Eastern); Lord Colville of Culross (Great Northern); and Lord Houghton.[85] On the second division the only three peers of the efficient interest who voted at all did so against the government and in favour of the Lords' amendment: the Liberals Lord Houghton and the Duke of

Sutherland (Highland and London & North Western railways) and the Conservative Earl of Feversham.[86] Representatives of the largest companies in the upper House clearly kept together.

In the division lobbies of the Commons the efficient interest displayed a remarkable solidarity.[87] On 31 March 1873 nine Liberals of the efficient interest disobeyed the Liberal whips in voting with eight Conservative and Liberal–Conservative directors against a government amendment to clause 3 of the Traffic bill.[88] Seventeen directors, including six Conservatives, voted against a backbench Liberal amendment to clause 10.[89] Ten directors, including five Conservatives, voted against allowing individual traders to make complaints to the Railway Commissioners, whilst none voted in favour of this proposal.[90] On Rathbone's amendment to protect clause 10 from an absolute right of appeal, seven of the efficient interest voted against Rathbone, and none for him.[91] An attempt the following year to amend the 1873 Act so as to allow chambers of commerce and private individuals to apply to the Railway Commission for a through rate, attracted the support of only one member of the efficient interest; but twelve directors, including one Liberal and one Liberal–Conservative, voted with the Conservative whips against it.[92]

The only hint of a true 'party' division amongst the interest came in a division on 7 April 1873, challenging the Order for the Consideration of the Traffic bill. Here eight of the interest, all Liberals, voted with the government and one, a Conservative, against. But the size of the voting, 103 to 23, is obviously too small to allow any important conclusions to be drawn from it, other than that the Liberal directors were not prepared to turn against a government bill to the principle of which they had already assented.[93]

On one question, not hitherto touched upon, which cropped up in 1873 and 1874, there was no division of opinion at all amongst the members of the efficient interest. Ten of them, including two Conservatives, voted with the Liberal whips on 29 April 1873 against a motion calling for the state purchase of Irish railways. Altogether only twelve of the entire railway directorate in the Commons – eight of them sitting for Irish seats and five of them Conservatives, and of whom eleven were directors of purely local lines – declared themselves in favour of this policy.[94] When a similar motion was brought forward a year later 19 members of the efficient interest voted against it (nine Conservatives, one Liberal–Conservative and nine Liberals) and none in its favour, thus indicating very clearly that the Liberal directors were as opposed to the purchase of Irish railways by the State as were the Conservatives.[95]

One welcome result of the threat to the railway companies in 1873 was that the Railway Association received a number of important new members including the North London Railway, the London, Brighton & South Coast Railway, the London, Chatham & Dover Railway, and Watkin's companies, the South Eastern and the Manchester, Sheffield & Lincolnshire, thus giving the association the character of a national representative body.[96] The campaign of 1873 itself displayed many of the features which the interest was to use for the best part of its pre-1914 career. First and foremost it reveals the immense energy of which the leading members of the interest were capable, an energy which makes nonsense of the claim that the bill of 1873 incurred no very strong opposition, or that such opposition as there was arose merely from Parliament being jealous of its own powers.[97] M.P.s with large business interests to defend would go to great lengths to defend them. This was emphatically so in the case of railway directors.

Such devotion transcended the bounds of party. In 1873 Leeman, Pease and Watkin were quite content to carry on a strenuous opposition to the Liberal government of which they were in other respects staunch supporters, and that too at a time when the government was at its weakest. But the means by which the opposition was organized was not, and could not be, a matter of a straight appeal to the division lobbies, for, as the division lists show, the efficient interest was too small by itself, and unless the companies could be sure of picking up the votes of malcontents from the government side, and of members of the opposition, their chances of defeating the government of the day outright on a vote were negligible.

Party loyalties, in any case, were not to be easily dismissed. Nor, of course, did the Railway Association possess machinery approaching that of the party whips; it could only rely on the brotherly sentiments of the members of the efficient interest. Such sentiments were not strong in 1872 but grew stronger in 1873 in the face of a common enemy, government legislation. In the main the interest relied on making a fuss. This it did equally well behind the doors of Whitehall and in the parliamentary lobbies as in public. Propaganda in public was important, for no goverment could brush aside the opinions of thousands of shareholders. But when a group of influential M.P.s who controlled the country's main means of communication threatened a revolt in connection with the policy of the administration, that administration was under strong pressure to make concessions. This is one political conclusion to be drawn from the passage of the Railway and Canal Traffic Act. The railway interest did not obtain everything it wanted in 1873. It would doubtless have preferred no legislation at all. Yet the government bill did not pass into law in its original form. That is the measure of the interest's success.

One further point needs emphasizing. Although the interest was not able to get all it wanted in the Commons, it was more successful when the bill reached the Lords. There, though the interest was numerically much weaker than in the Commons, there was a ready supply of peers more than willing to come to the defence of property. In 1873 the railway interest used the House of Lords as a revising chamber. It was to do so when similar legislation was again threatened.

# Chapter 3

# The safety
# of the public

In 1874 the attention of the railway interest turned to the question of accidents. The problem of safety on the railways had grown acute in the early 1870s, largely through a succession of serious railway accidents which naturally aroused public indignation. In the matter of railway safety, as in that of railway rates, the demand for state intervention had grown. The railway M.P.s saw their task as being the prevention of state interference with railway management, not merely because such interference was felt to be reprehensible in itself, but because, as regards the actual day-to-day safe working of the lines, it was felt to be positively dangerous.

Then, and later, much scorn was poured on the railway directorate and its parliamentary arm for having prevented the universal adoption of allegedly proven safety devices. But from the viewpoint of the companies the record of state interference with railway working had been far from satisfactory. In the early days of railway operation no one knew as much about the working of a railway system as the companies themselves. When, in 1840, the Railway Department of the Board of Trade was set up, its inspectorate, forbidden by law from having close ties with the railway companies, had to be drawn from the ranks of the Royal Engineers.[1] As the Act of 1840 clearly showed, the main concern of the legislature was to fix a personal responsibility for the safe working of trains. Clause 5 of the Act gave the Board of Trade a power to inspect railways, but not to prevent their being opened. The board had no powers to lay down even minimum safety requirements.[2]

With these powers the Railway Department itself was not satisfied. A report issued by the officers of the department on 25 January 1841 declared that "The maximum degree of safety is far from being attained in practice."[3] Though "the Government should not attempt to interfere in questions of an experimental nature . . . nor . . . to regulate matters of detail, so as to take the management of the railways out of the hands of . . . the Directors and their officers", yet, the report continued, "As matters stand at present, the Government has the responsibility [for public safety], without any of the powers which ought to accompany it."[4] The report went on to recommend "that a general power should be given to the Board of Trade of issuing regulations for enforcing upon railways in general, or upon any railway in particular, such arrangements and precautions as from experience appear necessary for the public safety."[5] Lord Melbourne's government introduced a bill based on the report.

The subsequent history of this bill revealed the attitude which the railway companies were to maintain towards government intervention virtually down to 1914.[6] Even before the Board of Trade report had been issued, the companies had themselves taken steps to reach some sort of agreement on codes of signals and related topics.[7] On 19 January 1841 a large gathering of railway directors, engineers and managers took place at Birmingham to consider the causes and circumstances of railway accidents. Glyn, of the London & Birmingham, was in the chair; Hudson of the York & North Midland was also present; most of the principal railway companies were represented.

After deprecating "sudden and hasty legislation", the meeting went on to propose rules, regulations and codes of signals recommended to be observed on all railways.[8] If Brunel is to be believed, this was purely a propaganda exercise intended simply to placate public opinion.[9] More important was the setting up of a committee to keep an eye on government proceedings. Its policy was not to prevent the issue of specific regulations, but to prevent wide and undefined discretionary powers being given to the Board of Trade. Thus the committee did not offer outright opposition to the government's bill, but proposed to substitute a clause which would in fact have given the board wider powers than it actually obtained the following year, though they were narrower than those proposed by the Whigs. Under the committee's clause the board would have been prevented from issuing regulations designed to "impede or interfere with the business and traffic of the railways", and from prescribing "anything of an experimental nature."[10] Even so, the committee's proposals aroused hostility in railway circles, and there were sighs of relief when the bill was referred to a Select Committee of the House of Commons.[11]

The Select Committee was of opinion that no discretionary power of issuing regulations for the prevention of railway accidents should be delegated to the Board of Trade, and recommended that "the supervision of that Department [the Railway Department] should be exercised in the way of suggestion rather than in that of positive regulation."[12] In early June, a few days after the Select Committee had reported, Melbourne's government was defeated and its bill lost. But the fears of many railway directors proved well-founded. The new Conservative government was no less averse than its Whig predecessor to railway regulation. However, the bill of 1842 avoided the more controversial provisions of that of 1841, and passed into law with little fuss.[13] No general power was given to the Board of Trade to issue what regulations it pleased; but clause 6 gave it the power to postpone the opening of a railway where such opening was likely to be attended with danger to the public using the same, "by reason of the Incompleteness of the Works or permanent Way, or the Insufficiency of the Establishment for working such Railway."[14]

This clause gave the Railway Department a useful instrument of persuasion. It was by persuasion that accident inquiries were carried out and safety devices adopted.[15] The powers of the Board of Trade were limited not merely by this legal framework, but by what was technically feasible; technical feasibility had to be based on experiment and experience, both of which took time to develop. Moreover, the board's recommendations had always to be cheap enough for a company to think it more economical to comply than to resist.[16] The directors, for their part, were doubly wary of adopting new methods of working: any increase in capital expenditure might mean a reduction of dividend to the proprietors of the line; and any failure in the working arrangements would reflect upon them rather than upon a remote government department. Economics and their own prestige dictated prudence.

Nor was it by any means certain that the Railway Department knew its business better than the companies. On the question of safety the Royal Commission of 1865–7 had concluded that any attempt to regulate matters of railway safety by authority "would necessarily tend to check all efforts on the part of the railway companies themselves to improve these details of working", and had intimated that the protection of the public was to be gained not by interference on the part of the Board of Trade, but by reliance on the Common Law and Lord Campbell's Act.[17]

Notwithstanding these strictures, the 1868 Regulation of Railways Act included a clause ordering companies to provide such a means of communication, between passengers and company servants, on all trains which carried passengers more than 20 miles without stopping, as might be approved by the Board of Trade.[18] The companies themselves had experimented with systems of communication, but felt they could not recommend any one system for general adoption.[19] In due course, however, the Railway Department gave its approval to a system of cord communication designed by T. E. Harrison, engineer-in-chief of the North Eastern Railway.[20] But the Harrison Cord proved so inefficient that in the summer of 1872 the Department gave notice of its intention to withdraw its approval of the cord as from 1 January 1873.[21]

This experience, whilst reinforcing the companies' own view that the responsibility for the safety of passengers should be left to them, also proved a powerful argument against all legislative interference with the actual running of the railways. The *Railway Times*, in perfect sincerity, attacked

> the presumed necessity of further and constant interference with the free action of those who are both personally and pecuniarily responsible for the efficient working of the undertakings respectively placed under their control, in order, as it is alleged, to protect the public from accident, and compel the adoption of what the Board of Trade, or some other departmental body, constituted for the most part of gentlemen who, after all, can be nothing more than amateurs in railway work, may think proper to direct.[22]

Within the Board of Trade opinions amongst the inspectors were by the 1870s sharply divided on the comparative merits of legislation and the persuasive power of public opinion as a means of securing the adoption of safety devices.[23] Moves in Parliament to invest the board with greater powers to deal with companies making incorrect returns of accidents to their servants elicited from W. R. Malcolm, the Assistant Secretary for the

Railway Department, the rejoinder that "The suggestion which has been made to the effect that the Board of Trade should send agents about the country to hunt up cases against the Companies is hardly in accordance with the Spirit of our Government".[24]

For two decades after the passing of the Act of 1868 the emphasis in railway safety legislation was put not on compulsion but on giving vent to public pressure through wider publicity. With this policy the railway interest had no quarrel. If the companies were to be regulated at all, they much preferred flexible regulation by the Board of Trade to rigid regulation by Parliament; they preferred permissive to compulsory legislation. In 1871 a vigorous opposition was organized against the Conservative Sir Henry Selwin-Ibbetson's bill which sought to give the Board of Trade wide powers to inspect railways and enforce methods of safe working. After some hesitation Fortescue was persuaded to oppose the bill.[25] But later in the same session Fortescue's own bill was allowed to pass through both Houses without any debate. This measure legalized the holding of inquiries into railway accidents, and provided for more formal investigation of serious accidents; it also authorized the Board of Trade to call for accident returns.[26]

The Act was the compromise measure of a minister who himself had no policy on the question of railway safety, but was content to conciliate as many interests and to relieve as many pressures as possible. It achieved neither end. The reason lay in the series of serious collisions which bedevilled the railways in the late 1860s and early 1870s, traceable to inadequate brakes or methods of signalling, or to both.[27] Most of the larger companies were already in the process of adopting the block system of working, designed to prevent more than one train being on any one section of line at a time, and interlocking, to prevent the conflicting and contradictory movements of points and signals by a signalman. The merits of different systems of brakes were, however, far from clear; a committee of the Railway Association felt unable to recommend any one braking system for general adoption.[28]

The publicity which the Act of 1871 was designed to give affected parliamentary opinion more forcefully than it did the companies. Less than two years after its passing Lord Buckhurst (later Earl De La Warr), an early friend of the Amalgamated Society of Railway Servants and one of the principal antagonists of the railways in Parliament at this time, introduced in the upper House a bill making the block system and interlocking of points and signals compulsory on all new lines at once, and on all existing lines after 1 January 1875. The bill was not welcome to the railway interest, preoccupied with the Railway and Canal Traffic bill. Fortescue, however, regarded it as a useful opportunity unofficially to launch an inquiry into the matters it raised, and gave some help in getting it drawn up.[29]

The railway companies took a cautious view of the bill; mindful of public opinion, they raised little objection when it was referred to a Select Committee. This took the bill out of the political arena and placed it in the hands of a committee of thirteen peers, of whom four were railway directors. The Railway Association decided that "the Block and Inter-locking Systems were both good, but not infallible or necessary in all cases."[30] Thus the general managers and engineers who gave evidence before the committee set out to prove that the companies were already spending large sums on the block and interlocking systems, whose enforce-ment was thus declared to be unnecessary and also dangerous, because of the complacency those systems allegedly induced in engine-drivers.[31] But it was the evidence of Thomas Farrer, Permanent Secretary at the Board of Trade, which seems to have settled the fate of the bill. "I should be very sorry", he declared, "to see that responsibility [of defining a uniform block system for general adoption] thrown upon the Board of Trade at all."[32]

It was little wonder, therefore, that when the draft report came to be considered, Buckhurst found himself isolated. Much of the report was taken up with a catalogue of the progress being made by the companies in adopting the block and interlocking systems. Reference was made to the dangers of indiscriminate obligatory use of these systems. Buckhurst's bill was condemned. But a recommendation was included for further in-formation as to the progress being made in installing these modes of working on all passenger lines.[33]

The report was as pleasing to the government as it was to the railway companies. When the struggle for the Railway and Canal Traffic bill was all but over, Fortescue found time to introduce a bill providing for returns to be made by railway companies of their progress in adopting the inter-locking and block systems.[34] The Railway Association did not impede its progress; it became law after very little debate in the House of Commons and none at all in the Lords.[35]

The mounting frequency of railway accidents in the late summer of 1873 ensured that the government would derive little respite from Fortescue's Act. The situation was widely regarded as a national scandal.[36] Queen Victoria stepped in, and on 30 October wrote to Gladstone that "if a Director was bound to go with the Trains we shld soon see a different state of things!"[37] Gladstone passed on the letter to Fortescue, but further legislation was out of the question. The government's position was weak, its ministers in disarray, its support falling off. Fortescue decided to deliver a stern public admonition to the railways; he had a circular drawn up which he submitted for the Cabinet's approval and then sent to the companies.[38] The circular took the form of a sharp rap on the knuckles from the President himself. It spoke of "methods of working and mechanical contrivances, the value of which has been thoroughly ascertained, [which] have been too slowly introduced". There was a reminder that the government might "at any time [consider] the expediency of legislation."[39]

This threat, such as it was, merely brought forth paragraphs of indignation from the railway chairmen. Richard Moon, hurt and annoyed, voiced a deep-felt suspicion of mechanical appliances which induced in men a false sense of confidence. Gooch, making the same point, reminded Gladstone's government of its own false sense of confidence in the Harrison Cord.[40] The companies preferred to adopt new methods in their own time. At the end of 1873 all double lines on Watkin's South Eastern and Metropolitan railways were worked on the absolute block system; on the Manchester, Sheffield & Lincolnshire Railway, however, the mileage of double lines so worked was only one-eighth. On the London & North Western over half the points and signals were interlocked; on the Sheffield company less than one-sixth.[41] The replies to Fortescue's circular made it plain that any further government interference would be considered an unfriendly act. Yet at the same time the continuing series of accidents excited public and parliamentary attention. Gladstone thus bequeathed to Disraeli a problem which demanded a solution, but which promised much trouble if a solution were found.

Disraeli's Cabinet was singularly ill-placed to be able to reach definite decisions on any question involving the Board of Trade. R. A. Cross bore witness, in old age, to the absence of policy formation, especially on the part of Disraeli himself, who "had to rely entirely on the various suggestions of his colleagues."[42] The Board of Trade had no voice of its own in the Cabinet, for Charles Adderley, upon whom Disraeli's choice as its President fell, was expressly excluded from that inner circle, probably on account of his habit, in the 1850s, of voting against the party.[43] Between Disraeli and Adderley no love was lost. At Disraeli's wish Sir Stafford Northcote, the Chancellor of the Exchequer, undertook to serve as Adderley's spokesman in the Cabinet.[44] This arrangement did not work well, and broke down in 1875 over merchant shipping legislation, after which the Prime Minister made a clumsy attempt to remove Adderley from office. Squabbles between the two men continued till finally, in March 1878, Adderley left the Board of Trade for a seat in the Lords.[45]

In this strained atmosphere relations between Adderley and Disraeli were at their smoothest when no controversial Board of Trade legislation was being contemplated. In any case Conservative thinking itself fostered a policy of inaction where railways were concerned. By 1874 the fortunes of the Conservative Party were already felt to be too tightly bound up with commercial and industrial property to admit of great interference with them by a Conservative government. Disraeli openly favoured permissive legislation.[46] Though in his address to the Buckinghamshire electors he had promised to support "all measures calculated to improve the condition of the people", he stressed as well that he did not consider "this great end is advanced by incessant and harassing legislation."[47] On this point at least Disraeli and Adderley were in agreement.

> I am quite convinced [Adderley wrote] that the way to deal with the Railway Cs. is to cease harassing them by requirements of this & that, & to turn to aiding them to serve the public as they are liberally trying to do & keep in good will with them.[48]

In 1874 this policy was put to the test. The Conservatives had been in office less than two months when Earl De La Warr renewed his attack on the railway companies' safety record, and moved for a Royal Commission. The government did not resist this move, neither did the companies.[49] The railway interest, in fact, played the whole subject in a low key, allowing it to pass speedily from the uncertain world of politics into the realm of technicalities. The *Railway Times*, whilst warning against the expectation of "Utopian results", hoped that "the report of a body of practical railway authorities . . . may tend to satisfy the public mind that no available means of safety are neglected."[50]

The Royal Commission, which included T. E. Harrison of the North Eastern, dealt with two distinct questions. The one, involving technical matters concerning interlocking, the block system and brakes, was quite expected by the companies. The other, concerning accidents to railway servants and overwork, was certainly less expected. Michael Thomas Bass, the Liberal brewer, M.P. for Derby, large Midland Railway shareholder, and earliest patron of the infant Amalgamated Society of Railway Servants, was instrumental in having William Galt, a noted railway reformer and engineer, put on to the commission "to watch over the men's interests."[51] De La Warr was also on the commission. So it could not have been too difficult for Bass to have persuaded the commissioners to hear evidence from ex-railwaymen connected with the Amalgamated Society, including F. W. Evans, general secretary 1874–83 and Edward Harford, general secretary 1883–97.[52]

Fortunately for the companies the society's heart was not in this work. It regarded the commission "as a means, no doubt, of shelving railway difficulties as long as possible – perhaps to be ultimately bequeathed as a legacy to some future ministry", an assertion in which there was much truth.[53] In common with other sections of the trade union movement it concentrated on the reform of the law of employers' liability, and achieved no real success in this field until well after the Royal Commission had reported. In the history of the reform of the law of employers' liability the proceedings of the Royal Commission on Railway Accidents were of no great importance. Nonetheless it is noteworthy that at this time the railway interest took little notice of the Amalgamated Society, less still of its parliamentary friends. It was fortunate for the interest that the society's evidence before the Royal Commission was presented as ineffectively as its historian asserts.[54]

The Royal Commission sat for nearly three years.[55] The evidence given by the Board of Trade inspecting officers was conveniently ambiguous. Colonel Yolland urged greater powers for the Board of Trade to enforce the block system on all lines, but agreed that there was no difference of opinion between the board and the companies as to the advisability of its adoption.[56] He thought that a uniform brake system for the whole country was desirable, but did not wish to "create a difficulty which appears . . . likely to arise by insisting upon uniformity."[57] On the question of overwork a colleague agreed that twelve consecutive hours was "a fearfully long time" for a signalman to be on duty, but could point to no case in which excessive hours of work of a signalman had caused an accident.[58] Henry Tyler exonerated the companies from the charge of deliberately overworking their men, and spoke highly of the value of publicity, rather than interference with railway management, as a means of securing a more equitable arrangement of working hours.[59]

In this respect the picture which emerged from the evidence of railway servants was of a benevolent despotism exercised by the companies over their men for the latter's own good.[60] That there was substantial discontent over excessive hours of work is beyond dispute. Yet there was much that was deferential in the attitude of railway employees: higher wage packets meant much more to them than shorter hours.[61] Though some witnesses demonstrated vague agreement as to the desirability of improved safety appliances, others displayed an equally vague prejudice the other way.[62] Thomas Farrer once again poured cold water on the idea of enforcing systems of block working, interlocking and brakes; they were not, in his view, "things which can be settled once for all."[63] This was exactly what the companies felt, and it was doubtless for this reason that they played such a willing part in what proved to be the most spectacular episode of the commission's work, the brake trials at Newark.

The trials at Newark in the summer of 1875 formed the only extensive piece of propaganda which the railways undertook at any time before 1914. The idea originated with the commission, but needed the willing cooperation of the companies. The Railway Association appointed a committee of general managers and directors to discuss the location and details of the experiments with Edward Woods, an engineer appointed by the Royal Commission to represent it at the trials.[64] The trials took place in early June, six companies sending a total of eight engines fitted with different systems of 'continuous' brakes, which might be applied to every vehicle of a train.[65] But the results of the trials were inconclusive. Woods and Colonel Inglis, in their report to the Royal Commission, thought it "neither fair nor desirable at present to pronounce definitely either for or against any particular invention brought before the Royal Commission."[66] In the late summer and autumn of 1875 the general managers and other railway officials themselves gave evidence, assuring the public of the vigilance of the companies, and deprecating the idea of compulsion in the matter of brakes, or of any other safety precaution.[67] In May 1876 the Earl of Aberdeen, who had succeeded the Duke of Buckingham as chairman, warned that the Royal Commission could not be expected to choose between the different forms of brakes.[68]

The companies had, meanwhile, taken steps, as they had done in 1841, to forestall any drastic action against them. At the end of 1874 a committee of superintendents of the principal companies met to attempt to draw up a uniform system of rules for working all the railways of the country.[69] Between 1874 and 1876, under the auspices of the Railway Clearing House, a comprehensive manual of regulations was agreed to, though complete unanimity of practice was not attained.[70]

Anticipation of Board of Trade requirements was also tackled by the companies at this time. In March 1876, at the request of several chairmen, Leeman approached Farrer on this subject. Farrer's suggestion, that meetings be held between representatives of the companies and the inspecting officers, to discuss the latter's requirements and "the common and general adoption of improvements" was enthusiastically endorsed by the Railway Association.[71] They, and Farrer, seem to have had in mind a permanent consultative and advisory body. Adderley, fearful of too much responsibility being placed on his department, vetoed this suggestion; but it was agreed that, as occasion arose where new regulations were contemplated, a committee of railway and Board of Trade representatives would be appointed to discuss them. The arrangement promised to give the companies some say in their own regulation, and they accepted it. The agreement was embodied in a formal letter from Farrer to Leeman on 25 July 1876.[72]

This agreement, and the set of rules agreed in the same year, were the only tangible results of the commission's work. For there was no unanimity in the report which the commission presented in February 1877. The Majority Report, signed by six of the original nine commissioners, including Aberdeen, Harrison and Galt, recommended that discretionary powers be conferred upon the Board of Trade to enforce a miscellany of safety requirements, including the block and interlocking systems, and speed restrictions; but all such orders were to be subject to review by "a competent appellate tribunal." A change in the law of civil liability of railway companies for accidents to their servants was also contemplated. In tracing the causes of railway accidents, however, human fallibility was considered the main culprit. On the crucial subject of brakes there was comparative silence, other than a recommendation that sufficient brake power should be made obligatory, whether by hand brakes or by continuous brakes.[73] Harrison added a proviso warning of the false sense of security engendered by the absolute block system, and protesting against railway companies being singled out for special treatment in the matter of employers' liability.[74]

De La Warr refused to sign the report at all, and submitted his own conclusions, remarkable chiefly for the light they throw on the doubts and difficulties surrounding railway safety, as experienced by the man in whose protests the Royal Commission had originated. De La Warr thought it should be made obligatory on all railway companies to provide block and interlocking systems, and to employ sufficient brake power on all passenger trains. He too recommended a change in the law of employers' liability. But he did not think it desirable to confer any additional powers on the Board of Trade "which would lessen the responsibility of railway companies in working the traffic", and he envisaged a scheme whereby the board, having made a recommendation to a company without a favourable response, might itself appoint some higher tribunal "for final decision."[75]

Such inconclusiveness was welcomed both by the companies and the government. Adderley, who in 1876 was all but overwhelmed by the task of promoting merchant shipping legislation, had discountenanced the idea of comprehensive legislation on railway accidents long before the Royal Commission had reported.

> I cannot think that much legislation or government interference will be found desirable – though a great mass of faults in detail will appear in the Report. Everything is in a state of experiment, & the public sense of danger, & the Companies own interests are making them take every effort to improve. If this Department [the Board of Trade] is charged with prescribing improvements much more mischief & danger will accrue.[76]

When the report had been published, and De La Warr gave notice to ask whether the government proposed to legislate, Northcote advised Disraeli to "simply say that as the Govt. have not yet had time to consider the Report of the Commission you cannot give an answer."[77] In the Lords the Prime Minister made it clear that the government could not undertake to legislate at all in 1877.[78] The Eastern Question and Irish obstruction made comprehensive legislation on railway safety less and less likely that session, whilst growing divisions in the Cabinet over Turkish policy rendered such legislation politically inadvisable. Stafford Northcote himself was occupied with another delicate railway problem, that revolving around growing demands for the repeal of the passenger duty. Moreover just at this time relations between Adderley and Disraeli reached their nadir when the Prime Minister challenged Adderley's right to appoint to a vacant Railway Commissionership.[79] No one in the government was in a mood to meddle with the railways, especially on the basis of such contradictory evidence as the report of the Royal Commission afforded.

But gestures had to be made. Adderley discussed with Leeman the possibility of the companies agreeing to the appointment of a committee to consider the question of brake power.[80] The companies had naturally welcomed the Royal Commission's report; but the government's latest proposal was treated with caution. At a special meeting of the association a committee was appointed to meet the Board of Trade and "assure them that the Railway Companies are fully alive to the necessity of adopting some improved mode of stopping Trains and that the leading Companies are at this moment testing various systems for the attainment of that object."[81] This reply provided Adderley with a reasonable answer to awkward parliamentary questions, especially as he appeared to have thrown the ball firmly into the railway companies' court; consultation was to be the prelude to legislation.[82]

In fact Adderley was thinking solely in terms of creating correspondence to be laid before Parliament, to prove beyond doubt that the government was putting pressure on a responsive and responsible industry, and that therefore legislation would be an unnecessary waste of everyone's time. This idea pleased the Railway Association, which responded warmly to suggestions from the Board of Trade regarding the construction and contents of the correspondence.[83] To emphasize the folly of legislating on questions of such a technical nature Viscount Bury, a Liberal director of the London & South Western Railway, brought forward a motion in the Lords, that "direct legislative interference with the details of railway management tends rather to increase than to diminish the danger of accident by dividing responsibility" between the government and the companies. Bury's motion was not sponsored by the association, but received its subsequent approval.[84] It gave Disraeli an opportunity to expose the weaknesses and contradictions in the Royal Commission's report. Lord Houghton assured Parliament that "if there was delay in the adoption of any particular brake, it proceeded . . . solely from the conflicting opinions of experts."[85]

But the government was eventually, and much against its will, forced to legislate precisely because of the point Houghton had stressed: conflicting opinions. In due course Oakley forwarded to the Board of Trade statements from the companies regarding the action they were taking to install continuous brakes.[86] Taken individually the replies amply justified the view that "While the [Royal] Commissioners have been sitting, considering, and reporting for two years or more, the railway companies have been acting, spending large sums of capital to provide . . . means for the prevention of accidents."[87] But the possibility of the adoption of a uniform and efficient braking system over the whole country seemed as remote as ever. The Great Western had tried no less than seven brakes. The Manchester, Sheffield & Lincolnshire board had chosen the vacuum brake "as on the whole the least objectionable", but had decided against continuous brakes, which, they considered, "showed that new sources of danger were produced in practical operation."[88] In general the returns showed more diversity of opinion than the government had expected. Moreover, the Board of Trade's General Report upon Railway Accidents for 1876 insisted that "the time has now come when it is incumbent upon the Railway Companies to agree amongst themselves as to which of the various systems of continuous breaks [sic] . . . is best adapted for general adoption."[89]

There was a serious risk of pressure for further government action. On

30 August 1877, therefore, the board addressed a letter to all the companies, setting out conditions essential, in its opinion, to "a good continuous brake".

The companies and their officers [it warned] . . . would do well to reflect that if a doubt should arise that from a conflict of interest or opinion . . . they are not exerting themselves, it is obvious that they will call down upon themselves an interference which the Board of Trade, no less than the companies, desire to avoid.[90]

Mounting pressure for legislation worried the railway interest no less than Adderley. In December a deputation saw him, only to be told "that unless the Companies could show that they were progressing, the Government would not be able to resist legislation in the ensuing Session."[91] Leeman promised that the association would itself extract further information from the companies, and present it to the Board of Trade in time for the session of 1878.

This information was forwarded at the end of February. Once again the replies indicated great activity but little unanimity on the question of continuous brakes.[92] A special difficulty was that there was no regular means by which companies could exchange information; and, as Leeman pointed out to Adderley, even practical men had their differences on technical questions.[93] No doubt, too, considerations of professional pride entered into company policy; when a company engineer declared for one or other of the brakes available, his reputation was at stake if he subsequently changed his opinion. One writer on the subject of railway accidents has criticized the British companies severely for being "extraordinarily parochial" and rejecting the Westinghouse air brake "simply because it was American".[94] In fact, several companies adopted this brake. If they did not all adopt it at once, this was because they approached it, as they approached the block and interlocking systems, with caution, even suspicion. In the course of time the companies did adopt either this brake or the automatic vacuum brake, both of which satisfied the Board of Trade's conditions.[95] Lord Henniker summed up the government's own view when, replying to criticisms of government inaction, he declared that in a few years the companies "would have settled this important matter for themselves."[96]

A month later the government bowed to the critics of the railways and of its own railway policy, by legislating. The political situation was itself now somewhat more conducive to action. Although in March Lord Derby had resigned from the government, Adderley's own departure from the

Chapter 3

Board of Trade had brought in as the new head of that department Viscount Sandon, a competent man with a place in the Cabinet. In the Lords, on 11 April 1878, Lord Henniker introduced a government bill empowering the board to call for returns from the railway companies of the continuous brakes in use on passenger trains on each railway in the United Kingdom, and the types of brake used.[97]

This was a proposal merely to bring the law on the subject of continuous brakes into line with that governing the interlocking and block systems. Lord Houghton, for the companies, gave the measure an unenthusiastic blessing.[98] The bill passed through both Houses without amendment and became law in June; as the *Railway Times* was quick to point out, its main purpose was to "dissipate groundless fears and strengthen public confidence."[99] The companies continued to make experiments. In 1881 and 1882 conferences of general managers were held.[100] 'The Battle of the Brakes' continued. Aided by a Conservative government as anxious as the companies to avoid the taking of compulsory powers in the matter of railway safety, the railway interest was able to put off such compulsion until they no longer feared it. When such powers were eventually taken, in 1889, and another government, also Conservative, made Orders upon the companies, it was in the main preaching to those who had already been converted.

# Chapter 4

# Employers' liability

The campaign which the railway companies staged against serious interference with their working in matters of safety taught them some lessons
of lasting value. They gained experience of the workings of government
departments, experience which showed that much more could be achieved
by negotiating with governments than by fighting battles in the parliamentary arena. The sympathy with which the Conservative administration
regarded railway points of view could not have been plainer. Moreover, the
controversy over safety had brought the railway companies face to face
with the railway workers. But at this time the concern of railway workers
was not with accidents and overwork; their concern was with employers'
liability. The battle over employers' liability followed hard upon that over
railway safety. The tactical and political lessons of the former were reinforced by the latter.

The subject of employers' liability had been raised only incidentally during the Royal Commission of 1874–6. Yet it was one which peculiarly concerned railway companies, though they held aloof from it until legislation was almost on top of them. The Railway Association was certainly as well equipped to deal with this question as it was to deal with other hostile moves in the legislature. It is true that, as a body, the Railway Association never interfered with labour relations, within individual companies or with the industry as a whole, until it was forced to play some part in resolving the crisis of 1911. But this attitude arose quite naturally from the fact that the conditions of labour in each company were so different as to admit of no common line of action, save in the most exceptional circumstances.[1] Nor should it be forgotten that the association was a voluntary organization with limited and mainly political and parliamentary aims. Companies certainly did consult together on labour matters, especially when the object was to defeat or forestall combination among railway servants.[2]

At the same time, the unique conditions of the railway service made it especially resistant to trade unionism for far longer than was the case with all other large industries. This very isolation provided a good reason why the railway interest should have stayed in the background when other employers and their organizations fought the moves to legalize trade union practices. The principal railways inherited from the early years of railway growth a military structure, often with ex-military men in control, and a military discipline.[3] Of the ten railway strikes which occurred between 1830 and 1870, only four were not defeated. Petitions and memorials had to be presented separately, and personally, by the men in each grade.[4] Paternalism flourished. In railway towns the companies provided churches, schools, hospitals, public baths and gasworks. Many companies subsidized compulsory friendly societies, and some ran savings banks.[5]

But above all, railway employment brought security. In times of economic distress companies might dismiss casual labourers, but the many skilled workers employed by the companies had little fear of being 'laid off'.[6] There was much discontent, especially with hours of work. Yet although trade unionism on the railways can be traced back at least to 1848, none of the early organizations survived. Many of them had a friendly society atmosphere, with little importance attached to militancy. When the Amalgamated Society of Railway Servants appeared on the scene at the end of 1871, it too had something of this atmosphere, emphasized by its middle-class patrons, such as Michael Bass. For the remainder of the decade, strike action continued to be unpopular and generally unsuccessful, and in 1879 the footplatemen seceded to form their own union.[7]

In addition to these social and industrial factors, a peculiar development of English law had given the railway companies a most useful form of immunity from the effects of trade union combination. This was the doctrine of 'common employment', first laid down in Priestley v. Fowler (1837), by which a master was held not to be liable to his servant for any injury caused by the negligence of a fellow servant with whom the servant injured was engaged in a common employment. In Wilson v. Merry (1868) the Lords decided that the doctrine extended to managers and superior persons.[8] Thus established, the doctrine afforded much protection to all employers from claims for compensation by their workmen for injuries sutained in the course of employment. In the case of the railways, which had a complicated but hierarchical structure, the doctrine proved doubly effective, for there were very few railway servants who could not be said to be working in a common employment with some other servant in the same company.

Hence by the nature of railway employment and of the law governing that employment, railway directorates had reason to fear nothing from industrial trade unionism in the 1870s. The Railway Association played no part in the passing of the Employers and Workmen or Conspiracy and Protection of Property bills promoted by Disraeli's government. But such aloofness could not survive an attack on the law of employers' liability for injuries to their workmen. It was here, in the legislative sphere, rather than on the industrial front, that the Railway Association and the Amalgamated Society of Railway Servants first clashed.

The immediate origins of the foundation of the Amalgamated Society lay in a movement, for higher wages and shorter hours, in which Michael Bass played a prominent part.[9] Bass raised the matter in Parliament, and in letters to the chairman of his own company, his fellow Liberal M.P. W. P. Price, he attacked the management of the Midland Railway as "oppressive and illiberal towards their workmen, inconsistent with public safety, and injurious to the permanent interests of the shareholders."[10] In 1873 Lord Buckhurst, alarmed by the numbers of railway servants killed and injured, called on the companies to "provide a system of compensation for the benefit of the survivors of those killed in their service."[11] In December Bass publicly accused the Lancashire and Yorkshire Railway of making false returns of accidents to their servants; the Board of Trade placed the matter in the hands of the Treasury Solicitor.[12] Further revelations followed in September 1874, when the Lancashire & Yorkshire was again the main target.[13] De La Warr, as noted in the previous chapter, had obtained an examination of the whole question of railway accidents by a

Royal Commission in which the Amalgamated Society, through the efforts of Bass, was able to play a part. But even before the Royal Commission had begun to hear evidence, the question of employers' liability had been raised in Parliament, and legislation proposed, by no less a person than Edward Watkin.

The origins of the bill introduced by Watkin on 5 May 1874 "to amend the Law relating to Compensation for Injuries suffered by Persons in the course of their Employment" are still obscure.[14] In November 1873 Watkin, out of Parliament since 1868, stood as Liberal candidate in the Exeter by-election. The Conservative candidate, Arthur Mills, was a director of the North Staffordshire Railway. Exeter was an important railway centre, with railwaymen's votes to be won. The Exeter Tories accused the South Eastern Railway of being notorious for its accidents. Watkin replied by promising support for a compensation bill, and the statutory limitation of hours of work, and was thereby able to obtain the backing of the local Amalgamated Society branch in the election campaign.[15]

Watkin was defeated, but on being returned for Hythe next year he affected to redeem his promise by introducing a compensation bill himself. The bill sought to abolish the doctrine of common employment as a valid plea against claims for compensation by employees, but limited the amount of compensation payable to one year's wages. Contributory negligence was excluded from actionable cases. Clause 3 allowed employers and servants to make separate arrangements as to the amount of compensation. Allowances from sick and provident funds were to be taken into account by courts when assessing the amount of compensation for injury.[16]

The Mining Association took the bill seriously enough and issued "Reasons" against it as a "direct attack on the Mine Owners" who, the association alleged, could only exercise a general supervision over their men. Yet the restrictive nature of the bill suited the railway companies, and the parliamentary committee of the Railway Association gave it no more than passing mention.[17] But the bill received no support from the Trades Union Congress or the Amalgamated Society. Bass had already drawn up a Compensation bill, and F. W. Evans accused Watkin of deliberately introducing his own bill, with its "peculiar notion of compensation", in order to forestall the passing of "an honest measure".[18]

Watkin's bill was dropped. The executive of the Amalgamated Society continued to support Bass's bill.[19] In May 1875 Watkin again introduced a compensation bill, but its terms were now somewhat altered. The amount of compensation payable, instead of being limited to one year's wages, was limited to £200, while of any allowance from sick or provident funds, only the proportion contributed by the employer liable to pay compensation was to be taken into account by courts in assessing such compensation.[20] Evans supported the bill. The Parliamentary Committee of the Trades Union Congress opposed it, mainly on account of the restrictions it would have placed on the amount of compensation.[21] Godfrey Lushington, the Home Office Counsel, was particularly scornful of clause 3 which, he maintained, would "enable Railway Companies to snap up consents in an unjustifiable manner."[22]

The Railway Association briefly noted the bill's existence.[23] It was withdrawn at the end of June, by which time the Conspiracy and Protection of Property bill, of far more immediate concern to a far larger number of trade unions, was passing through the Commons. In July the Amalgamated Society's executive condemned Watkin's bill, but promised support if it were reintroduced without the limitation on compensation.[24] Watkin's real motives in introducing this bill, and that of 1874, can only be surmised. The bills cannot be dismissed as an electoral device. The bill of 1874 was not introduced until after the meeting of the new Parliament; there was no reason, politically, to introduce a bill at all in 1875. At Hythe Watkin had found a safe seat, which he retained continuously from 1874 to 1895, even after turning Unionist. Nor is there any evidence that the bills might have been promoted by the railway interest as a red herring. The Railway Association never opposed or supported them. It seems best to regard the bills as exclusively Watkin products.[25] Probably the philosophy behind them was that to give the railwaymen something of what they wanted in the way of reform of the law of employers' liability was better than waiting until the trade unions grabbed all they wished for, leaving the railway companies open to vast amounts of costly litigation. But neither the railway companies nor the government appeared interested.

In 1876 the campaign against the doctrine of common employment took a more serious turn. In February Alexander Macdonald, Michael Bass and other Liberals introduced a bill to abolish the doctrine, with a time limit on claims for compensation but no limit to the amount payable.[26] The mining interest, thoroughly alarmed, despatched a deputation to R. A. Cross to protest against the proposal. A number of the most prominent coal owners were also railway directors. Thomas Knowles (1824–83), the Conservative M.P. for Wigan, besides being a colliery proprietor and leading spokesman for the mining interest was also on the board of the London & North Western Railway. The parliamentary committee of the

Railway Association may have taken the view that, if displeasure was to be incurred by those who opposed Macdonald's bill, such opposition was better left to others. Either by design, or through sheer pressure of work created by the Royal Commission on Railway Accidents, the parliamentary committee passed the question of employers' liability on to the individual companies, advising them to instruct their own M.P.s on the measure.[27] Knowles attacked the bill as a measure which would "encourage nothing but carelessness and idleness." Another Conservative coal owner, Robert Tennant, M.P. for Leeds and a member of the Great Northern board, was less hostile to the bill and favoured a committee or commission. Joseph Pease of the North Eastern, whilst not opposing the measure outright, pointed out that the leading railway companies all had special funds for their workmen and that "Morally, if not legally, the liability was acknowledged by the masters in their contributions to these institutions."[28]

At the Home Office, Lushington advised "no legislation until the matter has been carefully considered as a whole."[29] The government accepted this advice. When a Conservative lawyer, Benjamin Rodwell, moved the rejection of Macdonald's bill, Cross promised a Select Committee, whose appointment, "to inquire whether it may be expedient to render masters liable for injuries occasioned to their servants by the negligent acts of . . . [those] to whom the general control and superintendence of workshops and works is committed", opened up a new phase in the question.[30] The railway companies feared most of all exceptional legislation affecting them alone, and so were content when the terms of reference were known.[31] But the parliamentary committee of the Railway Association considered it essential that the companies be represented on the inquiry. Two of their nominees, Knowles and Sir Henry Jackson, the Liberal chairman of the London board of the Northern of Canada Railway, were made members of the Select Committee; so too were Gooch and Tennant.

Having thus obtained acceptable representation on the inquiry, the parliamentary committee of the Railway Association took no further interest in its work, beyond giving a general directive to its solicitors to act as they thought best.[32] At this stage the railways, though opposed to any special legislation aimed simply at their own industry, which might be upheld later as an embarrassing precedent, did not, in the industrial and political climate of the day, consider it worthwhile to carry on a systematic opposition to attempts at altering the law of employers' liability.

The Select Committee sat for two sessions. But the companies played a minor part in its proceedings. In February 1877 the report of the Royal

Commission on Railway Accidents caused some alarm, for the Majority Report recommended changes in the law so that "the company should in every case be liable to its servants for the negligence of those to whom it delegates its authority as master."[33] In April 1877 senior officers of the major companies were instructed to give evidence to the Select Committee. George Findlay prepared a statement of facts regarding the practice of the London & North Western, and on 3 May, with James Grierson of the Great Western and Henry Oakley, he was instructed to give evidence the following day.[34]

Findlay was the principal railway witness. He directed his remarks to show that any alteration in the law would lead to antagonism between the companies and their servants, and indiscipline, and that in any case nearly all accidents on railways were due to the negligence of workmen. He also warned that if the law were altered, railway companies would be discouraged from supporting benefit societies. Grierson and Oakley agreed with and supported these statements.[35] When the Select Committee came to draw up its report two drafts were presented, one by the chairman, Robert Lowe, and one by Sir Henry Jackson. With few exceptions Gooch and Knowles voted in favour of Jackson's document, which became the committee's report.[36] It was a cautious and conservative review, recommending no change in the law of employers' liability, except "where the actual employer can personally discharge the duties of masters"; in such cases "the acts or defaults of the agents who thus discharge the duties and fulfil the functions of masters, should be considered as the personal acts or defaults of the . . . employers." The report pointed out that "The fact of such a delegation of authority would have to be established in each case."[37]

From the point of view of the railway companies this report created a most unsatisfactory situation. The report appeared in late June 1877. In April the Liberal Duke of St Albans had introduced a bill in the Lords specifically aimed at the companies, to restrict the employment of railway servants to twelve consecutive hours in any twenty-four. The Railway Association left it to be dealt with by the general body of peers, a trust well founded as the measure was withdrawn without a division.[38] But the fact that railways were being singled out for special treatment in the matter of employers' liability was not encouraging, especially as Liberal party opinion appeared to be turning in this direction. At Oxford, in January 1878, Sir William Harcourt, the future Liberal Home Secretary, spoke of the need for legislative interference with railway employment where the safety of the public was at risk, and attacked the doctrine of common employment as applied to railway work.[39]

The Amalgamated Society of Railway Servants, also sensing the changing mood of parliamentary, and especially Liberal, opinion, and working on the theory that many M.P.s who were not railway directors would support a measure dealing exclusively with railwaymen, decided to press for such a bill. On 18 January Bass and Macdonald introduced a bill substantially that of 1876.[40] The railwaymen found a champion of some stature in Thomas Brassey, Liberal M.P. for Hastings and eldest son of the famous railway contractor. On 30 January Brassey presided over a meeting in London called for the purpose of urging Parliament to pass a measure of compensation for injuries to railway servants; Gladstone, Dilke and Lowe sent messages of support.[41] On 22 March Brassey took a deputation from the Amalgamated Society to see Cross and ask for his support for a bill based on the recommendations of the Select Committee and the Royal Commission, including the question of compensation to servants. Cross declined to commit the government, though he did give an assurance "that the matter would be dealt with as soon as public business would permit."[42]

When Macdonald's bill came in for second reading, Tennant moved an amendment that "any alteration in the Law of Liability of Employers for Injuries to those in their employ should be founded on the Report of the Select Committee of last Session on the subject; and that, considering the importance of the question, affecting, as it does, all classes of the community, any measure on the subject should be introduced by [the] Government." Brassey protested that "the feeling of the great mass of those who were interested in railways" was in favour of reform. The debate which followed brought out a great diversity of opinion. Conservatives like J. E. Gorst supported the bill; Liberals like Shaw Lefevre thought it went too far. The Attorney-General, John Holker, promised to bring in a bill based on the Select Committee's report, and Macdonald's measure was 'talked out'.[43]

These events clearly caught the government and the railway companies off their guard. Privately at this time the government leaned towards the employers' view. Holker looked forward to a law absolving employers from liability to anyone simply for the negligence of their servants, but at the same time making all carriers of passengers by land insurers against loss. In 1878 this was just not practical politics. So Holker submitted to Cross a draft bill narrowing somewhat the definition of common employment, though not abolishing it, but making employers liable for the negligent acts of servants "in authority", who, in the case of railways, were to include general managers, traffic managers and station masters.[44]

This was at least a bold attempt to define the delegation of authority in industry. It was above all in the case of the railways that the question of extent of delegation became politically explosive. Sir Matthew White Ridley, M.P. for North Northumberland and Under-Secretary of State to Cross at the Home Office, posed this question in a memorandum written in July 1878; as Ridley joined the North Eastern board after the fall of Disraeli's government, and rose to become chairman of the company, the memorandum has a more than academic importance.[45] Ridley inclined towards a limitation of the defence of common employment "as everybody seems agreed should be done", but he did not see this as the end of the problem and, like Holker, suggested "compulsory insurance on both sides", though he could not see how "the insurance coming all out of the employers' pockets" could be avoided. He dismissed arbitrary distinctions between railway and other companies.[46]

Lushington, now Assistant Under-Secretary, also feared making an exception of the railway companies should employers generally be absolved from liability for their servants' negligence; but he feared equally a move to make all carriers insurers, because he felt the companies would resist either course.[47] The prospect of making all employers liable for their servants' negligence gave rise to visions of employers insisting on 'contracting out', with "strikes and lock outs all over the kingdom." Lushington's opinion was that:

> Notwithstanding . . . the pledge that the Government has given I think it would be inadvisable for them to commit themselves to a Bill that has not been completely considered. Perhaps some light might be thrown on the subject by a Royal Commission.

By November, with the government much troubled over affairs in Africa and Afghanistan, Henry Thring, the parliamentary counsel, advised against even the consolidation of the law surrounding employers' liability, for the dangers of falling foul either of the masters or of the servants was too great, and "Parliamentary considerations would be alone fatal to a consolidating Bill."[48] But Holker was beginning to have second thoughts.

Railway opinion was less undecided but far from clear. No one defended the law as it stood.[49] Gooch had supported Jackson's report, which had become that of the Select Committee, and which Tennant had upheld in the Commons. Much obviously depended on definitions, particularly the definition of agents fulfilling "the functions of masters", as the report of the Select Committee put it, and the definition of a master's responsibility towards his employees. Railway directors were prepared to be answerable for officials with whom they were in immediate contact. They were not prepared to shoulder responsibility for the actions of every one of their employees, particularly as this might mean constant and costly litigation which could upset labour relations and set aside the companies' own benefit funds.

The Amalgamated Society, however, was a new and unknown factor. Public attention was already focused on the problem of railway safety and accidents by the Royal Commission and its meagre results. Liberal M.P.s were flirting with trade unionism. The slackening rate of growth of the economy was already apparent. The net revenue of the companies dropped in 1878, and further still in 1879; in the latter year dividends on ordinary capital, which had risen slightly in 1878, were down by an average rate of over 8 per cent.[50] The Engineering and Iron Trades Association sought the support of the railway companies in an effort to extend working hours in the engineering and iron trades, and sent a deputation to the Railway Association; Gooch told them the Railway Association had decided "not to interfere".[51]

If this decision sprang from hesitancy, the spectre of legislation on employers' liability soon dispelled doubts. In October 1878 F. W. Evans had drafted another bill, well supported by Liberal M.P.s, which sought to deprive employers of the defence of common employment. This formed the substance of a bill introduced by Brassey in the Commons in February 1879; De La Warr introduced a practically identical bill in the Lords.[52] At the same time Macdonald brought in a bill of his own.[53] Then, in March, Holker astonished the railway companies by introducing a bill on behalf of the government.

As regards railways Holker had been influenced more by the findings of the Royal Commission on Railway Accidents than by the Select Committee on Employers' Liability. He had come round to the view that, comforting though it might have been to have had a law which rendered "no exception admissible" to the general principle that employers should not be liable to anybody for the negligent acts of their servants, railway companies and other "special classes of employers" would have to be dealt with by "special legislation".[54] His bill did not seek directly to abolish the doctrine of common employment. But, in respect of certain types of employment, it laid down that where servants suffered injury through the negligence of "servants in authority", the fact of common employment would henceforth be no bar to a right of action against the employer by those injured or by the "personal representatives" of those killed. The greatest danger to the railway companies came from the bill's definition of a "servant in authority"; in reference to a railway this phrase was declared to mean "Any person entrusted by the Company with the management of the railway, or of the traffic, or of any particular part of the railway or traffic, or of any station on the railway, or of any works connected with the railway, and no other person."[55]

The text of Holker's bill forced the railway companies to play a far greater part in the employers' liability controversy than they had hitherto done. It demonstrated too that if the companies could no longer rely on the sympathies of the Liberal party, Conservatism was not reliable in all circumstances either. It is, of course, a moot point as to whether, in the light of the subsequent obscurity into which the bill fell, Holker ever intended seriously to press on with it. J. S. Beale, one of the Railway Association's honorary solicitors, "felt convinced that the Attorney-General . . . did not intend the Bill to go so far as it really does."[56] After some thought the companies decided they could take no risks. Beale and R. F. Roberts, the London & North Western solicitor, saw Holker; they obtained nothing beyond a statement "that it was the intention of the government to include only chief and not subordinate officers" within the definition of a servant in authority.[57]

Other employers were no less worried. The National Federation of Employers of Labour wrote to the Railway Association suggesting a joint conference, with representatives from the Mining Association and the National Association of Factory Occupiers, "with a view to united action in Parliament" regarding the government's bill. The railways responded warmly, appointing a committee of chairmen and deputy chairmen to meet the National Federation and its allies.[58] By the time the conference took place, at the Westminster Palace Hotel on 25 April, the National Association of Master Builders of Great Britain, and the Central Association of Master Builders, London, had also joined the movement. Knowles was the central figure, for he was by then President of the Mining Association, and thus straddled two key industries; it was to him that the conference entrusted the task of arranging a deputation to Disraeli "for the purpose of urging upon him that the Bill be limited to the lines laid down in the Report of the Select Committee." Gooch and Moon declared themselves prepared to recommend the adoption of this course to the Railway Association.[59]

This was a strong indication that the companies as a whole took refuge behind the Select Committee's report. Prior to the interview with Disraeli on 9 May the Railway Association held a policy meeting. Gooch surmised that if Holker's bill was indeed based on the report of the Royal

Commission, as opposed to the Select Committee which had been specially appointed to deal with the subject, this itself was a tactical mistake. C. B. Denison thought legislation should be delayed till public opinion was better informed. But when all the representatives of the employers' associations held a preliminary conference, George Leeman's resolution, that the Prime Minister be requested to withdraw the bill, was carried unanimously.[60]

This is indicative of a split in the ranks of the Liberal Party, not in the ranks of the railway companies. Gooch was a good party man, not given to embarrassing his government. His political colleague, Knowles, had fewer reservations. When the deputation met Disraeli, Cross, Holker and the Lord Chancellor, Earl Cairns, Knowles told them that further legislation between employers and employed was "undesirable and unnecessary"; if the government's bill became law, "it would open the door for a continuous state of litigation between masters and men, and make it simply a case of employers *versus* trades unions." Gooch also urged the withdrawal of the measure: "Railway companies", he said, "had hitherto managed affairs with their men very well, and on the Great Western line there had not been a strike for 40 years." Richard Moon attacked Disraeli's administration for taking upon itself "paternal cares"; he continued,

> Workmen were well able to take care of themselves, they could leave at any time, and they fully understood the nature of the work which they engaged in. This was the worst time at which such a Bill could be introduced, when trade was never in a worse condition, when competition was such that they were beaten not only in foreign but also in home markets, and looking at the question from all points, he hoped that the Bill might be postponed for, at least, another year.[61]

The Amalgamated Society of Railway Servants had already written off the government's bill as a measure of no practical value to their members. On 30 July the bill was withdrawn.[62]

The Conservatives did introduce an identical bill the following year, though in the House of Lords. Referred to a Select Committee, it aroused the instant opposition of the Railway Association, which decided to call a conference of employers' associations as in 1879.[63] But this elaborate preparation proved unnecessary; the Cabinet was about to decide in favour of a dissolution, which was announced on 8 March.

The Liberal victory of 1880 made legislation on employers' liability virtually certain. The manner in which the Liberals espoused the cause of reform in the matter of employers' liability was in itself important. For the first time the efficient railway interest in Parliament, though far from identifying itself with Conservatism, found itself in opposition to a purely Liberal policy. Speaking against a motion calling for special treatment of railway servants as regards the doctrine of common employment, Watkin, supported by Knowles, deplored attacks on the railways in some constituencies for party purposes.[64] The Amalgamated Society's machine was swung behind Liberalism. Prominent Liberals, if they had not already done so, ranged themselves on the side of the unions. Circulars sent out by the Amalgamated Society to parliamentary candidates, asking their support for Brassey's bill, brought replies in the affirmative from nearly 300 of the M.P.s elected.[65]

Gladstone, once more Prime Minister, was lukewarm on the subject of employers' liability, identifying it at this stage with Ireland and other issues "one wd. like to meet . . . as far as may seem practicable."[66] But J. G. Dodson, President of the Local Government Board, had already reminded him that the "Employers' Liability Bill should not be lost sight of – Many classes of working men are most anxious about it."[67] The bill was to be Dodson's own contribution to radicalism. A committee of the Cabinet examined the different schemes, and decided to adopt Brassey's.[68] On 21 May Dodson presented to the Commons a bill identical with Brassey's bill of 1879, giving an employee the same right of compensation for personal injury by reason of the negligence of his employer, or of those acting under the employer's orders, as was enjoyed by non-employees.[69]

The railway companies had expected such a proposal, but were not prepared for Dodson's single-minded tenacity of purpose. The Railway Association's consulting solicitors asked him to postpone the second reading but were met by a blank refusal. Knowles reported that the Mining Association, whilst naturally opposing the bill, had suggested a scheme of mutual insurance. At Brabourne's suggestion the Railway Association decided to approach Gladstone direct, and at the same time to request Benjamin Whitworth, the Liberal Home Ruler and director of the Metropolitan Railway, to ask Dodson in the House whether the second reading would be postponed while employers gave their views to the Prime Minister. This forced Dodson's hand. On 28 May he told Whitworth that the second reading had been postponed till 3 June.[70]

This was a welcome breathing space; yet the efforts needed to obtain it showed that the Railway Association could not hope to do much more single-handed. The time gained was therefore used to whip up opposition to Dodson's bill. It was decided to call a gathering of industrial clans to demonstrate against the measure. This was an act of political realism. With legislation imminent the railway companies and other industries decided that mutual insurance was preferable to the universal enforced liability of employers for their servants' injuries. The meeting, at the Westminster Palace Hotel on 1 June, found employers in complete agreement on this point. A resolution condemning legislation which went beyond the Select Committee's report, and asking that the government's bill be itself referred to a Select Committee, with power to investigate the proposed scheme of insurance, was moved by Alfred Barnes, Liberal M.P. and important Derbyshire colliery owner, seconded by Gooch, and carried unanimously. At the same time the policy to be pursued before Gladstone was discussed, and it was arranged "that as many Members of Parliament as possible should be asked to attend with the Deputation."[71]

When Gladstone saw the combined employers' deputation the following day he was evidently impressed. Only two Liberal directors of large railway companies had accepted the government's bill, Hugh Mason and Samuel Laing, and then only in principle.[72] To Gladstone's face Watkin denounced the bill as "a barrel of gunpowder prepared by Her Majesty's Government" chiefly to conciliate the trade unions. Richard Moon pointed out that the railway companies were "quite willing to be responsible for the acts of a manager or some person in authority."[73] Gladstone asked for the proposals to be put on paper, and assured the meeting that nobody would be taken "by surprise".[74] In private, however, Gladstone was suspicious of the plan to send the bill to a Select Committee.[75] Immediately after the employers withdrew, Samuel Morley, the Liberal M.P. and hosier, introduced a deputation from the Amalgamated Society of Railway Servants, to urge the government not to accede to demands for compulsory insurance. But Gladstone had left the room; Dodson had to face the railway servants himself.[76]

The revolt of Liberal industrialists against the bill continued to grow. During the second reading debate the measure was criticized not only by Knowles from the opposition, but from the government's side by Sir Andrew Fairbairn, head of the Leeds firm of machine makers and a Great Northern director, Sir Henry Jackson of the Belfast Central and Northern of Canada railways, David Davies, and by Watkin, who bitterly referred to "Hon. Members who come from the hustings reeking with pledges to the working men [and who] might be disposed to follow the Prime Minister's lead in this matter."[77]

The following day the bill was committed by the government *pro forma*, and emerged with material alterations.[78] These demonstrated that the government was still thinking in terms of a measure which would satisfy all sides. A new clause 3 limited the sum recoverable as compensation to the estimated earnings of the three years previous to injury. A new clause 4 laid down that actions for the recovery of compensation must be commenced within six months of the injury. The most important innovation was a clause 6 which defined "a person who has superintendence entrusted to him" as "a person whose sole or principal duty is that of superintendence, and who is not ordinarily engaged in manual labour", and an "employer" as including "a body of persons corporate or unincorporate." *Prima facie* this alteration favoured employers; clause 6 certainly narrowed down the number of persons for whose actions railway directors were to be liable. But it could be argued that, by narrowing down the area of an employer's responsibility, the bill made litigation more certain. There can be little doubt that the tendency of the amended bill to pinpoint more accurately the limits of an employer's responsibility led trade unionists and their Liberal allies to press for the insertion of similar provisions defining the extent of an employer's responsibility more accurately also. In the case of the railway companies this was to have serious repercussions.

Certainly none of the alterations made the railway companies any happier. Subsection 3 of clause 1 imposed a liability on an employer for an accident to a workman sustained "By reason of the negligence of any person in the service of the employer to whose orders or directions the workman at the time of the injury was bound to conform, and did conform." As far as railway companies were concerned this really amounted to an outright abolition of the doctrine of common employment, without any regard for the inevitable remoteness of the railway directors from the vast majority of their employees. As subsequent divisions on the bill showed, the railway interest supported provision being made for laying down the amount of compensation payable, provided it was limited to the sum proposed in the amended text.[79]

The immediate concern of the companies was to gain acceptance of the idea of mutual insurance. At Watkin's suggestion Knowles agreed to press for a Select Committee to consider this question. On 6 July Knowles duly moved for the Committee. In reply to Watkin Gladstone promised that the government would give full consideration to a carefully framed plan of insurance. The motion was lost by 259 votes to 130.[80]

Events made it impossible for Gladstone to demonstrate his sincerity. On 3 August the Lords threw out his Irish Compensation for Disturbance bill. Already discontented radicals looked to the government for redress, and Gladstone determined, in spite of the lateness of the session, to persevere with some of the ministry's other schemes, particularly in the domestic field.[81] A stern Employers' Liability bill was to be part of this policy. At the same time, and doubtless influenced by the ease with which Knowles' motion for a Select Committee had been defeated, many employers were induced to give up the struggle against the measure. A meeting was arranged between employers' representatives and trade union delegates, the latter including Macdonald, Henry Broadhurst, Thomas Burt, Ben Pickard and F. W. Evans; Gladstone agreed to defer the committee stage while these talks took place. But the truce was anathema to the Railway Association. Whilst requesting director-M.P.s to oppose subsection 3 of clause 1, the association refused to send any representatives to meet the union leaders.[82]

The effect of this decision was twofold. It isolated the railway companies as the most unreasonable, and therefore the most reactionary, amongst the employing classes; and those Liberal M.P.s who belonged to the efficient railway interest found that they were now firmly placed on the right wing of Liberalism, though in fact they had not altered their views at all since the days of Conservative rule. They considered it most unreasonable, as did their Conservative colleagues, that railway companies should be made liable for every injury sustained by their servants, whilst at the same time contributing, voluntarily, to funds "the very object of which is to provide for those whom they employ that which the law at present denies them."[83] The view of the companies was that the railway employer should be able to opt for the latter without incurring extra obligations. To this the Amalgamated Society of Railway Servants and its Liberal allies were adamantly opposed, ostensibly because they regarded these proposals as an evasion of liability, but also because anything which strengthened the ties between the companies and their employees weakened union solidarity.[84]

Proceedings in committee on the bill demonstrated the position in which Liberal railway directors now found themselves. The amendment to leave out subsection 3 was proposed by Joseph Bolton, the Liberal merchant from Stirling and deputy chairman of the Caledonian Railway, and received guarded approval from Joseph Pease; it was negatived without a division.[85] Pease and Henry Jackson both had to oppose an amendment put forward by Samuel Morley, their fellow Liberal, designed to further increase the liability of railway companies for injuries to their servants occasioned by servants working in other departments.[86] Watkin proposed to confine actions under the bill to places where "no mutual insurance fund . . . is established", but this proposal was negatived also.[87] The proviso as to contributory negligence was struck out without a division, on the motion of James Bryce, the Liberal member for Tower Hamlets.[88]

When the Railway Association took stock of the situation on 10 August, the feeling was "that any attempt to modify the Bill [in the Commons] would prove futile."[89] But the worst was yet to come. On 13 August Sir Hardinge Giffard, the former Conservative Solicitor-General, moved a new clause, specifically depriving railway companies of the defence of common employment in any action brought against any railway company under the Act. Two other Conservatives, W. T. Makins and Sir Henry Tyler, both of the Great Eastern board, opposed the clause, which was negatived on a division. Later the same day, however, an amendment proposed by Samuel Morley, imposing upon employers liability for injuries to their servants "by reason of the negligence of any person in the service of the employer who has charge or control of any signal, points, locomotive engines, or trains upon a railway", was agreed to without a division.[90]

This amendment turned the Liberal Employers' Liability bill into an avowedly anti-railway measure. Lord Brabourne, newly arrived in the upper Chamber, offered his services there to the railway companies. The Railway Association accepted, and Brabourne was asked "to oppose the exceptional class legislation proposed by this Bill", to have Morley's amendment struck out and, if possible, "to add a clause to the Bill on the question of Insurance, and to limit the amount of damages to a sum not exceeding £200." Brabourne duly gave notice to omit subsections 3 and 5 (Morley's amendment), to limit the amount of compensation to £150, and to move a new clause the object of which was to legalize schemes of mutual insurance in lieu of claims being made under the Act, that is, insurance plus contracting out.[91]

On the second reading Brabourne attacked the bill vigorously. He did not move his clause limiting compensation, and he failed also in committee to have Morley's amendment struck out. But his motion to omit subsection 3 was carried by 75 votes to 49.[92] When the Commons naturally disagreed with this amendment, Brabourne at once wrote to Lord Rowton (Montagu Corry) in the hope that Disraeli, who had shown himself to be sympathetic to the views of the railway companies, might be persuaded to throw his weight against the reinsertion of the subsection.[93]

But there was to be no clash between the two Houses. On 3 September the Lords decided not to join issue with the lower House; a few days later the bill became law.[94]

One thing which the Act of 1880 did not prohibit was the contracting out of its own provisions. R. F. Roberts consulted the Solicitor-General, Sir Farrer Herschell, and other lawyers, and reported that they considered that railway companies and their servants could contract out of the provisions of the Act, though "great care should be exercised in framing the Contracts, as they would not be binding without some valuable consideration to support them."[95] On the London & North Western, contracting out, with simultaneous membership of the company's insurance societies with increased scales of benefits, became obligatory. Similar though less stringent arrangements were put in force on the London, Brighton & South Coast Railway. On the Great Eastern deductions were made from the company's contribution to the men's insurance fund if a man obtained damages by litigation. Elsewhere, however, there was no contracting out.[96]

But in the courts subsection 5 of clause 1 of the Act, Morley's amendment, was deprived of much of its intended force.[97] The Amalgamated Society of Railway Servants pledged itself to the abolition of the doctrine of common employment, as well as of contracting out, stoutly defended by the London & North Western.[98] The dilemma was not resolved until, by enacting the Workmen's Compensation Act in 1897, the Unionists were able to replace the law of employers' liability by a compensation scheme which was in practical terms not far removed from the system of insurance for which the railway interest had pressed 17 years before.

These developments, however, could not be foreseen in 1880. In that year the railway interest had suffered its first reverse in the field of the actual working of the railways, as distinct from railway economics, rates and traffic arrangements. It was a reverse in which the Amalgamated Society of Railway Servants played a substantial part; and it was a reverse in which, though errors of judgment, of tactics, played a part, party politics proved the decisive factor. The railway interest approached Gladstone in the belief that he controlled the destiny of the bill. This was not so. In matters of secondary importance, particularly in the domestic field, Gladstone allowed himself to be led by his left wing. In any case, in 1880 Gladstone was too preoccupied with imperial and Irish affairs. Dodson was the driving force behind employers' liability reform. He wrote to the Prime Minister:

> May I repeat to you what I wrote to Chamberlain yesterday – viz that I hope when once the bill is approached that it will be pushed on day after day with the shortest possible interval even between its different stages. . . . Such a course shows 1. determination on the part of the Government 2. It leaves the minimum of opportunity to get up speeches, invent amendments, & organize resistance inside the House or out of it.[99]

It is certainly surprising that the railway companies never approached Chamberlain on the subject of employers' liability in 1880. Chamberlain, at the Board of Trade, was still very much an untried figure. His appointment had been a political one, in deference to the demands of the National Liberal Federation. He came to the Board with a reputation as an active radical; the railway interest may instinctively have fought shy of him, though they fared no better at the hands of Dodson or Gladstone. Moreover, though Leeman had been elected chairman of the Railway Association in 1880, with Gooch as deputy chairman, he took no part in the running of the association that year. The chair was taken by Gooch or Richard Moon. Leeman retired in 1881 and was replaced by Gooch, with Moon as his deputy. Thus from February 1880 the association was led by two men who had nothing in common with the leading Liberals. This naturally did little to smooth matters.[100]

The negotiations with the Liberal government showed that it was prepared to take up and press left-wing measures of industrial reform, and that it was prepared to conciliate Labour rather than Capital. It is clear that, in this respect, the accession to power of the Liberals in 1880 strained loyalties amongst the Liberal members of the railway interest. On Knowles' motion to have the employers' liability bill referred to a Select Committee, seven Liberals of the efficient interest voted with their party, but five voted against the Liberal whips and joined eight Conservative members of the efficient interest in voting with Knowles. The five were J. C. Bolton, S. C. Glyn, Henry Robertson, C. R. M. Talbot and Edward Watkin.[101] One division in committee found three Liberals of the efficient interest, Lord F. C. Cavendish, Sir Andrew Fairbairn and Alexander Matheson, voting with their whips, but four, Robertson, J. W. Pease, L. L. Dillwyn and Sir G. MacPherson-Grant, voting with three Conservatives in defiance of their whips.[102] When Morley moved an amendment to extend the operation of the bill to workmen working in separate or distinct branches or departments for an employer, no Liberal member of the efficient interest voted for it, though ten voted with the whips against it. Similarly, on an amendment to secure a clearer definition of a person having superintendence entrusted to him, only one member of the efficient interest, Hugh Mason, voted in favour of it whereas seven Liberals voted with their whips against it, and were joined by three Conservatives, W. W. B. Beach, Thomas Bruce and R. W. Cochrane Patrick.[103]

If these figures are evidence merely that the Liberal railway interest stood on the right wing of the party rather than on the left, voting in the Lords demonstrated that the Conservative vote there was showing itself to be the railway companies' best friend. In a division on Brabourne's motion to omit subsection 3 of clause 1, support came from a number of Conservative directors, and from Disraeli. The only railway directors to vote in favour of the subsection were Liberals, and none of these were directors of large companies.[104] As if to press home the point, it was Disraeli himself who moved to insert a time limit to the bill, providing for the expiration of the measure at the end of 1882, unless extended by Parliament.[105]

The contrast between the relationship of the companies to the government under Disraeli's regime, and the treatment the railways received at the hands of Gladstone's administration in its first months of office, could not have been more complete; indeed the comparative ease of the railway interest's position under Disraeli may well have put its members off their guard. In February 1881 Watkin proposed that the Railway Association should be reorganized, with a paid chairman, solicitor and secretary, to secure uniformity of action, and efficiency. He "cited instances in both Houses of Parliament, when there had not been any of the Railway representatives present to support Peers and Members, who had endeavoured to protect the Railway Interest when legislation affecting it was pending."[106]

This was certainly true of the later stages of the Employers' Liability bill. In the division on Pease's clause regarding mutual insurance societies, besides Pease who was acting in defiance of the Liberal whips, no member of the efficient interest declared himself in favour of the proposal; yet only two, both Liberals, voted with their whips against it.[107] Lord Randolph Churchill's clause regarding mutual insurance schemes attracted no support from the companies; but only four Liberal members of the efficient interest, and no Conservative member, voted against it.[108] When an amendment was moved to restrict the operation of Samuel Morley's new subsection 5 of clause 1, although Thomas Burt, Henry Broadhurst, Lord Randolph Churchill and Drummond Wolff supported the amendment, no director of a large railway company did so; but only two members of the efficient interest, both Liberals, Lord F. C. Cavendish and Sir Andrew Fairbairn, voted against it in obeisance to the Liberal whips.[109] Finally, in the division on whether to agree with the Lords' amendment, as amended in the Commons, limiting the operation of the Act till 31 December 1887, no member of the efficient interest voted against the Lords' amendment, as amended; yet only one, the Liberal Lord F. C. Cavendish, who had close family ties with Gladstone, voted with the Liberal whips in its support.[110]

These divisions, which all took place on or after 6 August, would appear to add substance to Watkin's criticism. In the later stages of the bill there was a most meagre attendance by both Liberal and Conservative members who sat on the boards of the large railway companies. Conservative M.P.s may have been afraid, for political reasons, of appearing to oppose the bill. Possibly the railway interest as a whole was fearful of drawing attention to itself by opposing popular provisions, or by supporting unpopular ones such as Lord Randolph Churchill's mutual insurance clause.[111] In many cases there certainly must have been acute clashes of loyalty, between loyalty to the party and loyalty to the company. Abstention was a neat way of solving the problem. This, however, was far from being universally true in the case of the Liberal directors.

Years before, Watkin had written to Lord Salisbury congratulating him on his appointment as Secretary of State for India, and promising him

> in advance, never to give a mere party vote against *any* Government of which you are a member. Indeed, I hope to vote for, and with, a Government of which you are at the head – some day.[112]

Those Liberal M.P.s who, like Watkin, were most active as members of the railway interest were by nature the sort of M.P.s who could be persuaded to desert their party, provided the brand of Liberalism which they supported, a brand developed in the days of *laissez-faire*, free trade agitation, and rabid hostility to landowners, no longer found favour with the party which called itself Liberal, no matter by whom it was led. Liberalism was slowly passing from an individualist to a collectivist philosophy.[113] This was recognized by contemporaries, who looked forward to the period "more or less remote, when the two great sections of Liberalism should fall definitely apart, and fuse on one side with the great Radical body, . . . [and] on the other, with its natural opposite, the Conservatism of the time."[114]

The Conservative members of the efficient interest knew from their experience during 1874–80 that post-1868 Conservatism would give them a sympathetic hearing. To the Liberal members the Employers' Liability Act was both a warning and a signpost. Gladstone's Irish policy pointed in the same direction: more dictation by a Liberal government less determined than any previous Liberal government to maintain the rights of property and the inviolability of private interests. By the beginning of 1882 Lord Brabourne was able to say how much he would rather support a government with Lord Salisbury at its head "than one inspired by Chamberlain & Co. as the present seems to be." The general public, he added, "do not recognise the great departure from *moderate* Liberalism to which his [Gladstone's] Government has led their party" since 1880.[115]

During the passage of the Employers' Liability bill in 1880 there were 14 divisions in the Commons. Four Liberal members of the efficient interest voted against their whips on two occasions: J. C. Bolton, Henry Robertson, Hugh Mason and J. W. Pease. Five others voted against their whips on one occasion: S. C. Glyn, C. R. M. Talbot, Sir E. W. Watkin, L. L. Dillwyn and Sir G. MacPherson-Grant. This must not, of course, be exaggerated into a 'revolt'. Dillwyn, Pease and Bolton remained loyal to Gladstone throughout the Home Rule crisis. Watkin did not. Brabourne had parted company with Liberalism much earlier. David Davies, Andrew Fairbairn and Sir G. MacPherson-Grant turned Unionist in 1886.[116] Henry Robertson also signified his break with Gladstone.[117] For such people, signs of the shifting principles of Liberalism in the 1880s left no alternative but to rethink political allegiances.

# Chapter 5

# The railway passenger duty

Although relations between the Liberal government and the railway interest suffered a discouraging start when the Employers' Liability Act was pushed through, that measure had not directly involved the man charged by Gladstone with the overall superintendence of railway affairs. Indeed, the exact position Joseph Chamberlain would take up in regard to railways had yet to be revealed, or even worked out, for his knowledge of the subject was vague and his first inclinations were to let sleeping dogs lie.[1] But this was not to be. He was obliged to deal both with railway rates and with the railway passenger duty; these were questions aggravated by social and economic conditions set against a background of constant political turmoil. Moreover, once obliged to cast about for solutions to these problems, Chamberlain's radical zeal led him to adopt policies and postures which brought him and the railway interest into bitter conflict.

The railway passenger duty provided the battleground for the first trial of strength. The problem had, in fact, engaged the attentions of railway companies, and of successive governments, for many decades. In the early stages of the dispute Gladstone himself had played a central part as President of the Board of Trade under Peel. Forty years later Gladstone's own government attempted to settle the question. Here was another area of railway administration in which the practices of Liberalism resulted in further alienation of the railway interest.

The railway passenger duty was almost as old as the public passenger-carrying railway. It was first imposed by Lord Althorp in 1832 at the rate of one halfpenny per mile for every four passengers carried. Difficulties were experienced in obtaining the necessary information, and in 1842 the tax was changed to a duty of 5 per cent upon the gross receipts from all passengers conveyed.[2] Two years later, however, the nature of the duty was altered fundamentally by clauses which Gladstone inserted in his Railway Regulation bill as part of his policy of giving inducements to the companies in order to extract from them better facilities for the public, in this case the third-class passenger, whose use of main-line trains the companies had hitherto discouraged.[3] Sections 6 to 10 of the 1844 Act compelled all passenger railways to run at least one train every weekday from end to end of the line, in each direction and stopping at every station, at a fare not exceeding one penny per mile, at such times and under such conditions as were approved by the Board of Trade. In return such companies had remitted to them the duty otherwise payable in respect of the receipts from the conveyance of such passengers.[4]

In the following decades there was tremendous expansion in third-class rail travel. In 1845 only just over 17 per cent of all passengers carried on United Kingdom railways were third-class; thirty years later that proportion had risen to over 77 per cent.[5] In 1842 the duty yielded to the government £153,000; by 1868 this had risen to £500,000, and reached about £800,000 in 1882.[6]

The railways had acquiesced in the original imposition as a matter of justice, for similar duties – notably stage-carriage mileage duties and licences – were then paid by horse-drawn traffic. As these duties were repealed, the justice of maintaining a duty on railway passengers became less obvious.[7] At the same time the rise in working expenses of railways in the 1870s lent added impetus to the movement for the repeal of the duty.[8] But Gladstone's Act, and the expansion of third-class rail travel which it encouraged, made a straightforward repeal of the duty financially difficult and politically dangerous, especially as the Reform Act of 1867 made governments more vulnerable to working-class opinion. The railway interest demanded the repeal of the duty as a matter of strict justice, with no strings attached, but was met with the cry of 'monopoly' and counter-demands, that if the country was to give up such a considerable sum, the companies should be prepared to come forward with a *quid pro quo*. It was a situation of which Joseph Chamberlain could be expected to take full advantage. From the point of view of the railway interest there appeared to be little room for manœuvre.

The attempts of the companies to obtain some modification of the duty, culminating in the bargain which the Railway Companies' Association reluctantly struck with the government in 1883, reveal the railway interest at its most flexible, using every means available to bring pressure to bear upon successive governments, at administrative and parliamentary levels, and making use of other interested parties wherever possible. The responses of these governments also underline important differences of treatment which the interest experienced at the hands of Conservative and Liberal administrations.

Gladstone continued to interest himself in using the duty to obtain more concessions for the working classes. In 1863 some negotiations took place between him, then Chancellor of the Exchequer, and the railways, on the basis of exempting from duty all third-class passengers at fares not exceeding one penny per mile; but nothing definite emerged.[9] Then, as a result of an administrative squabble between the Board of Trade and the Board of Inland Revenue, the government of which Gladstone had become Prime Minister made overtures unilaterally. The cheap train provisions of the 1844 Act had long outgrown their usefulness. The third-class passenger was no longer frowned upon by the companies, nor was it any longer expected that a train, to enjoy exemption from duty, should have to stop at every station. The Board of Trade had accordingly dispensed with this condition, but in 1866 was advised that it had no power to do this.[10] For the companies a literal enforcement of the Act threatened a drop in revenue, or an increase in duty payable, or both. When it came into office at the end of 1868, Gladstone's government faced the prospect of having to administer, to the detriment of third-class passengers, an Act regarded as superfluous by the Board of Trade and as obsolete by the Inland Revenue.[11] So when, in 1869, Cardwell pressed the companies to reduce charges for the conveyance of troops by railway, Robert Lowe, the Chancellor, held out the possibility of some remittance of the passenger duty. As the Inland Revenue was now badgering companies for payment of duty on trains not stopping at every station, the companies naturally pricked up their ears.[12]

But Lowe's proposal, to replace the duty on passenger traffic by a 1 per cent duty on all traffic, thus taxing goods and mineral traffic for the first time, produced a sharp difference of opinion among the companies. Under the influence of northern companies, like the North Eastern, the proposal was rejected. The southern companies, whose revenue came mainly from passenger traffic, threatened independent action to obtain a total repeal of the duty.[13] A suggestion from the Board of Trade, that companies should run extra third-class and workmen's trains in return for a partial remission of the duty, produced a mildly encouraging response, but Lowe, with an eye on government revenue, poured cold water on the idea, ominously introducing the argument that the duty was the price the railways had to pay for their monopoly.[14] There, for the time being, the matter rested.

No further approaches were made until, in 1872, the Attorney-General commenced proceedings against the North London Railway to determine whether, in fact, the Board of Trade had the power to dispense with the requirement that trains, to qualify for remission of duty, must stop at every station.[15] When Leeman raised the matter on behalf of the Railway Association in the House of Commons, Lowe declared that the collection of the duty on fast and express trains was

> just and fair; because it is notorious that the exemptions were granted under an idea which prevailed at the time [1844] that it would be a losing business to carry third-class passengers at a penny a mile, whereas it has turned out to be a very lucrative one.[16]

At the end of the year the Railway Association decided to make a personal appeal to Gladstone and accordingly sent a large deputation to Downing Street to ask for the complete abolition of taxes on locomotion and, more immediately, for the removal of the threats of legal proceedings. Gladstone remained totally unmoved.[17] In revenge, two days later, the North London solicitors revealed that the Conservative lawyers Lord Cairns and Sir William Bovill had in 1866 assured that company that they were correct in resisting the claims of the Inland Revenue.

> It may have been merely a coincidence, but it was curious that Lord Cairns and Sir William Bovill having been shortly afterwards appointed Attorney and Solicitor General, nothing was heard of the proceedings previously threatened until some time after those gentlemen had been succeeded by other [i.e. Liberal] law officers of the Crown.[18]

The following year the railway companies were too preoccupied with questions of safety and traffic legislation to feel able to reopen on any scale that of the passenger duty. In the west country, however, Henry Ellis, a director of the Bristol & Exeter Railway, and a prominent shareholder, was busy circularizing companies with a view to organizing shareholders' petitions to the Treasury.[19] Edward Watkin kept the question before the government by acting as spokesman for a deputation to Lowe on 26 March.[20] But Lowe's budget, containing no remission of the duty, came as a disappointment. "Mr. Gladstone's Government", the *Railway Times* observed, "has not quite come up to the high expectations formed of it . . . in 1868", and the paper accused Lowe, with reason, of trying to curry favour with the multitude.[21] In any case the government, immersed in a pool of disillusion, was by now too weak to undertake such a controversial financial reform. When, in June, Gladstone made a private approach to Leeman, to ascertain what concessions the companies might be prepared to offer, the reply was that they had only one counter-proposal to make: total abolition of the duty.[22]

The formation of a strong Conservative government the following year gave rise to greater hopes for the settlement of the question. Though the companies were not prepared to abandon their demand for total abolition without conditions, they could expect a sympathetic hearing from a Chancellor of the Exchequer who had himself been a railway director, and from an administration wedded to principles of legislative serenity.[23] In the spring of 1874 Henry Ellis and Sir Antonio Brady, a director of the Cornwall Railway, formed and became honorary secretaries of a Railway Passenger Duty Repeal Association, an unashamed pressure group which received the blessing of the companies.[24] Together, the Railway Companies' Association and the Repeal Association lost no time in arranging a joint pre-budget deputation to Northcote.[25]

For a time the idea of remitting the duty appealed to the Conservative Chancellor. Gladstone had left a large surplus. Northcote confided to Adderley that there was a possibility the duty would be given up.[26] To Disraeli, on 22 March, Northcote put forward a plan to abandon the idea of reducing income tax, and instead to turn the budget into a scheme of remissions of various taxes, including the railway passenger duty. At the Chancellor's suggestion a committee of the Cabinet was set up to negotiate with the railway interest.[27]

But other claims weighed heavy on Northcote's mind. The prospect of being able to relieve local taxation, abolish the sugar duties, and take a penny off the income tax, was too bright to be ignored.[28] It soon became clear that even Northcote was not prepared to run the risk of remitting the passenger duty, without obtaining some concession which he could parade before Parliament and the country. When the joint deputation saw him on 17 March, Leeman, whilst making a strong plea for total abolition, was able to offer nothing in return.[29] The problem thus remained no nearer solution.

Within the railway interest there were occasional apostles of compromise.[30] But the case against the North London Railway, heard before the Court of Exchequer in June and July, tended to harden attitudes. The company lost, Baron Amphlett's judgment containing a declaration that only cheap trains, approved by the Board of Trade, which stopped at every intermediate passenger station on the line could be exempted from duty under the 1844 Act, whether the fares exceeded the prescribed or parliamentary rate, or not.[31] At a special meeting of the Railway Association, Gooch, Moon and Watkin urged a policy of militant non-co-operation, by which only those third-class trains which stopped at every station would continue to be run, and all fast cheap trains would be withdrawn.[32] By October there was broad agreement among the companies to a series of resolutions proposed by Leeman, the net effect of which was that the passenger duty was to be added to all third-class fares wherever this was practicable.[33] It was an attempt to have "the practical bearing of the question" brought home to the public "by the fear of the *argumentum ad pecuniarum*", and next month the London & North Western, Great Western, and South Eastern railways announced an increase of 5 per cent in all third-class fares.[34]

In 1875 the railway companies made further efforts in the same direction of arousing public opinion. Under the auspices of the Repeal Association a large public meeting was held in London on 16 March, and a memorial against the duty was sent to Northcote and Disraeli.[35] The following week Lord Houghton and the Marquis of Londonderry led a deputation, representing 200,000 shareholders, to the Chancellor, only to be answered with the familiar request to propose some concession "so as to meet the wants of the lower classes".[36]

Legislation was out of the question. On the financial side, with money needed for naval purposes, Northcote considered he was in no position to sacrifice revenue. Moreover, in respect of the passenger duty his own attitude had hardened too, inasmuch as he now considered that the case for exemption, granted in 1844, "had now pretty well collapsed in consequence of the great increase and profitableness of third-class traffic".[37] Nor could the question of cheap trains and the passenger duty be any longer isolated from the much wider problem of working-class housing and the relief of overcrowding. The passing of the Artisans' Dwellings Act in

1875 proved that the Conservatives were alive to this issue. One possible solution, especially in London, was to move the working classes out of slum areas into the suburbs, but this was only practicable where cheap transport was available; here the penny-a-mile rate prescribed by the 1844 Act was too high.[38] Consequently, some companies, such as the Great Eastern, North London and London, Chatham & Dover, had been compelled to run certain very cheap workmen's trains by the terms of their private Acts. Others, including the London, Brighton & South Coast, Metropolitan and South Eastern railways, had been providing cheap fares for workmen voluntarily since the mid-1860s. But these developments only affected the London area. It remained true that the Act of 1844 was the only general method of obtaining cheap trains for the working classes. No Conservative government at this time could be expected to repeal the relevant clauses of that Act without providing something in their stead.[39] Thus as the problem of working-class housing became more acute in the late 1870s, Disraeli's government, fettered by its own social policy, was obliged to make some gesture in respect of the passenger duty. Its chance came when the House of Lords dismissed with costs the appeal of the North London Railway against the judgment of the Court of Exchequer, in February 1876.[40]

This case was the signal for the companies to return once more to parliamentary action. On 7 March F. L. Spinks, the Conservative M.P. for Oldham, moved "That in the opinion of this House, the Railway Passenger Duty ought to be reduced at an early date, with a view to its ultimate repeal".[41] Spinks was not a railway director, but his speech was a concise statement of the companies' demands, and both he and Benjamin Rodwell, who moved for a Select Committee, had previously been in touch with the Repeal Association and officials of the Great Eastern and London, Brighton & South Coast companies.[42] The Railway Companies' Association saw in a Select Committee a grand opportunity to put over its own case in public; Leeman, acting on a resolution passed the same day, supported Rodwell.[43] Northcote, grasping at a chance to shelve the question, also supported Rodwell's amendment, which was thus carried comfortably by 137 votes to 23.[44]

The Railway Association made certain that the Select Committee was a well-managed affair. Co-ordination of evidence was placed in the hands of a strong subcommittee of directors, managers and M.P.s (Leeman and Watkin), with the solicitor of the North London Railway acting as legal representative.[45] With so much agreement between the Inland Revenue authorities and the Board of Trade as to the necessity for modification of the Act of 1844, it was not difficult for the companies to present a damning case against the passenger duty as then administered. To previous arguments touching the injustice and financial burden which the duty imposed were added new ones designed to convince public opinion that the duty actually hampered the development of travel facilities for the working classes.[46] George Findlay went so far as to undertake that if the duty on third-class traffic were removed, "we would at once remove, to the extent that we had previously added, the five per cent that we are empowered to charge".[47] But on the question of a fresh concession the companies were adamant. "You have no right", declared Forbes, chairman of the London, Chatham & Dover Railway, "to ask me for an equivalent as a condition of removing from me that unjust tax".[48]

The report of the Select Committee gave formal expression to the views of the companies, and stands as a testimony to the work done by the railway director–M.P.s. A demand for the entire repeal of the duty was inserted by nine votes to six, with the help of the votes of Lord Claud Hamilton of the Great Eastern, Sir Harcourt Johnstone of the North Eastern, T. C. Bruce, and Knatchbull-Hugessen. A proposal to exempt from duty all fares up to sixpence for a single journey in urban and suburban districts was made by Alexander Macdonald, amended to ninepence on the motion of Knatchbull-Hugessen, and also carried on a division. In addition the report, issued in June, called for the abolition of duty on all fares up to one penny per mile.[49] These were strong indications to the government of the extent to which working-class representatives were now interesting themselves in the effect of the duty on working-class travel.

But the recommendation to remit the duty in full "whenever the state of the public revenue will permit", proved to be the government's escape clause. Northcote certainly wished to alter the tax in some way provided the companies would make an equivalent concession, and he rightly perceived that the tax was "one which we shall hardly be able to maintain for ever."[50] But he was never again in a position to offer more than partial remission. Military expenditure, the Eastern Crisis, the raising of income tax and the Zulu War left no room for financial largesse in favour of railway companies on such a controversial matter. To representatives of the Railway and Repeal Associations, led by Lord Houghton, on 22 February, the Chancellor replied frankly that "he was not in a position to talk very much about remissions of taxation at present."[51] In April Knatchbull-Hugessen, with the support of the Railway Association, made a final attempt to raise the matter in the Commons, and in a fine speech called for the implementation of the Select Committee's proposals. Northcote would commit himself to nothing; the debate developed into a slanging match between the railway interest and its more implacable opponents, and the motion was withdrawn.[52] Northcote had already confessed to Sir William Stephenson, chairman of the Board of Inland Revenue,

> Looking to the experience of former attempts to legislate for the benefit of passengers, I think that non-intervention is the better policy for the State to adopt.[53]

For its part the Railway Association took no further initiative in the matter either. It was much concerned at this time with railway safety, and with the recurrent problem of rates. Moreover the passenger duty threatened to divide the railway interest once more on a geographical basis, especially as its incidence had now increased. *The Times* pointed out that those companies with relatively little goods traffic felt the impact of the duty severely.[54] These were the companies operating commuter services in London, and those operating in southern England, where goods and mineral traffic was light. Thus in 1876 the North Eastern Railway paid approximately 0.5 per cent of its total gross receipts in passenger duty, whilst the South Eastern paid 2.2 per cent.[55] It was these southern companies which pressed most strongly for the total abolition of the duty.[56] The fear of an open breach amongst the companies on this issue may well have accounted for the way in which the Railway Companies' Association allowed the topic to lapse during the last years of Disraeli's ministry.[57]

That the issue was kept alive at all at this time was due to the efforts of a very different body, the Travelling Tax Abolition Committee, formed on 30 October 1877 by the veteran atheist, agitator and Co-operator George Jacob Holyoake, with a latter-day Chartist, Collet Dobson Collet, as secretary. Working-class leaders such as Thomas Burt and George Howell were also members of the committee, whose aim was to take up the question of the passenger duty solely in the interest of the working classes, and to press for its "unconditional abolition".[58] Supporters of the committee in Parliament included Spinks and Rodwell. Officially the committee had no connection with the Railway Association and was, Holyoake asserted, in no way subsidized by the companies; but Watkin kept in close touch with it and some companies, especially the South Eastern and London, Brighton & South Coast, afforded travel facilities.[59] Brady and Ellis, of the Repeal Association, also had some contact with Collet when he read a paper on "The Prejudicial Effects of the Railway Passenger Duty upon the Travelling Public" at the Society of Arts on 26 February 1877.[60] In the

Upper House Lord Houghton acted on the committee's behalf, particularly in the presentation of petitions.[61]

The committee was certainly an active body. The *Gazette* which it issued free, at irregular intervals from April 1878, was sent to every M.P., the principal railway officers, and the chief newspapers, and gives a good indication of the scope of its activities.[62] These included the sending of letters to M.P.s, petitioning Parliament, memorializing governments and reprinting important articles and papers.[63] The results of such propaganda are not easy to assess. The committee must be credited with having kept the issue of the passenger duty alive, before Parliament and government, at a time when there was "a regrettable absence of unanimity" on the part of the railway interest on this question.[64] But Holyoake's boast that the committee was "mainly instrumental . . . in obtaining the repeal of the penny a mile tax on all third class fares . . . in 1883" must be taken as a wild exaggeration.[65]

The most that can be said of the committee is that, at a time when social reform was again becoming a political issue, it had a certain nuisance value. In 1878 Thomas Farrer at the Board of Trade regarded the committee as "really the R.[ail] W.[ay] interest looking out of another window"; both he and Lord Sandon were disposed to ignore it.[66] In February 1880 the committee adopted new tactics, by suggesting that tramways were railways and should also be made to pay the passenger duty, an attempt, as Farrer pointed out, "to get rid of the R[ail] W[ay] Passenger Duty, and to use the non taxation of Tramways as a lever".[67] Though the Permanent Secretary remained unmoved, Joseph Chamberlain was obviously worried.[68]

The passing of the Employers' Liability Act in 1880 created the worst possible atmosphere for the development of relations between the railway interest and Gladstone's administration. This was so not simply on account of the details of the Act, but because the manner in which it was passed put the interest on its guard – a hostile guard – against each and every overture made to it by the Liberal government for the settlement of railway problems. Nor were the railway companies pleased with the appointment of a man of Chamberlain's radical zeal. His political apprenticeship in Birmingham had left him with a suspicion of tightly-organized business groups, and his particular dislike of the railway interest was something he did not conceal.[69] It is curious that Chamberlain's biographers have virtually ignored his work at the Board of Trade, contenting themselves, at best, with a mere résumé of the principal measures touching that department which were passed during his term of office there.[70] It is true that he went to the Board of Trade not altogether happily, and in matters of day-to-day administration was in the hands of his permanent officials. But for a man who, it is alleged, "hated bureaucracy and central direction",[71] Chamberlain proved surprisingly partial to the use of stern administrative and legislative measures. This was especially the case with the problem of cheap trains and the passenger duty, where issues of pure administration merged with those of social policy and working-class politics. In June 1882 the report of the Select Committee on Artisans' and Labourers' Dwellings, appointed the previous session, drew attention to the urgent need for a more adequate service of workmen's trains, especially between London and its suburbs.[72] Here was a subject to which Chamberlain was drawn by past experience, natural inclination, and political opportunism.

In fact, Chamberlain had already encountered the problem in the spring of 1882. In March Edward Watkin, stung by the refusal of the government "to make any concession of any description" regarding the passenger duty, informed Plumstead Board of Works of the intention of the South Eastern directors to discontinue the service of workmen's trains between Plumstead, Woolwich and London.[73] Such action seemed likely to rebound on the already harassed Liberal government, for many of the workers involved were government "slop-makers", employed making army clothing.[74] At the suggestion of the Plumstead board, Chamberlain authorized an approach to the Earl of Redesdale, Chairman of Committees, to have inserted in the South Eastern's private bill, then before Parliament, clauses enforcing the continuance of the workmen's service. To Chamberlain's annoyance the clauses were not inserted, but pledges were given to continue the trains in question.[75]

Recurrent complaints, and questions in Parliament, concerning the overcrowding in and inadequacy of workmen's train services in the London area, prompted Chamberlain to inquire deeper into the matter.[76] On 13 November he placed in Farrer's hands a memorandum authorizing an official inquiry, into the subject of workmen's trains on the Metropolitan lines, by Major Marindin, a Railway Department inspector, with a view to laying the report before Parliament.[77] This report, submitted in February 1883, urged the need for more third-class accommodation, more workmen's trains, and the provision of weekly as well as daily cheap tickets for workmen.[78] Chamberlain grasped the chance to turn this into a further belated instalment of the Liberalism long demanded by the left wing of the party. By April the Railway Department was able to inform Plumstead Board of Works that the government intended to legislate on the basis of the report "at an early date".[79]

Chapter 5

Any modification of the provisions of the 1844 Act, however, needed the approval of the Chancellor of the Exchequer, Hugh Childers. Already with a good surplus, and the prospect of increasing revenue next year, he was able to oblige.[80] In his budget speech he announced a proposal to abolish the duty on fares of one penny per mile, and to levy only a 2 per cent duty on railways in urban districts; at the same time, the Board of Trade was to be given powers to insist, subject to an appeal to the Railway Commissioners, on the running of additional workmen's trains.[81]

Childers' proposals were in the nature of a bargain, an offer to meet the companies halfway; they did not square with the policy of the companies, which had hitherto been to press for total and unconditional repeal. But the treatment the railways had suffered at the hands of the Liberals over employers' liability made for a cautious approach. Increased working costs, and the knowledge that the government might have to act to pacify traders on the question of railway rates, probably also counselled conciliation. The southern companies apart, the railway interest seemed prepared to examine the government's proposals sympathetically, the more so when it became known that the urban areas envisaged would cover centres of over 100,000 population, with a radius of 12 miles.[82]

Yet though the Railway Association resolved not to oppose the second reading of the bill when it was published at the beginning of June, its details, and especially the proviso that companies would lose the benefit of remission of duty where they refused to comply with an order of the Board of Trade, or of the Railway Commissioners, requiring suitable accommodation for workmen and penny-a-mile passengers, shocked even moderate railway opinion. Here was an attempt to perpetuate the "mixing-up" of the question of the passenger duty with that of cheap travel, embodied moreover in a plan to give the government powers of interference with both the details of railway working arrangements and with the structure of railway charges. Soon after the second reading of the bill a strong committee was appointed to see Childers and Chamberlain and discover how far the government would bend.[83]

Chamberlain in particular turned out to be patiently stubborn.[84] When the bill was committed *pro forma*, the government did concede a closer definition of a workmen's train, and an amendment requiring the Board of Trade, at the request of any company, to refer to the Railway Commissioners any order they might make concerning the running of workmen's trains and third-class accommodation.[85] At the committee stage proper, Childers accepted further amendments of detail proposed by the Conservative M.P. Joseph Bolton, chairman of the Caledonian Railway, on behalf of the Railway Association.[86] But from the railway interest as a whole there was no strong opposition to the measure in Parliament. At such a late date in the session the interest preferred the half-a-loaf offered to a struggle whose hopelessness was proved when the third reading in the Commons was carried by 70 votes to 8; the bill became law on 20 August.[87]

Only Watkin, annoyed at the supineness of the Railway Association, continued the struggle in public. After the companies in the association had refused to adopt a more militant tone, he formed, on 8 August 1883, his own Association of Railway Shareholders to fight for the protection of railway property.[88] Watkin's association was never a very influential body. It drew its support mainly from his own companies, but, since one of its objects was to "minimise the interference of irresponsible State officials" in the running of the railways, it naturally attracted politicians of the extreme right such as Lord Wemyss, head of the Liberty and Property Defence League, and Sir Edmund Beckett.[89]

There was probably some truth in Brabourne's contention that the Railway Companies' Association was initially jealous, or at least suspicious, of the shareholders' organization.[90] Such feelings did not last long, for the Association of Railway Shareholders disappeared into obscurity after 1886. But, as an index of railway opinion at this time, its formation was symptomatic. The difference between Watkin and the other director-M.P.s was really one of strategy, not policy. The point which irked the entire railway interest was that, on an issue of strict principle, whether or not a duty should continue to be imposed on railways after it had been removed from, or was not levied on other forms of transport, the Liberal government of Gladstone had forced a compromise. Chamberlain knew this to be so, for in 1884, in evidence before the Royal Commission on the Housing of the Working Classes, and in a phrase which must have caused much annoyance to railway directors, he declared,

> the repeal of the passenger duty can be justified on public grounds quite independently of any question of the provision of workmen's trains.[91]

Of course the Cheap Trains Act of 1883 did not require the railways to provide workmen's trains and suitable third-class accommodation; but if a company failed to satisfy the Board of Trade in either respect, it risked losing the benefit of remission of duty under the Act. This was the essence of the "bargain" which Henry Calcraft of the Railway Department admitted in 1884 before the Royal Commission.[92] The determination of the Board of Trade to see that the bargain was carried out became apparent in a strongly-worded circular sent out by Farrer in October 1883.[93]

Complaints by the companies next year proved how dependent they were upon the Act in obtaining any remission of duty.[94]

These facts showed how much weaker the companies' position in respect of the duty had become, for after 1883 it was much harder for them to argue convincingly for its unconditional abolition, as a matter of right, simply on the strength of the pre-1883 situation. After 1883 the companies, with no hope of a further early modification of the duty, increasingly found themselves the victims of pressure on the Board of Trade by radical organizations, such as the London Reform Union, to increase workmen's facilities.[95]

In its immediate context the Act of 1883 further embittered relations between Chamberlain and the railway interest at a time when cordial co-operation between the government and the railways was about to suffer a further setback. For both had been pushed unwillingly into grappling with yet another railway issue which the Tories had shelved, and the most explosive. This was the problem of railway rates, destined to dominate railway politics for the entire decade.

# Chapter 6

# Confrontation with liberalism

The re-emergence of railway rates as a political issue in the 1880s was a direct result of the fall in prices which, following the boom of the early 1870s, continued almost unrelieved until 1891 and was accompanied by a fall in profits and by an ominous decline in the rate of growth of industrial production. It is now generally recognized that this particular slackening of the rate of growth of the British economy cannot be regarded as an isolated period of 'great depression'. Some trends, such as the rise in real wages, suggest it was not a period of 'depression' at all.[1] Nonetheless it is clear that this was a period of "doubts, self-questioning and disenchantment."[2] In 1881 the Fair Trade League was formed to campaign on behalf of home producers for protection from foreign competition. The basic tenets of economic free trade were beginning to be questioned.

From the general fall in profits the railways did not escape. Decreasing rates of production naturally affected railway receipts, whilst capital expenditure and running costs continued to increase. The companies were not entirely blameless in the matter of their deteriorating economic position; failure to improve operating techniques had predictable results. At the same time the companies could maintain, with some justice, that the refinement of their own techniques depended on progress in other sectors of British industry.[3] But whatever the reasons for the deterioration of their economic position, the effects were unmistakable. From the late 1870s labour productivity on the railways remained virtually stationary. The proportion of net receipts to total paid-up capital fell from 4.74 per cent in 1872 to 4.15 per cent in 1879, rose to 4.29 per cent in 1883, and then fell continuously to 1886 when it stood at 3.99 per cent.[4] From 1884 to 1888 there was a prolonged fall also in the average rate of railway dividends.[5]

By then the railway companies were being confronted by torrents of abuse from traders and farmers. Faced with higher costs and stiffer competition, especially from abroad, those who had their goods carried by rail had expected that the railways, like other industrial concerns, would naturally lower their rates and charges. But, with working expenditure rising, the railways needed high rates to maintain dividends. Only in regard to bulk produce imported from abroad did the companies feel inclined to charge special low rates.[6] Thus within the British Isles high rates and anomalous rates, lightly regarded in the years of plenty, now seemed doubly burdensome.[7] The late 1870s witnessed a stream of complaints touching on unlawful charges, unequal mileage rates, and allegedly preferential rates in favour of foreign goods. These complaints were of two types. Firstly, and more generally, there were complaints alleging an 'undue preference' by a railway company. Where such a preference appeared to favour one locality rather than another, the defence of the companies was that, in a competitive system, the general rate must be dictated by the company having the shortest route. Where (more contentious still) the preference favoured goods imported from abroad as against home-produced goods, the companies argued that, when faced with sea competition (as, for example, the London & South Western Railway was for goods carried between Southampton and London), special import rates were necessary to gain the traffic.[8] Secondly there were complaints grouped around the alleged illegality of certain 'terminal' charges railway companies made, over and above the maximum rate, for the use by traders of stations and siding accommodation.[9]

Soon, however, specific complaints about preferential rates and excessive terminal charges turned into a general demand for an all-round reduction of rates and a reclassification of the charges for different classes of goods, as laid down in the numerous private Acts of the railway companies. By the common law the charges of a carrier had to be reasonable; about 1845 a maximum rate clause became general in railway Acts, but in practice many goods were carried at rates well below the parliamentary maxima. Since the apportionment of individual rates was more of an art than a science, and since companies were determined to make as much profit as possible, the principle, resented so much by the traders, arose of charging "what the traffic will bear"; this principle received statutory recognition in section 90 of the Railway Clauses Consolidation Act of 1845.[10] Moreover, owing to the monthly rate conferences, the more important of which had grown up between 1873 and 1881, no single railway could reduce competitive rates unilaterally.[11] Thus it came as no surprise that coupled with complaints about excessive charges were demands for the reform of the constitution of the Railway Commissioners. Their powers were said to be too limited, thus preventing their decrees from being enforced; litigation before the court was said to be expensive, and to lead to complainants against a railway company becoming 'marked men'.[12]

The Railway Commissioners themselves, in their fourth annual report, drew attention to the weaknesses of their own constitution. They suggested that powers be given to them to order the reduction of unreasonable as well as unequal charges, and to vary the amount of a through rate demanded by one company over the lines of another.[13] The appearance of the report was well timed, for the powers of the Railway Commission were due to lapse in 1878, when the whole question would have to be considered afresh.

The Associated Chambers of Commerce had in fact already broached the subject of maximum rates with the Board of Trade in March 1877.[14] Disraeli's government was so unwilling to consider the question of the Railway and Canal Traffic Act of 1873, involving, as it did, "the raising of some big questions", that the Cabinet almost overlooked the subject.[15] But economic conditions made it certain that this would not be allowed to happen. In April 1878 the Associated Chambers again raised the matter with Adderley, asking this time for the implementation of the Railway Commissioners' own proposals and for a *locus standi* for chambers of commerce before the commission. In January 1879 Lord Sandon, Adderley's successor, approached the Railway Association for its views.[16]

Chapter 6

The complaints of the railway companies against the commission were as formidable as those of the traders. In a statement read to Sandon on 12 February they instanced its expense, its apparent incitement of complaints against companies, and the inadequate right of appeal given by the 1873 Act; the companies also demanded the repeal of those sections of the Act which gave the commissioners powers as to through rates, on the grounds that these powers were "unjust . . . and useless".[17]

Sandon was evidently taken aback. It was out of the question that any such controversial legislation would be attempted by the government at this time. Sandon did indeed produce a bill, but it was nothing more than a measure to continue the Act of 1873 until 31 December 1882. The bill passed through both Houses without a word of debate, and became law on 15 August.[18]

The Railway Association did not raise the matter again during the lifetime of the Conservative government. But the railway rates controversy grew steadily fiercer, and developed political complications. On 28 April 1879, at the Westminster Palace Hotel, the Farmers' Alliance was inaugurated, a tenant body whose object was to promote "such legislation as will tend to agricultural advancement". One of its founders, James William Barclay, the Liberal M.P. for Forfarshire, a merchant, shipowner and farmer, soon busied himself together with the Liberals Professor W. A. Hunter and the Marquis of Huntly, and others, in organizing "an agitation to obtain the revision and reduction of railway charges for the conveyance of agricultural produce".[19] Disraeli's government was out of office too soon for this campaign to have much effect. In May 1880, however, the alliance was joined by the Central Chamber of Agriculture in denouncing preferential railway charges for foreign produce.[20] The following month the Associated Chambers of Commerce sent a deputation to Chamberlain to press for a uniform classification of railway goods, and the bestowal upon the Railway Commissioners of powers to revise the rates of the companies and to order through rates.[21]

There is no evidence to suggest that Chamberlain was in any sense conversant with the details and finer points of the rates controversy. He confessed to a railway deputation in March 1884 "that he did not know the complexity of the subject [of railway rates] until he had been informed of it by the Railway Companies".[22] But his political senses told him that he risked being caught in the cross-fire of farmers and industrialists from all political camps. Even at a purely constituency level, the acute feelings of Birmingham on the subject were well known.[23] Chamberlain was certainly anxious to please the chambers of commerce. But against this, as he told

Farrer, had to be weighed the cost of incurring the displeasure of the railway interest:

> I am . . . rather doubtful whether it will be good policy to attempt this question at all next session. We are likely to have a stormy time and other matters will no doubt more urgently require attention. Whatever we do will be stoutly opposed by the Railway Companies and it will be for us to consider whether it is worth while to irritate the interests affected by proposing anything until we are quite sure of being able to carry it out.[24]

Thus a policy of caution became one of delay. When, on 15 February 1881, Bernhard Samuelson, the Liberal ironmaster and engineer, and M.P. for Banbury, moved for a Select Committee "to inquire into the charges of Railway Companies for the conveyance of merchandise, minerals, agricultural produce, and parcels . . . and into the working of the Railway Commission of 1873; and to report as to any amendment of the laws . . . that may be desirable", the government offered no opposition to its appointment.[25]

Initially the railway companies were not enthusiastic. They were still smarting after the struggle with the Liberal government over employers' liability. They remembered Liberal policy towards the rights of landowners in Ireland, and expressed anxiety about a similar "confiscation of railway property" – compulsory reduction of rates – in England.[26] Yet, with the experience of the Joint Select Committee of 1872 and of the Select Committee on the Passenger Duty, of 1876, the Railway Association was able to turn the Select Committee on Railways, 1881–2, to its own advantage in brilliant fashion.

The Select Committee, when appointed, had among its 27 members seven prominent railway directors. These consisted of four Liberals: J. C. Bolton, Lewis Dillwyn, Joseph Pease and Edward Watkin; and three Conservatives: Gooch, Sir Henry Tyler, and William Lowther of the London & North Western.[27] It was at once determined that the Parliamentary Committee of the Railway Association should set up its own liaison committee of railway officers and solicitors, to keep in constant touch with the Select Committee and to convey to the railway members on it the views of the Parliamentary Committee.[28] The traders, by contrast, were hardly organized on such a scale. The Central Chamber of Agriculture did have a committee to watch proceedings, and could naturally count on a number of Conservative M.P.s on the Select Committee for support. But the Association of British Chambers of Commerce was hampered by the fact

Chapter 6

that many of its constituent chambers were small, weak, apathetic, and incessantly suspicious of each other. It was not till February 1882, halfway through the Select Committee's proceedings, and when the bulk of the traders' evidence had already been taken, that industrialists and farmers, realizing the value of a central body to match the Railway Association, formed the Railway and Canal Traders' Association "for mutual protection in the matter of railway rates".[29]

The result was, that when the farmers and industrialists appeared before the Select Committee in the spring and early summer of 1881, the impact of their evidence was marred by a lack of precision, of uniformity in the remedies offered for the ills complained of, and by the obvious unresolved jealousies between different areas. At that time traders seemed not to realize that a statement that a railway company was charging rates to the detriment of one district was also evidence that these rates encouraged trade in the districts 'preferred'.[30] As Farrer told the Select Committee in a printed memorandum of July 1881, "If there is to be competition, rates must be unequal. If rates are to be equal throughout, there can be no competition".[31] In some instances witnesses refused to give definite answers, or admitted their inability to produce statistics in support of their case; some witnesses offered drastic solutions, such as the setting aside of existing Acts of Parliament, whilst others could offer no solution.[32]

The Railway Association, whilst taking advantage of these mistakes, was determined to repeat none of them. Towards the end of June 1881 a full meeting of the Association considered in detail the evidence the companies would offer, and the points to be brought out.[33] Thus the railways, with James Grierson and George Findlay as their leading witnesses, were able to present a well-documented case, insisting on their right to charge terminals, arguing against the Railway Commissioners having powers to fix rates, and repudiating any deliberate policy of preferential rates for foreign goods. Above all, they insisted that the public interest was their main consideration.[34] The same meticulous care over the preparation of evidence was taken when the Select Committee was reappointed in 1882, and the companies then saw their main task as being the rebuttal of traders' evidence.[35]

When the Select Committee finished hearing evidence, at the beginning of May 1882, and began considering its report, the railway interest was able to take advantage of Liberal troubles to further its own ends. Barclay, on behalf of the traders, let it be known that he would submit his own draft report; there could be little doubt as to its contents and conclusions. So Evelyn Ashley, Parliamentary Secretary to the Board of Trade, and a member of the Select Committee, approached Gooch "to have any amendments or suggestions from the Railway Companies", presumably with the object of avoiding any excuse for controversial legislation. Gooch reported back to the Railway Association, which instructed the general managers and consulting solicitors to draw up suggestions. The association was also able to obtain a copy of Barclay's draft report in advance of its presentation to the Select Committee, and sent annotated copies of it to the railway directors on the committee.[36]

Although it was Barclay's draft, not Ashley's, which the committee adopted as its working document, the seven railway directors were able, by the use of their block vote, to turn the draft into a document thoroughly acceptable to the railway industry. Out of a total of 111 divisions the seven directors showed a split vote on only 22 divisions. A paragraph calling for parliamentary recognition of station and service terminals was carried by twelve votes to nine. J. C. Bolton's amendment condemning equal rates was carried by nine votes to seven; his paragraph alleging that inequalities of charge benefited the public was inserted on a vote of twelve to nine. A paragraph acquitting the railways "of any serious causes of offence" was inserted by ten votes to nine. Finally, a proposal to give the Railway Commissioners power to modify preferential rates for foreign goods where these were less than the rates for similar home produce was defeated by nine votes to eight. In each of these cases the block railway vote, never less than six out of the possible seven, ensured the approval or rejection of the clauses and paragraphs in question.[37]

Thus the Select Committee's final report called for parliamentary recognition of the right of railway companies to charge the much-disputed station terminals, and praised lawful differential rates as giving the public the advantages of industrial competition. On the question of the Railway Commission, the report recommended that it be made permanent, but that litigants before it be given a right of appeal; there was also a recommendation that it be given the power to order a through rate on the application of a private trader. The report urged that railway companies be "required to consolidate their special Acts, in so far as they affect rates or charges imposed upon the traders". And the report declared

> that on the whole of the evidence they acquit the railway companies of any grave dereliction of their duty to the public . . . the rates for merchandise . . . are, in the main, considerably below the maxima authorised by Parliament.[38]

The report was a document which the association viewed with obvious satisfaction; and, provided any legislative proposals followed it closely, and in full, Chamberlain could hope to carry out a useful reform without further alienating the railway interest from the Liberal Party.[39]

In 1883 Chamberlain had no time to bother with such a reform. Bankruptcy and patents interested him more, and had the attraction of being topics which did not arouse bitter parliamentary opposition. Corrupt election practices required attention. The Liberal government, already out of favour with its followers over Ireland, was suffering further divisions as a result of radical hostility to Gladstone's Egyptian policy; franchise reform had once more to be postponed. Moreover, within the field of railway reform, the passenger duty was already being tackled. Early in the same session, 1883, farming interests pressed the government to push forward an Agricultural Holdings bill.[40] So the reform of railway rates could certainly not then be contemplated.

But the trading interests and their supporters would not allow Chamberlain to forget the subject, and he himself had still to make important policy decisions concerning it. This policy emerged slowly but unmistakably. When the Conservative Sclater-Booth moved a new standing order, making it obligatory upon the Board of Trade to report on all railway bills seeking higher rates, the government refused to oppose it, and it passed without a division.[41] On 4 May 1883 Bernhard Samuelson rose in the House to call attention to the report of the Select Committee, and to move

> That it is expedient that the Railway Commission should be made permanent and a Court of Record; and that, in general conformity with the recommendations of the Committee, the power of the Commission be extended; and that, on application by a Railway undertaking for Parliamentary powers, a locus standi be afforded to Chambers of Commerce and Agriculture, and similar bodies, and to persons injuriously affected by the rates and fares sought or already authorised in the case of such undertaking.[42]

Chamberlain offered no opposition, and this motion too was passed without a division.[43]

Here, then, was a clear indication of the way Chamberlain's policy was developing. In any struggle between the railways and the traders he meant to favour the latter at the expense of the former. But he meant equally to minimize his difficulties as much as possible. When the subject of legislation was taken in hand, in November 1883, the Board of Trade took care to seek early consultations with the Railway Association. What Chamberlain had in mind, however, outraged railway opinion. The plan of the companies was threefold: legal recognition of terminal charges; a new classification of goods; and a new model schedule of maximum rates. But they emphasized "that the scheme shall be taken as a whole, & that they shall not be asked to abandon their present maxima without getting what they want in the form of a right to terminals & an higher maximum of mileage rates for short distances".[44]

Chamberlain thought this proposal "right in principle, but we cannot accept it en bloc . . .".[45] Instead of a measure to deal simply with the rates question, and embracing all the recommendations of the Select Committee and no others, Chamberlain proposed an omnibus bill to make the Railway Commission permanent, with a right of appeal, and to give chambers of commerce and agriculture, and others, the opportunity of bringing before it all questions of preferential rates; individual traders were also to have the right to apply for through rates. The question of a uniform classification of goods was also to be dealt with, and terminal charges defined. Furthermore, interlocking and continuous brakes were to receive attention in the same measure.[46] All this was a formidable pill for the railways to swallow; the only inducement was the proposal to give legal recognition to terminal charges.

Whatever chance there might have been of the railway interest accepting such a measure and allowing it to become law, as non-controversial legislation, was thrown away by Chamberlain during the following weeks, as a result of his attempting to bargain with the railway companies on the question of terminals, whose legal recognition the companies, relying on the report of the Select Committee, demanded as a matter of right.[47] By 4 March 1884, in an effort to exclude from the bill as much controversial material as he could, Chamberlain had abandoned the idea of either proposing the classification or of scheduling it to the bill, and thought that in the circumstances, the legalizing of terminals would be unfair.[48] This decision, to deal neither with the classification of goods, and hence with the amount of rates, nor with the question of terminals, seemed to the railway companies to be a great betrayal and a sign of weakness, the more so when Chamberlain advised them to each bring in bills of their own next session, with the classification annexed to each bill.[49] On 28 March he pleaded, with some truth, that "He could not pledge himself to carry the Terminal Clause, as it might be struck out in the House of Commons"; but the appeal fell on deaf ears, for the Parliamentary Committee of the Railway Association rejected any attempt to carry out only a portion of the Select Committee's recommendations.[50]

In April Chamberlain made a proposal which convinced the companies that his true sympathies lay with the traders. The proposal was to deal with the question of terminals and classification, but also to introduce a clause empowering the Railway Commissioners to revise and amend the classification at the behest of "any party interested" or where the rate authorized was "unreasonable". Grierson likened this proposal, which would have placed the companies under the threat of perpetual revision of their charging powers, to "a descending staircase where there was no landing". On 8 April the association unanimously carried a strong condemnation of the entire scheme.[51] On 5 May Chamberlain replied, through Calcraft, "that if the Railway Companies insisted on having the Terminal Clause without condition, he considered that the negotiation must be at an end, and that he must be at liberty to take his own course."[52]

Chamberlain's flirtation with railway reform had now come to an end. A bill was introduced and given a formal first reading on 22 May, but this was no more than an empty gesture.[53] It was not from the railways that opposition to the bill sprang, for they were prepared to reason with Chamberlain still, in the hope of an agreed settlement.[54] The traders, however, led by Samuelson and Barclay, launched a strong attack on the measure and its author, their main objections being directed to the proposed legalization of terminals and the right of appeal from the Railway Commissioners.[55]

This was an attack to which Chamberlain proved sensitive, with good reason. Events in the Sudan had brought Liberal unrest to a new peak. The Franchise bill was also causing trouble, whilst the Merchant Shipping bill was posing grave problems which were Chamberlain's personal concern.[56] Disquiet on the government back benches had reached the point at which a revolt in the division lobbies was not unlikely. On 21 May Samuelson moved a new standing order to allow chambers of commerce and agriculture to petition against a railway bill on the grounds of injurious rates and fares proposed, or already levied, by the company. With trade and agriculture at a low ebb, this was a proposal Chamberlain feared to oppose; he told the companies that they "must take care of themselves with regard to Mr. Samuelson's Motion." On 9 July the standing order was approved, against Chamberlain's advice, by 94 votes to 84.[57] This was a symbolic defeat for the government, and a warning. The following day Chamberlain withdrew his bill.[58]

Chamberlain's refusal to give terminal charges statutory recognition, coupled with his failure to prevent traders from obtaining at least one of their demands, provoked the companies to engage in a rare display of legislative initiative. They were prompted by a remark which Chamberlain had rashly thrown out in the March 1884 negotiations, to the effect that, with reference to terminals and the classification of goods, "he thought the best way would be for four or five of the largest Railway Companies to bring in their bills next Session with the Classification annexed to each Bill".[59] In the autumn, acting on this advice, the directors of nine of the largest companies – the London & North Western, Great Western, Midland, North Eastern, Great Northern, Great Eastern, London & South Western, London, Brighton & South Coast, and London, Chatham & Dover – agreed to act together in promoting such bills in 1885. Great care was taken that the scales of rates, and especially the terminals clause, were alike in each bill.[60]

The nine bills, when published, produced strong protests from chambers of agriculture and commerce, the Railway and Canal Traders' Association, and their parliamentary friends in both the Liberal and Conservative camps. Major Craigie, of the Central Chamber of Agriculture, told a conference summoned by the Traders' Association on 14 January 1885,

> The sooner Parliament was made to understand that the recommendations of the Select Committee of 1882 would not be accepted by the country the better. Traders and agriculturists were at present in no position to listen to any proposals, however specious and plausible, which involved an increase in the rates of carriage.

The Conservative peer Lord Henniker reminded the same gathering,

> The Bills were seeking to establish by a side-wind that which Mr. Chamberlain sought to establish last year. They carried out the most vicious principles of Mr. Chamberlain's Bill, and had none of the compensating advantages of that measure.[61]

The traders evidently meant business, for the support they were able to obtain from Liberal and Conservative M.P.s to oppose the bills was such that Henry Oakley took the rare step of sending to *The Times* a letter inspired by, but not attributed to, the Railway Association, defending the companies in bringing forward their bills.[62] In February, when a conference was suggested between the traders and the companies, with the Board of Trade as mediator, to remove "misapprehensions", the companies willingly agreed.[63]

Farrer, the inspirer of this policy, and doubtless mindful of the railway interest's ability to work against governments by a combination of brilliant committee work and astute publicity, viewed the whole business with grim and none-too-steady composure. The affair, he told Chamberlain, had been blown up to look other than it really was, "a matter of tactics, rather than policy", and he urged that the Board of Trade should "keep the position of an arbitrator and not become partisans". If there was a "violent move on the House by the Traders", then the railways would be forced to "come to us cap in hand, and we shall be able to impose terms on them".

> For yourself, I cannot think that it will be well to make an enemy of the highly organized, lasting, deep-pocketed R[ail] W[ay] interest, or to encourage them to Join in the cry which is raised against you as an assailant of property. The wrath of the Traders is a fire of chaff blown into a sudden blaze by bad times. The wrath of the Companies is red hot steel.[64]

But at this time Chamberlain was nothing if not an "assailant of property", and he gloried in it. He was now absorbed in popularizing the Radical Programme, the campaign having started on 5 January with his famous "What ransom will property pay?" speech at Birmingham.[65] The traders of Birmingham were particularly vocal on the subject of the railway bills, so much so that Chamberlain, in a letter to the Birmingham Railway and Canal Rates Association, denied that he intended to support the second reading of them.[66] He had no intention of bringing pressure to bear on the traders on this issue, or even of appearing to do so. As more industrial centres and organizations declared against the bills, and petitioned against them, Chamberlain went so far as to deny allegations that he had inspired or prompted the railway companies at all in their action.[67] Finally, in Parliament, Chamberlain declared that if the bills came on for second reading, "he would offer an outright opposition to them".[68]

This statement was the death warrant of the scheme. Angry and annoyed both at Chamberlain's betrayal of the companies in the matter of the bills, and at his refusal to implement the recommendations of the Select Committee, the Railway Association decided to take the entire matter out of Parliament and beyond Chamberlain's reach. On 24 April Sir Joseph Pease, in a statement authorized by the association, announced that the bills would be withdrawn, and this was done the following week.[69] At the same meeting Oakley had read a letter from the solicitors to the London, Brighton & South Coast Railway, imparting the news that the company had succeeded in inducing the Railway Commissioners to state a special case to the Divisional Court "in regard to their recent decision on the application of Messrs. Hall & Co. disallowing our claim for terminals". The chance was too opportune to be missed. Up to this time the Railway Commission had held steadfastly to the view that charges for the use of stations and siding accommodation were part of the maximum rate, and could not therefore be charged in addition to it. Now there was a chance to have the ruling reversed. The association at once offered the Brighton company the use of its own solicitors in the preparation of the brief. The case was heard in the Queen's Bench Division on 30 June 1885. The companies emerged with a judgment reversing both the decision of the Railway Commission and the previous policy of that court.[70]

By taking the issue to the courts, and beyond Chamberlain's reach, the railway interest proved true to Farrer's words. Their flexibility, in switching from one line of attack to another, swept away the foundation of Chamberlain's railway policy, the use of statutory recognition of terminals as bait to win concessions from the companies, whose position was of course now much less vulnerable to such bargaining techniques. Chamberlain had gone out of office with the whole of Gladstone's government before Hall's case was heard. But the judgment clearly had some impact on his thinking, for a deputation to him from Lord Henniker's "Railway Rates Parliamentary Committee", led by the Mayor of Birmingham in October, learned that

> he had always felt that there were strong arguments in favour of terminal charges, and that there was really no ground for asking the railway companies to sanction a revision of their rates as against themselves, unless they were given an opportunity of reconsideration in their own favour.[71]

As Chamberlain left the Liberal Party the following year, this *volte-face* on the subject of railway rates was without practical importance or effect, for his views on the matter ceased to have any hold on Liberal thinking, though his experiences may well have swayed Conservative policy two years later. It is indeed in this respect, as experience, that Chamberlain's stay at the Board of Trade, though productive of little railway legislation, was important. He had forced a compromise with the companies on the issue of the passenger duty; he had tried to bargain with them also, in favour of the trading interests, on the question of railway rates. Even critics of the railways found such a mode of procedure "impolitic and unstatesmanlike".[72] The memory of Chamberlain's tactics remained with the railway interest in the eventful years which followed.[73]

# Chapter 7

# The swing
# to the right

The general election of 1885 produced a dramatic drop in the total number of railway directors in the House of Commons, from 108 to 84.[1] Of these 84, 28 were sitting for the first time, whilst just over half had sat in the previous Parliament. The decrease in the total railway representation in the Commons came about largely through a drop from 53 to 32 in the number of M.P.s who sat on the boards of local lines. Here, as between the two major parties, the Liberals bore the brunt of the loss, from 29, in 1884, to 16. The net result was that in January 1886 railway representation in the Commons was more evenly divided than ever before between Liberals and Conservatives.

In the Lords the efficient railway interest remained a strong Liberal preserve, the Tory peers dominating the local lines.[2] But it was true of the railway interest in both Houses that, in the fluid political situation of

1885–6, any significant move to the left in the Liberal Party might result in a revolt such that the interest, less attached to Liberalism and faced with fundamental issues of the extent and scope of government control in a new era of state intervention, would be constrained to find a new political wing under which to shelter. It was this process which was completed during the remaining years of Gladstone's political life.

By the mid-1880s there were few railway directors who viewed the economic position of their undertakings with optimism. By the summer of 1886 the economic position of the major English lines was felt to be so bad that chairmen and general managers met during the latter half of the year to discuss ways of co-operating to reduce working expenses.[3] Goods revenue, net revenue, and average rates of dividend fell sharply.[4] Though they were to rise again by the end of the decade, the immediate effect was to make the companies more disinclined than ever to entertain proposals from traders for the revision and reduction of their charging powers. With Hall's case settled, the right to charge terminals was beyond dispute. The railway companies could look governments squarely in the face.

There was little doubt that the reform of railway rates would be a major political topic in 1886. The Liberals were committed to it on the strength of Chamberlain's bill of 1884. Now Tory newspapers were joining in the attack on preferential rates, given by railway companies to imported goods, as a "positive scandal":[5]

in any event, when the interests of the public clash with the interests of the railway companies, there can be no question as to which is entitled to first consideration. The railways exist for the public, not the public for the railways.[6]

Bernhard Samuelson, acting on the instructions of the Associated Chambers of Commerce, carried out an investigation into British and Continental railway rates, to the detriment of the former; his report, published in January 1886, urged a revision of the British system, and received such publicity that the Railway Association felt obliged to consider an official reply.[7]

Salisbury's caretaker government of 1885–6 had already taken the matter in hand. All the major commercial and industrial organizations were pressing for legislation on railway rates. Lord Henniker's committee included 15 peers, and had the support of 45 M.P.s both in the Parliament dissolved in 1885 and in the new Parliament the following year, thus giving it an effective representation in the lower House actually greater than that possessed by the railway companies.[8] It is certain that the complaints of agriculturists had made the Tory leadership fully alive to the importance which rank-and-file Conservative opinion attached to the subject.[9] In a Cabinet Memorandum and Draft Bill dated 14 January 1886, Edward Stanhope, the President of the Board of Trade, outlined the difficulties in the way of legislation.

Stanhope recognized at the outset that the decision in Hall's case meant that "we no longer have a bribe to offer to the railway Companies to induce them to agree to other changes". His plan, embodied in the draft bill, was simply that the companies should, collectively or individually, within twelve months of the passing of the Act, submit to the Railway Commissioners revised classifications of rates and schedules of maximum rates and terminals; that the Commissioners should hear and determine objections; and that the scales of charges as settled by them should be embodied by the Board of Trade in provisional schemes, to be laid before Parliament for six weeks and thus pass into law. Any railway company or authorized public authority was to be allowed to propose alterations in the classifications or schedules "at any time", but here again the Railway Commissioners were to have complete jurisdiction to decide whether or not to allow the alterations, which were also to need parliamentary approval. Stanhope proposed to make the Railway Commission permanent, and to allow complaints to be made to it by public authorities and chambers of commerce and agriculture; but appeals were to lie to a superior court of appeal on questions of law. In deciding whether any railway charge did or did not create an undue preference, the commissioners were to be empowered to "take into consideration whether such charges are necessary for the purpose of securing traffic in respect of which they are made".[10]

Stanhope's proposals cannot be regarded as final Conservative policy. Later in the year he took great pains to point out that the bill which Mundella had hastily introduced within two months of coming into office was Mundella's measure alone, and that the Conservative cabinet had never agreed to the provisions of any bill on the subject.[11] Stanhope certainly intended to consult the companies prior to introducing legislation, for an invitation to meet him to discuss the question was sent to the Railway Association on 27 January.[12] His draft bill, in contrast to Chamberlain's proposals, had the merit of dealing simply and straightforwardly with one issue, without threats or demands for equivalents. It was never made public, but it is important in providing a link with the measure which the Conservatives successfully passed two years later.

Within three weeks of submitting his memorandum, Stanhope was out of office. The return of Gladstone to Downing Street brought at the head of the Board of Trade the Nottingham manufacturer and pioneer of labour conciliation A. J. Mundella, an advanced Liberal who had helped found the Association of Chambers of Commerce in 1860, and who had no love for, nor, it seems, experience of British railways. On coming into office he found Stanhope's draft awaiting further action.[13] But Mundella was too sensitive to traders' opinions to resist the temptation to introduce a measure less simple but more attractive to railway users. The traders had already taken an early opportunity to impress their views upon him.[14] On 19 February Lord Henniker led a deputation of 26 Liberal and Conservative M.P.s and four peers to Mundella, urging him to institute "a very strong Railway Commission", easily accessible to traders, to determine the classification of goods and fix through rates on the application of a trader, and deal with undue preference of any sort. Mundella not only promised a careful consideration of these views, but arranged for the deputation to meet the Lord Chancellor and go clause by clause through the measure he proposed to lay before Parliament in March.[15] With the railway companies there was no such consultation.

In the debate on the introduction of his bill, on 11 March, Mundella received support not merely from Liberals, but from Conservatives and even Irish Nationalists.[16] The bill followed the outline of Stanhope's draft, though Stanhope asserted that the Conservative cabinet had given its sanction to none of the proposals, but had postponed consideration of the matter in order to receive representations from railways and traders.[17] Mundella had listened only to the latter. His bill made provision for appeals on matters of law only, and under no circumstances on matters of undue preference (clauses 14, 15, 25). As in Stanhope's draft the jurisdiction of the commissioners was to be extended to special as well as to public Acts (clause 17). However, the rates revision clause (clause 24) gave the task of settling a revised classification and schedule to the Board of Trade, which, in cases of disagreement between companies and objectors to the new scheme, was empowered to draw up a scheme of its own to be submitted to a Joint Committee of both Houses. Moreover, subsection 7 of this clause provided that, even when a new scheme had been approved by Parliament, any railway company or chamber of commerce or agriculture could apply later to the Board of Trade to "revoke, amend, or vary" any Provisional Order by a further Order, thus giving the government a "recurring power of revision" over railway charges. Clause 28 gave the board wide powers of mediation, though no power of decision, between companies and persons complaining of unreasonable charges. By clause 29 the board was given a blanket authority to call for additional railway statistics.[18]

Mundella's bill amounted to a large slice of state intervention, supported widely by agriculturists and traders. The Railway and Canal Traders' Association thought it inadequate; but both they and the Associated Chambers of Commerce gave it full backing.[19] The railway companies were shocked at the extent of the Liberal proposals:

> the custom seems to have gained ground of late of regarding the railways, not as commercial concerns, as they really are, struggling for a return upon the capital invested, but as national institutions, existing merely for the benefit of the public.[20]

In a detailed report the general managers and solicitors of the Railway Association laid stress on the compulsory nature of the proposals: the compulsory revision of rates, the prohibition of any appeal on the question of undue preference, the unlimited power of the Board of Trade to require statistical returns, and the 'Conciliation Clause' (clause 28):

> it will be the first step towards giving the Board of Trade direct control over the actual charges of Railway Companies; and the indirect power which the Board of Trade possess (and have already exercised) of enforcing compliance with their reports, when Railway Companies promote Bills in Parliament, shows the danger of grandmotherly legislation of this character.[21]

The Railway Companies' Association prepared for action on a broad front. At its meeting on 23 March, with 47 members present, representing 16 of the largest companies, the unanimous decision reached was to enlist the support of shareholders at special meetings of each of the companies, "with a view to secure a strong and united opposition to the compulsory revision of the present authorised tolls and rates, on the security of which the Railway capital of the country has been subscribed".[22]

The news of these indignation meetings came in the midst of political crisis. With the resignations of Chamberlain and G. O. Trevelyan from the Ministry on 26 March, the struggle over the Home Rule bill moved into its final stages. There was much political and economic uncertainty. News that two of the companies, the London & North Western and the Midland, had issued manifestos denouncing Mundella's bill, and calling upon shareholders to influence M.P.s to ensure its defeat, "startled the Stock Markets" and led to a sharp fall in railway stocks.[23] A mood of gloom prevailed in investment circles.

Such an unworthy attempt to take advantage of the rights of property indicates a desire on the part of the Government to treat the railways upon principles analogous to those which have been applied to the freedom of contract respecting landowners and tenants in Ireland.[24]

In this sense the railway campaign, though it did not initiate a revolt of property against Liberalism, certainly added much fuel to the fire. It is significant that when the Employers' Liability bills of Arthur O'Connor and Thomas Burt were referred to a Select Committee, the Railway Association felt it prudent to confer with engineering and shipbuilding employers as to the best means of opposing them.[25] In their campaign against Mundella's bill railway propagandists were careful to lay special emphasis on the extent to which it raised "the whole question of the inviolability of Parliamentary contracts".[26] There were threats that companies might abandon building projects if the bill passed. These feelings were not dispelled by the special meetings called by some of the larger companies in April, and the circulars which issued from their offices. The companies also enlisted, perhaps using some pressure, the support of railway workers, by stressing the adverse effects Mundella's bill would have on conditions of employment in the industry.[27] Even the Conservative *Globe* felt itself bound to congratulate the companies on "having thoroughly done the work of the *advocatus diaboli*".[28]

But the Tory leadership was not so sneering. Whatever Conservative policy may have been in January, the ostentatious way in which Liberal M.P.s, especially county members, supported government action to settle the railway rates question, made it imperative for Conservatism to avoid being identified with the Liberal bill, but also to avoid any commitment to any other.[29] The Conservative hierarchy had a strong link with the railway companies at this time, for in 1884 R. A. Cross had joined the board of Watkin's Manchester, Sheffield & Lincolnshire Railway.[30] On 1 April 1886 Stanhope issued his statement disclaiming for himself and for the late Conservative government any responsibility for the measure which Mundella had introduced.[31] Cross took up the same theme with Watkin, who wrote to Oakley on 5 April,

My colleague, Sir Richard Cross assures me that any such Bill as Mr. Mundella's was never before a Conservative Cabinet, or ever ordered to be prepared by them; that he is entirely opposed to the delegation of authority as to all our rates and fares to the Board of Trade, and that Lord Salisbury is of the same opinion.[32]

Cross also mentioned the matter in a letter to Salisbury on 9 April, and discussed the subject with the leader of the opposition in the Commons, Sir Michael Hicks Beach.[33] The nature of these discussions remains a mystery but, in the light of subsequent developments, it is probable that they centred on the problem of making as much political capital as possible out of Mundella's bill without actually having to vote against it and thus antagonize Tory farmers and traders, and tie their own hands.

For by now trading and agricultural interests had come out firmly in support of Mundella. The Railway and Canal Traders' Association issued a whip to M.P.s to support the second reading, as did the Central Chamber of Agriculture.[34] At least 172 M.P.s are known to have come out in support of the bill.[35] Against this the total number of railway directors in the Commons was just over 80, and the efficient railway interest totalled only 39. The total number of Liberal directors returned in 1885 was 43, but of these only 18 were to defect from the party in June 1886.[36] Even if all the Conservative directors had decided to vote against Mundella's bill – which was most unlikely as some of them, such as the ironmaster Alfred Hickman, were active supporters of the measure – and excluding the two Irish Nationalist directors, the Railway Association could not have counted on the support of many more than 50 M.P.s. Defeat of Mundella's bill, given Conservative policy towards it, was out of the question.

There were signs, however, that the Conservative leadership, whilst not prepared to vote against the bill, would look sympathetically upon amendments of it. The Conservative peer Lord Colville of Culross, chairman of the Great Northern Railway, told a meeting of the Railway Association on 4 May,

> the feeling of several of the prominent members of the House, was that they would not support a direct negative of the Bill, but that in Committee they would be glad to consider suggestions for amendments, with a view to reasonable and fair treatment of the Railway Companies being assured.[37]

Secure in this knowledge, the association decided upon a change of tactics. The railway interest ceased to oppose the bill root and branch. As a meeting of managers and solicitors pointed out, the main objection of the companies was not to reclassification and revision of maximum rates, but to this being carried through by compulsion, at the whim of the government. The amendment which the Caledonian chairman, Joseph Bolton, moved on the second reading of the bill, approving of its general objects but deprecating "any compulsory interference with or diminution of those

powers of earning revenue granted by Parliament to Railway Companies",
was exactly what the association had agreed upon two days before.[38] But
there was no division. Bolton withdrew his amendment, and Mundella's
Railway and Canal Traffic bill was given its second reading.[39]

At this stage Irish affairs once more intervened. There could be no
further progress with Mundella's bill till after the second reading of the
Home Rule bill. On 8 June Home Rule was defeated in the Commons by
343 votes to 313, 93 Liberals voting in the majority. On 10 June the Railway and Canal Traffic bill was withdrawn.[40] A general election followed
next month.

The extent to which Mundella's bill contributed to the fall of Gladstone's government has already been the subject of some controversy
amongst historians.[41] The precise extent cannot be calculated, for this
would require detailed evidence of the state of mind of all the Liberal
railway directors who voted against Home Rule. Liberal directors of the
large companies were clearly worried by the proposed railway legislation.
This is seen most clearly in the case of Joseph Pease. Worried by talk of
extending the provisions of the 1881 Irish Land Act to England and Scotland, Pease distinguished himself on 25 January 1886 by being the only
Liberal railway director to vote with the Conservative whips against Barclay's amendment to the Address.[42] In mid-May Pease wrote to Gladstone
urging him to withdraw the Home Rule bill and so forestall "a great break
up of the Liberal party"; he had already urged the Railway Association to
seek an interview with Mundella before the second reading of the Railway
and Canal Traffic bill.[43]

But in proportion as Mundella and the Liberals proved intransigent,
the Conservatives proved reassuring. Cross, who was present at a meeting
of the Railway Association on 13 May, gave what amounted to an official
denial by the Conservative leadership that the Salisbury government of
1885–6 had ever discussed the question of giving the Board of Trade
power over railway rates; after entering a protest against Mundella's clause
24, Cross assured the association that he felt himself "at liberty to move the
rejection of it in Parliament".[44]

Nonetheless, of the 40 Liberal railway director-M.P.s left in the House
of Commons by June 1886, only 17 turned against Gladstone.[45] Whilst this
number would just have been sufficient to have ensured the second reading
of the Home Rule bill, it can hardly be supposed that all 17 were motivated
by a hatred of Mundella's railway bill. One of them, W. C. Quilter, not
only supported Mundella's bill, but campaigned for a stronger measure.[46]
Others, such as J. C. Corbett and Sir H. H. Vivian, had railway interests so

small that they could not possibly have played a large part in determining political loyalties.[47] Moreover, it must be remembered that several very prominent Liberal members of the railway interest, including Bolton, Dillwyn and Pease, remained loyal to Gladstone throughout the crisis.

It is, however, within the efficient interest that figures become more meaningful. Of the Liberal members of the efficient interest, 20 in January 1886, 11 turned against Gladstone and left the party. This compares with 29 per cent of the entire parliamentary party.[48] The significance of this figure is plain. For many years Liberal policy towards the railway interest had been suspicious and hostile. In the cases both of Chamberlain and Mundella, the railways were alienated not merely by the content of their proposals, but by the manner in which the proposals were thrust upon them with little hope of compromise or discussion. Nor was it only amongst Liberal directors that the swing to Unionism occurred; the movement permeated the administrative grades. Lord Stalbridge informed Lord Salisbury in 1890 that George Findlay, general manager of the London & North Western, had declared himself a convinced Liberal Unionist.[49] Myles Fenton, general manager of Watkin's South Eastern, was another Unionist devoted to the "great cause".[50] Another prominent railway administrator who turned Unionist was Sir James Allport, till 1880 general manager, and afterwards a director, of the Midland Railway. Lord Claud Hamilton, the Conservative M.P. and deputy chairman of the Great Eastern Railway, advised Salisbury in December 1886 that as Allport not only enjoyed great prestige amongst the rebel Liberals, but had actually come out in support of Salisbury's government, his political friendship was worth cultivating.[51]

For Liberal directors and managers alike, the events of 1886 did not come as a great traumatic experience; the writing had been on the wall for some time. The Conservatives promised and had proved to be accommodating and sympathetic. As Liberalism moved in a more Radical direction it lost touch with the great industries, like the railways, whose interests it no longer served. After the election in the summer of 1886, the view in Liberal circles was that when the Conservatives legislated on the subject of railway rates, as they intended to, they would "enjoy much more favour than did Mr. Mundella from the railway chairmen and leading directors."[52]

The elections of 1886, 1892 and 1895 reflected the parting of the ways between Liberalism and the railway companies.[53] The Conservative victory of 1886 led to an increase in the number of Conservative directors in the Commons, from 39, in 1885, to 48. In subsequent years railway companies preferred to take on to their boards Conservatives rather than

Liberals, or even Liberal Unionists, so that by 1890 the Conservative interest had risen to 57, more than double the number of Liberal directors. During this period the number of Liberal Unionist directors remained between 10 and 12, and the number of Liberals, 20 after the 1886 election, rose to its highest, 24, only in 1891.

Liberal Unionism was clearly more symbolic of the changing political structure of the railway interest than a cause of it. Of the 17 Liberal directors who turned Unionist in June 1886, nine failed to return after the election, and, of these, seven were directors of large companies.[54] In the Parliament elected in 1886 only three directors of large companies were Liberal Unionists, compared with eight who were Liberals, of whom one, Sir M. A. Bass, went to the Lords in the same year. This meant that Liberal and Liberal Unionist directors of large companies, combined, only totalled 11, as against 23 Conservatives, compared with 20 Liberals and 19 Conservatives in 1885. In 1891 the figures were nine Liberals, six Unionists, and 24 Conservatives.

But it was amongst the directors of the smaller railways that the decline in Liberal representation was most marked. Here, as with the large companies, there was a tendency for Conservative representation to increase, from 14 in 1885 to 23 in 1890. In 1885 the Liberal figure had stood at 16. Of these only seven turned Unionist and only five were returned in 1886; these, with two additions in that year, brought the 1886 total also to seven, as against eight Liberals. But between then and 1891 the Liberal total reached only ten, and the Liberal Unionist total actually declined to five. By 1891, therefore, the Liberal and Liberal Unionist totals combined were actually lower than in 1885, whereas the Conservative total had increased by 50 per cent from 14 to 21.

These trends were confirmed in the last decade of the nineteenth century. In spite of the Liberal victory of 1892 the total number of Liberal directors in the Commons actually fell. The Conservative total fell too; only 34 of the 55 Conservative directors who were sitting in the House in 1891 sat there after the 1892 election. But of the total railway interest the Conservative proportion rose, and in 1894 was just over 60 per cent, slightly higher, in fact, than in 1891. This proportion remained about the same after 1895. In the election that year the Liberal proportion fell to under 25 per cent. Of the 18 Liberal railway directors then returned to Parliament, only nine sat on the boards of large companies; by contrast there were 30 Conservative and Liberal Unionist M.P.s on these boards. Thus at the outbreak of the Boer War the efficient railway interest in the Commons was an overwhelmingly Unionist body. Liberalism and railway direction were rapidly losing the common ground they had once possessed.

In the Lords the pattern was still more pronounced. The number of Liberal peers who sat on the boards of small British railways had always been very low, only three in 1885 and only two in 1889.[55] In 1885 the efficient railway interest in the Upper House had included 14 Liberals. This number dropped steadily in the next decade, as Liberal peers who ceased to hold directorships with the large lines were not replaced by politicians of the same party. By 1892 the number had fallen to seven, and by 1899 stood only at five. The number of Liberal Unionist peers in the efficient interest remained about the same: seven in 1886, nine in 1894, seven in 1899. The introduction of Conservative peers into the direction of large companies was rapid. In 1885 there were only four such directors; in 1892 there were ten, and in 1899 14. Of these, only four, Lords Cross, Muncaster, Newlands and Rathmore, were new creations; Cross and Rathmore had, in any case, held their directorships before elevation to the peerage.[56] In the Lords, as in the Commons, the transformation of the efficient railway interest into a Conservative body was not a mechanical result of the Liberal split, but the effect of deliberate company policy.

In the Commons the total railway interest became numerically weaker. As has been noted earlier, this was due primarily to a decline in the number of M.P.s on the boards of the small domestic lines, from 32 in 1885 to 23 in 1899; the number of Conservative directors of such railways fell from 14 to 11, and of Liberals from 16 to 9. This was probably the result of the disappearance of many smaller lines, swallowed up by the larger companies. In 1880 *Bradshaw* listed 352 separate railway companies in the United Kingdom; the number fell to 302 in 1890, and stood at 256 in 1900. At the same time the total number of directors of large companies increased from 39 in 1885 to 46 in 1899, when these directors accounted for more than half the total number of director-M.P.s. Of these 46, only 11 were Liberals.

The swing away from Liberalism had a further important effect on the political structure of the railway interest: its leading spokesmen ceased to be Liberals. Dillwyn, who had always taken a back seat, died in 1892. Joseph Bolton retired from Parliament in the same year. Pease, though he continued to speak on behalf of the railways almost to the time of his death in 1903, was too conciliatory and lukewarm, and his company, the North Eastern, soon found itself gravely out of step with other railway managements on the question of collective bargaining. The directors who led the railway interest in Parliament after 1886 were of a very different mould; all were Unionists. They included Gladstone's former chief whip, Lord

Stalbridge, who remained a father-figure in the railway interest till his retirement from the London & North Western Railway in 1911, and William Lawies Jackson, a man with a thoroughly Conservative and commercial background, who was M.P. for Leeds, a member of Lord Salisbury's government, and the most promising of the Great Northern Railway directors.[57]

In their changing political structure the railways did not develop as an isolated industry. The period after 1885 witnessed an increasing percentage of new peers being drawn from industrial and commercial backgrounds.[58] J. A. Thomas had already traced statistically the extent to which the representation of other industrial interests in the Commons, notably finance, shipping, transport, engineering and brewing, had become Unionist by the end of the century.[59] For all these interests, as for the railways, Liberalism, which had once stood for individualism and the freedom of trade from interference, lost its *raison d'être* when its practitioners began preaching ideals of 'State Socialism' and interference with the hitherto undisputed rights of freedom of property. The alienation of property from Liberalism began long before 1886; it reached a point of no return that year because the pretext for a formal breach was too great to be ignored.[60]

Though the effect of this transformation on the Liberal party was, in the short term, centrifugal, creating a manpower vacuum which Gladstone, for another eight years, was able to hide but not fill, in the long run the reorientation of property left the field clear for younger radicals, less overawed by the mystique of property, to propagate and later carry through new collectivist ideas. The effect of the new political alignment on Conservatism was less clear-cut. Certainly the party was becoming less neurotic about the Land and the Church. The social and economic questions which arose in the late 1880s gave Conservative individualists new food for thought. Salisbury declared that Conservative policy was "the upholding of confidence".[61] This was not the same as the policy of "leaving well alone" which Frederic Harrison believed had won for the Conservatives the election of 1874.[62]

That policy had suited the railway interest perfectly. Now, however, the marriage between commerce and Conservatism brought the party new responsibilities to a variety of conflicting interests. Conservatism relied increasingly on large urban constituencies for support. And, unlike Liberalism, it did not have a history of opposition in principle to State interference. Pragmatism was its keynote. Though the railway interest could expect treatment more lenient or, depending on one's viewpoint, more just, it could not expect to escape scot-free from a government which saw fit to pass an Allotments Act in 1887, a County Councils Act in 1888, a Free Education Act in 1891, whose Irish Land Act of 1887 was a measure avowedly designed to break contracts previously made, and whose Factory and Workshops Act of 1891, with its concept of dangerous industries, opened a new chapter in State control of industry.[63] The domestic legislation of Salisbury's second Ministry was largely reflected in, if not actually inspired by, Lord Randolph Churchill's "Dartford programme"; that programme included the remodelling of railway rates "so that the home producer should not be underbid by the foreigner."[64]

The Railway Association held no illusions about the likelihood of rates legislation under the Conservatives. In continuing adverse economic conditions, complaints from traders and farmers about differential rates on home and foreign produce could not be ignored.[65] The Railway Association was aware, too, that its position in the new Parliament, *vis-à-vis* the agricultural interest, was weak, and that it might be better to try and enlist support from agriculturists than to fight them.[66] Since the farmers had made it quite clear that they would not accept legislation solely on the basis of the report of the 1881–2 Select Committee, the companies favoured a new parliamentary inquiry into the import and export rates charged by railway companies. Lord Stanley of Preston, the Conservative President of the Board of Trade, a shy man with a resolute mind, met this request with a polite refusal.[67] The government was already under pressure from farmers to act on high and preferential railway rates. The final report of the Royal Commission on the Trade Depression, published in January 1887, though not condemnatory of the railways, drew attention to the need for greater railway facilities and lower charges. On the last day of February Lord Stanley presented his rates bill in the Upper House.[68]

The bill as presented perpetuated some features of Mundella's measure.[69] Clause 7 provided for complaints by public authorities to the Railway Commission, and by traders' associations which obtained certificates from the Board of Trade. Clause 17 provided for appeals only on questions of law. As in Mundella's bill, clause 24 compelled companies to submit revised classifications of goods and schedules of maximum rates to the Board of Trade; after hearing objections, in cases where no agreement could be reached, the board was to draw up classifications and schedules which, in the board's opinion, it would "be just and reasonable to substitute for the existing rates and charges of the railway company as fairly applicable thereto", and submit them to Parliament (subsection 6) as Provisional Orders. There was also a 'Conciliation clause' (27) and a statistical returns clause (28). Clause 29 compelled companies to exhibit lists of their rates and classification at every station. By clause 25 a differential rate "for the same or similar services", as between individual traders, different districts, or British and foreign goods, was put into the category of an "undue preference", unless a company could prove otherwise to the satisfaction of the Railway Commissioners. But, under subsection 2, the commissioners were enjoined to "take into consideration whether such lower charge or difference of treatment is necessary for the purpose of securing the traffic in respect of which it is made." When the bill came on for second reading, Henniker objected to this provision; but, on behalf of the traders, he gave the bill a general approval.[70]

As the directors of the Manchester, Sheffield & Lincolnshire Railway recorded, the most objectionable feature of Mundella's bill, the proposal to give the Board of Trade perpetual powers of rates revision, was absent from the Conservative measure.[71] Nonetheless Stanley's bill was greeted with dismay in railway circles, though in fact it probably represented the maximum he was prepared to concede to the traders. A week before the second reading, the Railway Association decided to send a strong deputation to Lord Stanley and the Prime Minister. Its appeal was directed as much at Salisbury, a former railway chairman, as at Stanley. Richard Moon put the case thus:

> the Railway Companies would be very sorry not to assist the Government in carrying out a fair Bill. What they objected to was that their earning powers should be interfered with . . . the Railway Companies now looked to the Prime Minister, as head of the Government, to say that he did not mean anything in the Bill to take away the powers granted to the Railway Companies.[72]

Salisbury responded warmly. The government, he avowed, "had not the least intention of permitting anything in the nature of confiscation." He invited the companies to submit modifications to the bill. Secure in the knowledge of such a declaration of intent, the railway interest did not divide on the second reading, though through Brabourne, Stalbridge and the Marquis of Tweeddale, they gave full vent to their objections.[73]

Both sides now set to work in earnest to press amendments upon the government. Lord Henniker's committee objected to terminal charges, and there was much pressure from traders to make all differential rates illegal. Arguments revolving around protection for home industries proved, however, to be a double-edged weapon. On 21 March Lord Stanley was urged by a deputation from the "Northern Counties" to retain subsection 2 of clause 25. This plea was also put forward by local port interests, campaigners for cheap food, and, naturally, the shareholders.[74] The Railway Association, which entrusted their amendments to Brabourne, sent out letters to peers urging support at the committee stage.[75]

This appeal had excellent results. The peers, willing as ever to come to the rescue of property and the *status quo*, agreed with Brabourne in opposing a new clause, moved by the Earl of Jersey on behalf of the traders, which would have obliged railway companies to furnish through rates on request. An amendment to restore the law to what it had been before Hall's case was withdrawn. Tweeddale succeeded in obtaining the approval of the Lords to an alteration in clause 24, providing that the revised classification of goods and schedule of rates, as settled by the Board of Trade, should be "equivalent to" the existing rates and charges, thereby safeguarding the companies against loss of revenue. An attempt by the Earl of Jersey to delete subsection 2 of clause 25 was defeated on a division. The conciliation clause, on Tweeddale's motion, and with Stanley's approval, was struck out, as was clause 29 on Brabourne's initiative.[76]

The railway companies received further testimony of the government's goodwill on the report stage, for then the only alteration to be seriously interfered with was that relating to the publication of classification tables.[77] Brabourne advised the railways "to support the Government in their endeavour to carry it [the bill] through . . . the House of Commons . . . in its present shape."[78] The alterations and amendments constituted a notable parliamentary victory for the railway companies, pointing to the fact that if they were less powerful in the Commons, in the Lords their influence remained strong. Now, indeed, it was the traders who opposed the bill. The Farmers' Alliance declared it would not acquiesce in the measure unless subsection 2 of clause 25 was withdrawn. On this point the Railway and Canal Traders' Association gave notice of its intention to use "every means in their power to oppose this provision in the House of Commons." The Central Chamber of Agriculture also promised "the most strenuous opposition" to this provision.[79]

As *Herapath* noted, the bill had "merely passed through the first and by no means the most important stage".

> The real fight will take place in the Commons, and it must be noted that Lord Salisbury himself has given strong indications that the Cabinet as a whole will not object strongly to the evident sense of the lower House.[80]

The railways and the traders both realized this. The bill passed the

Lords on 5 May and reached the Commons on 16 May.[81] Brabourne urged the Railway Association to be content with the measure as it was, to put down as few amendments as possible in the Commons, and to assist the government in assuring the bill's speedy passage through the lower House.[82] The policy of the traders was naturally the reverse. They had been looking forward to a measure which would enforce lower railway rates; this, as Lord Stanley later remarked, the bill was never intended to do. The government naively hoped for a second reading *pro forma*; instead the opposition was felt to be so great that the bill was withdrawn without its second reading in the Commons even being proposed.[83]

But the issues were now very clear: the maximum charging powers of the companies, and the extent to which they were to be allowed to vary their actual charges, for similar items carried over similar distances, depending on their point of origin. For a Conservative government this latter issue was particularly delicate, for it touched the thorny subject of protection for home produce, which the Fair Trade League and other bodies were bringing into prominence once more. Watkin, who most feared government interference with the companies' charging powers, favoured the assimilation of home and foreign rates for produce, to "take the sting out of the objections to Railways".[84]

The traders, not content with whipping up opposition to the government's bill in 1887, decided they could no longer trust the Salisbury government to bring in a suitable measure, and that they must promote legislation themselves. In January 1888 the National Sea Fisheries Protection Association drew up a bill, providing for a uniform scale of rates for the carriage of fish, which its president, the Conservative M.P. Sir Edward Birkbeck, introduced in the Commons on 10 February.[85] On the same day Sir Bernhard Samuelson, whose guest Mundella had been in January, presented a bill of his own to give perpetual powers of rates revision to the Board of Trade and to impose equal mileage rates over the whole field of railway charges.[86] Both bills were anathema to the railway companies, but it is significant that they treated both bills very seriously.[87] There was no doubt that the government would have to attempt legislation once more. For the companies, the main worry was not the acceptance of the government's measure; that they had already done. The problem now was to support that measure to their utmost and ensure its safe passage in the form in which it had left the Lords in May 1887.[88]

But this was to prove impossible. In February 1888 Lord Stanley was appointed governor-general of Canada. His successor at the Board of Trade, Sir Michael Hicks Beach, knew something about railways, for he had helped promote the East Gloucestershire Railway in 1863 and was now its chairman.[89] This did not make him a friend to the railway interest. Hicks Beach openly sympathized with the traders. His views on railway rates were much nearer than Stanley's to those of the trading interests, and Salisbury had misgivings about asking him to defend Stanley's bill in the Commons, if Stanley should still be allowed to pilot the bill through the Upper House.[90] Parliamentary time in the Commons was, however, so scarce that this was the course taken. On 14 February 1888 Stanley introduced in the Lords a bill virtually identical with the measure as it had left the Lords the previous year.[91]

The second reading of the bill passed smoothly enough, a move by Lord Jersey to reject the bill being defeated by 72 votes to 45.[92] Jersey, however, who had just entered upon a term of office as chairman of the Central Chamber of Agriculture, was not prepared to let the matter rest. Agriculturists and chambers of commerce started intensive lobbying and propaganda campaigns.[93] When Jersey announced his intention to move an amendment in committee prohibiting different rates for British and foreign merchandise, Oakley warned the Parliamentary Committee of the Railway Association that "he was not alone in thinking that as there was much opposition to contend with the amendment might be carried on a division". The following day, in spite of a personal plea by Salisbury, Jersey's amendment was carried by 69 votes to 63.[94]

Though this was a defeat, and a setback, railways and government alike knew it had meaning only as a symbolic act of defiance by the trading interests. "The enforcement of a statute embodying this amendment", *Herapath* declared, "would work untold mischief on all kinds of traffic, on agricultural as much as any."[95] The rigid enforcement of equal rates for home and foreign produce was bound to hit the trade of ports hardest. Richard Moon suggested securing the co-operation of the traders and shipowners of the great ports, making known to them "the ruinous way in which this Clause would effect their interests", and inviting Lord Hartington, the Liberal Unionist leader and chairman of the Furness Railway, to use his influence on their behalf.[96] Hartington, who was present with ten other director-M.P.s at a large meeting of the Railway Association's Parliamentary Committee on 10 May, the day of the bill's second reading, recommended pressure on traders and shipowners as the best course. A deputation from the Parliamentary Committee to Hicks Beach on 18 April pledged general support for the bill, providing the undue preference clause was altered. The association also drew up circulars for distribution to traders and shipowners by individual companies.[97]

Southampton was one locality where this campaign had greatest effect. The local press there was loud in condemnation of Lord Jersey's amendment, and a deputation, including representatives of the chamber of commerce, the corporation, the Harbour Board and the Dock Company, travelled up to see Hicks Beach on 30 April.[98] Even the Railway and Canal Traders' Association lost its enthusiasm for an amendment which was as likely to result in a levelling up of home rates as in a levelling down of foreign ones, and, with the chambers of commerce and agriculture, began stressing instead the need to reduce rates and restrict terminal charges.[99]

When the bill, together with Samuelson's measure, was referred to the Standing Committee on Trade, Hicks Beach was placed in an embarrassing position. Mundella determined to press the government to carry as many points as possible in favour of the traders.[100] The time taken up by the Local Government bill made it imperative that the Railway and Canal Traffic bill be proceeded with as quickly as possible. But the conflicting views of different sets of traders, especially regarding preference, made agreement on amendments difficult, placing the government in a "somewhat unstable position".[101] Chamberlain, under pressure from local chambers of commerce, threatened to add to this instability, and, anxious to show his anti-railway and protectionist leanings, pressed upon Hicks Beach a number of amendments with which the latter was loath to argue.[102]

The sending of the bill to the Standing Committee put the railway interest at a grave disadvantage. Out of a total of 85 members the Standing Committee included only eight members of the efficient interest, of whom one, Sir M. W. Ridley, was appointed chairman.[103] The Railway Association attempted to get its representation increased, but was unsuccessful.[104] Nor did Hicks Beach give any firm assurance to its Parliamentary Committee that he would resist amendments proposed by Samuelson and others, with the object of removing the safeguards inserted by the Lords in the 1887 bill to protect the companies from interference with their maximum charging powers.[105]

This issue proved one of the most contentious, for the Standing Committee spent four days considering it without making any amendments acceptable to either the companies or the traders.[106] Two days were spent discussing undue preferences, the wrangle ending only when Hicks Beach moved that the clause in question, clause 25, be formally negatived to allow him to bring up a new section on report. It was not till 9 July that the committee finished dealing with the clauses already in the bill.[107] Little time was left for the completion of the remaining stages. Hicks Beach therefore decided to bow to the traders' wishes. He acquiesced in a new subsection to the rates revision clause, to give any person or railway company the right to apply in future to the Board of Trade to amend any classification or schedule "by adding thereto any articles, matters, or things." This, whilst not as extensive as subsection 7 of Mundella's clause 24, nonetheless savoured of the perpetual revision to which the companies had objected in 1886.[108] Hicks Beach was actually defeated in an attempt to alter clauses agreed to at the instance of William Hunter, giving the Railway Commissioners power to fix through rates at the behest of traders. The President's new undue preference clause, whilst avoiding the dangerous narrowness of Lord Jersey's amendment, was framed in its spirit. Another clause moved by Hicks Beach gave the Board of Trade wide powers to call for statistical returns from the companies.[109] The bill which emerged from the Standing Committee was thus hardly to the liking of the Railway Association. But, as the solicitors pointed out, there was little probability of securing further amendments in the Commons or in the Upper House. The measure thus had a smooth journey through its final stages, and became law on 10 August.[110]

The Railway and Canal Traffic Act of 1888, though the culmination of five years of attempts to revise and consolidate railway rates, itself marked merely the beginning of a period of intense activity by the companies and the traders. Under the terms of the Act, the companies themselves were each to submit to the Board of Trade revised classifications of merchandise and schedules of maximum rates which they proposed to adopt. It was left largely to the Board of Trade to try to arrange agreements between the companies and objecting traders. As there were, at the time of the passing of the Act, about 900 separate railway Acts dealing with the charging powers of 976 companies, and involving millions of separate rates, this proved a gigantic task, not made easier by the vague wording of the 1888 Act, which gave little strict guidance as to the principles which should govern the new schemes.[111]

The revised classifications and schedules were submitted to the Board of Trade on 9 February 1889, Oakley thereafter acting as the principal railway representative in the negotiations.[112] The board then invited objections to the proposals, and over 120 meetings were arranged throughout the United Kingdom between the traders and the companies to endeavour to arrive at agreed schemes.[113] Traders and farmers who looked forward to substantial reductions were disappointed with the companies' proposals. Chambers of agriculture banded together to co-ordinate their opposition.[114] The Railway and Canal Traders' Association set up its own negotiating body, whilst local authorities, chambers of commerce, and traders, in Lancashire and Cheshire, formed a "Conference on Railway and Canal Rates" for the same purpose.[115] In July, at the instance of the radical Lord Mayor of London and former merchant, Sir James Whitehead (1834–1917), these two bodies joined with a large number of chambers of commerce and agriculture, and local authorities, in forming the Mansion House Association, "for general and united defence".[116]

With such a high level of combination and determination on both sides, and even with Board of Trade officials acting as neutral chairmen, agreement proved impossible.[117] Hicks Beach then set in motion a formal inquiry, into the objections, by two of the Board's officials, the Parliamentary Secretary Lord Balfour of Burleigh, and Courtenay Boyle, whom Mundella had appointed Assistant Secretary in charge of the Railway Department in 1886. The hearings commenced in London on 15 October 1889. They were later transferred to Edinburgh and then Dublin, and did not terminate till 21 May 1891, having occupied 85 days in all.[118]

The proceedings were as acrimonious as they were prolonged. The railway companies contended that it was the duty of Lord Balfour and Courtenay Boyle merely to codify rates. The traders argued that they also had a duty to alter the maximum charging powers so that rates would in practice have to be reduced.[119] "At the end of it all", *Herapath* remarked truly, "no single principle in dispute has been settled, no contested point disposed of".[120]

During June and July 1890 the Board of Trade officials embarked upon the task of drawing up schedules of charges, to be submitted to Parliament, which would satisfy both sides. It was an attempt to reconcile the irreconcilable.[121] When the first completed schedules, those of the London & North Western and Great Western, were forwarded to the Railway Association, they were greeted with general disgust bolstered by anger at Hicks Beach's determination to make the matter public, and so force the companies' hand. Beale, of the Midland Railway, felt the board's proposals "almost amounted to confiscation." Richard Moon complained that the board "had largely reduced the rates for coal and other traffic without being asked to do so by the traders", and that this was contrary to the assurance given by Lord Salisbury in March 1887.[122]

A deputation of railway managers and solicitors, led by George Findlay, which was received by Hicks Beach on 28 October 1890, estimated that the proposals of the Board of Trade would involve losses of revenue to the companies ranging from £117,700 for the Midland Railway to £4,000 for the London, Brighton & South Coast company, losses "of so serious a character as to make it absolutely impossible for the Companies to accept those Schedules in their present form." But Hicks Beach, eager to please the traders, insisted on full publicity being given to the demands of the companies for reconsideration. In a sentence which gave the companies little cause for hope, the President promised merely to consider "whether there is any ground for departing from the conclusions at which I have already arrived."[123]

Such determination on the part of a Conservative minister on this question was indeed a danger signal for the companies. Though some members of the railway interest clearly hoped for a political solution to the problem, the truth was that the conditions of 1886 could not be repeated. The traders had acquired political strength, and meant to derive the utmost benefit from it.

# Chapter 8

# Political isolation and its results: railway safety

The advance of state control of railway rates under Conservative rule was matched by a similar considerable widening of government powers in matters of railway safety. Here however the railway interest was more successful in the meeting of its demands, for the leading advocates of compulsion in safety matters did not include, or draw support from, large numbers of Conservatives, but came instead from the ranks of left-wing Liberalism and the Amalgamated Society of Railway Servants.

In industrial terms the Amalgamated Society remained weak during the 1880s, following the complete collapse of a Nine Hours Movement in 1881–2. Only in 1887 did the society's membership reach the 10,000 mark. But in parliamentary terms it continued to win friends amongst the Liberals, and after its victory over Employers' Liability in 1880 the society turned its attention to matters of railway safety, particularly continuous automatic brakes. Joseph Chamberlain proved a willing listener; his proposals to legislate on brakes as part of his omnibus bill of 1884 may well have been a reflection of the society's influence, the more so as it had sponsored Earl De La Warr's bill in 1882. Another matter in which the society took the initiative between 1881 and 1886 was the design and adoption of automatic coupling devices, to lessen the risk of accidents to shunters.[1]

One Liberal upon whom the propaganda of the society had a deep effect was Francis Allston Channing, a Fellow of University College, Oxford, who was first elected to Parliament for East Northamptonshire in 1885, holding the seat continuously till 1910.[2] Channing never ceased being a thorn in the side of the railway interest. He joined the committee of the Farmers' Alliance, and early in his career struck up a firm friendship with the Amalgamated Society, whose various causes he promoted in the Commons.

Channing's views reflected the increasingly harsh and unsympathetic attitude of Liberalism towards the railways in the 1890s, which must in turn have helped the reorientation of the railway interest towards the Conservatives. An admirer of Chamberlain's abortive merchant shipping and railway legislation in 1884, he was one of those left-wingers who believed earnestly in the value of the 'Labour Plank' in the Liberal platform, who supported and would have strengthened the Newcastle Programme, and for whom, with the secession of the Liberal Unionists, the field was left clear to shape a new species of radical Liberalism.[3]

The high number of fatalities in railway work formed one of Channing's main themes in his election campaign in November and December 1885.[4] When the new Parliament assembled he introduced a bill which proposed to confer powers upon the Board of Trade to order railway companies to adopt the block system, the interlocking of points and signals, and to fit all passenger trains with an approved continuous brake. The bill also sought to give the board powers to compel companies to fit all vehicles in goods and mineral trains with "such improved apparatus for coupling and uncoupling the vehicles as shall make it unnecessary for men to go between them for the purpose of coupling or uncoupling". There was also a clause requiring companies to make monthly returns to the Board of Trade of all employees on duty for more than 12 hours, or who resumed duty without a full nine hours' rest.[5]

Channing's bill had wide Liberal support. Five other Liberals put their names to it. Mundella, who was being pressed by Channing to give a grant to the Amalgamated Society to assist in the testing of railway couplings, did not wish to appear hostile to the measure. But his own Railway and Canal Traffic bill had already run into difficulties. When Channing's measure came up for second reading, on 19 May, Mundella confessed himself "somewhat reluctant to take all the responsibility which this Bill would put on the Board." He pointed out that the companies were steadily proceeding with many of the improvements the bill sought; whilst hoping the bill would be given a second reading, he recommended it be sent to a Select Committee. The Railway Companies' Association had already decided to ask director-M.P.s to oppose the measure. Perhaps because they were better judges of the temper of the House, none of the director-M.P.s who spoke offered an outright opposition, but all, and especially the Liberals Pease, Robertson and Bolton, took up Mundella's suggestion of a Select Committee, to which the House agreed.[6]

The second reading of Channing's bill meant its acceptance in principle by the Commons. It therefore seems pertinent to ask why the railway companies did not offer a more vigorous opposition to what was, after all, only a private member's measure. Probably the progress made by the companies since the mid-1870s in the adoption of the block system, interlocking, and continuous brakes, had taken the sting out of some of Channing's proposals, and also out of the former objections of the companies to any state interference at all in railway safety. Where there was no longer any necessity for state interference, there was no longer any need to fear it, This being so, the railway M.P.s may have felt it better to have the bill amended than to obstruct it from the start.

The fall of Gladstone's government, within days of the appointment of the Select Committee, killed Channing's measure. Though he reintroduced the bill in 1887 and 1888, under the Conservative government it never reached the second reading stage.[7] Nor is there any indication that either Lord Stanley or Hicks Beach, both absorbed with railway rates, ever contemplated introducing, as considered government policy, any bill in the terms for which Channing wished. When Channing brought forward a motion on the subject, on 8 May 1888, Hicks Beach, though giving a vague promise to legislate, declared:

> He thought it would be most unwise on the part of Parliament to alter the general policy which had been adopted in this matter by doing anything which would tend to hand over the direction or administration of the Railways to the Board of Trade.[8]

The most he would concede was to use the powers under the Railway and Canal Traffic Act in order to obtain returns as to couplings, a policy reminiscent of that pursued by Adderley and Lord Sandon ten years before.[9]

In any case, by 1888 the question of the adoption of the block system, interlocking, and continuous automatic brakes had been largely settled by the railways themselves. Ninety-seven per cent of the English and Welsh lines had adopted the block system, and 99 per cent of the Scottish. On English and Welsh lines, 93.5 per cent of the points and signals were interlocked, and 82 per cent on the Scottish lines. By 30 June 1889 75 per cent of the engines on the railways of Great Britain were fitted with continuous brakes which complied with the requirements of the Board of Trade, and 72 per cent of the coaches. Only the backward and impoverished Irish lines lagged behind. In Ireland only 59 per cent of points and signals were interlocked, and the block system was installed on just 31 per cent of the lines; on the Great Northern Railway of Ireland the figure for the block system was as low as 14 per cent.[10]

It was on the Great Northern of Ireland that an accident occurred at Armagh, on 12 June 1889, which altered Conservative policy. The Armagh disaster involved a loss of between 70 and 80 lives, many of the victims being young children. An overloaded excursion train fitted only with a simple – i.e., non-automatic – continuous brake, had been purposely divided on a bank; the rear portion, running backwards, collided with the following train, itself despatched only because the line was worked on the time-interval system, not the space-interval system which was the essence of block working.[11] Major-General Hutchinson, in his report, drew attention not merely to the advisability of making the adoption of continuous automatic brakes compulsory, but also to the "grave question whether legislative power could not be sought to make the block system compulsory on old lines as it has been for many years on new lines."[12]

The outcry produced by the "hideous butchery" of Armagh demanded a bold response from the government.[13] Channing naturally raised the matter with Hicks Beach, who on 15 July produced a bill which was, in its essentials, Channing's own measure of 1886.[14] It gave the Board of Trade powers to order railway companies to adopt the block system and interlocking, and to provide continuous automatic brakes on all passenger trains in regular use. It also obliged companies to adopt a system of coupling approved by the Board of Trade, and to make periodical returns of all employees, whose work involved the safety of trains or passengers, who worked for more than 12 hours at a time.

The major companies represented by the Railway Association had no intention of frustrating the principal purposes for which the bill had been introduced, but they objected strongly to the coupling clause because, as a deputation told Hicks Beach on 25 July, investigations into systems of coupling wagons had not been completed, and there were great difficulties with regard to private owners' wagons.[15] In fact the main objections to the coupling clause came not from railway companies, but from the many private owners of wagons, including the coal-owners.[16] Oakley was instructed to communicate with M.P.s with a view to obtaining a postponement of the second reading.[17]

The railway servants, with the help of Channing, Burt, Charles Bradlaugh and other radicals in the Liberal and Irish Nationalist parties, launched a counter-campaign in favour of the retention of the coupling clause.[18] Hicks Beach, anxious to pass his bill before the end of the session, agreed in deference to the companies and the private owners to omit the clause; but when the radical M.P. Storey objected to the bill being proceeded with on such terms, the entire measure was withdrawn on 29 July, and a new bill, minus the coupling clause, was introduced the following day.[19]

The bill, now simply a measure to remedy the situation revealed at Armagh, and providing also for returns of more than 12 hours' continuous work, received Channing's blessing; though in committee he moved a coupling clause, which would have entailed the use of the coupling pole, the amendment was withdrawn without a division. The bill passed its remaining stages with only one noteworthy alteration, an amendment to the overtime returns clause, leaving it to the discretion of the Board of Trade to fix the exact number of hours worked above which returns would have to be made.[20]

The measure became law on 30 August. In October the Board submitted to the companies draft orders it proposed to issue under the Act. But it was not till more than a year later, and after consultation between Hicks Beach, board officials, and general managers, that a final, modified order was issued to the companies, which, Oakley reported, "might be generally adopted by them."[21]

The passing of the Act of 1889 closed a chapter in the history of state regulation of railway safety, but only so far as passengers were concerned. The provision made in that Act for returns of overtime drew attention publicly to the connection between safety and overwork, and pointed to the new direction from which further demands for legislation were to arise. In 1888 the Amalgamated Society of Railway Servants had adopted the "Darlington Programme", calling for a guaranteed week's pay, a ten-hour day, and eight hours for shunters in busy places; the same year the society had approved a rules alteration, deleting the need for a ballot of all members before a strike could be called. These were the principal features of a new mood of militancy to which the union had turned even before the advent of 'New Unionism'.[22] The following year saw the foundation of the General Railway Workers' Union, attracting the lower railway grades, and sponsored by John Burns, fresh from his victory in the London docks.[23] In 1890 there was a series of labour disputes affecting railway companies throughout the United Kingdom.

These developments necessitated some reassessment by the companies of their policy towards the unions. Most of them, like the Great Western, grasped instantaneously at non-recognition.[24] But not all. In March 1890 the North Eastern Railway entered into direct correspondence with Edward Harford of the Amalgamated Society.[25] In August a strike on the Taff Vale, Rhymney, Bute Docks, and Barry Dock companies was settled when James Inskip, the Taff Vale chairman, met Harford and negotiated a settlement conceding the guaranteed week's pay.[26]

At the time of the South Wales dispute there were rumours that the principal railway companies had promised co-operation and support to the Welsh companies not to concede the demands of the men.[27] If this is true, no evidence for it exists in company records, though the managers of the London & North Western, Midland, and North Eastern railways had been in touch with the Rhymney Railway, regarding 'recognition', in May and June.[28] In any case, with the retirement of Inskip the following year, and the appointment of Ammon Beasley as general manager, the Taff Vale embarked on a militant anti-union policy.[29] On the London & North Western, at Crewe, where an alliance dating from 1880 between leading Conservatives and the company's chief mechanical engineer, F. W. Webb, had led to control of the town council by the Tory party and "railway nominees", the intimidation of Liberal trade unionists reached its climax at the end of 1889 with the foundation there of a branch of the General Railway Workers' Union and the dismissal from the railway works of the chairman of the local Liberal Association and the secretary of the Liberal Club.[30]

Even the events at Crewe, however, did not match the drama and bitterness of the strike for a ten-hour day which began in December 1890 amongst the employees of the Glasgow & South Western, North British, and Caledonian railways, and which broke up, only after riots and evictions of railwaymen from houses owned by the Caledonian company, at the end of January 1891. Here the questions of long hours, non-recognition, and the refusal to grant a ten-hour day, were coincident. "There was also the feeling", one observer wrote, "that in resisting the claims of the men, the companies were fighting the battle of the commercial world against the New Unionism."[31]

Scottish M.P.s raised the matter of the working hours of railway servants with Hicks Beach before the Christmas recess. The President of the Board of Trade had already sensed the growing importance of the issue, for he had mentioned it in a speech at Kilmarnock in October.[32] On 26 November Calcraft circularized the companies and the Railway Association on the subject of long hours and accidents, with particular reference to signalmen, drivers and guards.[33] The numbers of railway servants killed and injured in accidents had risen yearly, from 377 killed in 1888 to 517 in 1891, and from 2,081 injured in 1888 to 2,977 in 1891.[34] Accidents to railway servants, and long hours, both already causes of industrial unrest, were about to become political issues too.

The prospects which faced the railway interest at the end of 1890 were therefore grim. The year itself marked the beginning of a new downswing in the trade cycle, destined to continue to 1894.[35] The percentage of working expenditure to gross receipts, which had remained static at 52 per cent from 1886 to 1889, rose to 54 per cent in 1890, and by 1893 had reached a new peak at 57 per cent.[36] This heightened the alarm with which the companies greeted the schemes of the Conservative government under the 1888 Railway and Canal Traffic Act, by which they prophesied large losses of revenue. It heightened their resolve to resist collective bargaining and the demands of the trade unions. The 1888 Act provided for large-scale interference by the State in the hitherto sacrosanct charging powers of the individual companies. The Regulation of Railways Act of 1889, though it contained in itself nothing the companies could seriously complain about, was nonetheless viewed by them as "part of an objectionable system of Parliamentary interference" with the liberty and rights of capital invested in trade.[37] A year after the passing of the Act, advocates of railway nationalization established the "Railway Reform Association" to campaign for the state purchase of the railways.[38] From the Conservatives, within whom the railway interest now formed merely one of a number of often conflicting commercial groups, it could certainly expect sympathy; this was no guarantee that it could expect much more protection.

The Scottish railway strike had, moreover, brought into prominence the hours of railway servants at a time when labour conditions generally were already under public scrutiny and were about to become the subject of a Royal Commission. As a Board of Trade return for the months of September 1889 and March 1890 showed, it was not at all unusual for goods guards

135

to work over 12 or even 13 hours per day, whilst for engine drivers such working hours were quite common.[39] The state regulation of railway hours was advocated at Annual General Meetings of the Amalgamated Society from 1890 onwards.[40] Channing determined to take the matter further. In January 1891 he brought forward a motion directly related to events in Scotland, condemning the United Kingdom railways for perpetrating "a grave social injustice" in the matter of excessive hours of labour, and calling for the State regulation of the working hours of railway servants.[41]

The party political overtones in Channing's speech were undisguised. In the Parliamentary Committee of the Railway Association, Charles Parkes, chairman of the Great Eastern, thought it would be very desirable "if some Members on the same side of the House as Mr. Channing would speak against the motion."[42] None did so. On the contrary, many Liberal M.P.s who spoke in the ensuing debate had no qualms about giving the state some powers of interference with the conditions of work of adult railwaymen, on the now familiar grounds that the companies enjoyed virtual monopolies which the State had granted them.[43]

But the most surprising speeches came from the Conservative benches. Some Conservatives favoured an inquiry, perhaps to save themselves from having to vote either for the motion, or against it. Others, however, spoke openly in support of Channing.[44] In a phrase which reveals an important shift in Conservative thinking, Arthur Baumann, Conservative M.P. for Peckham, declared that he was "in favour of limiting the labour of railway servants for their own sake, not for the sake of public safety."[45]

Although Channing's motion was defeated, the margin, 141 to 124, was too small to be brushed aside. With the whips on, twelve Conservative and Liberal Unionist members of the efficient railway interest voted against Channing. But three Conservative and two Liberal Unionist M.P.s voted against the government. Liberal members of the efficient interest were conspicuous by their absence; whilst none voted against the motion only two, James Joicey of the North Eastern and D. A. Thomas of the Taff Vale, voted for it.[46] The *Railway Review* gave prominence to the political implications of the debate, whilst many branches of the Amalgamated Society wrote to their M.P.s.[47] On 27 January the Railway Association decided to support a Select Committee in preference to legislation. On 3 February, on the motion of Hicks Beach, the terms of reference of such a committee, "to inquire whether, and, if so, in what way, the hours worked by Railway Servants should be restricted by legislation", were approved by the Commons without a division.[48]

The railway interest was well represented on the Select Committee, so

well, in fact, that the indignation of radical M.P.s was taken to the point
of dividing against the inclusion of one railway director, Gathorne-Hardy.
In the end, out of 26 members of the Select Committee, there were seven
directors of large companies; four Conservatives: Gathorne-Hardy (South
Eastern), Sir Herbert Maxwell (Glasgow & South Western), C. T. Murdoch
(Great Western) and Sir Henry Tyler; two Liberals: Miles MacInnes
(London & North Western) and Joseph Pease; and one Liberal Unionist,
G. R. Vernon (Caledonian).[49]

But sheer weight of numbers was not enough. Channing and Edward
Harford were able to produce startling evidence of long hours. Harford,
moreover, called not for a statutory limit, but for Board of Trade powers to
limit hours to ten per day where they considered it necessary.[50] In reply
the railway companies adopted three lines of attack: to show "that it
would be impossible to work the railways if the proposed powers . . .
were given to the Board of Trade"; "to produce to the [Select] Committee
some of their servants to say that they were quite satisfied with their employment"; and, of course, to refute specific complaints made by railwaymen.[51]

It was in carrying out the first two of these tasks that the companies
overplayed their hand. Findlay, in evidence before the committee, dismissed as utterly impracticable any idea of a legal eight- or ten-hour day,
insisting that the hours of labour "must be regulated according to supply
and demand."[52] Henry Tennant, of the North Eastern, proved equally
unbending, almost insulting the committee by advising it to

> complete its evidence; no doubt a great amount of valuable information
> will be found in the evidence when completed, and then when the
> volume is completed let the Board of Trade send a few copies to the
> secretary of each railway company.[53]

This attitude of complete unwillingness to compromise was dictated
partly by issues of principle current in railway circles for decades, and
partly by falling dividends and higher working expenses. But it was
prompted to some extent by fear of trade unionism, not in industrial terms,
but in the context of the growing alliance between the Amalgamated
Society of Railway Servants and the Liberal Party. Hence the endeavour to
belittle the society as much as possible, and to bring forward railwaymen
to contradict union policies. In some cases this was relatively simple, for
the Associated Society of Locomotive Engineers and Firemen was as much
opposed to a legal maximum of ten hours per day as were the railway
managements. Other railwaymen, particularly North Eastern mineral

guards, simply did not agree with the policy of the Amalgamated Society.[54] The Great Eastern Railway used methods of gentle persuasion, by cutting hours of work so that drivers and firemen, compelled to be away from their homes and to accept reduced earnings, willingly complained to the committee.[55] But the dismissal of stationmaster Hood by the Cambrian Railways' directors in August 1891, after he had given evidence to the committee, focused public attention on the committee's proceedings in a manner which was bound to do the railways the greatest possible amount of harm.[56]

Hood's case raised in dramatic fashion the issue of the inviolability of parliamentary witnesses from intimidation, and led to the passing of the Witnesses (Public Inquiries) Protection Act in June 1892.[57] The Select Committee, reappointed in 1892, made a special report on Hood's case in March. On 7 April the former manager of the Cambrian Railways and three directors, including the Conservative M.P. J. W. Maclure, were publicly admonished by the Speaker, but only after a stormy debate in which Irish Nationalists and some Liberals had pressed for compensation for the unfortunate ex-stationmaster.[58] Hicks Beach thus found himself having to defend the Cambrian directors; his speech was characterized as "a plea for mercy for the strongest and not for justice to the weak."[59]

The Conservative government suffered from Hood's case almost as much as the railways.[60] With a general election only weeks away, the matter assumed a new importance. Earlier in the year Hicks Beach had, in fact, privately approached Findlay and Oakley to obtain the views of the companies generally on the question "whether some power could not be given to the Board of Trade to inquire into the cases of overwork on Railways and that the Board should have power to impose penalties on Railway Companies failing to carry out the Board's orders." But the Railway Association declined to be drawn.[61]

The Amalgamated Society, however, seized the opportunity provided by the forthcoming elections to send out questionnaires to all candidates; the replies, published in the *Railway Review* between 15 April and 15 July, showed clearly that the Liberals formed the bulk of those in favour of a legal ten-hour day and six-day week. Yet of those who favoured this solution, nearly a quarter were Conservative candidates. Though the way of Liberalism in the matter seemed clear, Conservative policy was in danger of falling between the two stools of railway management and railway labour.[62]

Both Hicks Beach and Channing presented draft reports to the Select Committee.[63] On certain points, notably the difficulties in the way of laying down a fixed legal maximum applicable to all grades on all railways, the drafts were in agreement. Both admitted the main complaint of the railway unions, that the companies could do far more to ensure reasonable hours of railway work. The President's report, however, stressed that not all the companies were equally blameworthy, that well-managed lines, such as the London & North Western and the Great Eastern could do, and indeed had already done, much to mitigate the evils complained of. Laying down a desirable maximum of ten hours per day for signalmen, and 12 hours per day, or 66 hours per week, for drivers, firemen and guards, the President's report proposed to attain these largely through the force of public opinion acting upon published returns from the companies. Only in the case of specially recalcitrant companies, and only after accidents deemed to involve "habitually excessive" hours, was the Board of Trade to have powers to call upon such companies to submit and put into operation satisfactory schedules of booked time. Even here, the board's powers were to be limited to approving or rejecting proposals from the companies concerned. Hicks Beach's draft stressed its disapproval "of anything which would relieve the companies from that responsibility by imposing upon the Board of Trade the duty of making regulations for the working of the traffic by the officers and servants of the companies."

Channing's draft report started from a quite different assumption: that "Railways are State-granted monopolies, and the State has the right and the duty to insist on safe working and just conditions of labour, including reasonable hours." He proposed to give the Board of Trade full powers, when complaints were made, to inquire into allegations of overwork and to have the authority, if necessary, to enforce its own recommendations as to maximum hours of work, the Railway Commissioners acting as a court of appeal. Channing also turned his attention to non-recognition, which he regarded as a product of reactionary obstinacy; he clearly hoped that the role of the trade unions in sending complaints to, and thus being recognized by the Board of Trade, would lead also to their being recognized by the railway companies.

Only the block vote of the railway directors ensured the second reading of Hicks Beach's draft in preference to that of Channing.[64] The continued use of this block vote was responsible for the defeat of a number of amendments put forward by Channing and his supporters. Thus Hicks Beach's draft emerged generally intact as the final report of the Select Committee in June 1892.[65] But Hicks Beach did not have the task of legislating upon it. Parliament was dissolved in July, and a Liberal majority returned at the elections.

As noted earlier, the Amalgamated Society took the opportunity afforded by the elections to bring maximum pressure to bear on M.P.s and candidates. Channing's draft report was serialized in the *Railway Review* and issued as a pamphlet.[66] Channing himself, "in view of the nearness of the Election & the importance of the subject", had sent a copy of his draft to Gladstone even before it was put before the Select Committee, adding that "a broad & generous sympathetic attitude" by the Liberal party towards the railwaymen "will not be thrown away politically".[67] This was indeed the case. In Maclure's constituency, the Stretford division of Manchester, the Liberals called in the services of the Amalgamated Society and ex-station-master Hood.[68] Maclure kept his seat. But the narrow defeat of T. Milvain, the Conservative candidate at Durham city and a member of the Select Committee, was widely attributed to the railwaymen's campaign, which may also have played a part in the Conservative defeats at Doncaster and West Islington.[69] With the return of Mundella to the Board of Trade, legislation on the subject of railwaymen's hours was certain.

Gladstone had the subject in mind at least as early as November 1892.[70] Channing was able to obtain all-party backing for a bill of his own, introduced in February 1893 and framed in the terms of his draft report.[71] A bill brought in by John Burns and Keir Hardie sought to enforce an eight-hour day on all railways.[72] Conservative back-benchers, led by Sir Seymour King, brought in a bill of their own, to enforce the ten-hour day for shunters, porters, platelayers, drivers, firemen and guards, and the eight-hour day for signalmen, but allowing companies to apply to the Board of Trade for permission to exceed these limits.[73] Mundella's bill was mild by comparison. Introduced on 6 February and given a second reading on 22 February, it followed more nearly the report of the Select Committee, giving the Board of Trade powers to order the submission and adoption of schedules of reasonable hours of labour for railway servants in any company if the hours worked appeared, upon inquiry, to be excessive.[74]

Faced with the choices represented by these various proposals, and considering the political circumstances, the Railway Association resigned itself to a tacit acceptance of Mundella's bill, which it had already decided not to oppose on second reading.[75] The Amalgamated Society, however, sought to influence supporters of the government to persuade Mundella to adopt many of Channing's proposals, particularly the legal recognition of the right of railwaymen to send in complaints themselves, or through union officials, to the Board of Trade for investigation.[76] Channing failed, in the Standing Committee, to have an explicit reference to trade union officials inserted, but, on Mundella's own motion, words were added allowing complaints of excessive hours to be made to the Board of Trade by railway servants themselves, or by persons "on behalf of the servants . . . of any railway company".[77]

As these proceedings showed, the main contest surrounding the bill was not between the government and the railway companies, but between the government and its own left wing backed by the railway servants.[78] The main weapon of the companies was not, and could not be, political at this time; efforts were concentrated instead on giving facilities to drivers and firemen to protest against parliamentary interference with working hours.[79] Edward Harford retaliated by accompanying a deputation of North Eastern Railway signalmen to Mundella on 24 April, to urge "the insertion [in the bill] of a *maximum*" with regard to signalmen's hours.[80] But, at the bill's consideration stage, a clause proposed by the Conservative Sir John Gorst, to make hours exceeding eight per day for signalmen, and ten for other railwaymen, *prima facie* excessive, was overwhelmingly defeated.[81]

In the Upper House Lord Colville accepted the bill on behalf of the railway companies. But the Conservative peers, eager even now to frustrate Liberal legislation, and in any case preferring to base any interference with the hours of adult males upon the solid grounds of public safety, provided the railway companies with some comfort. This was in the form of an amendment, proposed by Lord Balfour, to exclude from the operation of the Act all railwaymen who were not, in the opinion of the Board of Trade, "directly or indirectly engaged in or concerned with the movement of traffic." Salisbury gave this amendment his support, and it was carried by 64 votes to 26. Mundella declared himself against such an alteration; but he accepted an alternative proposed by Hicks Beach, excluding from the operation of the Act all railway servants "wholly employed in clerical work or in the Company's workshops." In this form, on 27 July, the bill became law.[82]

The Act of 1893 was a landmark in the history of state regulation of industry in Great Britain, being the first occasion on which Parliament had sought to regulate the hours of work of adult males. Its operation was, of course, entirely permissive, depending upon the attitude taken by the board in any case brought before it. The right of trade union representatives, in practice, to make complaints to the board was another notable innovation. Courtenay Boyle, in a letter to Oakley on 19 September, made it clear that the board expected the companies to allow their employees to make use of the Act "without fear of consequences"; and the board refused to supply companies with names of complainants.[83] As the first and second reports of the board on the working of the Act showed, companies co-operated willingly in cases the government brought to their attention.[84]

Much of the early success of the Act was due to the work of Francis J. S. Hopwood, a young solicitor who had entered the Board of Trade in 1886, and who in 1893 replaced Courtenay Boyle as secretary to the Railway Department when the latter succeeded Calcraft as Permanent Secretary.[85] Calm and detached, Hopwood earned the confidence of the Amalgamated Society, and its praise.[86] But no effort on his part could make up for the limitations of the Act, the principal one, in the eyes of the union, being that it failed to stipulate the maximum length of a working day. The persistence of 'twelve-hour' signal boxes illustrated this. Nor did the Act lead to a diminution in the accident rate among railway employees. In 1895 the Annual General Meeting of the Amalgamated Society called for an eight-hour day; but with further government legislation in this direction unlikely, industrial action seemed the only way of achieving this goal.[87]

The fact that the railway interest did not pursue its opposition to state regulation of railway hours with greater vigour requires some explanation. Mundella's proposals of 1893, quite apart from their direct effect on railway working, threatened also to interfere with timetables and perhaps with rates of pay, and hence with dividends.[88] But the interest could not hope to defeat the bill. Much of 1893 was taken up with the second Irish Home Rule bill, which passed the Commons only in September; the passage of the Railway Regulation Act by Mundella thus assumed an added importance as the only noteworthy redemption that session of election promises made barely a year before. Particularly after the Scottish strike of 1890–1 and Hood's case, an agitation against the principal features of Mundella's bill was likely to damage the reputation of the companies far more than the policies of the government. Hood's case made the parliamentary representatives of the companies particularly sensitive on this point. In May 1892, after the Select Committee had received complaints concerning alleged interference with witnesses by the Amalgamated Society, Gathorne-Hardy and Tyler urged that a special report be made in these cases also. The motion was, however, defeated by eleven votes to six, four Conservatives and two railway directors voting in the majority.[89]

The voting here illustrates another, and probably the most decisive factor against vigorous opposition to the bill; namely that its principles had the support of an important section of the Conservative Party, which could not therefore be mobilized against it. At this very time the railway interest faced a similar problem over a far more crucial question which was arousing members on all sides of the House. Ultimate control of hours of labour had now been taken from the companies; control of maximum railway rates was about to undergo a similar transformation.

# Chapter 9

# Political isolation and its results: railway rates

The campaign over hours of labour, culminating in 1893, pointed to new political realities with which the railway interest was now faced. These realities were, however, being made even clearer by the simultaneous struggle over railway rates which was about to reach its climax. The dismay with which the railway companies had greeted the draft Provisional Orders of the Board of Trade for new classifications of goods and schedules of maximum rates under the 1888 Act, and the losses of revenue in which it was feared they would result, has already been noted.[1] But here, as with the inquiry into hours of labour, there was no possibility of outright opposition. Although sections of the railway press urged the companies "to fight every detail" before the Select Committee to which the draft Orders were to be referred, the more experienced railway administrators concurred with George Findlay that "the Companies should accept as much of the Scheme as they could and oppose the remainder."[2]

But from the first, opinion within the railway interest was divided as to the best methods of dealing with the draft Orders. The Provisional Order Confirmation bills of the first nine of the leading companies showed still further reductions.[3] Conservative peers like Lord Colville and the Earl of Wharncliffe saw no point in further haggling with Hicks Beach, and favoured instead a direct and bold approach to Lord Salisbury. Liberals and Liberal Unionists like Lord Stalbridge and Sir Frederick Mappin (Midland Railway) favoured a course less charged politically, the withdrawal by the nine companies of their bills of the present session involving new lines and additional expenditure; this was the course recommended at a meeting of the chairmen, deputy-chairmen, managers and solicitors on 3 March 1891.[4] Behind this recommendation was clearly an attempt to repeat the tactics of 1886. But the political circumstances were not the same; the opposition was certainly not prepared to take up the companies' case. The *Economist* declared:

> The companies, in fact, propose to abdicate their monopoly rights, and, if they do, it will be for Parliament to see that no restrictions are placed upon others who wish to step in and supply the traffic facilities which the existing companies refuse any longer to afford.[5]

Their bluff called, the companies settled down to the complex task of considering amendments to the Order Confirmation bills. These were referred to a Joint Select Committee of the Lords and Commons. In this situation the Railway Association provided a common meeting ground for the settlement of a large number of policy decisions involving detailed fixing of maximum rates and classification of goods within the areas served by each company whose Provisional Order was under consideration.[6] But the proceedings were really in the nature of private contests between each company and its traders, the companies having to defend their own cases individually. There was, however, general agreement that the companies should seek to amend the proposed classification "wherever this has been reduced below the Railway Clearing House Classification." The general managers laid particular stress on giving as much publicity as possible to the reductions with which it was proposed to burden the companies.[7]

The Select Committee sat from 9 April to 17 July 1891, to deal with the bills of the nine principal companies, and again between March and May 1892 to deal with 26 other bills.[8] But with the passage of the first nine bills, which received the Royal Assent on 5 August 1891, the main issues had been settled.[9] Findlay was able to report that the hearings had been "most impartial", and that several proposals made by the traders had been rejected; but, he warned, the maximum rates "had . . . been dealt with very severely".[10]

The maximum rates now assumed crucial importance. The upswing in the trade cycle between 1886 and 1890 had given way to another depression, unrelieved till 1894, and a consequent fall in prices. This worried traders, who looked forward to lower railway rates to help boost sales.[11] The railway companies were no less worried, especially as they faced increased coal charges and higher wage bills; from 1892 to 1895 the companies as a whole suffered severe falls in goods revenue, net revenue, and average rates of dividend.[12] As the new schedules of the nine principal companies were due to come into force on 1 August 1892, this left barely a year in which to rearrange the millions of special rates granted to traders by the companies, many of them below the old parliamentary maxima, to conform with the new maxima.[13] It was under these conditions that the idea arose of doing away with the special rates, and simply charging the new maximum rates authorized by Parliament.

This circumstance – it can hardly be called a plan – originated at a special meeting of the goods managers held on 21 and 23 October 1891, when it was decided to recommend "as the basis of revision" that "all Class Rates . . . be fixed on the full maximum powers". The idea seems to have been merely to see, as a test, how far such rates would be accepted by the traders, for the general managers added that the revision of local rates should be left to the discretion of each company. Findlay and other London & North Western officials were clearly in favour of the experiment. But Oakley, with his more intimate political knowledge, thought "it would be undesirable, or even inadvisable to increase rates all round simply because the Companies had the power to do so."[14]

For a time the subject dropped; but as August 1892 approached, with the work of revision still far from complete, it gained currency once more. At a meeting of the goods managers on 28 April 1892 it was decided to put into operation the idea mooted in October 1891 "in the revision of through and competitive rates", but only "as far as practicable."[15] This left the final policy decision in the hands of the general managers and the directors. That the nine companies were still sincere in wishing to revise their rates is evident from the fact that they decided to apply to Hicks Beach for an extension of time till 1 January 1893.[16] At a meeting of managers and solicitors at Euston in October 1892 it was certainly envisaged that if all the special rates were not revised by December, they could be inserted as soon as possible afterwards.[17] But the idea of taking the full pound of flesh granted by Parliament, now that the opportunity and the excuse had arisen simultaneously, proved irresistible. If any plans did exist ultimately to revise all rates, neither the traders nor the station-masters were informed. Instead, traders who examined the new rate books in late December found only the new parliamentary maxima inserted; these were the actual rates which the stationmasters were compelled to charge them in the new year.[18]

The raising of rates to the legal limit may be regarded as the equivalent, in political terms, with respect to charging powers, of the Scottish railway strike and Hood's case with respect to hours of labour. Short-term gains were offset by long-term loss of sympathy and support from the political community.

The farmers, already suffering heavily from loss of trade, were in up-roar.[19] Industrialists and coal-owners were hardly less concerned.[20] Even where rates had not been increased, the companies sought to recoup them-selves by withdrawing privileges which had come to be taken for granted, such as the carrying of drovers free with livestock, or the carriage of coal at 21 cwt to the ton.[21] None of this was illegal. But it demonstrated to traders and farmers that whatever changes had been brought about by the 1888 Act, if they wished their goods to be carried by rail they were still wholly in the hands of the companies as to the costs involved. The Con-servative M.P. Sir Albert Rollit, in introducing a deputation to Mundella from the London Chamber of Commerce on 17 February 1893, declared that maximum rates, which were "intended to be a shield for the traders", had become "a sword in the hands of the companies".[22] The Conservative *Morning Post* observed:

> Whereas they were formerly chastised with whips, the traders and agriculturists allege that it will now be in the power of the Railway Companies to scourge them with scorpions.[23]

The Mansion House Association, to which many of the traders sent their complaints, determined to hold a conference early in the new year to co-ordinate action.[24] Meanwhile local meetings were held, especially by the farmers, to bring their complaints before M.P.s, a procedure which naturally involved the Conservative opposition, the more so as the Liberal majority was so slender.[25] But only pressure on the government was likely to bring quick remedies. The farmers of Leicestershire brought the subject before Mundella in December.[26] Many complaints were sent direct to the Board of Trade. The Lancashire and Cheshire Conference arranged for a deputation to see Gladstone.[27] In late January 1893 a deputation of farmers and Liberal M.P.s urged Mundella to give the Board of Trade and the Railway Commissioners powers "to deal with all unfair and unreasonable rates, whether or not within the *maximum*."[28] A similar resolution was adopted a few days later at a large meeting called by the Mansion House Association and attended by many chambers of commerce and agriculture, county council representatives, and M.P.s of all persuasions, from Conservatives like Alfred Hickman and Alfred Baldwin to advanced Liberals as represented by Channing and James Whitehead.[29]

Nor did the traders ignore purely parliamentary tactics. On 1 February 1893 alone three bills were introduced by Liberal back-benchers to deal afresh with the rates question. Radical M.P.s threatened to block all railway bills unless the companies modified their rates.[30] A Conservative M.P., Sir Frederick Dixon-Hartland, actually took this step, and on 7 February handed in a blocking notice "in respect of every private Bill which has so far been introduced in the interest of a railway company."[31] This campaign of pressure by the traders reached a crescendo on 15 February, when nearly 200 M.P.s, led by Whitehead and Channing, laid their demands before a harassed Mundella, who agreed that the railway companies were "straining the patience of the trading public to the very uttermost", but asked that the traders wait till Easter.[32]

The political implications of this campaign were evident, for Gladstone's government, with a majority of only 40, depended for its existence on the continued support of its left wing and the Irish Nationalists. Home Rule once again occupied the centre of the political arena. Mundella himself was occupied with the hours of labour of railway servants. So he looked to the railway companies to lessen his difficulties, as well as their own.

On 2 January Courtenay Boyle addressed Oakley on the subject of the increased charges.[33] The general managers seem to have been genuinely surprised at the volume of complaints. Findlay felt that "many of the cancelled rates would have to be restored". A reply to Courtenay Boyle, drafted by the managers, assured the Board of Trade that "the rates at present entered in the rate books are not to be taken as necessarily final"; that the Railway Association had appointed a committee of managers to confer with the traders; and that "many of the alleged grievances will disappear before the end of February, by which date the completed scales of rates will be inserted in the rate books".[34]

That the initiative in the raising of rates had come from the goods managers and general managers is not surprising, for it was they who, during the previous four years, had been most closely concerned with the details of the new rates and their effect on company finance. Now the initiative swung back to the parliamentarians. Experienced members of the railway interest, like Pease and Jackson, took time off from defending the companies in Parliament to try to save the companies from themselves. For by the end of February complacency had given way to fear, both of loss of revenue if rates were reduced, and of public opinion and government action if they were not. On Oakley's initiative the subject was again considered by a large meeting of the association on 20 February. John Dent Dent, chairman of the North Eastern, urged that the railway companies "had a right to be treated with fairness, but . . . there was no doubt that many rates charged at or within the new maximum would have to be lowered." William Cawkwell, of the London & North Western, agreed that the companies "ought to put themselves right with the public." The veteran Liberal Sir Joseph Pease, who felt the political dangers more than most, referred

> to the excitement in the House of Commons caused by the increase of certain rates, and . . . strongly advised a settlement as far as possible, at the rates in force on the 31st December last . . . The Companies ought to put the Board of Trade in a position to say that they were doing their best to settle the complaints of the Traders on reasonable terms.

On the Unionist side the desire to avoid a head-on clash with the Liberal government on this issue was no less intense. It was evident that if a clash came, the Conservative leadership would not risk a split in its own ranks by coming to the defence of the railways. Sir Julian Goldsmid, the Liberal Unionist director of the London, Brighton & South Coast Railway, advised a return to the old rates rather than that "the Board of Trade should intervene, and obtain an increased control over the Companies." David Plunket (later Lord Rathmore), a Conservative director of the London & North Western, reinforced the view that at this particular time the Commons "were prepared to pass anything unfavourable to the Railway Companies." Jackson, the man most in touch with Conservative opinion, advised

> that the Companies should try and wade the stream at the shallowest place. The House of Commons was, no doubt, much disturbed on this question of increased rates, and so was the President of the Board of Trade. The Managers and Solicitors ought to be able to find a way out of the difficulty . . . The Companies should revert to the former rates, or as near to them as possible.[35]

As a stopgap, Oakley provided Mundella with a list of rates reduced since the beginning of the year, and Mundella was able to parade these before the traders.[36] As to their ultimate policy, however, the railway interest was far from united. Fear of parliamentary interference gave way to fear of revenue losses. The Railway Association met again on 24 February, when 23 companies were represented. The Midland Railway favoured a plan by which the companies would agree voluntarily to limit any increase on the 1892 rates to 5 per cent. The London & North Western directors felt unable to accept any limit; they were supported in this view by the Great Western representatives. The Lancashire & Yorkshire Railway agreed to a limit in principle, but not to a figure as low as 5 per cent. Final settlement of the question was again deferred.[37]

This procrastination in the face of mounting hostility from the traders and mounting impatience from the government proved fatal to a quick settlement of the issue. On 28 February Courtenay Boyle again wrote to Oakley:

> the President of the Board of Trade is unable to satisfy himself that the revisions which have already taken place would not result in a material increase of the rates which were charged in 1892, and I am to state that, in the opinion of the Board of Trade it will be impossible to remove the almost universal dissatisfaction which prevails unless there is at least a general return to the basis of the 1892 rates . . .
>
> I am, therefore, directed by Mr. Mundella to earnestly press upon you the importance of making as speedily as possible such concessions as may satisfy the reasonable requirements of Trading Communities of the United Kingdom, for, unless this is done, and done as speedily as circumstances will permit, legislation to accomplish this purpose will become inevitable.[38]

A growing sense of political isolation prepared the way for panic and paralysis. The directors of the major companies looked to their general managers for a lead; the managers threw the ball back firmly into the directors' court.[39] On 28 February Joseph Pease pointed out

> that if the case of the Railway Companies was serious last week, it was more serious now . . . the policy of the Companies was, in his opinion, to bow to the great pressure put upon them by all shades of parties . . . and to look forward to better times when they might be enabled to raise their rates again.

The Lancashire & Yorkshire Railway agreed to fall in with the 5 per cent maximum increase, but the London & North Western and Great

Western companies refused.[40] Now a new fear arose, that if Mundella was informed that the companies could not agree on a settlement, he would use this as a pretext for forcing a settlement upon them. In a state of collective confusion, the Railway Association finally managed to agree upon a resolution recommending the companies individually to make "as speedily, as possible, such concessions as may satisfy the reasonable requirements of the Traders." This decision was communicated to Courtenay Boyle by Oakley in a letter of 1 March which appeared in *The Times* two days later.[41]

It is questionable whether Mundella really intended to legislate, as he told the companies. Certainly legislation on such a topic would have been extremely difficult in the overcrowded session of 1893. But the reply of the companies satisfied no one. On 3 March a motion condemning the railway rates as "most prejudicial" to the industries of the country, and calling upon the government to legislate, was brought forward by the Conservative Sir Albert Rollit, at this time President of the Associated Chambers of Commerce, and seconded by the Liberal Sir James Whitehead.[42] Earlier in the day Mundella had signified his agreement with a suggestion from William Hunter, that a Select Committee be appointed. From the Conservative side Hicks Beach announced his consent. Rollit's motion, in a modified form, was thus carried without a division.[43]

In March and April some of the companies did carry out considerable rate reductions, and they assured the Select Committee that as soon as rates were finally fixed, overcharges would be refunded – in itself an admission of the traders' case.[44] On 12 April Oakley assured Courtenay Boyle that "The work of revision has been continuously carried on" on the basis of a 5 per cent maximum increase on the 1892 level, and that "the Companies believe that the general dissatisfaction which found expression in the month of January last, has been now to a great extent, if not altogether removed".[45] Agriculturists and traders were convinced neither of the permanency nor of the sincerity of these moves. The action of the companies "had impressed the public mind with the feeling that they cannot be trusted, and that they must be continually watched."[46] On 17 April Whitehead introduced a bill, sponsored by members of all parties, to declare illegal all rates in excess of those in force on 31 December 1892, unless approved by officers of the Board of Trade.[47] A week later the executive committee of the Mansion House Association resolved to recommend the public "not to pay, or agree to pay, any rates or charges in excess of those actually being paid in 1892."[48] On 16 May the promised Select Committee was appointed:

to inquire into the manner in which the Railway Companies have exercised the powers conferred upon them by the Railway Rates and Charges Order Confirmation Acts, 1891 and 1892, and to consider whether it is desirable to adopt any other than the existing means of settling differences between the companies and the public with respect to the rates and conditions of charge for the conveyance of goods, and to report what means they recommend.[49]

Out of a total membership of 19 on the Select Committee, the railway interest could count on the support of only four M.P.s: Goldsmid, Jackson, Pease and Plunket; whereas the traders had at least six prominent supporters: Hickman, Hicks Beach, Hunter, Rollit, Samuelson and Whitehead. Such representation as the railways achieved was more by accident than by design, and unanimity between the companies was absent. Plunket wished for greater representation; Liberal members of the London & North Western board agreed to use their influence in this direction.[50] But Jackson, in reply to an inquiry from the Conservative Chief Whip, Akers-Douglas, expressed himself strongly against putting any railway directors, as such, on the committee, on the grounds that the presence of any representative of the railway interest, however inadequate, would be used against the companies.[51]

Jackson's letter betrays a fatalistic mood. It underlines the disunion and disarray in the ranks of the railway companies. They had no clear idea of the defence they should put up before the Select Committee, though there was a consensus that the defence ought to be fashioned to fit the complaints the traders were expected to make.[52] The traders could not, of course, attack the legality of the raising of rates. So they chose to stress instead the unreasonableness of this action and its effect on the trade of the country. They accused the companies, in general, of trying to make excess profits, and their representatives demanded that the Board of Trade be given 'teeth' to prevent this happening.[53]

These notions were quite foreign to the ears of the railway managements. They regarded the Order Confirmation Acts of 1891 and 1892 as solemn contracts, against the letter of which there could be no argument. They had regarded the multitude of separate railway acts, which those of 1891 and 1892 superseded, in the same light. Thus their first line of defence before the Select Committee was to plead that in 1893 they had simply sought to recoup themselves for reductions in some cases by raising actual rates in others.[54]

Had this been the main defence of the companies, a strongly legalistic one, it would have needed little further amplification. But it obviously did not answer the complaints of the traders, whose pressure on the government made it most unlikely that Mundella would allow the companies to hide behind it. Thus, though the companies believed they had a perfect right to raise rates, they were reluctant to use this as their only reply to the traders. So a second defence was put up, that there had been an unfortunate misunderstanding; that there had not been time to revise every special rate before December 1892; and that the insertion of the maximum parliamentary rates in the rate books had been merely a temporary expedient.[55]

There was certainly, as has been shown, some truth in this argument. But the companies had not made these facts public until the first week of January 1893.[56] It did not square with the claim made by the companies to a margin of at least 5 per cent above the 1892 rates.[57] Nor did it square with the fact that the stationmasters had not been informed that the new maximum rates were provisional only.[58] It smacked of justification *ex post facto*.

The draft report which the Liberal minister G. J. Shaw Lefevre presented, in late November, dismissed the argument of insufficient time, but accepted the first argument, that "the course of the companies was mainly actuated by their determination to recoup themselves to the fullest extent by raising the rates of articles when the maximum rates were above the actual rates." For so doing the companies were condemned for "dislocating trade and alarming so many interests". The draft report took the view "that it was not the intention of Parliament that the companies should raise their non-competitive actual rates even by 5 per cent. all round". The report continued:

> some greater security should be provided against the arbitrary increases of rates for the conveyance of goods, even though they should be within the maximum charges fixed by recent Acts. . . . The railway companies cannot be considered as exempt from the ordinary fluctuations in the trade of the country, or as being justified in raising their rates at any time in order to maintain their dividends at the expense of the other traders.

The report concluded with a recommendation that the Board of Trade should be able to authorize complaining traders to go before the Railway Commission, which would be empowered to decide whether an increase of rates in 1893 was or was not "just and reasonable", but without the power to award costs on either side.[59]

These pronouncements were of a very far-reaching character, amounting to a complete break with *laissez-faire* principles in regard to railway charges and profits, in the very year when the same principles had been abandoned in relation to hours of labour on the railways. The remedy proposed, however, was mild by comparison, and the railway representatives on the Select Committee chose not seriously to challenge it. The traders were far from satisfied. Rollit managed to expunge the reference to the Board of Trade before a trader could appeal to the Railway Commission.[60] But the commission continued to be regarded as an expensive and long-winded tribunal.

The report thus agreed was submitted on 14 December.[61] Any hopes that Mundella and his colleagues may have had that it would satisfy the traders were soon dashed. The report's conclusions, far from satisfying the traders, confirmed them in the righteousness of their campaign. On 19 February 1894 a conference of traders' organizations, municipal corporations, peers and M.P.s, called by the Mansion House Association, carried a series of resolutions approving of the report as far as it went, but declaring that any satisfactory legislation must provide "for an appeal against any unreasonable or excessive charge whatsoever"; doubts were cast on the ability of the 1888 Act to deal with preferential rates given to foreign merchandise, and here a test case, followed by further legislation, if necessary, was approved.[62] A general meeting of the Mansion House Association, in January, had already decided to recommend traders to continue to refuse to pay any increased rates.[63]

At the Railway Department Hopwood decided to press Oakley for an assurance "that the Railway Companies are prepared to adopt such steps as they can properly take in order to meet the wishes of the traders".[64] The general managers still hoped to avoid or at least to minimize legislation, by adopting the main recommendation of the Select Committee, for a reference to the Railway Commissioners of the reasonableness of any increase of rates made since 1892, should traders so wish, each party paying its own costs; a meeting of 50 members of the Railway Association, representing 17 companies, agreed to reply to the Board of Trade in this sense.[65]

It is unlikely that the traders, now in full pursuit of their quarry, would have been satisfied with anything less than legislation. For the government, legislation on railway rates assumed a new importance. The resignation of Gladstone on 6 March left the Liberal party without effective leadership and bereft of political direction. The House of Lords had killed Irish Home Rule outright, dealt a fatal blow to Asquith's Employers' Liability bill, and mauled H. H. Fowler's Parish Councils bill. This shattering of policies made the government more sensitive to new proposals for legislation in other fields.[66] Hopwood was inclined to accept the offer of the Railway

Association of 6 March, but felt that "we must bring in our bill & make it an Act as soon as Parliamentary circumstances will allow."[67] Courtenay Boyle informed Oakley on 14 March that the Board of Trade was "unable to concur in the view that the proposed arrangement will make fresh legislation unnecessary."[68] Mundella bowed to political considerations and commercial pressure, and on 12 April introduced a government bill.[69]

Mundella's proposals followed closely the recommendations of the Select Committee: the Railway Commission was to be empowered to hear and determine complaints regarding any increase in railway rates since 31 December 1892, provided the complaint had first been considered by the Board of Trade; in any case so brought, the onus of proving before the commissioners that the rate complained of was reasonable, was to be put upon the railway company, and for this purpose the bill specified that it would be no defence merely to show that the rate was within the limits fixed by an Act of Parliament or by a Provisional Order Confirmation Act. No costs were to be awarded on either side, except in cases of frivolous or vexatious actions. At a meeting of the Parliamentary Committee of the Railway Association on 18 April, these proposals were accepted, mainly on the grounds that they were infinitely preferable to the proposals which traders were making for an appeal against all unreasonable rates and charges, whether increased after 1892 or not.[70]

At this point Mundella's personal misfortunes impinged on the rates question. A public inquiry into the affairs of the New Zealand Loan and Mercantile Agency, of which Mundella had been a director, led to his resigning the Presidency of the Board of Trade on 12 May.[71] *Herapath* would have preferred as his successor John Morley, on account of the "judicial temper of his mind, unquestioned probity, and proverbial honesty".[72] Instead Lord Rosebery's choice fell upon the jurist and historian James Bryce. This appointment filled railway circles with alarm. Bryce was suspected as a "bookish man" and feared as a radical. The most *Herapath* could find to say of him was:

> His Radicalism, at any rate, is leavened with Constitutionalism and a respect for the sanctity of law. The railways want no partiality, but they do desire rest from the chopping and changing of recent years, inspired solely by political considerations.[73]

These fears proved well-founded. The traders regarded Bryce's accession to office as a splendid opportunity to renew pressure on the government. On 15 June over 60 M.P.s of all parties, led by Albert Rollit, saw Bryce at the House of Commons to point out how "very inadequate to the occasion" was Mundella's bill. Channing protested against "the crystallising of the standard of rates of 1892 and creating a legal presumption that the railway companies are perfectly right if they charge up to that standard." Bryce was anxious to pass the bill with as little controversy as possible; but he admitted the justice of the traders' contention that many rates were unreasonable even though they had not been increased.[74]

The possibility that Bryce would be induced to agree to some amendments in order to satisfy the traders led the Parliamentary Committee of the Railway Association to arrange a deputation of their own.[75] The committee tried to persuade Bryce to alter clause 1 of the bill so as to make it clear beyond doubt that only the amount of any increases added to 1892 rates, and not the whole of a rate, would be submitted to the Board of Trade and the Railway Commissioners; Bryce refused to be moved.[76] The point at issue here was not whether all 1892 rates were to be open to review; Bryce agreed they would not be, and offered to insert words to this effect. But where a rate had been increased after 1892, Bryce refused to clear up an apparent ambiguity to limit the jurisdiction of the Railway Commissioners simply to the amount of the increase. This was less than the traders demanded, but more than the companies had bargained for.[77] Stalbridge advised the Railway Association "to oppose the passage of the Bill with all the force at their command."[78] This was an empty threat so far as the House of Commons was concerned, but not so with the Lords, where, as Bryce had pointed out to the traders on 15 June, the chances of the bill coming to grief were strong. On 10 July the association agreed not to oppose clause 1, if Bryce agreed to insert the desired amendments and to withdraw the bill if outvoted on this point.[79]

The traders, anxious for the bill to pass before the close of the parliamentary session, moderated their terms.[80] David Plunket appeared as a go-between, and on 11 July saw Bryce, Whitehead and Hickman; the two latter agreed to try to arrange for the 1892 rates to stand "subject to certain advantages with regard to Sidings and other matters." The Railway Association approved of this in general terms, and agreed to the suggestion of Rollit and Whitehead for a joint conference.[81] This meeting took place on 16 July, Bryce acting as neutral chairman. Rollit and Hunter, for the traders, agreed to the amendment of clause 1, whilst Plunket, the principal railway spokesman, accepted amendments asked for by the traders, relating mainly to increases of rates through alterations of conditions of carriage and to access to the rate books of 1892. By the beginning of August the concessions by both sides had been determined.[82] With the measure largely agreed, the committee stage in the Commons was completed in two days. On 15 August the bill passed the Lower House; it went through the Lords without debate, and became law on 25 August.[83]

The Act of 1894 closed, for the foreseeable future, the legislative phase of the rates question. But the effects of the Act were felt by both sides more keenly each year. Prior to 1894 the power of railway companies to raise or lower rates within the maxima laid down by Parliament had never been controlled by statute, save in the cases of undue preference and through rates. The virtual freezing of the rates at their level on 31 December 1892 made for a degree of rigidity in railway finance which the companies could only accept by strict economy themselves in other fields.[84] At first attempts were made to increase profits by increasing facilities, typified by the 'races' between east- and west-coast companies to Aberdeen in 1895. But competition soon gave way to combination, sometimes openly, and sometimes with parliamentary approval, but often secretly, thus increasing public and governmental suspicion, and lending support to demands for nationalization. It was in 1895 that the Railway Nationalisation League was formed to press for the implementation of the state purchase clauses of Gladstone's Act of 1844.[85]

But it was in the field of labour relations that the effect of the legislation of 1894 was most marked. Whether the demands of the unions were for increased wages or shorter hours, the companies found that the Act of 1894, coupled with that of 1893, had driven them into a corner, for they saw little hope of being able to pass on to the public even a proportion of higher labour costs.[86] Economic pressures thus breathed new life into the doctrine of 'non-recognition', which was bolstered also by the knowledge that in 1894 the Amalgamated Society of Railway Servants had espoused the cause of railway nationalization.[87] Moreover, whilst many companies ignored the Amalgamated Society, some combined to attack it.

These developments helped delineate the railway interest as not merely a Conservative group, but a breed of the extreme right. Fear played a part, fear of the unknown and of the uncertain. It was fear of reduced profits which led the companies into the confusion resulting in the legislation of 1893–4. The London & North Western Railway had already prophesied that control by the Board of Trade of working hours "would constitute such an interference with the management of the railways as could only prove to be the first step towards the Government purchasing the railways of the country."[88] Now that interference had come about.

By tacit agreement on both sides the railway interest and the bulk of the Liberals now regarded each other as hostile, the mood of confrontation being strengthened by the way in which the Liberal party allowed itself to be used to foster the beliefs of interests hostile to the companies. The legislation of 1893–4 was enough to make this clear. Yet it emerged in other ways too, not least in the struggle over Asquith's Employers' Liability bill in 1893, when it was freely admitted that a sustained and well-timed campaign by the London & North Western Railway and its employees and supporters in Parliament, in favour of the retention of contracting out, had resulted in the bill's demise.[89] This experience unnerved the Liberal party and gave it a sharp reminder that the railways were not to be treated lightly.[90] A bewildered Lloyd George found himself having to defend his party, over Asquith's bill, before a meeting of railwaymen at Bangor early the following year.[91]

For the diminishing number of Liberal members of the efficient railway interest the dilemma was plain, as the division lists show: their abstentions on Channing's motion of 23 January 1891; the voting of Liberal directors on both sides in the debate on Hood's case in 1892; and a similar occurrence on the question of contracting out.[92] Nonetheless, it is evident that the hostility of Liberals was not the main reason why the companies were not more successful in opposing the Acts of 1893 and 1894. They were powerless to prevent legislation, or to impose major alterations in projected legislation, because in the issues involved they could not count on the support of any other political group to act as a buffer between themselves and interests increasingly hostile and increasingly powerful. There was far too much overlap between trading interests and the Conservative Party for the latter to be able to speak out against the massive dose of state interference sanctioned by the Railway and Canal Traffic Act of 1894. There was far too much odium attached to the railways in the matter of excessive hours of work for the Conservative leadership to feel free to come to their rescue in 1893. What is most remarkable about the part played by the Conservative leadership in both years is the silence it managed to maintain on both issues.[93]

But of the two major parties there was no doubt that it was the Conservatives whom the railway interest preferred to see in office, and with whom the companies preferred to deal. The question of preferential rates for foreign produce and protection for home industries, particularly agriculture, remained for some months a source of embarrassment. A conference on the Depression of Agriculture, organized by Conservatives at the beginning of December 1892, had passed a strong Protectionist resolution.[94] The National Agricultural Union, formed the same month on the initiative of the Conservative peer Lord Winchelsea, had as one of its objects the abolition of preferential railway rates for foreign produce.[95] But a case against the London & South Western Railway, brought ostensibly by the Mansion House Association, though actually by a group of London docks, alleging preferential rates in favour of produce imported through Southampton, and which was heard before the Railway Commission in March and April 1895, resulted in a stalemate.[96] The farmers turned more attention to their own businesses, and to the means by which they could combine to send consignments properly packed in quantities large enough to secure lower railway rates.[97]

Thus whilst the railway trade unions campaigned on behalf of Liberals in the general election in the summer of 1895, the railway interest looked forward to, and applauded, the Conservative victory. The *Railway Times* declared:

> the self-appointed spokesmen of the railway workers, in common with the declared enemies of the railway industry, have identified themselves so strongly with the party of revolution that we cannot refrain from expressing our satisfaction at the triumph of those forces which make for stability and order.[98]

It remained to be seen to what extent the governments of Lord Salisbury and A. J. Balfour would prove true to this description in their dealings with the railway companies. The old relationship, the relationship as it had existed in the days of Disraeli, and even during Salisbury's first and second Ministries, had vanished beyond recall. The Acts of 1888 and 1889, and of 1893 and 1894, had brought the government and the railway companies into a new and much closer relationship. Clerks from the Railway Clearing House had been borrowed by the Board of Trade to help with the work of rate revision and the tabulation of objections.[99] Circulars sent to railway companies in regard to the procedure to be followed in connection with the Provisional Orders, were submitted to Oakley by the Railway Department for his approval before being despatched.[100] The almost daily contact between board officials and representatives of the railway companies during the long inquiries into railway rates, 1889–94, took the companies into the machinery of administration, and took the Railway Companies' Association into the public eye; the knighthood bestowed on Henry Oakley in 1891 was a recognition of this.[101]

The closer relationship had come about through the operation of the Acts of 1888 and 1893. Reference has already been made to the working of the latter. In the case of the former, the 'Conciliation Clause' was the means by which the Board of Trade intervened in disputes between the railways and their customers, to try to resolve them.[102] Other groups were tempted to use the Board of Trade in a similar way. Thus in 1894 Bryce played the role of neutral chairman in discussions between railway companies and traders to agree the terms of the Railway and Canal Traffic bill. In December 1890 the London County Council called upon the Railway Department to arrange with the railway managers a conference to consider greater facilities for workmen's trains.[103] A meeting took place in 1891, and at a conference between the two sides at the Board of Trade on 28 June 1893 some concessions were made.[104]

By 1894 this closer involvement of the government in the running of the railways, and of the railway companies in the administration, if not the shaping, of government policy, had become so intricate that the general managers and consulting solicitors advised the Railway Association to consider the appointment of a full-time paid secretary, and the taking of permanent offices.[105] This itself was in the nature of an admission of a decline, in political terms, of the strength of the railway interest, which could no longer count on Liberalism but could not be sure of Conservatism either. The period 1891–5 witnessed the admission to the Railway Companies' Association of a number of the smaller English, Welsh and Irish companies, probably as a result of the detailed rates negotiations.[106] Their outlook and purpose was administrative only, not political. Whereas the cohesion of a political interest group, particularly one dominated by members of a single party, was to some extent guaranteed at the outset by identity of status and views, permanent organization was most necessary in the case of a non-political pressure group, more or less clearly involved in the administration of government policy; for the first time the Railway Companies' Association showed signs of becoming such a non-political group. And it was in the atmosphere created by this new relationship that, during the next decade, the dialogue between Conservative governments and the railway interest took place.

# Chapter 10

# Compromise
# with unionism

Lord Salisbury's third Ministry was well placed to enjoy good relations with the railway interest, for a number of its members were, or had once been, railway directors. Salisbury himself had been chairman of the Great Eastern Railway; Devonshire was chairman of the Furness Railway; Cross sat on the board of the Manchester, Sheffield & Lincolnshire Railway; Ridley, the Home Secretary, was a director of the North Eastern Railway; Walter Long, President of the Board of Agriculture, was a Great Western director; and Akers-Douglas sat on the London, Chatham & Dover board. The two most notable anti-railway ministers, Hicks Beach at the Exchequer and Chamberlain at the Colonial Office, were now in relatively weak positions from which to influence Board of Trade policy towards the railways. Moreover, though the Conservatives had not opposed the legislation of 1893–4, they could rightly disclaim responsibility for it.

But the developments in railway administration since 1888 left both sides less room for manoeuvre. Unless the government did nothing at all in the way of railway reform, it could not hope to please both the traders and the companies in matters concerning rates, nor could it hope to satisfy both the companies and the railway workers in matters of safety and trade union activities. For the first few years of its existence Salisbury's government remained on tolerably good terms with the railway companies. In 1899 the relationship boiled over. But owing to the Unionist government's manifold difficulties after 1902, and to the changing circumstances of railway regulation under Gerald Balfour, Arthur's younger brother, who went to the Board of Trade in 1900, A. J. Balfour's administration was able, by a policy of peace, to pour a little oil on its own troubled waters, and at the same time to create a new relationship with the companies.

The quietist policies of Gerald Balfour contrasted strongly with those of the man whom he succeeded at the Board of Trade, Charles Thomson Ritchie (1838–1906). Ritchie, a Conservative free-trader, had already outraged some sections of opinion in the party when, as President of the Local Government Board, he had made a determined attack on the squirearchy through his Local Government Act of 1888. Ritchie was admired by railwaymen's leaders, a rare distinction for a Conservative minister.[1] Always to the left of his party, he did not represent "the interests of true Conservatism", certainly not in the sense understood by the railway interest.[2] He and they were destined to come to blows.

But for the moment both sides wished to avoid conflict. The railway companies offered no resistance to the passage of the Conciliation Act in 1896. On the domestic front, however, the government's main concern on coming into office was with the plight of agriculture. The farmers were now groping towards combination to obtain lower rates for greater bulk. Ritchie proposed to aid the movement by making himself available as an intermediary. In December 1895 he suggested to Stalbridge that the chairmen of the London companies confer with him early the following year; and, as a result of a meeting on 30 January 1896, the companies agreed to do as much as they felt able to provide and publicize lower rates for large consignments.[3] Subsequently many companies met local farmers and agreed to make some reductions.[4]

This spirit of co-operation continued in 1897, and in a matter which might have aroused far more animosity, that of employers' liability. That issue, dormant since 1880, had sprung to life again in 1893, mainly on the question of contracting-out in Asquith's bill of that year. Whilst it was unlikely that a Unionist government would drop contracting-out, Chamberlain's call in 1892 for the recognition of "the universality of the right to compensation", thus by-passing the perils of common employment, pointed the way to a compromise.[5]

The railways viewed the prospect of general compensation for accidents, legislated for by the Conservatives, with far less alarm than that of prohibition of contracting-out enforced by the Liberals. The Act of 1880 had simplified their thinking, for they realized that the clock could not be put back on a settlement of 17 years' standing, which had effectively dealt the death-blow to the doctrine of common employment as it affected staff engaged in the movement of traffic. This left a straight choice between litigation on the one hand and contracting-out in favour of a company scheme, not less favourable, on the other. A few companies insisted on contracting-out; the vast majority did not. Moreover, even on the London & North Western, the value of a company-sponsored insurance scheme as a counterweight to trade unionism was certainly not as great in 1897 as it might have been in 1880. James Beale, the Midland Railway solicitor, one of those whom Chamberlain consulted prior to the introduction of the Workmen's Compensation bill, thought the railways would approve a scheme to give effect to general compensation, provided the railway companies "have a definite liability fixed, and can get rid of litigation."[6]

Personalities also played a part. It was well known that Chamberlain was the driving force behind the Unionist bill. But the minister who had prime responsibility for the bill, the Home Secretary Sir M. W. Ridley, was also a North Eastern director. Both Ridley and the Attorney-General, Richard Webster, argued against enacting a general unfettered law of compensation without contracting-out.[7] Ridley gave way to Chamberlain on the principle of general compensation. But Chamberlain lost the battle to exclude contracting-out.[8]

The Unionist bill of 3 May 1897 thus embodied two features which made it palatable alike to the railway companies and to other large employers.[9] For those companies who still wished to contract out, the bill allowed them to do so; for the rest the bill's principal feature, the formulation of the conditions as well as of the principle of a general compensation for injuries sustained in the course of employment, provided a welcome alternative to litigation. These two features were, in fact, in line with some of the proposals made by several members of the railway interest between 1878 and 1880.[10] The exclusion of shipping and agriculture from the list of industries affected by the measure precluded opposition from those quarters. The Railway Association, for its part, remained so unperturbed by the bill that it did not consider any action till after the second reading. Even then, when the bill was in the Commons the only concern of the general managers and solicitors was to limit the duration of compensation for incapacity; the amendments made to the First Schedule in committee seem to have satisfied them on this point.[11] When the bill reached the Lords the Parliamentary Committee of the association was similarly relaxed. A small subcommittee appointed to watch proceedings in the Upper House expressed itself content with the bill at the end of July.[12] The bill became law on 6 August.[13]

Most railway companies which had accepted liability under the Employers' Liability Act of 1880 continued to do so under the Workmen's Compensation Act of 1897. The London & North Western Railway Insurance Societies were reorganized in 1898 to provide, from members' contributions only, compensation supplementary to that payable by the company under the Act.[14] Only the Great Eastern Railway contracted out under an approved scheme to which both company and men contributed.[15] The issue of employers' liability, so far as it related to the railway companies, was dead. Neither during the passage of the Act of 1897, nor after it had become law, did the railway interest launch any great campaign, as they had done between 1878 and 1880, or play any prominent part in the discussion of the bill in Parliament. On this issue, as with that of the Regulation of Railways Act of 1889, the companies did not oppose what they did not fear.

It was on the labour front, however, where the position of the companies was none too secure, that the *modus vivendi* with the Unionist administration began to crumble. And as labour relations, especially after the passage of the Conciliation Act of 1896, were the more immediate concern of the Board of Trade, the attitude of that department assumed greater importance. The launching of separate national movements by the Amalgamated Society of Railway Servants on behalf of guards, shunters, signalmen and other grades, in November 1896, ushered in a period of renewed, more bitter, and more determined strife between the railway servants and the companies.[16] The companies took a first, uncertain step towards alliance against a common enemy. A meeting of general managers on 2 December 1896 decided to ignore the circulars sent out by Edward Harford in furtherance of the national movements.[17] But the dismissal of over 80 men by the London & North Western Railway prompted Ritchie to intervene to avert a strike. Negotiations were opened, under the Conciliation Act, at the Board of Trade. Though officials of the company and the Amalgamated Society never met, a settlement was reached on 11 December, and the dismissed men were reinstated.[18]

Ritchie's motives in this unprecedented intervention remain obscure.

It is possible that he feared the situation would otherwise have been exploited by the Liberals. But the reaction from other sections of industry was hardly flattering. The shipowners, whose Shipping Federation, formed on 2 September 1890 as a "fighting machine to counter the strike weapon", was having a fair amount of success, lamented the "ignominious surrender" of the London & North Western.[19] The anxiety of other railway companies increased at a special meeting of the Railway Companies' Association, called at the instance of Sir Joseph Pease late in March 1897, when he announced the decision of the North Eastern board to seek arbitration in its dispute with its employees. Though strenuous efforts were made by other companies to dissuade the North Eastern Railway from this course, George Gibb, the young general manager of that company, refused to give way.[20] The arbitration covered wages and conditions. Lord James of Hereford, the Liberal Unionist Chancellor of the Duchy of Lancaster in the Salisbury government, was chosen to conduct the arbitration and his award, published in August 1897, conceded some important points to the men, including the principle that each day stands by itself.[21]

Lord James's arbitration, besides marking a further deepening of the recognition afforded the Amalgamated Society by the North Eastern Railway, was an admission of outside interference in the running of a large company. Coupled with the surrender of the London & North Western a few months before it emphasized the part the government was willing to play in intervening in railway labour disputes. The pretensions of the Amalgamated Society began to be taken seriously, whilst the obvious lack of a united front in meeting the demands of the men, contrasted with the success of the shipowners and the engineering employers, gave rise to dissatisfaction at the inability of the Railway Association to unite the companies in common action.[22]

Thus, when, in October 1897, Richard Bell, Harford's successor as General Secretary of the Amalgamated Society, launched a National 'All-Grades' Programme, the railway companies did not wait to decide whether the object was to achieve recognition or merely national rates of pay. At a meeting of over 200 delegates on 4 November the companies set up a committee of the chairmen and general managers of the large English railways, including the North Eastern, to consider the whole problem and to decide on a uniform approach.[23] There was evidently some interest in the North Eastern arbitration, for representatives of that company "were present by invitation" at the meeting of 4 November to report on its working.[24] The possibility of fixing maximum rates of pay was also discussed.[25] But there were considerable differences of opinion amongst the managers as to whether they should settle with the Amalgamated Society, or combine against it in a federation analogous to those of the engineering and cotton employers.[26]

The details of these discussions were carefully kept from the public gaze. What is certain is that the companies were unable to agree. The interest shown in arbitration suggests that some companies favoured the policy of the North Eastern Railway. The large companies did not; uncertain economic prospects bolstered their determination to fight. A separate meeting of the general managers of the lines running from London to the north, called by Frederick Harrison, general manager of the London & North Western, at Euston station on 17 November, agreed on certain principles to be observed to minimize losses of revenue from strikes at competitive places. These principles included the division of receipts from traffic to or from a competitive point in the event of a strike there; rerouting of trains, and provision of trains by other companies, in order to maintain services; and agreement on maximum scales of wages and, if possible, hours of labour and overtime rates.[27] Not only was arbitration with the Amalgamated Society ruled out, but the companies agreed "not to accept any general programme providing for uniformity of pay or conditions of service such as the leaders of the Amalgamated Society of Railway Servants have drawn up and promulgated."[28]

By 2 December, when this anti-strike agreement came into force, other companies had been swung round against compromise.[29] Henceforth, while the North Eastern Railway followed a path of its own, all the other major railways in the United Kingdom refused to treat with the Amalgamated Society, taking refuge in a militant isolationist philosophy which, though it retained public sympathy for a few years, proved too unbending to remain popular indefinitely. For the moment, however, victory lay with the companies. Although on 3 December Bell wrote to Ritchie asking him to intervene and bring about a meeting between the two sides, Courtenay Boyle sent a cold reply the following day, declining to act, and pointing out that the policy of "endeavouring to deal with the companies as a body" presented "no prospect of success"; he added that "any attempt to force the claims of the men by a strike would be inconsistent with the exceptional position which the men have claimed from and which has been secured to them by the Legislature."[30] On 7 December the executive of the Amalgamated Society decided to abandon the all-grades movement and the strike threat, and to make overtures with a view to each company meeting its own men on a grade basis.[31]

The anti-strike agreement of 2 December had still to be tested in practice.[32] But its spirit created a new atmosphere of co-operation against trade unionism. An offer of assistance from the London & North Western speeded the collapse of strike threats on the Great Northern and Midland Great Western companies of Ireland.[33] In January 1898 a meeting of chairmen in London dissuaded the Midland Railway from giving general concessions to all grades.[34] At the Railway Association there was favourable reaction to an appeal from the Cork, Bandon & South Coast Railway for a grant towards expenses incurred in defeating a strike which had lasted from January to May 1898.[35]

The adoption of the December 1897 agreement clearly marked a new departure in company policy for, as its provisions indicate, its underlying principle was not so much that the unions could be fought directly, by the use of crude strike-breaking techniques, but that the best method of countering the strike weapon was by fighting the unions on their own terms, by helping each other to shoulder the economic consequences of strike action, and thus to 'hold out' long enough to wear down the men's organizations. Hence, no doubt, the desire of the companies to obtain compensation also through the law courts, as the Taff Vale succeeded in doing.

This is not to imply that the companies did not believe in the value of physical force and the use of 'free', or blackleg labour. Indeed, as the use made by the Cork company of substitute labour provided by the Free Labour Protection Association indicated, such methods could have useful results.[36] But except on the smaller lines, such as those in South Wales and Ireland, none of the companies could hope to recruit alternative skilled labour in sufficient numbers to defeat a strike outright. However, blackleg labour, maintaining a service of some sort, could have a profound effect on the morale of strikers.[37] This was why most of the large companies continued to have dealings with the free labour organizations well into the twentieth century.

Parliamentary returns for the years 1907 to 1910, obtained after the question of political contributions by railway companies had been raised in Parliament, show that the Labour Protection Association received no more than £35 per annum, all from small Welsh and Irish companies. The larger and more famous National Free Labour Association, however, collected sums worth on average £144 per annum from companies large and small throughout the United Kingdom.[38] Contributions from individual companies rarely exceeded £25. For such a small outlay, boards of direction probably regarded the subscription as a useful piece of insurance and a weapon of propaganda. Thus during the threatened strike in November

167

and December 1897 the Free Labour Protection Association placed advertisements in the London daily papers for "railwaymen of all grades". Later on it included Cheap Trains bills amongst objects of attack in its circulars.[39]

As a practical proposition the National Free Labour Association, founded, to combat the trade unions, in May 1893 by William Collison, was certainly more useful. Though its early origins are obscure, the association certainly had links with the Shipping Federation and the Federation's attack on the New Unionism.[40] The association attacked unlawful picketing, and in 1894 organized a campaign against the prohibition of contracting-out in Asquith's Employers' Liability bill, a campaign which coincided with and may have been connected with that of the London & North Western Railway employees.[41] By 1900 it had moved away from the shipowners and into the world of Lord Wemyss and his Employers' Parliamentary Council.[42] It was about this time that the railways turned to it for supplies of non-union labour in the event of a strike. Collison's organization was well equipped to fulfil this function. Free Labour Exchanges had been set up in various parts of the country.[43] In 1900, when the Taff Vale dispute erupted, Collison had already been called upon by the Great Eastern Railway to prepare a force of men in anticipation of a strike on its own line; this enabled him to supply the Welsh company with about 100 footplatemen, guards and signalmen at a day's notice.[44] He followed this success by circularizing all the general managers appealing for funds, and suggesting the establishment of branches of his association at railway centres.[45]

As the figures already quoted show, this appeal for funds did not fall upon deaf ears. From the parliamentary returns and the minute books of the major British railways, it is possible to say that the only companies in respect of which no record of subscription to the National Free Labour Association, or its Southampton counterpart, exists, are the Great Eastern (in spite of its willingness to use Collison's services), Great Northern, Great Western, London & North Western, and South Eastern railways, and, of course, the North Eastern.[46] It is no coincidence that these comprised the largest of the United Kingdom railway networks, where attempts to import free labour would have made least impact. The other major British companies, and many of those in Ireland, maintained some sort of link with Collison, certainly down to the crisis year of 1911. At least one company, the North British Railway, was still subscribing to the National Free Labour Association in 1914.[47] The companies indicated their approval of a plan put forward by the association to use discharged militiamen as a reserve labour force.[48] But they preferred to make their own arrangements to assist the Great Eastern Railway in anticipation of the strike threatened on that line.[49] And the small sums given to Collison bore no comparison with the £2,000 paid by the Railway Companies' Association to the Cork company, or with the £5,000 paid to the Taff Vale Railway as a contribution towards the legal expenses incurred in that company's action against the Amalgamated Society.[50]

To say, therefore, that the relationship of the railway companies to the National Free Labour Association at the turn of the century was that of "puppet–master" seems far-fetched.[51] Though the contributions towards free labour organizations continued, the services of these organizations did not figure largely in company policy after the period 1897–1900. When in 1901 the Rhymney Railway suggested that the Railway Companies' Association should establish its own organization, on the lines of that run by the Shipping Federation, with a reserve of men to replace strikers, no support from other companies was forthcoming.[52] The preference for 'splendid isolation', which had strong and deep roots among railway companies, persisted. But with governments, even Unionist governments, playing a greater part in the running of the railways, isolationism could not be pursued on all fronts. Its limits were revealed almost as soon as the companies had recovered from the troubles of 1897.

Ritchie's attitude towards the railway interest remained ambivalent. His intervention on behalf of the London & North Western Railway employees in 1896 had been followed by a refusal to take up the case of the Amalgamated Society in 1897. When in May 1898 Richard Bell approached the Board of Trade on the question of the victimization of men, Hopwood wrote to the companies concerned; yet in the case of the London & North Western Railway, which refused to allow the Board to interfere, Ritchie in turn refused to hold an inquiry, and subsequently Courtenay Boyle, in a letter to Oakley on 24 February 1899, exonerated the railway directors from all blame in connection with the union's allegations.[53] But the President's refusal to fall in with the wishes of the railway servants in matters of labour relations did not exhaust his policy towards them. At the very time when Courtenay Boyle's letter was sent exonerating company directors from blame in the matter of victimization, Ritchie was poised to spring upon those same directors a bill tailor-made to attract the support of the railway workers.

The origins of Ritchie's Regulation of Railways bill of 1899 are difficult to discern; thanks to the policy of destruction of public records it is most unlikely that the bill's origins will ever be known for certain.[54] But some influences are obvious. The Amalgamated Society had for a number of years been campaigning for the compulsory adoption of automatic couplings, to minimize accidents to shunters, and for the abolition of "stiff shackles", a form of screw coupling which the society regarded as a death-trap.[55] In 1893 Channing had introduced a bill on the subject.[56] Hopwood's influence in the matter, though without documentation, cannot be discounted. Moreover the former President of the Board of Trade, Hicks Beach, had included a coupling clause in his original bill of 1889.[57] Though that clause had been abandoned, this was primarily to ensure the passage of the other and, at the time, more important provisions. The question of couplings had not been abandoned, only shelved.

Ritchie, the unorthodox Tory with a reputation for shocking opinion in his own party, brought the question to life once again. The time was a favourable one. Casualties among railway servants as a result of accidents involving the movement of vehicles had risen from 1 to 928 killed and 1 in 167 injured in 1889 to 1 in 714 killed and 1 in 130 injured in 1892.[58] By 1897 1 in every 12 shunters and 1 in every 15 brakesmen and goods guards was being injured in the course of his employment.[59] By their embrace of Workmen's Compensation the Unionists had already shown themselves favourably disposed towards the alleviation of working-class hardship caused by industrial injuries. Two members of the Cabinet could certainly be counted on: Hicks Beach and Chamberlain. To prepare the ground still further, in the summer of 1898 Ritchie announced his intention to send Hopwood on a mission to the United States to study the methods adopted there following the passage through Congress of the Safety Appliances Act in 1893.[60]

Hopwood's report, dated 20 December 1898, was as uncomplimentary to the British railway companies as it was complimentary to those across the Atlantic. Hopwood did not actually advocate compulsory legislation, but by a subtle use of words made his meaning plain.

> It is not too much to say that the onus rests heavily upon our Railway Companies to show that it is impossible for them to discover and standardise for their use some form of coupler which will couple automatically, and prevent the necessity of a man having to go between the trucks to couple and uncouple. . . . It would, I apprehend, be of great assistance to them if the Board of Trade asked Parliament for legislative power to order the companies to apply a coupler in terms similar to that conferred upon the Department as to block working, the interlocking of points and signals, and the use of continuous brakes.[61]

Even before Hopwood's report had been presented and published there were strong rumours that Ritchie contemplated such compulsory legislation.[62] The radical press campaigned to this end.[63] In January and February 1899 the Amalgamated Society also mounted a campaign aimed at individual M.P.s, and Richard Bell wrote to Salisbury and Ritchie.[64] Probably this propaganda dispelled doubts which had evidently been lingering in Ritchie's mind. Channing and other left-wingers were ready to make a political issue of the matter.[65] It was well known that the London Committee of the Amalgamated Society was at this time making overtures to both the Conservative and Liberal Parties concerning Bell's parliamentary candidature; it was well known too that the Amalgamated Society's Executive disapproved of this action. The probability of Bell being won over for the Conservative Party was remote indeed; but Ritchie may have felt that the line was worth baiting.[66] On 20 February he announced to the Commons his intention to introduce a bill, and to refer it to a Select Committee to allow the companies to put their case.[67]

The introduction of the bill a week later naturally caused a great deal of alarm among the companies. They were to be compelled to provide, on all carriages and wagons, couplers coupling automatically by impact, and capable of being uncoupled without the necessity of men going between the ends of the carriages or wagons to uncouple them. They were also to be compelled to provide labels on both sides of goods wagons, to fit such wagons with brakes capable of being applied and released from either side, and to provide power brakes, instead of hand brakes, on all engines. After periods specified in the bill (five years in the case of automatic couplers) the Board of Trade was to be empowered to make orders upon the companies to carry out the bill's provisions; such an order having been made, a company was to be prohibited from allowing any engine, carriage or wagon to be used, on its railway, which did not comply with the terms of the order.[68]

It was the economic consequences of these proposals which the companies feared most. Their fears were shared by the private wagon owners, who had been the loudest to protest at Hicks Beach's coupling clause in 1889.[69] Both groups now sought to bring maximum pressure to bear on Ritchie to withdraw the bill before the second reading, and to institute an inquiry instead. It would be wrong, however, to see the struggle which followed, involving the Amalgamated Society, the Board of Trade, the railway companies and the private owners, as a contest between the advocates of collectivism and the defenders of *laissez-faire*. The arguments of the companies and private owners involved neither an attack on state control, nor a defence of economic freedom.

Although some members of the railway interest, notably Lord Claud Hamilton, were undoubtedly opposed to all collectivist legislation, the attack upon the bill was in purely practical terms. The large companies contested the view that the majority of shunting accidents were caused by shunting operations.[70] They questioned the assumption that what was applicable to American practice was applicable also to the conditions of railway operation in Great Britain. Most of all they were angry that legislation of such a technical nature was to be undertaken without any sort of previous impartial investigation. And they made no secret of the fact that the costs worried them. Statistics produced by the London & North Western Railway showed that compliance with the bill's provisions would involve not less than an estimated £2 per wagon, though in 1897 accidents in coupling and uncoupling had amounted to 3.8 per cent of the total in Great Britain, but to 12.6 per cent in the United States.[71]

When the Great Eastern board determined to send one of its locomotive superintendents to America to study the question in the light of Hopwood's conclusions, the Council of the Railway Association agreed to defray the expenses if some other companies could be persuaded to do likewise.[72] But the imminence of the bill's second reading made it imperative that more drastic action be taken. On 2 March Stalbridge wrote to Ritchie asking that the second reading be postponed.[73] The following day Claud Hamilton addressed a stiffly-worded letter to Salisbury, pointing out that the Great Eastern, Great Northern and Midland companies were about to send officials to America, accusing Courtenay Boyle of being on terms of intimacy with the Amalgamated Society, and charging Ritchie with having deliberately put the railway companies off their guard.[74] Four days later there appeared in *The Times* a letter from Claud Hamilton to W. W. Thompson Sharpe, M.P. for North Kensington, offering his resignation as President of the North Kensington Conservative Association, and announcing his intention not to support Salisbury's government.

> One attack has followed another upon property and capital . . . and the department specially created for the protection of trade proposes to impose upon the trade of the country an expenditure of many millions of unproductive capital, without previous inquiry . . . The Conservative party appears to me to have degenerated into a flabby party . . . They are like members of a trade union, afraid to call their souls their own.[75]

This move to bring the dispute into the open, and involve the unity of Salisbury's government, was eagerly taken up by other railway spokesmen. On 8 March the Railway Association's Council decided to write to *The Times* on its own account, to protest against "compulsory legislation without previous inquiry."[76] By now colliery proprietors and other private owners of railway wagons had joined in the protests. Midlands industrialists, based at Chamberlain's stronghold, Birmingham, pressed local M.P.s to oppose Ritchie's bill; the Liverpool Coal Traders' Association took similar action.[77] On 16 March a deputation, 200-strong, led by the Mining Association of Great Britain and representing the mining industries and various wagon-owners' associations, saw Ritchie to discuss the coupling clause. Their main complaint was that the mining industry ought not to be burdened with an expenditure of £5–6 million without an independent inquiry first. But the Conservatives amongst them made it plain that they meant business, thus taking up Claud Hamilton's theme, but making it far more potent. Sir Alfred Hickman, normally an opponent of the railway companies, pointed out that Ritchie's bill had placed Unionists "between the devil and the deep sea"; to support it would alienate the business vote; to oppose it would give ammunition to the socialists and their friends.[78]

Ritchie was now made painfully aware of the political implications of proceeding with his bill. His anxieties could not have been lessened by the suspicion that Campbell-Bannerman, just elected leader of the Liberal Party in the Commons, might seek to make of the bill an issue upon which to close the Liberal ranks.[79] When Jackson saw Ritchie in mid-March his impression was that the President still intended to proceed with a Select Committee. But the railway interest's enthusiasm for select committees, remembering the experiences of the select committees on Hours of Labour and on Rates, 1891–3, had soured.[80] A letter from Stalbridge to Ritchie on 17 March made known the desire of the companies to have a tribunal composed simply of persons "specially qualified to deal with the subject."[81] The Mining Association was more specific, and asked for a Royal Commission.[82] On 27 March Ritchie made it clear in the Commons that the bill, whose second reading had already been postponed, could not be passed that session. The following day he gave a strong hint that the bill would be dropped and a Royal Commission appointed.[83]

The *Railway Review* was probably correct in ascribing this surrender in part, at least, to the Cabinet.[84] A revolt such as that threatened by the Unionist railway directors and private owners of wagons had to be taken seriously. The Amalgamated Society failed to regain the initiative. Richard Bell enjoyed good relations with Tom Ellis, the Liberal whip, but was more interested in obtaining a seat in Parliament through this friendship than in carrying the fight over automatic couplers into the constituencies. It was the veteran F. W. Evans who, in April 1899, saw Ellis on the subject of Ritchie's bill, whilst Bell was in America inspecting automatic couplers there.[85] Ellis's death that month severed an invaluable link between the railwaymen and Campbell-Bannerman, more especially as there were still many industrialists allied to Liberalism. By 21 April Evans had concluded that the chance of Campbell-Bannerman officially espousing the railwaymen's cause was "remote".[86] By the time petitions from the Amalgamated Society's branches and from radical M.P.s had been organized, at the end of April, the battle had already been lost.[87] On 27 April Ritchie announced definitely that his bill would be withdrawn and a Royal Commission appointed.[88]

One miscalculation made by the Amalgamated Society was in believing that the railway directors were opposed to all the provisions of Ritchie's bill.[89] This was not so. The London & North Western Railway, for instance, was already fitting brakes to new and repaired wagons.[90] The London & South Western Railway was experimenting with improved coupling devices.[91] Early in 1900 the Great Northern, Great Central, North Eastern and North British railways began experimenting with trains fitted throughout with automatic couplers.[92] On 20 April 1899 the Council of the Railway Association resolved that Jackson should "take an opportunity unofficially" to inform Ritchie that if a new bill was introduced without the coupling clause, the railway companies would not object to it.[93] It was the coupling clause alone to which the railway interest objected. When the representatives of the railway companies arrived back from the United States, they came armed with extensive knowledge of automatic couplers and American experience of them.[94] This expertise, and single-mindedness of purpose, proved invaluable when the Royal Commission began hearing evidence.

The Commission, appointed on 30 May 1899 "to inquire into the causes of the accidents, fatal and non-fatal, to servants of railway companies and of truck owners, and to report on the possibility of adopting means to reduce the number of such accidents", was not quite the body of experts the companies had hoped for. At its head stood Lord James of Hereford; Walter Hudson was nominated to it by Richard Bell.[95] The railways were, however, represented directly by Sir Ernest Paget, chairman of the Midland Railway, and Sir Charles Scotter, a director of the London & South Western Railway, whilst another member of the Commission, the railway economist W. M. Acworth, could be considered benevolently neutral. By the time of the commission's appointment the Council of the Railway

Association was busily engaged in preparing detailed statistical and physical evidence. Scotter and Paget were of course brought into these deliberations, and on Scotter's initiative technical experts were on hand to suggest questions to be put to witnesses.[96]

The Royal Commission thus deliberated in an atmosphere wholly different from that of previous railway inquiries. The companies conceded most of the points at issue without a fight, throwing the responsibility for contesting them on to the private owners.[97] On the question of automatic couplings the companies based their opposition simply on the practical issue of the lack of a suitable coupling, and were able to produce models and the evidence of railwaymen in support of this claim.[98] Wagons were specially fitted with the various forms of coupling under scrutiny, and the Midland Railway placed its Brent sidings at the commission's disposal.[99] Railway witnesses tried to show that there was no ground for hostility between the Board of Trade and the railways; but they based their arguments on the contention that the railways were always ready to adopt proven safety devices, rather than on the dogma that the State should not, as a matter of principle, interfere with private enterprise; the principle of state interference was accepted, but declared to be unnecessary in the particular case of couplings.[100]

The commission's work thus resolved itself into an examination of technical matters, and the unanimous report which it presented in January 1900 was a technical document. In order to diminish accidents involving the movement of railway vehicles a number of suggestions were made, notably the provision of brake levers and labels on both sides of wagons, the covering of point-rods and signal-wires, the provision of adequate lighting where shunting operations took place, and the provision of air or steam brakes on all engines. These improvements in railway working were to be achieved by giving powers to the Board of Trade to make general rules or specific orders, the companies having a right of appeal to the Railway Commissioners. With respect to automatic couplers, however, the report accepted the view of the railway companies, that the differences between American and British practice were so great as to render direct comparison of very little value, and that there was still a long way to go before a device suitable for British conditions could be perfected.[101]

But the most significant part of the report was a two-and-a-half-page digression, showing beyond doubt that the work performed by goods guards, brakesmen, permanent-waymen and shunters, represented "a far more 'dangerous trade' than any other trade or process subject to State control except merchant shipping", and from that premise arguing forcefully that the state had a right and a duty to interfere with railway operation to safeguard such employments, as the principle of such interference with the conduct of dangerous trades was "well established."[102] For those who had missed the significance of the Acts of 1889 and 1893, these paragraphs administered the death-blow to *laissez-faire* doctrines in so far as such doctrines had ever been applied to railway operation.

Ritchie took all these remarks very much to heart. The bill which he introduced in February 1900 embodied the principle of 'dangerous trades' which Conservatives had already endorsed in the 1891 Factory Act. Besides giving the Board of Trade powers to make orders concerning the practices and devices specified in the report of the Royal Commission, subsections 2 and 3 of clause 1 also sought to give the department a blanket authority to make rules concerning any operation in the railway service which it might consider an avoidable danger, and to order the use or disuse of any appliance in connection therewith. Objectors to any rule were to be given the right to appeal to the Railway Commissioners, who were to take into account whether the rule "would materially interfere with the trade of the country, or with the necessary operations of any railway company." But, by clause 11, the Board of Trade was to be at liberty to inspect any railway to see if a rule needed to be made, or if rules already made were being complied with.[103]

Though automatic couplers were not specifically mentioned in the bill, the companies feared that the powers proposed to be given to the Board of Trade by subsections 2 and 3 of clause 1 would lead to compulsion, in this matter, by a backdoor.[104] But there was no chance of amending the bill to allay these anxieties. The second reading passed without a division. Out of a total of 84 members of the Standing Committee to which the bill was referred, the railway interest could expect support from only eight M.P.s, of whom the two Liberals, Sir Joseph Pease and Sir James Joicey, both of the North Eastern Railway, could not be relied upon. Pease, in fact, withdrew from the Standing Committee rather than take part in the proceedings on the bill.[105] Attempts by Charles Bine Renshaw, of the Caledonian Railway, to curtail the powers of the Board of Trade as set out in clause 1, were unsuccessful.[106] On the floor of the House, however, Jackson and Renshaw were able to persuade the government to accept an arrangement which gave any person affected by a rule made under the Act 18 months in which to require the Board of Trade to refer the matter to the Railway Commissioners.[107]

Members of the Railway Association were even then not entirely satisfied with the bill's provisions. Lord Claud Hamilton urged a determined opposition in the Upper House to obtain further powers of appeal; Jackson, acting as a buffer between railways and government, was able to dissuade the association from such an attempt. The bill passed through the Lords with little debate, and received the Royal Assent on 30 July.[108]

The passage of Ritchie's bill marked a watershed in the history of state regulation of railways in the United Kingdom, in the development of relations between the government and the railways, and in the evolution of the railway interest. With respect to the first two of these processes, the significance of the Act is obvious. Taken together with the Factory Act of the following year, it gave the government almost complete control over the conditions of railway operation and hours of labour. The only sector of railway labour relations in which the government had not, as yet, directly intervened was that covering relations with the unions and the fixing of wages. If and when that happened, the government would in fact be assuming ultimate control of the railway system, thus usurping the functions of the railway directors. Indirectly the government already played a part in the fixing of wage levels, through the freezing of railway rates, carried through by a Liberal government and not repealed by the Unionist government which succeeded it.

In retrospect it is easy to see that the amount of government interference prescribed by Ritchie's measure represented the very limits of regulation by the government without actual participation. Whether the railway interest realized this is less clear. But the radical revision of the constitution of the Railway Association, carried out in the same period 1898–1900 (and described in the following chapter), suggests that what was taking place was recognized by some, like Jackson, and accepted by the remainder. The objections which the railway interest raised to the bills of 1899 and 1900 were based on practical grounds of what was suitable and what was possible; very little time was wasted on arguments, now seen to be anachronistic and artificial, which centred on *laissez-faire* doctrines of political economy. As one Liberal Unionist M.P., not a railway director, put it on the second reading of the 1900 bill:

> This Bill . . . embodies a tendency which is very frequent of putting additional work – I may almost say legislative power – on one of our great Departments of State. It is far too late now to object to such a tendency.[109]

And Lord James of Hereford paid a handsome tribute in the Upper House to the "genuine desire on the part of the representatives of the railway companies to assist in carrying out legislation which will protect the men working on the railways from accidents."[110]

At the very least this was proof of a willingness on the part of the railway companies to accept that the clock should not be put back. The pace at which it was to go forward was another matter.

# Chapter 11

# Coexistence
# with unionism

At the turn of the century the railways of the country faced grave problems, though they were not yet such as to warrant an appeal to the government. The price of coal had increased as a result of the Boer War; whereas coal had accounted for only 6.9 per cent of working expenditure in 1896, by 1901 it accounted for 10.7 per cent.[1] The proportion of working expenditure to gross receipts, which had stood at 56 per cent in 1894, jumped to 62 per cent in 1900.[2] Road competition, especially electric tramways, posed a new threat. Dividends fell from an average of 4 per cent for the period 1885–95, to $3\frac{1}{2}$ per cent for the period 1895–1905. Shareholders, worried by increasing capital expenditure, called for and formed movements to campaign for stricter economy.[3] Where possible the companies reacted by raising their charges, but the restrictions of 1894 offered little scope in this direction. In 1903 efforts, though without success, were made through the Railway Association to secure co-operation between railways, with a view to serving public needs whilst observing economy in working and avoiding "needless conflicts in and out of Parliament."[4]

Combination of railways to eliminate wasteful competition offered a more hopeful solution, and the working union of the South Eastern and London, Chatham & Dover companies, which received the blessing of Parliament in August 1899, set an important precedent in this field.[5] But whether, as in this case, the agreement was an open one, involving parliamentary approval, or whether, as in the case of the London & North Western and Lancashire & Yorkshire railways in 1904–5, a secret agreement was reached, such action invited government interference sooner or later.[6]

The pressures acting upon the railway interest were not only economic. In spite of the Unionist triumph at the polls in October 1900, the efficient railway interest in the Commons showed no appreciable increase in strength, and its numbers dropped slowly to 33 M.P.s in 1905.[7] Of these, however, the Liberals were no longer absolutely dependable, so the effective strength of the interest in the Commons was nearer 35 in 1900, and only 28 in 1905. In the Lords during this period the total of the efficient interest remained at about 27.[8] But there were limits to what could be done in the Upper House, fast gaining a reputation as a haven of blind reaction.

Under these conditions the policy of the railway interest in the early years of the twentieth century became one of 'holding the line' and of coexistence; that is, of accepting the closeness of the relationship between government and companies, and working within the framework of that relationship, without giving cause for it to be made any closer. On the labour front the railway companies could expect broad support from the government, support received the more eagerly as the Khaki election had brought Richard Bell into Parliament as M.P. for Derby. The connection between the companies and the purveyors of free labour, as has been shown, amounted to no more than a flirtation, and was not an affair of the heart. The companies, as determined as ever to resist collective bargaining, put up their own defences. After 1900 even the North Eastern board was unwilling to give general concessions or meet 'all-grade' deputations.[9]

On the political and administrative fronts the policy of coexistence likewise met with the approval of the Unionist government. There were two reasons for this. After 1900 the Unionist government was never sufficiently strong to feel able to take issue with the railway companies on any major point of railway policy; sometimes its weaknesses in this respect led to embarrassments in the Commons, as when on 25 February 1902 a motion calling for a return of railway hours was carried, in the face of Gerald Balfour's misgivings, by 151 votes to 144.[10] The troubles caused by education and by Tariff Reform after 1901 re-emphasized the need for caution, especially as the Unionist railway interest was a solid body of Tariff Reformers.[11]

But probably just as important was the change at the head of the Board of Trade. In the Cabinet reshuffle which followed the 1900 elections, Ritchie succeeded Ridley at the Home Office, and his place at the Board of Trade was taken by Gerald Balfour (1853–1945), who held the office of President till March 1905. Gerald's reputation undoubtedly suffered at the time from comparison with his resourceful elder brother Arthur, his dynamic predecessor Ritchie, and his eager Permanent Secretary Hopwood. But the picture often painted of him as an "ornamental head" owed its origin largely to trade union and Socialist propaganda.[12] While trade unionists complained of his inaction, Lord Claud Hamilton, now gaining a reputation for himself as leader of the militant right-wing anti-unionist railway directors, found occasion to complain to Lord Salisbury that his nephew, who had then been in office less than three months, was paying too much attention to the Amalgamated Society and its secretary, Richard Bell.[13] The truth lay somewhere between these two views.

Gerald Balfour was far from being an inactive President of the Board of Trade. One of his first acts as President was to sanction Hopwood's scheme for the appointment of an Advisory Board, to include company representatives and Richard Bell, to assist in preparing draft rules under Ritchie's Act of 1900; it was this proposal which brought forth the letter, referred to above, from Claud Hamilton to Salisbury.[14] The Railway Association took the view that this was an attempt to force the association, and hence its constituent companies, to recognize the Amalgamated Society, and so refused to have anything to do with it.[15]

Perhaps this experience had a sobering effect on Gerald's policy. That policy, like that of the railway interest, emerged as one of coexistence. Balfour was prepared to work strenuously within the existing limits of authority allowed to the Board of Trade by the legislature. But he refused to extend those limits. In the matter of cheap trains for workmen, for instance, in which the Parliamentary Committee of the Trades Union Congress was now interesting itself, he refused to support proposals to amend the Act of 1883 unless the railways were given an equivalent.[16] So far as legislation was concerned, he would only take action where there was a large measure of consent amongst the parties concerned.

This policy fitted in neatly with the attitude of the railway companies after 1900. At the same time it left plenty of scope for co-operation and progress, particularly in complicated matters of technical and administrative change. The problems and possibilities are well illustrated by the long negotiations to lay down rules under the 1900 Prevention of Accidents Act, though here the story can only be briefly told.

After the Railway Association had refused to co-operate with the Board of Trade in the actual drafting of the rules, Balfour set up a departmental committee, under the chairmanship of Lord James of Hereford, which presented a set of draft rules in April 1901. These were then sent to the railway companies, the Mining Association and other private owners of wagons.[17] In June 1901 the Council of the Railway Association, in conjunction with six general managers, was empowered to effect a compromise.[18] Negotiations proceeded throughout the latter part of 1901. In December over 40 United Kingdom companies, some of them not members of the association, agreed to be represented by it at a formal hearing at the Board of Trade.[19] In January 1902 Lord James's committee submitted revised draft rules; but as final agreement on these proved impossible, the matter was taken to the Railway Commissioners, with the London & North Western appearing in support of the objections of all the companies.[20]

The main concern of the companies was with the first of the draft rules, that dealing with the provision of 'either-side' brakes on goods and mineral wagons. The companies had been experimenting with such brakes since the mid-1890s.[21] In 1901 the Railway Clearing House had already appointed a committee of traffic officers and mechanical engineers to examine various either-side brakes; by July 1902 five had been passed as suitable.[22] The companies now wanted the draft rule altered to exempt wagons of peculiar or large construction, provided such vehicles were fitted with alternative apparatus, and to exempt wagons fitted with automatic brakes.[23]

On 29 July 1902 the Railway Commissioners confirmed all the rules except that concerning either-side brakes, which was referred back to the Board of Trade for redrafting, to accommodate the objections of the companies.[24] Once again there were consultations between the two sides.[25] But in July 1903 the Railway Commissioners adjourned the case *sine die* to enable further experiments to be made. With the assistance of Guy Granet, now secretary to the Railway Association, the London & North Western Railway was persuaded to provide facilities for these trials in 1904.[26] The results were such as "would hardly warrant the expectation that the Court would pronounce in favour of the rule now before them."[27]

Even Richard Bell thought further experimentation desirable, and Gerald Balfour agreed.[28]

The tests which followed in 1905 also had the full support of the Railway Association. These tests, too, failed to produce an appliance which the Board of Trade inspectorate felt able to recommend the board to press the companies to adopt.[29] In July 1905 an attempt was made by Sir Herbert Jekyll, head of the Railway Department, to frame a rule for a brake capable only of being applied from either side. The Amalgamated Society was at first inclined to accept such an arrangement, but later recanted.[30] Negotiations and further inquiries dragged on through 1906 and 1907.[31] In December 1908 the Board of Trade received another rebuff at the hands of the Railway Commissioners.[32] There were further negotiations in 1910. Finally, in October 1911, the commissioners approved a new rule which came into force in November, more than 11 years after the passage of Ritchie's Act.[33]

These proceedings, which reflected little credit upon the Board of Trade, gave much ammunition to the railway companies in their contention that they knew their business better than any set of men in Whitehall. This feeling was as strong on the eve of the First World War as it had been, with respect to the question of a communication cord, on the morrow of the Second Reform Act. Many problems of railway operation were becoming far too technical to admit of decisions based simply on political considerations, a fact borne out by the slow rate of progress in the matter of either-side brakes under the Liberals after 1905, a rate quite as slow as that achieved by the Unionists.

Caution was even more essential in relation to railway rates and traders' grievances. In 1903, when the Earl of Onslow became President of the Board of Agriculture, the companies accepted an invitation to a meeting with representatives of the Mansion House Association at the Board of Trade.[34] On 29 July the general managers of the leading lines attended a conference with Onslow, mainly to discuss the carriage of farm and dairy produce.[35] The question of preferential rates for foreign produce inevitably cropped up. In July 1903, when the chambers of commerce pressed for a Departmental Committee, Gerald Balfour was unwilling to grant it until satisfied "that the carefully considered provisions of the Railway and Canal Traffic Acts have failed to ensure their object."[36] The convulsions suffered by the Unionist party as a result of the Tariff Reform campaign led to a reconsideration of this position. On 24 March 1904 Onslow, in a meeting with some railway chairmen, announced that a Departmental Committee was to be set up to enquire into the preferential rates allegedly given to foreign and colonial agricultural produce.[37] The railway companies fell in with this proposal. The committee included Sir Charles Owens, general manager of the London & South Western Railway, and Alfred Baldwin, M.P., a director of the Great Western Railway.[38] Locally, companies agreed to meet representatives of chambers of agriculture to discuss their problems. But though farmers were adept at organizing demonstrations and deputations they were, as the government was forced to admit, reluctant to take the trouble to come forward and present their grievances before the committee set up to hear them.[39] Their disappointment with the results of the committee's deliberations is hardly surprising.[40]

In two small, though not unimportant matters, however, the government was able to agree to legislation, because in each case the initiative came from back-benchers, and in both cases the Board of Trade was able to arrange a compromise such that there was very little conflict in Parliament. These were the Private Sidings Act of 1904 and the 'Sparks' Act of 1905.

The Private Sidings Act had its origin in a series of court cases in the period 1901–2, as a result of which railway companies were declared not to be obliged to afford "reasonable facilities" to owners of private sidings or to acquiesce in the connection of private sidings with main lines.[41] In 1903 a bill to annul the effect of these decisions, and to regulate matters by statute rather than by agreement, was introduced by the Liberal M.P. Sir John Brunner, chairman of Brunner, Mond and Company Ltd, and was supported both by Liberal and Unionist M.P.s.[42] The bill, to the relief of the Board of Trade, never reached the second reading stage; but the Mansion House Association took up the matter with the board in the autumn.[43] In 1904 Brunner's bill was reintroduced, passing its second reading on 18 March.[44] By prior consultation a sharp conflict in the Standing Committee was avoided, and the proceedings there disposed of in a day.[45] Negotiations were more delicate when the bill returned to the floor of the House. Hopwood and Bonar Law, the Parliamentary Secretary, were eventually able to arrange a compromise on the question of appeal to the Railway Commissioners.[46] In the Lords the bill was passed as a government measure, and became law on 15 August.[47]

The Board of Agriculture was able to play a similar role in 1905 on the question of compensation for damage to crops caused by sparks from railway engines. This seemingly innocuous subject gave rise to more trouble than might at first sight have seemed possible. The bill was a farmers' measure, designed to make it easier for them to obtain compensation from railway companies where fires could be traced to engine sparks. When the subject had arisen in 1901, Amelius Lockwood declared "the most he could promise to do was to absent himself from a division", because he "had his constituents to consider"; Sir Herbert Maxwell "felt bound to support the Bill."[48] Feeling among Conservative M.P.s generally was so great that Charles Beilby Stuart-Wortley, a Conservative M.P. and director of the Great Central Railway, advised the companies to accept the best bargain possible; he and Renshaw worked to this end.[49]

A bill was reintroduced in February 1905.[50] But though the companies opposed it, there was no division on the second reading on 3 March. At that time the government expressed no opinion, leaving the matter entirely in the hands of the back-benchers.[51] Later, however, the Board of Agriculture stepped in, probably to ensure the bill's passage before the end of the session. In the Standing Committee the companies were able to obtain some useful protective clauses, particularly a proviso that the Act was not to come into force till 1 January 1908, and also the right to enter lands to take precautions against fire.[52] In this form the bill passed its remaining stages and became law on 4 August.[53]

It is thus possible to see that though the legislative record of Gerald Balfour's railway administration was small, the period was very much a seminal one in the history of relations between the government and the industry. It was a period in which the two sides worked closer together than ever before. The time of the Railway Companies' Association was consumed, not with feverish opposition to the government, but with constructive work in collaboration with it and in response to it. Committees of experts were set up to deal with such miscellaneous matters as the conveyance of cycles by rail and the rating of railways, to consider rules proposed by the Home Office for docks under the 1901 Factory Act, and to consider the regulations to be put in force by the Local Government Board under the 1903 Motor Cars Act.[54] Perhaps most significant of all was the setting up, on 22 January 1903, of a committee to inquire whether the statutory form of railway accounts then in force required any alteration, and whether greater uniformity could be obtained.[55] This body, which reported in 1905, was appointed entirely on the initiative of the companies. It reflected their willingness to carry out railway reforms without needless parliamentary conflict; the committee's work proved a valuable asset to the Liberal government which legislated on railway accounts in 1910 and 1911.

In these circumstances, less work devolved upon the directors and M.P.s acting as a body, and more upon the general managers and the specialized staffs of the companies. After 1900 much railway regulation by-passed Parliament and avoided political controversy; instead it boiled down to questions of pure administration. A. J. Balfour's extensive procedural reforms in 1902 emphasized the extent to which the initiative in the Commons was passing out of the hands of private members.[56] Party considerations inevitably grew in stature. The murmurings of Lockwood and Maxwell in regard to compensation for damage to crops in 1901 were signs that even a seat on the board of a large company could no longer guarantee the loyalty of a director-M.P. to that company. The needs and the role of the Railway Association had undergone a substantial alteration.

The troubles of 1897 had had important repercussions on the structure of the association. The possibility of appointing a permanent secretary had been raised earlier in the decade.[57] In March 1897 Henry Oakley agreed to continue as honorary secretary only after a special committee had been appointed to consider the question of his successor.[58] His wish to retire lent a new urgency to the matter. Moreover, the North Eastern Railway's 'betrayal' of other companies over recognition of the Amalgamated Society, and the inability of the Railway Association, now a large body, to reach quickly a decided policy towards the union, pointed to weaknesses in its own organization. As W. L. Jackson put it:

> recent events had emphasised the necessity of Railway Companies acting more effectively together than they had done in the past. It was difficult in a crowded room to deal with the business for which they were called together. Any re-organization of the Association should . . . take the form of some kind of executive to act in the interests of the Companies generally . . . They ought to have an organization where there should be a continuity of policy.

A committee, which included Stalbridge, Jackson and Oakley, was appointed to consider the subject, and met during April, May and June 1898.[59]

At this time, and since the formation of the association, the power of decision-making rested with the entire body of members alone, assisted only by a Parliamentary Committee whose members included, after 1874, all M.P.s and peers on the boards of member companies.[60] As the meeting on 4 November 1897 had shown, this arrangement made for unwieldy meetings with indecisive results. Thus the committee appointed to consider reorganization, in a report adopted by the association on 30 June 1898, recommended that, though ultimate authority should still rest with the full association, day-to-day conduct of affairs should be placed in the hands of a council, elected annually, and consisting of five members in addition to the chairman and deputy chairman of the association. The council was to have power "to represent the Railway Association on all questions affecting general Railway interests", and to be able to add temporarily to its number as circumstances might dictate. The council was to present an annual report. Ordinary meetings of the association were to be held only three times a year, and the tenure of the offices of chairman and deputy chairman was to be restricted to two successive years for any one person. Though it was proposed not to meddle with the constitution of the Parliamentary Committee, the power of summoning meetings of it was to be given to the council. Finally, the appointment was recommended of a paid secretary "thoroughly conversant with Parliamentary business", with offices near Parliament Street and a small staff. In all official matters the secretary, like the Parliamentary Committee, was to be subject to the council's authority.[61]

At the first meeting of the association in 1899 a council was elected in accordance with the decision of the previous year. The first members were: Earl Cawdor (Great Western); Lord Claud Hamilton (Great Eastern); Sir Ernest Paget (Midland); Henry Bonsor, M.P. (South Eastern); and James Bunten (Caledonian). But the council in this form did not survive long. It is not difficult to see why. With Stalbridge and Jackson as chairman and deputy chairman respectively, the council, with whom real power to represent the United Kingdom railway companies now rested, was almost exclusively controlled by the London-based companies operating north of the Thames. Southern and Scottish companies had only one representative each. The Welsh and Irish companies, at that time in the vanguard of the fight against the trade unions, had no representation; nor did some of the most important English companies not based in London, principally the Lancashire & Yorkshire Railway, the North Eastern Railway, and the Great Central Railway, whose London extension had only just been opened.[62]

It was a director of the Great Central company, Charles Stuart-Wortley, who in May 1900 first raised the question of revising the new constitution, not on the issue of the council's composition, but on that of the status of director-M.P.s. Under the new constitution the Parliamentary Committee was firmly under the control of the council, and its status considerably diminished. This was clearly a reflection of the view, apparent when the legislation of 1893–4 was under consideration, that by themselves the railway M.P.s could achieve little. This was not a sudden development. There was hardly ever an occasion after 1868, or even prior to that date, when the railway interest could defeat a government measure on the floor of the House. But the interest could threaten trouble, especially when the government of the day was in a weak position. Now that the Liberal Party had moved so far leftwards, that advantage had disappeared so far as Liberalism was concerned. With Unionism it still had some force, and in 1899 the Unionist railway directors could rightly point to a victory in forcing Ritchie to withdraw his Regulation of Railways bill and to appoint a Royal Commission instead. But now, in 1900, a similar bill had been introduced. On 17 May 1900 the second reading of a Cheap Trains bill, supported by Liberal and Labour M.P.s, had been defeated only by a majority of 29.[63] There was understandable annoyance at the limited facilities now offered director-M.P.s to communicate with the Railway Association. This was the complaint which Stuart-Wortley carried to the association in May 1900.[64]

In all, 22 director-M.P.s were involved, though the Railway Association minutes do not reveal their names. Jackson was certainly not amongst them, for as chairman of the association, at a joint meeting of the council and the Parliamentary Committee on 24 May, he defended the *status quo*.[65] Jackson's position was obscure and insecure. As chairman he was expected to speak and fight on behalf of the companies. As a former Conservative minister he found it difficult and embarrassing to engage in open conflict with the government. As the most influential figure on the council of the association he was able to deal with the government direct, bypassing the Commons. The revolt by back-bench railway directors, most of them Unionists, threatened his position.

At a special meeting of the association on 21 June 1900, Stuart-Wortley proposed to add three director-M.P.s to the council, any two of whom were to have the power to call meetings of all director-M.P.s. This, he explained,

> gave voice to the wishes of all Railway Members of the House of Commons . . . the present arrangements with regard to Parliamentary matters were not a success, members not being consulted on, nor armed against any Bills affecting Railway interests. . . . With regard to the Cheap Trains Bill, members were not summoned until the day before the Bill came on for second reading. For the Railway Bill they were not summoned at all.

Colonel Amelius Lockwood, London & North Western director, asserted that "most of the Railway Members were caught napping over the present Railway Accidents Bill", and that Stuart-Wortley's motion would prevent a recurrence of such a state of affairs. Charles Bine Renshaw, of the Caledonian, made the same point. Jackson was forced to acknowledge the justice of these complaints; with difficulty he managed to obtain a reference back to the council.[66]

The upshot of these criticisms was a proposed amendment of the Railway Association's constitution, agreed to by the council on 24 July and adopted by the association on 12 October, allowing M.P.s on the boards of member companies to elect three of their number to sit and act with the council "upon all questions pending in Parliament", with power to summon meetings of all director-M.P.s to discuss such questions, "all questions of general policy remaining as at present to be determined by the Council . . . or the Association."[67]

But the erosion of the 1898 constitution did not end there. The North Eastern Railway, ostracized by the other companies and excluded from the deliberations of the council, drew up a scheme to give it the representation it desired, and designed to attract support from other provincial, Scottish and Irish companies similarly excluded.[68] On this point, too, Jackson was forced to give ground, the more so when other companies, such as the Cambrian, rallied to the side of the North Eastern.[69] On 22 January 1901 the association gave its approval to important amendments to the constitution, enlarging the council to 15 members, including the chairman and deputy chairman, nine members to be elected by London companies, three by English and Welsh provincial companies, two by Scottish and one by Irish companies. Although the chairman and deputy chairman were to be elected by the association as a whole, the representation of the group of companies to which they belonged was to be diminished by one or two, as necessary. Three M.P.s were to be added to the council for parliamentary purposes. Ordinarily the members of the council were to be railway directors; but provision was made for companies to be represented by general managers if necessary.[70] On 25 February a meeting of director-M.P.s elected as their representatives on the council Stuart-Wortley, Renshaw, and the Liberal Imperialist Sir Edward Grey, a member of the North Eastern board.[71]

Expressions of dissatisfaction continued to be heard. At the association's meeting on 22 January, Scottish and Welsh representatives pressed for greater representation for their companies.[72] The Furness Railway made a similar complaint to the council on 25 February.[73] Notwithstanding the fact that the amended constitution had been approved on 22 January, at a meeting of 48 members representing 25 companies, Jackson felt it prudent to obtain a confirmation of the arrangements at another meeting of the association on 5 March. At that meeting the election of the council was proceeded with on the lines adopted in January.[74] But dissatisfaction with the arrangements lingered on. In the summer of 1905 rumours that the Scottish companies were about to secede were strong enough for Stalbridge to raise the matter at a council meeting, where assurances were obtained from Renshaw and Maxwell that no such action was contemplated.[75]

The importance of the constitutional changes of 1898–1901 in the history of the railway interest cannot be over-emphasized. The effect was to supersede the Parliamentary Committee completely, and virtually to eclipse the full meetings of the association. Though the Railway Association's minutes give little indication of the personal, as distinct from the company and regional interests involved, it is plain that Jackson, backed by Stalbridge, was primarily responsible for the attempt to streamline the association's organization, replacing what had become a large, unwieldy and slow-moving body by a small gathering, representative mainly of companies based in London, able to meet at short notice, and with the power to act quickly. These were the points stressed by Jackson in a letter to the companies in defence of his scheme.[76] It reflected astute thinking, based not merely on the events of November and December 1897, but on an appreciation of the changes in the relationship between the government and the companies brought about as a result of the legislation of 1888–94. As an isolated political group, allied to but normally outside the protective cover of the Conservative Party, the railway interest needed to rely less upon open conflict with governments, and more upon a cordial, if not close, relationship with the administration, able and willing to be taken without delay into the consultative process.

Jackson's plan was an attempt to mould the constitution of the Railway Association to fulfil this new function. That he did not entirely succeed was due to two factors. In the first place, the sectional interests of individual companies, which had prevented the formation of a Railway Association in the mid-nineteenth century, were still strong, and continued to be so down to 1914. Secondly the parliamentary representation of the railway companies was becoming dominated by militants on the far right of the Conservative Party. Their continued faith in the efficacy of political pressure was not wholly misplaced, especially when Unionist governments were in office and when the efficient railway interest could boast over 40 M.P.s in its ranks.

It was perhaps ironic that, in this attempt to maintain the Railway Companies' Association as an instrument of political pressure, the Unionist M.P.s should have been joined by the usually forward-looking board of the North Eastern Railway, which, in a memorandum accompanying its proposals, urged that the main work of the association was still the "organization of Parliamentary opposition to legislative proposals that are calculated to injure Railway interests."[77] But the heyday of such political pressure was past. One important point in Jackson's plans, a point which remained untouched, was the statement that the three M.P.s elected to the Council were there for parliamentary purposes only, and not to engage in the discussion of questions which did not involve the machinery of the legislature.

Jackson rightly prophesied that in future the railways would have less to do with Parliament, and more with Whitehall. As the status of the director-M.P.s declined, so that of the general managers, the administrative heads of the companies, increased. In December 1902, and without any of the fuss which had surrounded the innovations of 1898–1900, the association adopted a recommendation of the council that eight general managers, chosen by the Railway Clearing House, be added to the council at the beginning of every year.[78] It was a sign of growing professionalism in railway representation.

Meanwhile the association had taken important steps to provide itself with a permanent headquarters. In October 1900 a 21-year lease was taken on three rooms at No. 53 Parliament Street, as the offices of the association. The following month the council approved the engagement of a confidential clerk, an office boy and, in January 1901, a typist.[79] More important still, Oakley, having guided the association through its first 33 years, had stepped down to make way for the association's first full-time paid secretary, William Guy Granet, a young forward-looking barrister with a crisp, analytical mind and, as it turned out, excellent qualities as an administrator.[80] Though Jackson's original ideas had had to be altered to secure approval, the newly-constituted association was henceforth in a much better position to deal quickly and expertly, and at close quarters, with government departments.

On the eve of the great Liberal victory at the polls in January 1906 the Railway Companies' Association was, as it remained, a purely voluntary organization, with no powers to bind member companies. But with a total membership of over 40 companies, representing a total paid-up capital of over £1,119,000,000, it had come to occupy a quasi-official position as the authoritative organ of company opinion on most matters involving the government and the companies.[81] The only exception to this was what had become the most explosive area of railway administration, labour relations and collective bargaining. It was from here, where no understanding with the government had yet been reached, that many of the troubles encountered by the railway interest, in the remaining years down to 1914, were to flow.

# Chapter 12

# The confusions
# of liberalism

The Unionist débâcle of January 1906 resulted in a fall by nearly a half in the number of railway directors in the Commons. This fact alone emphasized the close ties between Unionism and the railway interest. It seems clear, moreover, that after 1906 the interest suffered in public esteem by being identified with militant Toryism, especially as spokesmen of the far right, like F. E. Smith, were always willing to come to the defence of the railway companies.[1]

There were now only 37 director-M.P.s, of whom only 18 were directors of large companies.[2] Though the total number of director-M.P.s rose slightly in the following years, the railway interest was never to regain its former political strength in the legislature.[3] At no time between 1906 and the First World War did the number of directors of large companies rise above 21, a figure reached only in 1913. Liberal directors, whose loyalty was suspect even in the days of a Unionist government, were no longer reliable railway devotees. A truer figure for the efficient railway interest in the Commons in 1913 would therefore be 17, hardly enough to give the companies power in a political sense.

It was no adequate compensation that in the Lords, one of the Liberal government's primary legislative targets, railway representation increased. In 1906 there were 56 railway peers. By 1914 the figure had risen to 76.[4] Of these the total strength of the efficient interest varied from 30, in 1906, to 41 in 1911. Here, too, the Unionist domination was complete; the number of Liberal peers of the efficient interest never rose above six. This was yet another indication that, from a parliamentary point of view, the railway interest occupied a position no higher than that of a pressure group within the Unionist camp. This perhaps explains why at least one railway journal criticized the publicity given to the loss of strength in the Commons.[5] In 1906 the Council of the Railway Association was no less concerned, and in February decided to set up an Advisory Committee of M.P.s and former M.P.s, to assist the secretary in parliamentary matters.[6]

This is not to say that the railway companies now lacked leading spokesmen in the Commons; the drawback was that those spokesmen were all, without exception, Unionists of the extreme right. C. B. Stuart-Wortley (1851–1926), who had led the revolt of the director-M.P.s against Jackson's constitution for the Railway Association in 1900, was probably the most able of them.[7] He had a clear and methodical business intellect. But his motto – "Haud fast by the Past" – typified his outlook.[8] Sir Frederick Banbury (1856–1936) was, if anything, more extreme still. A stockbroker by profession, he first entered Parliament, as M.P. for Peckham, in 1892. In 1906 he was defeated in that constituency, but re-entered the House later that year as M.P. for the City of London, where he remained until created Lord Banbury of Southam in 1924. Though he retired as a stockbroker in 1906, his election to the board of the Great Northern Railway three years before had given him a new interest, where his financial, administrative and political experience proved invaluable. On Allerton's death in 1917, Banbury became chairman of the Great Northern company, a post he held until the company was absorbed into the London & North Eastern Railway in 1922. In his frock-coat and tall hat, never afraid of opening his mouth in public whenever the established order was threatened, he made no secret of his view that most innovatory legislation was unnecessary and all of it suspect, opinions he voiced most loudly during the passage of the Railways Act of 1921, by which most of the old companies were swept away in State-enforced amalgamations.[9]

Most colourful and most extreme of all, however, was Lord Claud John Hamilton (1843–1925), whose long career on the railways reached its climax during the premierships of Campbell-Bannerman and Asquith. The manner of his entry into the railway directorate is itself revealing. The second son of the first Duke of Abercorn, he seemed destined for a military career and in 1862 he entered the Grenadier Guards. But politics attracted him more. In 1865 he entered Parliament as Conservative M.P. for Londonderry, and retired from the Guards two years later. A Lord of the Treasury in 1868, he sat for Londonderry 1865–8, for King's Lynn 1869–80, and for Liverpool 1880–8. It was as M.P. for King's Lynn, in the territory of the Great Eastern Railway, that Claud Hamilton gained a seat on that company's board of directors, in 1872; he became deputy chairman of the company in 1875, and was chairman from 1893 to 1922.

In 1888 Hamilton retired from Parliament. But his railway career had hardly begun; indeed he had left the former specifically to concentrate on the latter. His two pet hates were Tory radicals, like Ritchie, and the trade unions, his opposition to the unions having originated in the impression made upon him by the 'Sheffield outrages' and the revelations at the inquiry which followed them. Even before 1906 he had given ample proof of the lengths to which he was prepared to go to shield the railway companies from reformers. The advent of a Liberal government in 1906 confirmed his worst fears. He held the chairmanship of the Railway Association during the first two years of that government's existence. In January 1910, after an absence of 22 years, he re-entered Parliament as M.P. for South Kensington, a seat he held until his final retirement from Parliament in 1918. In the railway world he achieved fame as the embodiment of rigid hostility to the Liberal government and the Amalgamated Society of Railway Servants, and of rigid authoritarianism at a time when flexibility and broad-mindedness would have paid bigger dividends.[10]

Behind Stuart-Wortley, Banbury and Claud Hamilton there was gathered an extremist group of Unionist railway directors ready to defend the companies against the machinations of Liberalism: men like Amelius Lockwood (1847–1928), first Lord Lambourne, of the London & North Western board; Evelyn Cecil, later Lord Rockley (1865–1941), a member of the London & South Western board, whose parliamentary career had been prefaced by a period as assistant private secretary to his uncle, Lord Salisbury; and the two Baldwins, Alfred (1841–1908) and Stanley (1867–1947), the son succeeding the father both as M.P. for Bewdley and as a Great Western director. These men were apprehensive about the future, partly because of what they already knew of Liberalism, but mainly because of what they did not know, but feared to find out.

When the Liberals entered office in December 1905 they had no formulated policy towards the railways. Nationalization was certainly gaining ground amongst left-wing Liberals, Labour supporters, and even some anti-railway Conservatives, as the support given by members of all three parties to the formation of the Railway Nationalisation Society, in 1908, bore testimony.[11] Some Liberal leaders, including Lloyd George and Winston Churchill, perhaps in deference to their Labour allies, paid lip-service to nationalization, but not as a prospect in the foreseeable future.[12] Many Liberals delighted in attacks upon the railway companies, attacks made all the more easily since they could now be turned to political advantage. But the historian who sets out to discover the railway policy of the Liberal government will have embarked upon a fruitless search.

There was no policy. Neither Lloyd George nor Churchill nor Buxton, the three Presidents of the Board of Trade during the period 1906–13, had any established ideas on the subject, though Churchill had given the problem considerable thought. All three politicians waited upon events. What characterized the policy of all three was that, once faced with the problem of the railways, crude suspicion gave way to a deeper realization of the complexities of the issues involved. Trapped in the eternal triangle of the railway world – railway companies, railway traders and railway workers – Asquith's government found itself sucked into a whirlpool, damaging both politically and economically, from which only the outbreak of war provided an escape. Until 1914, however, the Liberal government, as a consequence of lack of policy, was driven from one expedient to another. When the war came the relationship between the Liberal government and the railway companies was far closer than either side had intended.

In 1906 suspicions on each side were rife. Lloyd George, in charge of the Board of Trade during Campbell-Bannerman's premiership, was regarded as "an able solicitor with little experience of business, and no particular sympathy with the aims of the mercantile community."[13] His hostility to the great railway companies was well known, and had its origin as much in his Welsh nationalism as in his radicalism.[14] Within weeks of his election he began making threats about legislation on the subject of workmen's trains.[15] In 1907, when the subject had been raised by C. P. Trevelyan, he threatened to legislate to stop railway companies from making financial contributions to political contests, "without, of course, mentioning any time" for the bill's introduction.[16] Here again his bark was worse than his bite. He was too preoccupied with social reform to tackle railway problems seriously.

In any case, some of the grievances felt against the companies were being dealt with by other ministers. The reversal of the Taff Vale decision was high on the list of Liberal priorities after the election. The Liberal triumph at the polls, as the companies realized, made outright opposition to the Trade Disputes bill both foolish and damaging. Officially the Railway Association took very little notice of the bill. Claude de Jamineau Andrewes, an honorary solicitor, explained that though amendments might be proposed, "there were, in his view, reasons which made it inadvisable to move them on behalf of the Association."[17] Of the railway M.P.s, only the loquacious Frederick Banbury, quite unofficially, sought to fight the measure.

This situation of self-restraint was destined to last no more than a year. Some railway problems were already attracting renewed public interest. The question of the form and reform of railway accounts, for which share-holders were pressing, was sent to a Departmental Committee.[18] It was the report of another Departmental Committee, that which Lord Onslow had appointed in 1904 to examine the question of preferential treatment by railway companies for foreign agricultural produce, which presented Lloyd George with a situation he could not ignore.

Partly because of the poor response of the farming community to the Departmental Committee's appeal for evidence, its report was a complete vindication of the railway companies' position, and was naturally welcomed by the Railway Association.[19] Farmers' representatives from both sides of the House called for remedial action, and at the end of July 1906 the Liberal M.P. for Dudley, A. G. Hooper, introduced a bill to make it easier for traders to recover compensation from railway and canal companies for injury or delay to traffic through gross neglect.[20] This was only a gesture. But by December, when, backed by a formidable array of Liberals, including Channing and Lord Brassey, the Mansion House Association took up the question of Hooper's bill with the Board of Trade, Lloyd George found himself faced with a railway rates problem which he, no less than his Conservative predecessors, would have liked to avoid. Politically, moreover, the attempt by traders to enlist the support of the Labour Party made his position even more vulnerable.[21]

When Hooper's bill was taken over and reintroduced in an amended form in 1907 by the Liberal Unionist M.P. F. W. Lambton, it promised to become a battleground upon which the government would be attacked by both companies and traders.[22] The main bone of contention was the owners' risk rate, a rate below that normally charged, and offered by the railway companies on condition that they were absolved from liability for loss or damage other than that occasioned by the "wilful misconduct" of their employees. In fact many companies had paid claims to which traders had not legally been entitled, in order to secure the traffic. But the establishment of a "Joint Claims Committee" by the companies in 1902, to secure equality of treatment, put an end to this practice.[23] Once Lambton's bill had been presented the companies lost no time in protesting to Lloyd George.[24]

Lloyd George's policy was to work for a compromise. The companies were willing to agree in principle, if an amendment acceptable to them could be found to the wording of consignment notes, which traders would accept instead of legislation.[25] This the traders refused to do. The bill was given a second reading on 15 March. Proceedings in Standing Committee were completed on 25 March, all amendments proposed by the railway companies being rejected.[26] But Lloyd George refused either to promote the bill or to oppose it, and the measure lapsed.

Already, however, other grievances had arisen. At the end of 1905 the companies had agreed, as an economy measure, to end the system by which freight agents had been allowed to give rebates to traders as an inducement to business; the agreement came into force on 1 January 1907.[27] The trading community naturally opposed such a plan on the grounds of increased costs to themselves. Wild rumours circulated that it was part of a "Great Railway Combine", projected by the large companies, to divide the country into "spheres of influence".[28] Arrangements by companies in Liverpool to 'pool' traffic there lent substance to the argument that the rebates agreement was "the thin end of the wedge", to be followed by a general raising of rates.[29] Whilst the Act of 1894 precluded such a possibility, demands made by railway chairmen for an amendment of that Act only served to deepen traders' fears.[30] Lloyd George remained noncommittal. He admitted "the general sense of dissatisfaction throughout the country with a good many of the principles upon which railway rates were charged", but would go no further than to express the hope that he would be able "to deal with the whole question in the next two or three years."[31]

In trying to keep the railways and the traders from each other's throats, and to put himself to as little trouble as possible, Lloyd George could at least take comfort from the fact that railway rates were basically a statutory affair. The companies might withdraw privileges they had been accustomed to give in the past; but though they might complain of falling profits, the Acts of 1888 and 1894 prevented them from increasing dividends at the expense of the trading community. In matters of labour relations, however, the law of the jungle still applied. It was here that the unsteady equilibrium of Lloyd George's handling of affairs broke down.

Though the Taff Vale decision had come as a tremendous moral and financial blow to the Amalgamated Society of Railway Servants, and had led to a temporary decline in membership, its long-term effect was to lead to a closing of ranks within the union, and to an augmentation of the authority of the Executive Committee and the General Secretary in regard to strikes. At the same time, the failure of the Liberal Party to give official support on the question of automatic couplers in 1899, the part played by the Amalgamated Society in the formation of the Labour Representation Committee, and the entry of Richard Bell and other labour representatives into Parliament between 1900 and 1906, had all led to a mood of independence and militancy, a mood reinforced by the passage of the Trade Disputes Act of 1906.[32]

Hours of labour remained high on the list of the union's priorities. But recognition was, as before, the main issue, the principle which lay behind the all-grades movement launched in 1906. When Richard Bell wrote to the companies individually in January 1907, and again in February and July, asking them to receive deputations of their men accompanied by union officials, he met with complete refusal.[33] But the policy of non-recognition had become harder to maintain. Some companies, like the Great Central Railway, had already agreed to recognize the Amalgamated Society of Engineers in railway workshops.[34] Non-recognition of rail-waymen's unions had come to signify an attitude of mind, that there was to be no interference by a third party in relations between railway directorates and railway servants. As a practical policy, the growth of unionism amongst railwaymen from 1906 made it more of a liability than an asset.

The story of the crisis of 1907, and of the literary warfare between the Amalgamated Society of Railway Servants and the companies, which preceded the strike threat in October, has been told many times; it would be superfluous to repeat it here.[35] The final outcome, the Conciliation Scheme which avoided the question of recognition pure and simple, should not, however, be regarded as a victory for the companies. In the heat of the battle cherished though obsolete principles were discarded.

In public, railway officials naturally gave prominence to a multitude of reasons for refusing to recognize the unions, stressing the fact that such a concession would impair discipline and warning of the dire consequences for the country in which this might result.[36] The companies boasted that of the 560,000 railway employees in the country, only 100,000 were members of the Amalgamated Society.[37] But they were loath to admit in public that the union could only represent 259,000 workers, of whom more than 100,000 could not afford the subscription. On some railways the Amalgamated Society had the allegiance of more than 60 per cent of the men.[38] There were inevitably comparisons with 1897. But though attempts had been made in 1906 to resurrect the agreement of 2 December 1897, Collison's optimistic offer of "20,000 ex-railwaymen and others", in the event of a strike, was never taken up.[39] Public opinion was hostile to the companies. The companies, in fact, looked to the government to help them out of trouble; and, indeed, it was Lloyd George's intervention, and his separate meetings with a committee of railway directors and with representatives of the Amalgamated Society and the Associated Society of Locomotive Engineers and Firemen, which produced the settlement announced on the night of 6 November 1907.[40]

Both sides claimed that the Conciliation Scheme was their victory. But, while the unions had everything to gain by accepting it, the companies gave ground in three important respects: firstly, the privilege of railwaymen to have grievances with respect to pay and hours of labour considered by the railway boards, which had formerly been a mere favour, was now agreed to by the companies as a right; secondly, there was henceforth permanent machinery for dealing with such grievances, with recognized channels of communication; thirdly, where the Sectional and Central boards failed to arrive at an agreement, provision was made for the appointment of an arbitrator, whose decision was to be binding on all parties.[41] The arbitration provisions were by far the most revolutionary for, in accepting them, the companies agreed not merely to third-party interference in relations between themselves and their employees, but also to ultimate control of pay and hours being given to someone other than the boards of directors, someone in no way responsible to, or elected by, the shareholders, and with no direct interest in company affairs.

In view of the nature of these concessions, the authorship of the scheme is of some importance. Lloyd George naturally claimed it as his own.[42] The general idea of a Conciliation Scheme, similar to those in operation in the iron, steel and coal trades, probably emanated from him.[43] But the final scheme was really the outcome of a stick-and-carrot policy on the part of Lloyd George, and a constructive attitude on the part of some of the railway managements.

Lloyd George combined captivating eloquence with ruthlessness and cunning. His policy was, as he told his brother, "Conciliation at first but, failing that, the steam roller."[44] He threatened compulsory arbitration, and authorized official 'leaks' to this effect.[45] At the same time, by his very manner, he inspired confidence. Directors like Claud Hamilton of the Great Eastern and Sir Herbert Maxwell of the Glasgow & South Western, who opposed recognition and were extremely suspicious of Lloyd George, were clearly won over by his charm.[46] Maxwell, indeed, has paid tribute to Lloyd George's persuasiveness; the directors, he recalled, had previously agreed not to allow any outside interference in the relations between managements and men; but, under the influence of the Welsh radical, "our opposition melted away and we left the conference having consented to the appointment of conciliation boards".[47]

In fact the railway boards were anxious to clutch at any straw which would be the substance of a settlement with the unions whilst retaining the form of a *fin de non recevoir*. Confirmed last-ditchers, like Claud Hamilton, had, however, made too many inflammatory statements against the unions, to be able now to sit down and propose a compromise.[48] It was left to a younger man, more interested in running the railways than in maintaining outmoded principles, to hammer out a settlement. This was Sam Fay, since 1902 general manager of the Great Central Railway. Of Huguenot origin, he had worked his way up in the railway world from being a junior clerk in the London & South Western Railway in 1872. Short-tempered, ill-mannered, and a disciplinarian, Fay nonetheless had little time for moral conventionalities either in business or pleasure.[49] He was able to bring a fresh outlook to bear on current railway problems.

Fay realized that non-recognition was a bankrupt policy, and drew up a plan for conciliation machinery, a plan which was adopted by both sides to the dispute as the basis of a settlement.[50] Lloyd George certainly hoped that some recognition of the unions would be given on the conciliation boards. The companies stuck to their point that only company servants were to be permitted to sit on them. But when negotiations were about to break down on this point, the companies themselves put forward the suggestion of arbitration, which the unions accepted.[51] Approved by the negotiating committee of railway chairmen and the principal railway boards, the entire scheme was submitted to Lloyd George on 6 November, and it was he who persuaded the Amalgamated Society's executive to agree to it.[52] Faces had been saved on both sides. When Richard Bell left the Board of Trade that evening, "He met the directors . . . and they were all very friendly."[53]

The railway unions did not, of course, know the true origins of the Conciliation Scheme.[54] But there was another side to the negotiations, also kept well hidden from both the unions and the public. The companies had said all along that they could not afford to make the concessions asked for by the unions; and the continuing rise of working expenses, which the railway negotiators brought up with Lloyd George, evidently made some impression on him.[55] He was "much impressed with the great waste which necessarily results from such cases as the working of three competitive routes to Scotland or four routes to Manchester."[56] Though accounts vary, it is clear that he agreed, in the course of the negotiations, and provided the companies would agree to a Conciliation Scheme, to look favourably upon schemes of amalgamation or combination which would eliminate wasteful competition, and to institute some sort of inquiry into the lowering of working expenses by reducing competition, and possibly also into the much larger question of the revision of railway rates.[57] As he had for some time been promising traders to consider their grievances against the companies, such an inquiry would have a double purpose. But its course was far from smooth.

The question of amending existing legislation, especially as regards rates and amalgamations, had been discussed by the Council of the Railway Companies' Association on 3 December 1907; and Lord Stalbridge had raised the subject in an interview with Lloyd George on 11 November.[58] The railway companies took Lloyd George's remarks during the negotiations of October and November as the green light to go ahead with schemes which had been in the air for some time, and which newly-formed Railway Shareholders' Associations, in England and Scotland, had been pressing directors to adopt.[59] Foremost amongst these was the attempt by the Great Central and Great Northern companies to amalgamate under an Act of 1858. By the end of November 1907 the Heads of Agreement had been approved.[60] The beauty of the arrangement, from the points of view both of the companies and the government, was that it did not require the approval of Parliament, but only confirmation by the Railway Commissioners. The companies did not anticipate trouble.

Lloyd George had, meanwhile, been pressing ahead with his promised inquiry. The reality turned out to be less than the expectation. Lloyd George really had in mind, not an inquiry, but an "informal Committee" of railway and manufacturers' representatives, to consider mutually acceptable alterations in the law "as may conduce to economy and elasticity of railway working and also provide for the equitable division of any advantages accruing therefrom among the various parties interested."[61] This was not at all to the liking of the companies. As Sir Charles Owens, general manager of the London & South Western, pointed out to Lloyd George on

19 December, the companies were being asked to pay twice for the same concessions:

> the men we pay once in accepting the principle of Arbitration Boards. We pay again by dividing any profit that may accidentally come to us by legislation with traders.[62]

The conference set up by Lloyd George began its sittings in February 1908 and reported in May 1909. The companies hoped to be able to consider amendment of the Act of 1894 "so as to secure greater elasticity in the making of rates", combination and amalgamation, and a host of minor matters, all with the object of increasing revenue.[63] The traders and manufacturers naturally wished to discuss ways of reducing rates.[64] In these circumstances it is hardly surprising that little was achieved.

On the all-important subject of amalgamation and combination, Lloyd George's conference reached no conclusion at all. The reason was that he had had to engineer a complete reversal of policy.[65] The news of the agreement between the Great Northern and Great Central railways had given substance to rumours of railway pooling agreements which had been current in commercial circles for some time, and crystallized opposition to them.[66] In these circumstances Lloyd George considered it prudent to announce that when the Great Northern and Great Central agreement came before the Railway Commissioners for ratification, the Board of Trade would oppose it.[67] On 2 March 1908 the commissioners gave judgment for the government.[68] This breaking of faith with the companies left Lloyd George's policy in ruins. It was as well for him, as for the companies, that he left the Board of Trade the following month, to become Chancellor of the Exchequer in Asquith's government.

The veto of the Great Northern and Great Central agreement, far from daunting the companies in their efforts to reduce expenditure, led to a redoubling of those efforts. In August 1908 an agreement to this end was announced between the London & North Western and Midland railways.[69] An Anglo-Scottish traffic agreement was concluded in September.[70] Anglo-Irish traffic was also 'pooled'.[71] In December the North London Railway's shareholders approved a take-over of their company by the London & North Western.[72] Once more fears were rife that the railway companies were about to spring a "great alliance" upon the public. The *Daily Express* treated its readers to a sensational report that the twin objects of the exercise were to divide the railways into "geographical groups" and "to unite in fighting the demands of labour."[73] There was certainly strong circumstantial evidence in support of the first contention, for the existence of the traffic agreements announced in the press was not denied.[74] Moreover, although the Railway Commissioners had declared against the Great Northern and Great Central agreement, those two companies had now come up with an even bigger scheme, a full working agreement involving their own companies and the Great Eastern Railway.[75] As it was proposed to seek parliamentary approval for this fusion, the Liberal government was once more faced with policy problems.

Winston Churchill, who had succeeded Lloyd George at the Board of Trade, had already been giving the problem of railway combination considerable attention. He realized that "the old competition alike with its waste & its safeguards" was at an end. "In its place", he told Asquith, "has come combination. And what we have to do & do quickly is to devise some form of state control".[76] Ever since the general election of 1906, Churchill had been toying with ideas of pragmatic collectivism to solve social and economic problems.[77] He greatly admired the social and industrial policy in Germany, "organised not only for war, but for peace. We are organised for nothing except party politics".

I say – thrust a big slice of Bismarckianism over the whole underside of our industrial system, & await the consequences whatever they may be with a good conscience.[78]

Labour exchanges, unemployed and sickness insurance, government-sponsored road-building programmes, and compulsory education till 17, were all part of this grand design. "Railway Amalgamation with state control" had a natural place in such a policy. Churchill was not prepared to allow railway companies to amalgamate at will. If they tried to do so, he would offer "obstruction by hook & crook; & rumours of Nationalization."[79] But he welcomed the bill to sanction the working union of the Great Northern, Great Central and Great Eastern Railways, providing the public could be safeguarded.[80] On 10 March 1909 he obtained the approval of the Cabinet to a plan whereby the government would support the second reading of the bill, providing the promoters agreed to the insertion of various protective clauses, and to the reference of the bill "to a strong Committee, with special powers to consider & report upon the large issues of policy involved in schemes of this character."[81]

But Churchill's scheme ran into trouble almost as soon as it was announced. Liberal M.P.s regarded it with the greatest suspicion, and its second reading only passed by the narrow majority of 136 votes to 111.[82] The next step in Churchill's plan was to obtain the reference of the bill to a Select Committee, before which the Board of Trade "should have an opportunity of making . . . the whole case of amalgamations in the public interest."[83] In an effort to quell Liberal opposition to the bill, he allowed the Select Committee to be enlarged from nine members to 15, and to receive all petitions against the bill.[84] As far as the companies were concerned, the terms of reference and scope of the proposed inquiry were now too wide for comfort; the bill was withdrawn.[85]

This turn of events signalized the failure of Churchill's railway policy. In June 1909 he announced the appointment of a Departmental Committee to inquire into the law relating to railway agreements, and to recommend "what, if any, general provisions ought to be embodied for the purpose of safeguarding the various interests affected in future Acts of Parliament authorising railway amalgamations or working unions."[86] With this committee under way, Churchill lost all interest in railway problems. He determined to move on to lusher pastures.

# Chapter 13

# The end of the railway interest

As events turned out, Winston Churchill's Departmental Committee on Railway Agreements and Amalgamations achieved little. But it was certainly not stillborn. The last public inquiry into amalgamations had been held in 1872, so there was plenty of work for a new inquiry to perform. Churchill meant his committee to be, above all, "authoritative".[1] It consisted of ten members only, with Temple Franks and J. S. Beale (now a director of the Midland Railway) representing the companies, and Sir Maurice Levy, M.P. and Alexander Siemens representing the traders and manufacturers.[2] The main aim of the companies was to present a united front; a committee of general managers was set up with this end in view.[3]

The Departmental Committee began hearing evidence on 29 June 1909. Sir Charles Owens, of the London & South Western Railway, agreed to give evidence on behalf of the Railway Association "upon questions where the Companies are in agreement."[4] On 21 July the general managers' committee took the decision of principle "that no change in the law was desired by Railway Companies"; Owens gave evidence to this effect.[5] The traders and manufacturers, however, tended to concentrate on specific grievances with respect to rates.[6] Though there were few witnesses completely hostile to railway amalgamations, many could offer no suggestions as to how they might be controlled in the public interest.[7]

The Departmental Committee ceased hearing evidence in July 1910, but took another nine months to produce a unanimous and lengthy report, dismissing any idea that competition amongst railway companies could be continued, and advocating formal agreements in which the public interest, as it concerned rates, fares, facilities and staff redundancies, would be protected. There were also recommendations that "the *bona fide* transference of powers between individual companies should not be a matter requiring the consent of Parliament", but that such agreements should be invalid unless published, and that, where any amalgamation took place, the maximum charges of the companies should be assimilated and levelled down.[8]

The immediate effect of the appointment of the Departmental Committee was to take the heat out of the amalgamation controversy. In the political turmoil of 1909–10 railway matters slipped into the background, a state of affairs which suited Churchill's successor at the Board of Trade, Sydney Buxton, a man who lacked Churchill's boldness and sense of destiny and Lloyd George's persuasiveness and bargaining ability. In 1910 his only move in railway affairs was to bring in a bill based upon the conclusions of the Departmental Committee which Lloyd George had appointed in June 1906 to consider railway accounts and statistical returns.[9] Its work had been uneventful and largely non-controversial, and it received support from the Railway Association, which made available to it the recommendations of the association's own committee of railway accountants appointed in 1903.[10] On the vexed question of ton- and passenger-mile statistics, the Departmental Committee declined to recommend their compulsory use.[11] The most novel feature of Buxton's measure was a subsection, inserted in Standing Committee, providing for a reference to Parliament, by way of a Provisional Order, in the case of objections made by the Railway Association to alterations proposed by the Board of Trade in the schedule of accounts and returns after the passing of the Act.[12] As the *Railway Gazette* pointed out, this was "the first occasion on which the Association had received direct recognition as the official mouthpiece of the railways by being cited in a Bill."[13] But the crowded parliamentary and political timetable of 1910 allowed insufficient time for the bill's passage; it was withdrawn on 21 November.[14]

In other respects in 1910 relations between the Liberal government and the railway interest almost imperceptibly took a turn for the worse. The companies had made concessions to their employees in 1907, most notably on the question of arbitration, on the understanding that the way would be smoothed for them, if not to raise rates at least to press ahead with agreements and amalgamations, and in this and other ways to conduct their affairs in a thoroughly commercial manner.[15] The evidence of Guy Granet before the Departmental Committee on Agreements and Amalgamations is illuminating, for Granet had acted as secretary to the companies' negotiating committee during the 1907 crisis. He complained:

> So far from having got any benefit we are rather in a worse position.
> The position now is that not only has the path not been smoothed, but
> even as regards the making of pooling agreements, as to which the
> companies have unquestionably the legal power to act, restrictions are
> now being proposed.[16]

The mood was one not so much of despondency as of frustration and anger. As the railway interest was now almost completely a Unionist body in Parliament, politics inevitably arose. In October 1909 the *Railway Times*, no doubt with the budget in mind, referred to

> The attack upon property by the present Government and its want of
> sympathy towards all Home industries . . . nothing but a change of
> Government can restore confidence . . . in the circumstances the
> prospect of a general election can only be hailed with gratification by
> those whose interests lie in the railway industry.[17]

The rejection of the budget by the Lords was applauded by the same journal.[18]

The return to power of Asquith's government in January 1910, and again in December, and the passing of the Parliament Act, served merely to re-emphasize that, in a parliamentary sense, the railway interest was almost completely powerless. Moderates and die-hards within the interest certainly differed in their attitude to trade unionism. But on one point they were in complete accord. Liberalism had to be lived with; it was not to be allowed once more to wriggle out of its undertakings.

The failure of the bill to create a working union of the Great Northern, Great Central and Great Eastern companies had not put a stop to inter-company agreements. In Scotland the Caledonian, North British and

Glasgow & South Western Railways entered into a series of working arrangements.[19] On the labour front, the conciliation machinery was worked according to the letter rather than the spirit.[20] Such an attitude of grim determination had, indeed, been bolstered by the trade recession of 1908–9, just when many of the arbitrators were meeting. Even where disputes went to arbitration, companies claimed the sole right to interpret the arbitrators' awards, whilst some companies took to changing names of grades to minimize the effects of settlements already reached.[21] On 10 November 1910 a deputation from the Amalgamated Society of Railway Servants warned Buxton that the scheme of 1907 was breaking down.[22] Nine months later the first ever national railway strike took place.

The 24-hour ultimatum, to concede recognition, which the joint executives of the railway unions gave the companies on Tuesday 15 August 1911, took the companies and the government by surprise. The first reaction of the companies was to proclaim their faith in the conciliation boards.[23] Underestimating the extent of support for the unions, assurances were given that "a shortened service of trains" could be maintained.[24] Acting on this information, Buxton promised protection to the companies in their endeavours.[25] But after the unions had rejected Asquith's offer of a Royal Commission, on 17 August, and the strike had begun, the government changed its views. There was the possibility of a transport workers' strike.[26] The Moroccan crisis was at its height, and the threat of war demanded the movement of troops and of coal for the navy.[27] There were outbreaks of violence in South Wales.[28] The Labour Party threatened to move a vote of censure, and it was said that the government would fall during the autumn.[29]

The extent of the strike served at least to show that the attitude of the die-hards within the companies was grossly anachronistic.[30] Few railway directors or general managers knew how many of their men were 'out'.[31] Reports were so contradictory that George Gibb, general manager of the North Eastern Railway, was called upon by the Home Office to draw up a report on the situation. His findings, presented on Saturday 19 August, revealed

> that in South Wales, and in the quadrangle contained between . . . Newcastle, Liverpool, Nottingham and Hull, the goods train services are suspended to such an extent that, unless more trains can shortly be run, the districts affected will be in grave danger of a failure of the food supply. . . . The general conclusion to be drawn . . . is that the strike has already attained to dimensions beyond the anticipation of the

Railway Companies and that they will not be able so long as the strike continues to run effective services in the districts above mentioned.[32]

So the decision was taken to stop wasting time trying to persuade the unions to agree to anything less than recognition, and instead to bring pressure to bear on the companies to concede recognition.

This had been made easier because on Friday 18 August the chairmen of the leading companies had given plenary powers to Granet, general manager of the Midland Railway, and Gilbert Claughton, chairman of the London & North Western.[33] In the negotiations on 18 and 19 August, Claughton, who had succeeded Lord Stalbridge at the head of the London & North Western, was the key figure. His succession to Stalbridge was itself significant. Stalbridge had inherited from Sir Richard Moon, his own predecessor, a rigid attitude towards trade unions and collective bargaining. Claughton, like Granet and Fay, had much less faith in such policies, and in the course of his railway career he built up a very favourable reputation with the railway unions.[34] He was noted for his approachability and magnanimity.[35] Moreover he knew Albert Bellamy, of the Amalgamated Society, a London & North Western driver and men's chairman on that company's Conciliation Board; on 15 August the executives of the railway unions had appointed Bellamy to be chairman of the "Joint Conference" to conduct the strike.[36]

In these circumstances, negotiations were made much easier. On Friday 18 August, Lloyd George had managed to obtain agreement on a basis of settlement, including the appointment of a Royal Commission. On Saturday, when it became imperative, from the government's point of view, that the two sides meet, Buxton and Lloyd George, "very gradually and somewhat insidiously, partly by persuasion and partly by pressure", were able to induce Claughton to meet, in an official capacity, first Bellamy and then the other members of the Joint Conference. At 11.30 p.m. on Saturday night the settlement of the strike was announced.[37]

Halévy, relying on published and official sources, explained Lloyd George's success by the fact of his having informed the railway companies and the men "in confidence of the danger of war and urged the bad effect which in the existing situation would be produced by a general strike."[38] This explanation of events in terms of the international situation has gained general credence. Thus Henry Pelling writes: "Lloyd George . . . played a new and unexpected card – warning of the danger of industrial strife at a time when the country might become involved in war with Germany over the Agadir affair."[39]

In fact the government acted with far less finesse. Lloyd George and Buxton threatened that unless the two sides met face to face on the Saturday afternoon, and agreed to accept the findings of the Royal Commission voluntarily, the Royal Commission would nonetheless be appointed, and its conclusions enforced by legislation.[40] On the matter of recognition, this ultimatum left Claughton and Granet little choice. But they realized that though Asquith's government might well have carried out such a threat, they would have done so with a great deal of reluctance, for there was sure to be trouble in the Commons if any recommendation of the commission hostile to the unions was embodied in a bill. So Claughton played a trump card of his own. He offered on behalf of the companies to accept in advance the commission's recommendations if, in return, the government would promise to amend the Act of 1894 so as to allow rates to be raised to offset additional labour costs incurred as a result of improved staff conditions. Lloyd George agreed, and the government's undertaking appeared in the newspapers on the Monday morning, as part of the official announcement giving details of the strike settlement.[41]

So far as the railway interest was concerned, although Claughton and Granet had met the union officials, the question of recognition was by no means settled. Apart from those actually concerned in the negotiations, no one knew, or was told, exactly what had taken place at the historic meeting on Saturday. The very fact of the meeting aggravated the ever deeper differences between moderate and die-hard railway directors and managers. Claud Hamilton had no doubt that recognition had not been conceded.

> of course, when you sit on one side of the table and there are human beings on the other you cannot help seeing them and you recognise them in that sense, but they were not recognised in the sense of any conference or arrangement of terms with them, but merely for the purpose of an explanation. That is what was explained to me, and I accepted it.[42]

On 8 September there took place at the Railway Association's offices a meeting of the chairmen of the principal railway companies of Great Britain and Ireland, when the question of recognition was thrashed out.[43] The prime movers behind the meeting were Hamilton, Allerton, and Sir Alexander Henderson, chairman of the Great Central. All three opposed recognition. Their aim was to bring the other companies round to this view, and thus obtain a mandate from the association "to give evidence in direct opposition to the claim for recognition."[44] Claughton, who had already called together a "committee of experts" to consider the preparation of evidence, urged a contrary view, pointing out that the companies had virtually conceded recognition at the arbitration stage in 1907. He disliked having to concede recognition, and ruled it out in disciplinary matters; but his view was that the companies now had to consider what was possible and what was acceptable to public opinion. The question of public opinion weighed heavily with the chairmen. Sir Charles Renshaw indicated:

> With regard to recognition . . . if they took up a position of uncompromising hostility they would place themselves in a difficult position. In the great industries such as steel and coal, recognition was to a certain extent conceded. It was therefore necessary to indicate the limits wherein recognition was least unsafe.[45]

The Irish companies were adamant in their opposition to recognition in any shape or form. The chairmen of the southern and of the larger Scottish companies, though opposed to recognition, realized that the Royal Commission was likely to concede something: "This would probably be recognition in some form, and it was their duty to modify it as far as possible."[46] Eventually a resolution was carried unanimously "that the recognition of the Trade Unions by the Railway Companies was contrary to the interests of the public and of the Companies and should be resisted by the Companies by every means in their power."[47] But another resolution declared

> that in the opinion of the meeting it was not desirable that the Railway Companies' Association should exercise any supervision over the Committee which had been formed to consider the preparation of the evidence.

The practical effect of the second resolution was to nullify the first, for it meant that when the companies gave evidence before the Royal Commission, there was no 'official' policy of collective opposition to recognition. Each company spoke for itself. In fact, the general tenor of the evidence given by the companies was not that they would not accept recognition, but that they had had sound reasons for refusing it.

> there is no doubt that the main object for which recognition is sought is to provide a means of increasing the membership of the unions by forcing non-unionist workers to join, and from the point of view of the union this is necessary in order to place the union officials in a position to bring about a general stoppage of work if at any time their demands, however unreasonable, are not acceded to.[48]

The appeals made by Sir Charles Owens to uphold the national interest in the matter of recognition, reflected the attempt to place the whole subject in the hands of the commission.[49]

The five-man commission reported in October, recommending an amended conciliation scheme which gave members of each conciliation board the liberty to select a secretary from "any source they may think proper."[50] The companies accepted the report but the railwaymen objected to a form of recognition which was, at best, partial only, and to the survival of petitioning in the scheme.[51] They demanded another meeting with company representatives, but this the companies at first refused to concede; another strike was threatened.[52] Ramsay MacDonald gave notice of a motion condemning the companies' attitude. On Friday 17 November, five days before the motion was due to be moved, a meeting took place at the Railway Association's offices of the representatives of some of the principal companies. Arrangements were made to secure the support in the Commons of George Cave, Bonar Law, and other prominent Unionists.[53]

The debate on MacDonald's motion, on 22 November, thus assumed crucial importance in the recognition struggle. The railway directors regarded it as a test of the government's loyalty to them and to the settlement of August which the government had forced upon them. The unions looked, in the debate, for signs of Liberalism's loyalty to the working classes.[54] Both sides were disappointed. Lloyd George proposed a resolution simply asking the government to use its good offices to bring about a meeting of the two sides "to discuss the best mode of giving effect to the Report of the Royal Commission." This was the resolution eventually carried.[55]

It was thus in the meetings which followed, in December 1911, rather than in the previous August, that the real concession of recognition took place. A meeting of the Council of the Railway Association on 1 December authorized Granet and Claughton to accept the government's invitation to a conference.[56] On 7, 8, 10 and 11 December, under the chairmanship of Sir George Askwith, a settlement on the basis of the Royal Commission's report was hammered out.[57]

There was genuine relief amongst the companies when the ordeal was over. But it had left its scars. At the meeting of the two sides on 7 December, a telegram from the Irish companies repudiated the authority of the company delegates to speak for them.[58] Already at the Railway Association's council meetings of 1 and 6 December, disagreement had been rife. Henry Bonsor dissented from the resolution of 1 December agreeing to the conference.[59] The Scottish companies evinced the greatest suspicion of the entire proceedings.[60] Claughton and Granet, and the companies they represented, were no longer trusted. Allerton, his mind plagued with misgivings, thought that six representatives should attend, including himself and Sir Alexander Henderson. Henderson declined to attend, but insisted that Sam Fay, the architect of the 1907 scheme which had so skilfully avoided recognition, should be present; unless the Great Central Railway was represented, they "would have to inform the Board of Trade that they withdrew from the negotiations."[61] A motion by Allerton to increase the number of company representatives to six was defeated but Granet, fearing for his own position at the negotiating table and subsequently, demanded that Fay be included, and this was eventually agreed to.[62] Thus as the year drew to its close, the railway companies' suspicion of the government was matched only by their suspicion of each other. The wounds, made deeper still by loss of pride and of face, were never properly healed, but remained to open up at the slightest touch.

The companies could, however, look forward to the fulfilment of the government's promise to amend the Act of 1894. But from the government's point of view this was the worst feature of the entire settlement, for it was certain to bring the companies and the traders into conflict once more, and to take that conflict into Parliament. Asquith's government had lost much prestige with the working classes in 1911, not least because of its intimidatory, even bloody, handling of the railway strike. There was no overriding reason why Labour M.P.s should prevent companies from raising rates to recoup themselves in respect of bigger wage packets; but there was nothing to suggest they would consent to such a scheme with any enthusiasm. The opposition of traders on all sides of the House was guaranteed. The government thus found that the settlement of the railway strike had created more problems than it had solved.

Whilst the government was preoccupied with the miners' strike and the minimum wage legislation associated with it, little could be done in the matter of railway rates. But in the winter of 1911–12 the government took the decision that the bitter pill of sanctioning rates increases would have to be coated with much parliamentary sugar if it was to pass through Parliament intact.[63] Fortunately the reports of the Board of Trade Conference of 1908–9 and of the Departmental Committee on Agreements and Amalgamations provided much material which could be used as a *quid pro quo*.[64] Thus when the Railways bill was introduced on 1 April 1912, instead of being the short measure the companies had hoped for, it turned out to be an omnibus bill, reminiscent of Chamberlain's measure of 1884. Clause 2 did indeed declare that increased expenditure due to the cost of improved conditions of labour was to be treated as a valid justification for increasing rates. Clause 8 conferred powers on railway companies to make working agreements. But clause 1 extended the operation of the 1894 Act to include withdrawal of facilities and increases in passenger fares. Clause 5 gave the Board of Trade power to amend the classification of goods, whilst clause 6 brought within the jurisdiction of the Railway Commissioners unreasonable company's risk rates, and generally extended railway companies' obligations in regard to owner's risk rates.[65] The bill, in short, was intended to please everyone, but succeeded in pleasing no one.

The main objection from traders and manufacturers was naturally to clause 2, and to a lesser extent to clause 8.[66] The Mansion House Association and Sir Charles Macara's new Employers' Parliamentary Association began agitating for major amendments.[67] Local chambers of commerce emerged from their proverbial indolence to campaign against the measure.[68] The opposition of the Labour Party was, if anything, more pronounced. The railwaymen were particularly worried that clause 8 afforded no protection for them, or security of employment, where amalgamations were sanctioned.[69] The *Daily Herald* called Buxton's bill a "Betrayal of the Workers", and invited "every public-spirited person in the land, to raise such a storm against this treacherous Bill as will smash it to atoms and compel the Government, if they are going to do anything at all with the railways, to nationalise them forthwith in the public interest."[70] The Parliamentary Committee of the Trades Union Congress decided to oppose the bill.[71]

The objections of the railway companies were threefold. They resented the proposed extension of the 1894 Act to passenger fares; they objected to alterations in the classification of goods at the whim of the Board of Trade, a proposal which "went to the root of the statutory rights of the companies"; and they resented the provisions affecting owners' risk rates.[72] The main question for the companies to decide was whether these disadvantages outweighed the advantages given by clauses 2 and 8. On 22 April they decided not to oppose the second reading, but to move amendments in committee; a deputation made clear these views to Buxton on 20 May.[73]

Buxton, however, was thinking in quite different terms. In June, impressed by the opposition to clause 2, he clumsily attempted to alter it, so that the Railway Commissioners were merely asked to "have regard" to improvements made by railway companies in conditions of employment, when deciding whether rate increases complained of were reasonable. This was rejected completely by the Railway Association.[74] Other matters, especially the transport strike, crowded in to occupy the attention of Buxton and his colleagues. It seemed that negotiations would break down.

The position of the companies was now critical. Many of them had made substantial concessions to their employees in the late summer and autumn.[75] The general managers and goods managers pressed for "a general all-round increase of rates." In a letter to Buxton on 1 November the companies hinted that, whatever the government might do, there would be a general increase of rates at the beginning of 1913.[76] On 7 November Asquith announced that the Railways bill, which had still not received a second reading, would be withdrawn, and a one-clause bill to redeem the promise of 1911 introduced in its stead.[77] Subsequently, when Claughton saw Buxton, the clause proposed to be enacted was communicated to him, and accepted by the council of the Railway Association "on the understanding that the Government would undertake not to accept any amendment which might be urged upon them from other quarters."[78]

The efforts of the much-harassed Liberal government to pass the one-clause bill were beset with difficulties. Morale in the Liberal Party was low. On 11 November, due to a poor attendance of Liberal and Labour M.P.s, a Unionist amendment to the financial clauses of the Government of Ireland bill was carried.[79] This was a small matter, but it shook an already frightened and weary Cabinet. Buxton told Claughton that the government "could not possibly risk another defeat over the Railways Bill", and urged the companies to allow the passage also of clause 6 of the original bill, that dealing with owners' risk rates.[80] To this the companies refused to agree.[81] It was thus with some reluctance that Buxton withdrew his original bill on 2 December and, two days later, introduced the promised one-clause bill.[82]

The reaction of the traders, manufacturers and farmers was swift and predictable.[83] That the bill passed at all was due as much to the divisions of opinion within the Liberal, Unionist and Labour Parties as to the determination of Asquith's government. Attitudes emerged clearly on the second reading. Whilst many Liberals supported Buxton's claim that the government had made a promise and had a duty to fulfil it, others suspected any measure designed to make life easier for the monopolistic railway companies.[84] It was the Liberal M.P. Sir Alfred Mond who moved the bill's rejection; that Mond's motion was seconded by the Conservative M.P. B. F. Peto, showed that that party too was divided over the issue, mainly because of its large farming element.[85] J. H. Thomas, for the railwaymen, looked forward to eventual State ownership of the railways, but naturally supported a move to facilitate wage increases; but his party colleague G. N. Barnes opposed the bill.[86]

Thus though the second reading passed by a large majority, the government's problems were by no means over.[87] When Claughton, Lockwood and officers of the Railway Association saw Buxton early in February, the latter proposed a series of concessions to ease the bill's passage. These included the exclusion from the bill's provisions of increases in the cost of working passenger traffic, and a provision that the Railway Commissioners, in sanctioning a rates increase, would be allowed to review the situation if, for instance, wages were later reduced. The first of these proposals met with great objection from the southern companies, who leaned heavily on passenger traffic; but, on a majority vote, the council of the Railway Association accepted Buxton's proposals in order to assist the Board of Trade.[88]

The acceptance of these amendments eased the bill's passage through the committee stage, where the only alteration of substance was the insertion of a clause excluding Ireland (whose railway companies had not accepted the settlement of 1911) from the bill's operation.[89] The crisis in the passage of the bill came over a move by the traders to limit the duration of its provisions. In committee a clause to limit the duration to three years, moved by the Unionist M.P. Charles Bathurst, a member of the Central Chamber of Agriculture and a director of Richard Thomas and Company, the tinplate manufacturers, was rejected on a division.[90] At the report stage, on 13 February 1913, the Liberal M.P. Frederick Whyte moved a clause to limit the duration to five years. This was the occasion for a first-class row on the floor of the House, with both Liberal and Conservative back-benchers accusing the government of indiscriminate use of the whips to force the bill through. While the debate was on, and fearing a mass revolt, Asquith authorized Buxton to accept a time limit, providing the Act were continued in the annual Expiring Laws (Continuance) Act unless Parliament determined otherwise. Now it was the turn of the railway interest, in the persons of Claud Hamilton and Frederick Banbury, to shout at the government. But Whyte's clause was agreed to without a division, and the bill given its third reading.[91]

The Railway Association took determined action. On 14 February a letter, in the name of the chairman, Sir George Armytage, was sent to Asquith, accusing him of breaking the pledge of August 1911. Asquith, heartily sick of the whole business, replied through Maurice Bonham Carter repudiating the charge. Further exchanges followed between Downing Street and Parliament Street.[92] But the companies were now confirmed in their view that they ought to give up all hope of satisfaction from the Liberal government. Fortunately another weapon was near at hand. Contact was made with Lansdowne and other Unionist peers, who were told that the companies were prepared to risk the loss of the bill rather than that it should be passed with a time limit; their Lordships obliged by throwing out the clause.[93] Before this alteration was considered by the Commons, Claud Hamilton wrote to Bonar Law urging him to support Lansdowne's stand.[94] By 154 votes to 45 the Commons agreed to accept the deletion of the time limit. On 7 March 1913 the bill received the Royal Assent.[95]

The Railway and Canal Traffic Act of 1913 was one of the most unpopular measures passed by Asquith's government. In May the railway companies gave notice of a 4 per cent increase in rates on goods traffic, to operate from 1 July.[96] The exasperation of the traders reached new heights.[97] Buxton tried to obtain the consent of the Railway Association to the enactment of clause 6 of the original Railways bill; he met with a blank refusal.[98] Buxton's mind now began to turn to the wider aspects of the railway problem which had so bedevilled the Liberal government, and previous governments: the extent to which a private industry which had become a public utility ought to be subject to public control. His idea, as he told the Cabinet in July, was to have a small Royal Commission.

> The terms of reference must be wide enough to admit the consideration of any proposals for alteration in the existing conditions – even up to Nationalisation – and at the same time to exclude safety of working, and conditions of labour, which would only confuse the issue; which should be, the relations between the Railway Companies as business concerns on the one hand, and the State as representing the community on the other.[99]

On 30 July the Cabinet agreed to this proposal.[100] Under the chairmanship of the former Liberal Lord Chancellor, Lord Loreburn, the Royal Commission's composition, and its terms of reference, "to inquire into the relationship between the railway companies of Great Britain and the State in matters other than safety of working and conditions of employment, and to report what changes if any are desirable in that relationship", were announced in October.[101] It was generally assumed that the merits and demerits of nationalization would figure largely in the Commission's deliberations, as was certainly intended.[102]

The railway companies had not been consulted about the commission's appointment or composition. It posed grave problems for them. The Railway Association tried to avoid having to say anything on the question of nationalization, save that if state purchase did take place, the provisions of the Act of 1844, settled long since the terms on which the railways could be acquired, and they assume that in so far as there are railways which are not subject to the provisions of that Act, at least as favourable terms as those set out in the Act of 1844 would be applied to those railways.[103]

In matters of labour relations the position of the companies at the end of 1913 was no more secure. The formation of the National Union of Railwaymen in 1913, and its decision in November of that year to terminate the Conciliation Scheme and negotiate a new one, threatened more trouble for the companies, the more so as the union was determined to press for full and unqualified recognition.[104] But in this respect at least the lesson of 1911 had been learned, and the old policy discarded. Quietly and unostentatiously, in the spring of 1914, the companies' parties to the scheme appointed a committee, including Sam Fay and Guy Granet, to negotiate with the Associated Society of Locomotive Engineers and Firemen and the National Union of Railwaymen.[105]

The outbreak of the war in August solved problems for all concerned. The government assumed control of the railway companies of Great Britain under the Regulation of the Forces Act of 1871, and the entire system was managed by the Railway Executive Committee, a collection of railway managers under the official chairmanship of the President of the Board of Trade.[106] Sittings of the Loreburn Commission were suspended and never resumed.[107] And in October representatives of the companies, the National Union of Railwaymen, and the Associated Society, met together, without any outside mediation, and agreed to continue the Conciliation Scheme in force "until either of the parties gives notice to determine otherwise."[108]

In these respects the war acted as a catalyst in relation to developments which had preceded it. The Railway Executive Committee had been formed as long ago as November 1912; indeed, consultation between the War Office and the railway companies dated from 1896.[109] The period of Liberal administration after 1905 saw a further deepening of the co-operation between government and companies, and the involvement of one in the running of the other. In preparing plans for the despatch of troops to France the companies had had to participate in the formulation of some of the innermost secrets of government policy. With contact between the railways and the government so close, at the administrative level, the need for a railway interest, as an amorphous body of M.P.s, directors and their advisers, to shield the companies from the government, was evidently less pressing. At the same time such a task had become more difficult to perform.

On a policy level the events of 1911 smashed the united front which the Railway Association had, with varying degrees of difficulty, been able to maintain since its foundation. The acute differences in 1911 over recognition have already been mentioned. But the splits were not merely between those who "represent the fighting policy", such as Claud Hamilton and Frederick Banbury, and those who "gave away" the companies in August 1911.[110] They were geographical and institutional as well. The Irish companies had struck out on a policy of their own. The North Eastern Railway and several smaller companies were a law unto themselves in matters of labour relations. The Railways bill of 1912–13 precipitated a new crisis. The acceptance by the Railway Association of Buxton's proposal to exclude increases in the cost of working passenger traffic gave rise to demands from the southern companies for stronger safeguards for "the position and rights of minorities."[111] A committee set up to review the situation recommended that in future decisions of the council should be by unanimous vote only. On 6 May 1913 the association adopted this proposal. Its effect was to give members of the council, who were anyway elected on a geographical basis, an absolute power of veto over the council's actions.[112]

The very fact that the plan found favour with the association was itself a sign of growing stresses amongst the companies, and of growing suspicions. The Railway Companies' Association had been conceived as a voluntary body. The feeling that the companies must at all times retain complete control of their own affairs lingered on, even though legislation over the past 20 years had done a great deal to erode that control. Thus, at a time when the railway companies were being subjected to increasing public attacks, particularly from advocates of nationalization, the Railway Association was able to do nothing by way of reply. In 1906 and 1907 the problem of press attacks on the companies had been discussed by the council, but no action had been taken.[113] The establishment of a press bureau was discussed in 1914, but foundered on the alarm expressed at the suggestion "of giving any man a free hand to express the views of the Companies."[114] This failure of the companies to hit back at their critics did not go unnoticed.[115] But nothing was ever undertaken in the way of publicity and public relations, before 1914, to compare with the "Square Deal" campaign launched by the Railway Companies' Association in the 1930s.[116]

The truth was that an entirely different sort of organization was needed. The increase in the number of general managers on the council, in November

1912, from eight to ten, was a sign of the times.[117] The director-M.P.s, now little more than an appendix to the Unionist party, had entirely lost their value to the companies. So, to some extent, had the boards of direction. Questions of policy were rapidly becoming simply questions of administration. This was reflected in the practice, as distinct from the theory, of the Railway Association's constitution in the years immediately preceding the Great War. A. B. Cane, the secretary, has left a description of the way things worked at that time.

> The three Honorary Solicitors and the Secretary constituted, in practice, an informal Standing Committee of the Association, who dealt in the first instance with all legislative and Departmental questions.[118]

Minor questions were often dealt with by this body directly "by informal negotiation with the Government Departments or Parliamentary action and the results reported to the Council afterwards." Major questions remained for the council to deal with. But the council was orientated in the wrong direction. It still placed faith in parliamentary action and in fighting the politicians. As one observer wrote prophetically:

> The future of the great Corporations will lie more and more in the Government offices and less in Parliament. It is hopeless to expect to influence Parliamentary majorities, who will act under prejudice when they do not act upon orders. But it may be possible to persuade administrators . . . The Association would gain immensely if it had something in the nature of an intelligence department or general staff, which would work out in anticipation the strategy of future campaigns. This want might be supplied, if there was an Executive Committee whose duty it was to report at regular intervals to the Council.[119]

The First World War, and the period of post-war reconstruction, solved some of these difficulties. The Ministry of Transport, from its foundation in 1919, "insisted on dealing with the Railway Companies through the Association." The passage of the Railways Act in 1921, by a Coalition government, demonstrated the futility of any longer relying on the Conservatives for protection. But the statutory amalgamation of the private railway companies into four large concerns – the London & North Eastern, London Midland & Scottish, Great Western, and Southern Railways – from 1 January 1923, offered new possibilities.[120] By drastically reducing the number of companies, and hence the number of directors and director-M.P.s, large-scale reconstruction of the Railway Companies' Association became possible. The council was swept away, and with it the parliamentary members and the honorary solicitors. In their place the general managers were constituted a Standing Committee of the association, aided by another Standing Committee of company solicitors.[121]

The parliamentary basis of the Railway Companies' Association thus disappeared. But these developments did not represent a break with the past as much as a recognition of changing conditions which the war had brought into sharper focus. The great parliamentary representation of the private railway companies, a representation which was the cornerstone of the railway interest but which was never as strong as mere numbers might have suggested, had outgrown its usefulness before the war began. Closer ties between the government and the companies, ties which the war irrevocably strengthened, eventually made the railway interest redundant.

# Chapter 14

# **Conclusion**

The role of interest groups in British politics in the nineteenth and early twentieth centuries has not hitherto been given the attention it deserves. Historians have generally been content to interpret political developments in this period in terms of a few outstanding issues and a few outstanding statesmen. Histories of political parties have often been nothing more than histories of political leaders. The back-bencher has been ignored, and his own interests given little weight in interpretations of the development of the party to which he professed allegiance. Some attempts have been made to delineate interest groups in the House of Commons in numerical terms. But, as the study of the railway interest shows, numbers alone meant very little.

Statistical contrasts and comparisons are misleading not least because they ignore personal motivation. Even in the framework of later twentieth-century politics, when party ties and party discipline hardened, it would be dangerous to underestimate the impact of personalities and personal loyalties. It would be doubly dangerous to do so with reference to the earlier period, when party discipline, as an imposition upon M.P.s, was relatively weak, and when the duty of the Chief Whip was still primarily to act as "general manager" of the party, not chief disciplinarian.[1] Discipline crept in slowly. It never had time to gain a strong hold on the Liberal Party. Its real grip on the Conservative Party came about mainly after 1914, not least as a response to the emergence as an alternative government of the Labour Party, with its high degree of regimentation and its suspicion of minorities.[2] It seems probable that on most matters which came before Parliament before 1914, M.P.s were able to vote in accordance with their wishes as individuals, and that where this was impossible they either abstained or voted as they thought prudent.

Here again, quantification is no substitute for the study of issues, personalities and negotiations. The increase in "party voting" in the latter half of the nineteenth century, to which A. L. Lowell drew attention in 1901, reflected the extent to which M.P.s were being prevailed upon, by a wide range of parliamentary and extra-parliamentary sources, to agree consistently; even in 1899 over 30 per cent of all divisions were not on "party" lines.[3] The number of divisions per session in which the government whips were defeated was, as Lowell demonstrated, much higher in the 1850s and 1860s, when it often rose above ten per session, than in the 1880s and 1890s, when it rarely reached five per session.[4] But it would be wrong to regard these figures as a reflection simply of increasing pressure upon M.P.s, from the party machine, to conform to the party "line". The figures indicate no less strongly that when faced with opposition amongst their own supporters, governments were more willing to do battle in the division lobbies in the mid-nineteenth century than in the latter half of that century. After 1868, as this study has shown, consultation increasingly preceded conflict, in order that political casualties might be kept to a minimum. It is for this reason that resort to the division lobbies cannot be regarded as a final test of party unity.[5]

This is not to suggest that after 1868 and before 1914 party loyalties were unimportant; such as assertion is obviously absurd. But the rise of the mass party political organizations after, and arising out of, the Second Reform Act, did not blot out all other factors which influenced the loyalties of individual M.P.s and party supporters. Party pressure became simply another limiting factor which had to be taken into account. As 1886 proved for the Liberals, and 1903 for the Unionists, the dominance of party loyalty was by no means assured. The conflict between party interests and business interests occupied a central position in this evolutionary process.

Of all the nineteenth-century interest groups, the railway interest was the most infamous. It had little in common with the landowning and farming interests, with whom it was often in dispute; was not a professional body, like the lawyers; and was often in conflict with other business interests. The railway interest represented big business at its most ruthless and at its most highly organized. The railway companies played a crucial part in the industrial development of the United Kingdom. The rise and fall of railway shares was regarded as a barometer of the country's economic state. At the same time the early years of the companies' growth were marked by bitter rivalries and cut-throat competition. It is hardly surprising, therefore, that the companies' own organizations, the directors, and especially those directors who sat in Parliament, should have been regarded with both suspicion and awe, feelings which were aggravated by the apparently large representation which the companies could boast in the legislature. This was a position which might have accorded well with eighteenth-century notions of the representation of interests, but which accorded ill with the Liberal individualism and radical collectivism of the nineteenth century.[6]

In fact in the period before 1868 the unity and strength of the railway interest was more apparent than real. Inter-company rivalry was too intense to permit the growth of a permanent organization catering for common ends. Nor did the fact that the interest, politically, straddled both major parties make the development of such an organization any easier. Companies planned together only in emergencies and, as governments were generally reluctant to interfere with them, such emergencies arose infrequently. Indeed the United Railway Companies' Committee of 1867 might have lasted no longer than previous *ad hoc* committees which had withered away after a few years' existence. That this did not happen was due to the stream of hostile legislation, actual or projected, which demonstrated the need for a permanent structure to protect company interests.

The steady growth of state intervention in the railway industry after 1868 was not the result of a carefully prepared plan, but sprang piecemeal from the efforts of all governments to deal empirically with different problems of railway administration. Both Liberal and Conservative governments recognized the need for railway regulation. They differed as to how far, and by what means, such regulation was to be achieved. Liberals,

Conclusion

regarding the companies as quasi-monopolies whose privileges had been conferred by the legislature, defended Parliament's right to interfere in order to protect the public interest by placing further restrictions and controls upon those companies. The Railway and Canal Traffic Act of 1873, the Employers' Liability Act of 1880, the Cheap Trains Act of 1883, Chamberlain's abortive railway bill of 1884, the restriction upon hours of labour in 1893, and the freezing of railway rates in 1894, all proceeded upon this view. Consultation with the companies was kept to a minimum, though radical views were allowed full play. The results often appeared to the railway interest to be both vindictive and high-handed.

Conservative governments, by contrast, used a much greater amount of tact. They listened to what the companies had to say, partly because this made for a quieter life, and partly because they placed more faith in the companies to know their own business. The unfortunate attempt to impose a standard communication cord upon the companies in 1868 was a lesson the Conservatives did not forget, and the controversies surrounding automatic couplers and either-side brakes provided further reminders. The companies did not refuse to adopt safety devices, but they preferred to adopt them in their own time, after trial and experimentation; they saw dangers in premature standardization and enforcement. The directors, the appointed guardians of the shareholders' interests, objected to additional financial burdens being placed upon the companies by the legislature, financial burdens which appeared to them to stem from unilateral alterations of the original private Acts of the companies, which Parliament and the promoters had entered into as voluntary and sacred agreements. In proportion as Liberal policies towards the railways grew more confiscatory, so Conservative policies and methods grew more attractive.

The events of 1886 thus confirmed to the business community that, whereas the Conservative Party was the party of order and stability, the Liberal Party could be relied upon only to counsel change and to promote uncertainty at a time when the economic outlook was bleak. By 1886 the railway interest, both in and out of Parliament, had become a distinctly Conservative body. But this did not give it the protection it sought. Business interests of many kinds had come in under the Conservative umbrella; now they vied with each other to catch the attention of the party leaders. Whilst only one of these groups represented the railway companies, many represented the railway users. Farming and manufacturing interests began to organize themselves on a large scale. An important section of Conservative opinion favoured working-class reforms. Politically between 1886 and

1900 the railway interest was more united than ever before. But this unity did not bring strength. Of the five important Acts of railway regulation passed during that period,[7] three were promoted and pushed through by Conservative and Unionist administrations.

State control altered fundamentally the relationship between the government and the railway companies. Whenever possible, conflict was replaced by co-operation. The railway interest was never in a position to defeat the government of the day; and since it saw its main duty as being the defence only of the companies, restrictions on the rights of private members in the Commons affected it little. Its most useful work was not on the floor of the House, but in committees, behind closed doors, where the relatively small number of M.P.s actively concerned with the defence of railway interests had more scope to exert pressure.

The railway interest worked mainly by deputation and demonstration, by making a fuss and by posing a threat, by seizing upon periods of government weakness and exploiting them to the full. Its members were, however, too many, too independent, and perhaps too proud to indulge in mass publicity campaigns, or to join with other business interests in so doing. After 1900 the Unionist government had no wish to remain in conflict with the railway companies, and the railway interest had neither the resources nor the desire to remain in conflict with the government. Increasing economic pressures, diminishing strength in Parliament, and the fear of renewed attacks from the trade unions, all made for a policy of prudence. Thus, whilst avoiding new areas of conflict, both sides explored the possibilities of joint action.

It was this very co-operation which helped make the railway interest superfluous. As the number of railway directors in the Commons dwindled, the actual political power of the railway companies disappeared. Only in the Lords could the railway companies exert any legislative authority, and then only because of the sympathy of extremists, not because of railway representation there alone. At the national level the ability of railway companies to influence elections had never been great, though it certainly existed in railway centres.[8] Locally such influence was more pervasive.[9] At Crewe the London & North Western Railway had attempted to run the town in alliance with the Conservatives in the 1880s; in 1906 several companies with termini in London used their influence and their money in the London County Council elections. Isolated though these instances were, the controversy to which they gave rise indicated a growing impatience with the attempts of big business to play politics on the American model.[10] By 1906, too, there was growing impatience with railway company attitudes to labour relations, attitudes which threatened to disrupt the economy of the entire country.

The period of Liberal administration after 1906 witnessed the demise of the railway interest as a parliamentary force. On a political level, the interest occupied a small place on the extreme right wing of the Unionist party. On an administrative level, the increasingly complex technical matters with which railway directors had to deal put them largely in the hands of their general managers and other staff officers. A few directors, like Claughton, moved with the times; but they were very much the exception to the rule. Railway directors had always had to contend with shareholders' complaints and 'rebellions'. But from 1900 onwards, especially as the economic position of the railway companies deteriorated, these complaints became more pronounced, and the rebellions more closely organized. It was alleged that the landed interest was over-represented on the boards of direction, that coalowners, brewers, shipowners and steelmasters on the railway boards put their own particular concerns first.[11] As one disgruntled London & North Western Railway shareholder put it: "in the vast majority of cases they [railway directors] are elected for every other reason than because they have expert knowledge of railway business."[12]

This was quite true. Railway directors were put on to boards for the local, national and political influence they might put at the disposal of the companies, and for reasons of prestige.[13] These functions had, however, become less important, for the relationship between the government and the companies was now such as to admit more readily of close consultation at departmental rather than at political level. Some attempts were made to gear the Railway Companies' Association to this new role, but they were not entirely successful, owing mainly to the deep desire of the individual companies not to surrender any of their independence in policy matters. Disputes over the recognition of trade unions and collective bargaining were followed by regional differences over policy in regard to the modification of the much-resented Railway and Canal Traffic Act of 1894. On the eve of the First World War the dilemma was as plain as it had been 70 years before: that the necessity for effective action in common was not easily reconcilable with the maintenance of the complete freedom of action of the separate railway boards.

Clearly, however, future relations between government and railway companies lay in the administrative sphere. Co-operation during the First World War pointed the way. The war also hastened the acceptance of collective bargaining. Once the Railways Act of 1921 had replaced the old railway companies with a few large concerns, the way was open, not for the resurrection of the railway interest, but for the rebuilding of the Railway Companies' Association as a tightly knit and centrally controlled pressure group, whose job it would be to work as much with governments as against them.

# Appendix

## Introduction

*Bradshaw's Railway Almanack, Directory, Shareholders' Guide, and Manual for 1848*, which was first published in 1847, contained a list of M.P.s returned to the Commons in the general election of 1847, distinguishing those whom *Bradshaw* considered "Railway Members". Such lists appeared annually in *Bradshaw* up to and including the issue of 1852. From 1853 to 1857 no such lists appeared, though there were lists of railway directors and other officials. But from 1858 until *Bradshaw's* last edition, in 1923, separate lists of railway directors in both Houses of Parliament were printed each year, in addition to the much larger lists of all railway directors and officials. From 1864 a separate list of Members of Parliament on the boards of "Auxiliary" companies – mostly canal and carriage and wagon companies – also appeared.[1]

As with any such work of reference, much care is needed in using the various lists *Bradshaw* published. The very early editions actually appeared at the end of the year previous to that to which they referred; the later ones appeared at the beginning of their appropriate year, in January or February, before the opening of the parliamentary session. It follows that the lists must be taken as, at the most, referring to the situation at the end of the previous year. This creates difficulties in compiling accurate lists from *Bradshaw*, more especially when referring to election years. For example, it is the edition for 1869, not 1868, which gives information regarding the state of the railway interest in Parliament immediately after the election of November 1868. As the 1874 election came at the beginning of the year, *Bradshaw*, in the edition of that year, was able to print lists which faithfully reflected the results of the election. But, by contrast, the 1906 edition refers to the 1905 situation; and the 1907 edition includes some M.P.s, like Sir Frederick Banbury, who were defeated in the 1906 election but managed to find seats at by-elections later in the year.[2]

Apart from these difficulties of interpretation, errors and omissions appeared in *Bradshaw* and have to be taken into account. *Dod's Parliamentary Companion* is, of course, invaluable for checking all M.P.s, though the individual entries rarely contain much information regarding directorships. From 1880 onwards all directorships can be checked with the *Directory of Directors*, though even this must not be regarded as an infallible guide, at least in its first years of publication.

The lists and analyses which follow are based primarily on the three abovementioned works of reference, supplemented by other parliamentary directories where necessary. The crucial operation is the division of the railway interest into its different parts. Railway director-M.P.s who held directorships only of foreign lines have been included in the column headed "Foreign r[ai]lw[a]ys"; these included colonial lines. The director-M.P.s of other, that is United Kingdom, lines, have been divided into "Local r[ai]lw[a]ys" and "National r[ai]lw[a]ys". The numbers given under the "National rlwys" category indicate the strength of the efficient railway interest in Parliament.

The decision to include an M.P. in the efficient interest has not been based merely upon the size of the railway of which he was a director, but also upon its importance, and upon the importance which the particular M.P. gave to his railway interests. Thus directors of the Cambrian and Furness railways, and of the Taff Vale, Somerset & Dorset, Bristol & Exeter, and London, Tilbury & Southend lines have been included in the efficient interest, as have those of the two most important London lines, the North London and the Metropolitan. But directors of other and smaller suburban lines, such as the Metropolitan District, have not been included. Nor have the directors of any of the Irish lines. Though the major Irish companies, like many of the smaller English ones, did join the Railway Companies' Association, they were in a perpetually impoverished condition, unable to speak with a united, truly independent voice. The Irish railways had few apologists in Parliament even among the British directors, who only opposed the solution of state purchase of Irish railways because they feared such a move would be the thin end of a wedge sooner or later to be applied to their own undertakings.

In one instance a director of some very minor lines has been included in the efficient interest, because this seems appropriate in view of his work on behalf of the companies as a whole. The man concerned was Henry Robertson, Liberal M.P. for Shrewsbury. Robertson, a civil engineer and ironmaster, and a director of several very small Welsh lines, including the Llangollen & Corwen and Vale of Llangollen, was a railway constructor who took to defending the railways on a number of occasions in the Commons.[3] It would be wrong to exclude such a person in any estimate of the strength of the railway interest in Parliament.

The numbers included in the "National rlwys." category must therefore be taken as indicating the maximum strength of the efficient railway interest in the legislature. No director of an "Auxiliary" company has been included in the railway interest at all. The interests of wagon or canal companies were by no means identical with those of the railways, nor did directors of "Auxiliary" concerns go out of their way to defend the railway companies in Parliament. M.P.s who classed themselves as "Liberal Conservatives" have been separately indicated for the 1874–9 period. In the lists for the House of Commons, and except where otherwise indicated, "New members" refers to those M.P.s who first held railway directorships in the years indicated. Peers whose political allegiance is not ascertainable, or who classed themselves as independent, have been classified as "Others".

The following are the companies whose directors have been included under "National rlwys.":

Bristol & Exeter
Caledonian
Cambrian
Furness
Glasgow & South Western
Great Central
Great Eastern
Great North of Scotland
Great Northern
Great Western
Highland
Lancashire & Yorkshire
London & North Western
London & South Western
London, Brighton & South Coast
London, Chatham & Dover
London, Tilbury & Southend
Manchester, Sheffield & Lincolnshire
Metropolitan
Midland
North British
North Eastern
North London
North Staffordshire
Somerset & Dorset
South Eastern & Chatham Railway Companies Managing Committee
South Eastern
Taff Vale

# Appendix

## Table 1
# The railway interest in the House of Commons 1868–73

|  | Total | %age | Govt office holders | New members[4] | Foreign rlwys | Local rlwys | National rlwys |
|---|---|---|---|---|---|---|---|
| **1868** | | | | | | | |
| Lib | 76 | 60.8 | 6 | 14 | 7 | 43 | 25 |
| Con | 49 | 39.2 | 0 | 8 | 1 | 35 | 14 |
| Total | 125 | | 6 | 22 | 8 | 78 | 39 |
| **1869** | | | | | | | |
| Lib | 71 | 58.2 | 4 | 5 | 8 | 43 | 20 |
| Con | 51 | 41.8 | 0 | 5 | 3 | 35 | 13 |
| Total | 122 | | 4 | 10 | 11 | 78 | 33 |
| **1870** | | | | | | | |
| Lib | 59 | 55.7 | 4 | 5 | 7 | 31 | 21 |
| Con | 47[5] | 44.3 | 0 | 5[5] | 4 | 28 | 15 |
| Total | 106 | | 4 | 10 | 11 | 59 | 36 |
| **1871** | | | | | | | |
| Lib | 66 | 54.3 | 3 | 8 | 8 | 34 | 24 |
| Con | 58[6] | 45.7 | 0 | 8[6] | 7 | 35 | 16 |
| Total | 124 | | 3 | 16 | 15 | 69 | 40 |
| **1872** | | | | | | | |
| Lib | 70 | 56.9 | 2 | 7 | 10 | 37 | 23 |
| Con | 53[6] | 43.1 | 0 | 3 | 6 | 33 | 14 |
| Total | 123 | | 2 | 10 | 16 | 70 | 37 |
| **1873** | | | | | | | |
| Lib | 71 | 53.9 | 2 | 6 | 10 | 39 | 22 |
| Con | 61[7] | 46.1 | 0 | 8[8] | 7 | 37 | 17 |
| Total | 132 | | 2 | 14 | 17 | 76 | 39 |

Number of director-M.P.s elected in 1868
who sat in the previous Parliament:

| | |
|---|---|
| Lib | 55 |
| Con | 39 |
| Total | 94 |

Table 2

# The railway interest in the House of Commons 1874–9

| | Total | %age | Govt office holders | New members[9] | Foreign rlwys | Local rlwys | National rlwys |
|---|---|---|---|---|---|---|---|
| *1874* | | | | | | | |
| Lib | 59 | 47.6 | 0 | 7 | 5 | 33 | 21[10] |
| Con | 54 | 43.6 | 5 | 11 | 4 | 33 | 17 |
| Lib-Con | 9 | 7.3 | 0 | 1 | 1 | 6 | 2 |
| Irish Nat | 2 | 1.5 | 0 | 0 | 0 | 2 | 0 |
| Total | 124 | | 5 | 19 | 10 | 74 | 40 |
| *1875* | | | | | | | |
| Lib | 64 | 49.6 | 0 | 15 | 7 | 33 | 24[10] |
| Con | 53 | 41.1 | 4 | 13 | 3 | 29 | 21 |
| Lib-Con | 9 | 7.0 | 0 | 2 | 1 | 7 | 1 |
| Irish Nat | 3 | 2.3 | 0 | 2 | 0 | 3 | 0 |
| Total | 129 | | 4 | 32[11] | 11 | 72 | 46 |
| *1876* | | | | | | | |
| Lib | 64 | 49.6 | 0 | 4 | 7 | 33 | 24[10] |
| Con | 54 | 41.9 | 3 | 5 | 3 | 29 | 22 |
| Lib-Con | 7 | 5.4 | 0 | 0 | 1 | 5 | 1 |
| Irish Nat | 4 | 3.1 | 0 | 1 | 0 | 4 | 0 |
| Total | 129 | | 3 | 10 | 11 | 71 | 47 |
| *1877* | | | | | | | |
| Lib | 61 | 48.0 | 0 | 2 | 7 | 29 | 25[10] |
| Con | 54 | 42.5 | 2 | 3 | 2 | 31 | 21 |
| Lib-Con | 8 | 6.3 | 0 | 1 | 1 | 5 | 2 |
| Irish Nat | 4 | 3.2 | 0 | 0 | 0 | 4 | 0 |
| Total | 127 | | 2 | 6 | 10 | 69 | 48 |
| *1878* | | | | | | | |
| Lib | 61 | 49.6 | 0 | 4 | 6 | 27 | 28[10] |
| Con | 51 | 41.5 | 2 | 3 | 3 | 27 | 21 |
| Lib-Con | 7 | 5.7 | 0 | 0 | 2 | 3 | 2 |
| Irish Nat | 4 | 3.2 | 0 | 0 | 0 | 4 | 0 |
| Total | 123 | | 2 | 7 | 11 | 61 | 51 |
| *1879* | | | | | | | |
| Lib | 59 | 49.6 | 0 | 5 | 3 | 31 | 25[10] |
| Con | 50 | 42.0 | 3 | 2 | 2 | 24 | 24 |
| Lib-Con | 7 | 5.9 | 0 | 0 | 2 | 3 | 2 |
| Irish Nat | 3 | 2.5 | 0 | 0 | 0 | 3 | 0 |
| Total | 119 | | 3 | 7 | 7 | 61 | 51 |

| Number of director-M.P.s | | |
|---|---|---|
| elected in 1874 who sat | Lib | 46 |
| in the previous Parliament: | Con | 39 |
| | Lib-Con | 7 |
| | Irish Nat | 2 |
| | Total | 94 |

# Appendix

Table 3

# The railway interest in the House of Commons 1880–4

| | Total | %age | Govt office holders | New members[12] | Foreign rlwys | Local rlwys | National rlwys |
|---|---|---|---|---|---|---|---|
| **1880** | | | | | | | |
| Lib | 56 | 57.7 | 5 | 13 | 3 | 34 | 19[10] |
| Con | 37[8] | 38.2 | 0 | 5 | 3 | 19[8] | 15 |
| Irish Nat | 4 | 4.1 | 0 | 0 | 0 | 4 | 0 |
| Total | 97 | | 5 | 18 | 6 | 57 | 34 |
| **1881** | | | | | | | |
| Lib | 53 | 53.6 | 5 | 3 | 2 | 29 | 22[10] |
| Con | 42[8] | 42.4 | 0 | 7 | 5 | 20[8] | 17 |
| Irish Nat | 4 | 4.0 | 0 | 0 | 0 | 4 | 0 |
| Total | 99 | | 5 | 10 | 7 | 53 | 39 |
| **1882** | | | | | | | |
| Lib | 56 | 52.3 | 4 | 7 | 3 | 32 | 21[10] |
| Con | 46[8] | 43.0 | 0 | 7 | 7 | 22[8] | 17 |
| Irish Nat | 5 | 4.7 | 0 | 0 | 0 | 5 | 0 |
| Total | 107 | | 4 | 14 | 10 | 59 | 38 |
| **1883** | | | | | | | |
| Lib | 54 | 53.5 | 4 | 3 | 5 | 29 | 20[10] |
| Con | 43[8] | 42.5 | 0 | 2 | 8 | 17[8] | 18 |
| Irish Nat | 4 | 4.0 | 0 | 0 | 0 | 4 | 0 |
| Total | 101 | | 4 | 5 | 13 | 50 | 38 |
| **1884** | | | | | | | |
| Lib | 55 | 50.9 | 4 | 5 | 6 | 29 | 20[10] |
| Con | 48[8] | 44.5 | 0 | 6 | 8 | 19[8] | 21 |
| Irish Nat | 5 | 4.6 | 0 | 1 | 0 | 5 | 0 |
| Total | 108 | | 4 | 12 | 14 | 53 | 41 |

Number of director-M.P.s elected in 1880
who sat in the previous Parliament:

| | |
|---|---|
| Lib | 33 |
| Con | 32[8] |
| Irish Nat | 4 |
| Total | 69 |

Table 4

# The railway interest in the House of Lords 1868–73

| | Total | %age | Govt office holders | New members[13] | Foreign rlwys | Local rlwys | National rlwys |
|---|---|---|---|---|---|---|---|
| *1868* | | | | | | | |
| Lib | 16 | 22.2 | 1 | | 0 | 14 | 2 |
| Con | 26 | 54.2 | 0 | | 1 | 21 | 4 |
| Lib-Con | 6 | 12.5 | 0 | | 0 | 3 | 3 |
| Total | 48 | | 1 | | 1 | 38 | 9 |
| *1869* | | | | | | | |
| Lib | 20 | 41.7 | 1 | 4 | 0 | 16 | 4 |
| Con | 22 | 45.8 | 0 | 0 | 1 | 17 | 4 |
| Lib-Con | 6 | 12.5 | 0 | 0 | 0 | 3 | 3 |
| Total | 48 | | 1 | 4 | 1 | 36 | 11 |
| *1870* | | | | | | | |
| Lib | 20 | 45.4 | 1 | 2 | 1 | 14 | 5 |
| Con | 19 | 43.2 | 0 | 1 | 0 | 15 | 4 |
| Lib-Con | 5 | 11.4 | 0 | 0 | 0 | 2 | 3 |
| Total | 44 | | 1 | 3 | 1 | 31 | 12 |
| *1871* | | | | | | | |
| Lib | 19 | 39.6 | 1 | 1 | 1 | 13 | 5 |
| Con | 20 | 41.7 | 0 | 1 | 1 | 15 | 4 |
| Lib-Con | 6 | 12.5 | 0 | 1 | 0 | 3 | 3 |
| Others | 3 | 6.2 | 0 | 3 | 0 | 3 | 0 |
| Total | 48 | | 1 | 6 | 2 | 34 | 12 |
| *1872* | | | | | | | |
| Lib | 19 | 36.6 | 1 | 1 | 1 | 14 | 4 |
| Con | 21 | 40.4 | 0 | 4 | 1 | 16 | 4 |
| Lib-Con | 8 | 15.4 | 0 | 2 | 0 | 5 | 3 |
| Others | 4 | 7.6 | 0 | 1 | 0 | 4 | 0 |
| Total | 52 | | 1 | 8 | 2 | 39 | 11 |
| *1873* | | | | | | | |
| Lib | 19 | 35.2 | 1 | 1 | 1 | 14 | 4 |
| Con | 21 | 38.9 | 0 | 0 | 1 | 16 | 4 |
| Lib-Con | 8 | 14.8 | 0 | 0 | 0 | 5 | 3 |
| Others | 6 | 11.1 | 0 | 2 | 0 | 6 | 0 |
| Total | 54 | | 1 | 3 | 2 | 41 | 11 |

# Appendix

Table 5

## The railway interest in the House of Lords 1874–9

| | Total | %age | Govt office holders | New members[14] | Foreign rlwys | Local rlwys | National rlwys |
|---|---|---|---|---|---|---|---|
| *1874* | | | | | | | |
| Lib | 16 | 37.2 | 0 | | 0 | 11 | 5 |
| Con | 16 | 37.2 | 0 | | 1 | 11 | 4 |
| Lib-Con | 9 | 20.9 | 0 | | 0 | 6 | 3 |
| Others | 2 | 4.7 | 0 | | 0 | 2 | 0 |
| Total | 43 | | 0 | | 1 | 30 | 12 |
| *1875* | | | | | | | |
| Lib | 16 | 34.8 | 0 | 2 | 0 | 11 | 5 |
| Con | 21 | 45.6 | 0 | 3 | 0 | 16 | 5 |
| Lib-Con | 8 | 17.4 | 0 | 1 | 0 | 5 | 3 |
| Others | 1 | 2.2 | 0 | 0 | 0 | 1 | 0 |
| Total | 46 | | 0 | 6 | 0 | 33 | 13 |
| *1876* | | | | | | | |
| Lib | 18 | 40.9 | 0 | 3 | 0 | 12 | 6 |
| Con | 18 | 40.9 | 0 | 1 | 0 | 13 | 5 |
| Lib-Con | 8 | 18.2 | 0 | 0 | 0 | 6 | 2 |
| Total | 44 | | 0 | 4 | 0 | 31 | 13 |
| *1877* | | | | | | | |
| Lib | 19 | 40.4 | 0 | 1 | 0 | 13 | 6 |
| Con | 20 | 42.6 | 0 | 2 | 0 | 15 | 5 |
| Lib-Con | 8 | 17.0 | 0 | 0 | 0 | 6 | 2 |
| Total | 47 | | 0 | 3 | 0 | 34 | 13 |
| *1878* | | | | | | | |
| Lib | 16 | 36.4 | 0 | 1 | 0 | 11 | 5 |
| Con | 20 | 45.4 | 0 | 2 | 0 | 14 | 6 |
| Lib-Con | 8 | 18.2 | 0 | 0 | 0 | 6 | 2 |
| Total | 44 | | 0 | 3 | 0 | 31 | 13 |
| *1879* | | | | | | | |
| Lib | 16 | 37.2 | 0 | 2 | 0 | 9 | 7 |
| Con | 19 | 44.2 | 0 | 2 | 0 | 14 | 5 |
| Lib-Con | 8 | 18.6 | 0 | 0 | 0 | 6 | 2 |
| Total | 43 | | 0 | 4 | 0 | 29 | 14 |

Table 6

# The railway interest in the House of Lords 1880–4

| | Total | %age | Govt office holders | New members[15] | Foreign rlwys | Local rlwys | National rlwys |
|---|---|---|---|---|---|---|---|
| *1880* | | | | | | | |
| Lib | 20 | 38.5 | 3 | | 0 | 10 | 10 |
| Con | 23 | 44.5 | 0 | | 2 | 17 | 4 |
| Lib-Con | 6 | 11.5 | 0 | | 0 | 4 | 2 |
| Others | 3 | 5.8 | 0 | | 0 | 3 | 0 |
| Total | 52 | | 3 | | 2 | 34 | 16 |
| *1881* | | | | | | | |
| Lib | 20 | 38.5 | 3 | 3 | 0 | 8 | 12 |
| Con | 22 | 42.3 | 0 | 2 | 2 | 15 | 5 |
| Lib-Con | 5 | 9.6 | 0 | 0 | 0 | 3 | 2 |
| Others | 5 | 9.6 | 0 | 2 | 0 | 5 | 0 |
| Total | 52 | | 3 | 7 | 2 | 31 | 19 |
| *1882* | | | | | | | |
| Lib | 20 | 39.2 | 3 | 1 | 0 | 7 | 13 |
| Con | 22 | 43.1 | 0 | 2 | 1 | 15 | 6 |
| Lib-Con | 5 | 9.9 | 0 | 0 | 0 | 4 | 1 |
| Others | 4 | 7.8 | 0 | 0 | 0 | 4 | 0 |
| Total | 51 | | 3 | 3 | 1 | 30 | 20 |
| | 19 | 37.2 | 2 | 0 | 0 | 5 | 14 |
| Con | 24 | 47.1 | 0 | 2 | 1 | 18 | 5 |
| Lib-Con | 5 | 9.8 | 0 | 1 | 0 | 3 | 2 |
| Others | 3 | 5.9 | 0 | 0 | 0 | 3 | 0 |
| Total | 51 | | 2 | 3 | 1 | 29 | 21 |
| *1884* | | | | | | | |
| Lib | 19 | 42.1 | 2 | 1 | 0 | 4 | 15 |
| Con | 20 | 44.5 | 0 | 2 | 1 | 16 | 3 |
| Lib-Con | 4 | 8.9 | 0 | 0 | 0 | 3 | 1 |
| Others | 2 | 4.5 | 0 | 0 | 0 | 2 | 0 |
| Total | 45 | | 2 | 3 | 1 | 25 | 19 |

# Appendix

Table 7
## The railway interest in the House of Commons 1885–91

| | Total | %age | Govt office holders | New members[16] | Foreign rlwys | Local rlwys | National rlwys |
|---|---|---|---|---|---|---|---|
| **1885** | | | | | | | |
| Lib | 43 | 51.2 | 0 | 12 | 7 | 16 | 20[10] |
| Con | 39 | 46.4 | 6 | 15 | 6 | 14 | 19 |
| Irish Nat | 2 | 2.4 | 0 | 1 | 0 | 2 | 0 |
| Total | 84 | | 6 | 28 | 13 | 32 | 39 |
| **1886** | | | | | | | |
| Lib | 20[17] | 24.7 | 0 | 2 | 4 | 8 | 8[17] |
| Con | 48[18] | 59.2 | 7 | 4 | 7 | 18 | 23[18] |
| L.U. | 11 | 13.6 | 0 | 1 | 1 | 7 | 3 |
| Irish Nat | 2 | 2.5 | 0 | 0 | 0 | 2 | 0 |
| Total | 81 | | 7 | 7 | 12 | 35 | 34 |
| **1887** | | | | | | | |
| Lib | 20 | 25.6 | 0 | 2 | 5 | 8 | 7 |
| Con | 47 | 60.3 | 5 | 4 | 6 | 20 | 21 |
| L.U. | 10 | 12.8 | 0 | 1 | 1 | 5 | 4 |
| Irish Nat | 1 | 1.3 | 0 | 0 | 0 | 1 | 0 |
| Total | 78 | | 5 | 7 | 12 | 34 | 32 |
| **1888** | | | | | | | |
| Lib | 20 | 25.1 | 0 | 1 | 5 | 7 | 8 |
| Con | 48 | 60.1 | 6 | 5 | 7 | 20 | 21 |
| L.U. | 11 | 13.8 | 0 | 0 | 1 | 6 | 4 |
| Irish Nat | 1 | 1.0 | 0 | 0 | 0 | 1 | 0 |
| Total | 80 | | 6 | 6 | 13 | 34 | 33 |
| **1889** | | | | | | | |
| Lib | 21 | 24.4 | 0 | 2 | 4 | 8 | 9 |
| Con | 53 | 61.6 | 6 | 7 | 9 | 22 | 22 |
| L.U. | 11 | 12.8 | 0 | 1 | 1 | 5 | 5 |
| Irish Nat | 1 | 1.2 | 0 | 0 | 0 | 1 | 0 |
| Total | 86 | | 6 | 10 | 14 | 36 | 36 |
| **1890** | | | | | | | |
| Lib | 22 | 23.9 | 0 | 2 | 4 | 10 | 8 |
| Con | 57 | 62.0 | 7 | 5 | 10 | 23 | 24 |
| L.U. | 12 | 13.0 | 0 | 1 | 1 | 5 | 6 |
| Irish Nat | 1 | 1.1 | 0 | 0 | 0 | 1 | 0 |
| Total | 92 | | 7 | 8 | 15 | 39 | 38 |

Table 7 (*continued*)

| | Total | %age | Govt. office holders | New members | Foreign rlwys | Local rlwys | National rlwys |
|---|---|---|---|---|---|---|---|
| *1891* | | | | | | | |
| Lib | 24 | 26.1 | 0 | 2 | 5 | 10 | 9 |
| Con | 55 | 59.8 | 6 | 1 | 10 | 21 | 24 |
| L.U. | 12 | 13.0 | 0 | 2 | 1 | 5 | 6 |
| Irish Nat | 1 | 1.1 | 0 | 0 | 0 | 1 | 0 |
| Total | 92 | | 6 | 5 | 16 | 37 | 39 |

Number of director-M.P.s
elected in 1885 who sat
in the previous Parliament:

| Lib | 29 |
|---|---|
| Con | 21 |
| Total | 50 |

Number of director-M.P.s
elected in 1886 who sat
in the previous Parliament:

| Lib | 15 |
|---|---|
| Con | 36 |
| L.U. | 10 |
| Irish Nat | 2 |
| Total | 63 |

Table 8

## The Liberal Unionist railway directors in the House of Commons 1885–6

| | Total | Foreign rlwys | Local rlwys | National rlwys |
|---|---|---|---|---|
| Liberal director-M.P.s returned in 1885 who turned Unionist in 1886 | 18 | 0 | 7 | 11[19] |
| Of whom these were returned to Parliament in the 1886 election | 8 | 0 | 5 | 3 |
| And of whom these were not returned in 1886[20] | 10 | 0 | 2 | 8[19] |
| Number of L.U. M.P.s who had sat in 1885 but only became railway directors in 1886 | 2 | 1 | 1 | 0 |
| Number of L.U. directors who sat for the first time after the 1886 election | 1 | 0 | 1 | 0 |

# Appendix

Table 9

## The railway interest in the House of Commons 1892–4

| | Total | %age | Govt office holders | New members[21] | Foreign rlwys | Local rlwys | National rlwys |
|---|---|---|---|---|---|---|---|
| *1892* | | | | | | | |
| Lib | 21 | 32.3 | 2 | 3 | 3 | 11 | 7 |
| Con | 38 | 58.5 | 0 | 4 | 8 | 13 | 17 |
| L.U. | 6 | 9.2 | 0 | 0 | 0 | 2 | 4 |
| Total | 65 | | 2 | 7 | 11 | 26 | 28 |
| *1893* | | | | | | | |
| Lib | 22 | 31.0 | 3 | 3 | 4 | 9 | 9 |
| Con | 43 | 60.6 | 0 | 5 | 9 | 15 | 19 |
| L.U. | 6 | 8.4 | 0 | 1 | 0 | 2 | 4 |
| Total | 71 | | 3 | 9 | 13 | 26 | 32 |
| *1894* | | | | | | | |
| Lib | 23 | 30.2 | 3 | 1 | 4 | 9 | 10 |
| Con | 46 | 60.6 | 0 | 3 | 10 | 17 | 19 |
| L.U. | 7 | 9.2 | 0 | 1 | 0 | 1 | 6 |
| Total | 76 | | 3 | 5 | 14 | 27 | 35 |

Number of director-M.P.s elected in 1892
who sat in the previous Parliament:

| | |
|---|---|
| Lib | 17 |
| Con | 34 |
| L.U. | 5 |
| Total | 56 |

Table 10
# The railway interest in the House of Commons 1895–9

| | Total | %age | Govt office holders | New members[22] | Foreign rlwys | Local rlwys | National rlwys |
|---|---|---|---|---|---|---|---|
| **1895** | | | | | | | |
| Lib | 18 | 24.7 | 0 | 2 | 2 | 7 | 7 |
| Con | 48 | 65.8 | 5 | 6 | 8 | 14 | 26 |
| L.U. | 7 | 9.5 | 0 | 1 | 1 | 2 | 4 |
| Total | 73 | | 5 | 9 | 11 | 23 | 39 |
| **1896** | | | | | | | |
| Lib | 21 | 28.0 | 0 | 4 | 1 | 11 | 9 |
| Con | 46 | 61.3 | 5 | 2 | 5 | 13 | 28 |
| L.U. | 8 | 10.7 | 0 | 1 | 2 | 1 | 5 |
| Total | 75 | | 5 | 7 | 8 | 25 | 42 |
| **1897** | | | | | | | |
| Lib | 20 | 27.0 | 0 | 1 | 1 | 9 | 10 |
| Con | 44 | 59.5 | 6 | 2 | 5 | 11 | 28 |
| L.U. | 10 | 13.5 | 1 | 2 | 2 | 3 | 5 |
| Total | 74 | | 7 | 5 | 8 | 23 | 43 |
| **1898** | | | | | | | |
| Lib | 22 | 29.0 | 0 | 2 | 2 | 9 | 11 |
| Con | 45 | 59.2 | 7 | 4 | 5 | 11 | 29 |
| L.U. | 9 | 11.8 | 1 | 1 | 1 | 3 | 5 |
| Total | 76 | | 8 | 7 | 8 | 23 | 45 |
| **1899** | | | | | | | |
| Lib | 22 | 28.2 | 0 | 0 | 2 | 9 | 11 |
| Con | 47 | 60.3 | 7 | 2 | 6 | 11 | 30 |
| L.U. | 9 | 11.5 | 1 | 0 | 1 | 3 | 5 |
| Total | 78 | | 8 | 2 | 9 | 23 | 46 |

Number of director-M.P.s elected in 1895
who sat in the previous Parliament:

| Lib | 15 |
|---|---|
| Con | 42 |
| L.U. | 3 |
| Total | 60 |

# Appendix

## Table 11
## The railway interest in the House of Lords 1885–91

| | Total | %age | Govt office holders | New members[23] | Foreign rlwys | Local rlwys | National rlwys |
|---|---|---|---|---|---|---|---|
| **1885** | | | | | | | |
| Lib | 18 | 38.3 | 0 | | 1 | 3 | 14 |
| Con | 23 | 49.0 | 1 | | 1 | 18 | 4 |
| Lib-Con | 5 | 10.6 | 0 | | 0 | 4 | 1 |
| Others | 1 | 2.1 | 0 | | 0 | 1 | 0 |
| Total | 47 | | 1 | | 2 | 26 | 19 |
| **1886** | | | | | | | |
| Lib | 15 | 30.0 | 0 | 3 | 0 | 4 | 11 |
| Con | 24 | 48.0 | 2 | 1 | 1 | 18 | 5 |
| L.U. | 10 | 20.0 | 0 | 3 | 1 | 2 | 7 |
| Others | 1 | 2.0 | 0 | 0 | 0 | 1 | 0 |
| Total | 50 | | 2 | 7 | 2 | 25 | 23 |
| **1887** | | | | | | | |
| Lib | 14 | 25.9 | 0 | 0 | 0 | 4 | 10 |
| Con | 27 | 50.0 | 2 | 6 | 0 | 20 | 7 |
| L.U. | 12 | 22.2 | 0 | 2 | 1 | 4 | 7 |
| Others | 1 | 1.9 | 0 | 0 | 0 | 1 | 0 |
| Total | 54 | | 2 | 8 | 1 | 29 | 24 |
| **1888** | | | | | | | |
| Lib | 13 | 25.5 | 0 | 0 | 0 | 4 | 9 |
| Con | 24 | 47.0 | 2 | 1 | 0 | 17 | 7 |
| L.U. | 13 | 25.5 | 0 | 1 | 1 | 4 | 8 |
| Others | 1 | 2.0 | 0 | 0 | 0 | 1 | 0 |
| Total | 51 | | 2 | 2 | 1 | 26 | 24 |
| **1889** | | | | | | | |
| Lib | 12 | 22.6 | 0 | 0 | 0 | 3 | 9 |
| Con | 26 | 49.1 | 2 | 3 | 1 | 16 | 9 |
| L.U. | 15 | 28.3 | 0 | 3 | 3 | 5 | 7 |
| Total | 53 | | 2 | 6 | 4 | 24 | 25 |
| **1890** | | | | | | | |
| Lib | 13 | 23.7 | 0 | 2 | 0 | 4 | 9 |
| Con | 27 | 49.1 | 2 | 3 | 1 | 16 | 10 |
| L.U. | 15 | 17.2 | 0 | 0 | 3 | 4 | 8 |
| Total | 55 | | 2 | 5 | 4 | 24 | 27 |

Table 11 (*continued*)

|  | Total | %age | Govt. office holders | New members | Foreign rlwys | Local rlwys | National rlwys |
|---|---|---|---|---|---|---|---|
| *1891* | | | | | | | |
| Lib | 13 | 25.5 | 0 | 1 | 2 | 3 | 8 |
| Con | 25 | 49.0 | 2 | 2 | 1 | 14 | 10 |
| L.U. | 13 | 25.5 | 0 | 1 | 3 | 3 | 7 |
| Total | 51 | | 2 | 4 | 6 | 20 | 25 |

Table 12

# The railway interest in the House of Lords 1892–4

|  | Total | %age | Govt office holders | New members[24] | Foreign rlwys | Local rlwys | National rlwys |
|---|---|---|---|---|---|---|---|
| *1892* | | | | | | | |
| Lib | 12 | 21.4 | 2 | | 1 | 4 | 7 |
| Con | 27 | 48.2 | 0 | | 1 | 16 | 10 |
| L.U. | 17 | 30.4 | 0 | | 5 | 4 | 8 |
| Total | 56 | | 2 | | 7 | 24 | 25 |
| *1893* | | | | | | | |
| Lib | 12 | 22.6 | 3 | 2 | 1 | 4 | 7 |
| Con | 24 | 45.3 | 0 | 0 | 1 | 14 | 9 |
| L.U. | 17 | 32.1 | 0 | 0 | 5 | 4 | 8 |
| Total | 53 | | 3 | 2 | 7 | 22 | 24 |
| *1894* | | | | | | | |
| Lib | 9 | 17.6 | 2 | 0 | 1 | 2 | 6 |
| Con | 24 | 47.1 | 0 | 1 | 1 | 14 | 9 |
| L.U. | 18 | 35.3 | 0 | 1 | 5 | 4 | 9 |
| Total | 51 | | 2 | 2 | 7 | 20 | 24 |

# Appendix

Table 13

## The railway interest in the House of Lords 1895–9

| | Total | %age | Govt office holders | New members[25] | Foreign rlwys | Local rlwys | National rlwys |
|---|---|---|---|---|---|---|---|
| *1895* | | | | | | | |
| Lib | 9 | 17.0 | 0 | | 2 | 2 | 5 |
| Con | 28 | 52.8 | 4 | | 2 | 15 | 11 |
| L.U. | 16 | 30.2 | 1 | | 4 | 4 | 8 |
| Total | 53 | | 5 | | 8 | 21 | 24 |
| *1896* | | | | | | | |
| Lib | 6 | 11.1 | 0 | 0 | 0 | 2 | 4 |
| Con | 32 | 59.3 | 5 | 5 | 3 | 17 | 12 |
| L.U. | 16 | 29.6 | 1 | 0 | 4 | 4 | 8 |
| Total | 54 | | 6 | 5 | 7 | 23 | 24 |
| *1897* | | | | | | | |
| Lib | 7 | 13.7 | 0 | 0 | 1 | 2 | 4 |
| Con | 28 | 54.9 | 5 | 1 | 2 | 14 | 12 |
| L.U. | 16 | 31.4 | 1 | 0 | 4 | 4 | 8 |
| Total | 51 | | 6 | 1 | 7 | 20 | 24 |
| *1898* | | | | | | | |
| Lib | 7 | 12.3 | 0 | 0 | 1 | 2 | 4 |
| Con | 33 | 57.9 | 5 | 5 | 2 | 15 | 16 |
| L.U. | 17 | 29.8 | 1 | 1 | 5 | 3 | 9 |
| Total | 57 | | 6 | 6 | 8 | 20 | 29 |
| *1899* | | | | | | | |
| Lib | 9 | 15.3 | 0 | 1 | 2 | 2 | 5 |
| Con | 33 | 55.9 | 5 | 2 | 2 | 17 | 14 |
| L.U. | 17 | 28.8 | 1 | 2 | 4 | 6 | 7 |
| Total | 59 | | 6 | 5 | 8 | 25 | 26 |

Table 14

# The railway interest in the House of Commons 1900–5

| | Total | %age | Govt office holders | New members[26] | Foreign rlwys | Local rlwys | National rlwys |
|---|---|---|---|---|---|---|---|
| **1900** | | | | | | | |
| Lib | 18 | 24.0 | 0 | 2 | 1 | 8 | 9 |
| Con | 51 | 68.0 | 4 | 6 | 3 | 18 | 30 |
| L.U. | 5 | 6.7 | 3 | 0 | 0 | 0 | 5 |
| Irish Nat | 2 | 1.3 | 0 | 1 | 0 | 1 | 0 |
| Total | 75 | | 7 | 9 | 4 | 27 | 44 |
| **1901** | | | | | | | |
| Lib | 18 | 22.8 | 0 | 1 | 1 | 7 | 10 |
| Con | 54 | 68.4 | 4 | 5 | 4 | 18 | 32 |
| L.U. | 5 | 6.3 | 3 | 0 | 0 | 0 | 5 |
| Irish Nat | 2 | 2.5 | 0 | 1 | 0 | 2 | 0 |
| Total | 79 | | 7 | 7 | 5 | 27 | 47 |
| **1902** | | | | | | | |
| Lib | 17 | 23.3 | 0 | 1 | 1 | 8 | 8 |
| Con | 49 | 67.1 | 4 | 2 | 3 | 16 | 30 |
| L.U. | 5 | 6.9 | 3 | 0 | 0 | 0 | 5 |
| Irish Nat | 2 | 2.7 | 0 | 0 | 0 | 2 | 0 |
| Total | 73 | | 7 | 3 | 4 | 26 | 43 |
| **1903** | | | | | | | |
| Lib | 18 | 24.0 | 0 | 2 | 1 | 10 | 7 |
| Con | 50 | 66.6 | 4 | 4 | 3 | 17 | 30 |
| L.U. | 5 | 6.7 | 3 | 1 | 0 | 1 | 4 |
| Irish Nat | 2 | 2.7 | 0 | 0 | 0 | 2 | 0 |
| Total | 75 | | 7 | 7 | 4 | 30 | 41 |
| **1904** | | | | | | | |
| Lib | 17 | 23.3 | 0 | 0 | 1 | 9 | 7 |
| Con | 49 | 67.1 | 5 | 0 | 3 | 16 | 30 |
| L.U. | 6 | 8.2 | 1 | 1 | 0 | 1 | 5 |
| Irish Nat | 1 | 1.4 | 0 | 0 | 0 | 1 | 0 |
| Total | 73 | | 6 | 1 | 4 | 27 | 42 |
| **1905** | | | | | | | |
| Lib | 15 | 23.1 | 0 | 0 | 1 | 9 | 5 |
| Con | 44 | 67.7 | 3 | 1 | 3 | 16 | 25 |
| L.U. | 4 | 6.2 | 1 | 0 | 0 | 1 | 3 |
| Irish Nat | 2 | 3.0 | 0 | 1 | 0 | 2 | 0 |
| Total | 65 | | 4 | 2 | 4 | 28 | 33 |

Number of director-M.P.s
elected in 1900 who sat
in the previous Parliament:

| | |
|---|---|
| Lib | 15 |
| Con | 43 |
| L.U. | 5 |
| Total | 63 |

# Appendix

Table 15

## The railway interest in the House of Lords 1900–5

| | Total | %age | Govt office holders | New members[27] | Foreign rlwys | Local rlwys | National rlwys |
|---|---|---|---|---|---|---|---|
| **1900** | | | | | | | |
| Lib | 8 | 13.8 | 0 | | 2 | 2 | 4 |
| Con | 36 | 62.1 | 5 | | 3 | 17 | 16 |
| L.U. | 14 | 24.1 | 1 | | 3 | 4 | 7 |
| Total | 58 | | 6 | | 8 | 23 | 27 |
| **1901** | | | | | | | |
| Lib | 8 | 14.5 | 0 | 1 | 2 | 1 | 5 |
| Con | 32 | 58.2 | 4 | 0 | 3 | 15 | 14 |
| L.U. | 15 | 27.3 | 1 | 2 | 2 | 5 | 8 |
| Total | 55 | | 5 | 3 | 7 | 21 | 27 |
| **1902** | | | | | | | |
| Lib | 9 | 15.5 | 0 | 1 | 2 | 1 | 6 |
| Con | 34 | 58.6 | 3 | 6 | 3 | 16 | 15 |
| L.U. | 15 | 25.9 | 1 | 2 | 3 | 4 | 8 |
| Total | 58 | | 4 | 9 | 8 | 21 | 29 |
| **1903** | | | | | | | |
| Lib | 9 | 15.8 | 0 | 0 | 2 | 1 | 6 |
| Con | 33 | 57.9 | 2 | 1 | 3 | 16 | 14 |
| L.U. | 15 | 26.3 | 1 | 1 | 2 | 4 | 9 |
| Total | 57 | | 3 | 2 | 7 | 21 | 29 |
| **1904** | | | | | | | |
| Lib | 8 | 14.8 | 0 | 0 | 2 | 1 | 5 |
| Con | 31 | 57.4 | 2 | 0 | 3 | 15 | 13 |
| L.U. | 15 | 27.8 | 1 | 0 | 2 | 4 | 9 |
| Total | 54 | | 3 | 0 | 7 | 20 | 27 |
| **1905** | | | | | | | |
| Lib | 6 | 11.5 | 0 | 0 | 2 | 1 | 3 |
| Con | 32 | 61.5 | 2 | 2 | 3 | 13 | 16 |
| L.U. | 14 | 27.0 | 1 | 2 | 2 | 4 | 8 |
| Total | 52 | | 3 | 4 | 7 | 18 | 27 |

Table 16

# The railway interest in the House of Commons
# 1906–January 1910

| | Total | %age | Govt offices holders | New members[28] | Foreign rlwys | Local rlwys | National rlwys |
|---|---|---|---|---|---|---|---|
| *1906* | | | | | | | |
| Lib | 15 | 40.5 | 0 | 3 | 2 | 8 | 5 |
| Con | 18 | 48.7 | 0 | 0 | 2 | 4 | 12 |
| L.U. | 2 | 5.4 | 0 | 0 | 0 | 1 | 1 |
| Irish Nat | 2 | 5.4 | 0 | 0 | 0 | 2 | 0 |
| Total | 37 | | 0 | 3 | 4 | 15 | 18 |
| *1907* | | | | | | | |
| Lib | 13 | 38.2 | 0 | 1 | 2 | 6 | 5 |
| Con | 16 | 47.1 | 0 | 1 | 2 | 4 | 10 |
| L.U. | 2 | 5.6 | 0 | 1 | 0 | 1 | 1 |
| Irish Nat | 3 | 8.8 | 0 | 1 | 0 | 3 | 0 |
| Total | 34 | | 0 | 3 | 4 | 14 | 16 |
| *1908* | | | | | | | |
| Lib | 13 | 36.1 | 0 | 1 | 2 | 6 | 5 |
| Con | 18 | 50.0 | 0 | 3 | 2 | 5 | 11 |
| L.U. | 2 | 5.6 | 0 | 1 | 0 | 1 | 1 |
| Irish Nat | 3 | 8.3 | 0 | 0 | 0 | 3 | 0 |
| Total | 36 | | 0 | 5 | 4 | 15 | 17 |
| *1909* | | | | | | | |
| Lib | 19 | 42.0 | 0 | 6 | 3 | 9 | 7 |
| Con | 21 | 46.7 | 0 | 4 | 3 | 6 | 12 |
| L.U. | 2 | 4.6 | 0 | 0 | 0 | 1 | 1 |
| Irish Nat | 3 | 6.7 | 0 | 0 | 0 | 3 | 0 |
| Total | 45 | | 0 | 10 | 6 | 19 | 20 |
| *January 1910* | | | | | | | |
| Lib | 16 | 37.2 | 0 | 1 | 2 | 8 | 6 |
| Con | 23 | 53.5 | 0 | 3 | 4 | 7 | 12 |
| L.U. | 1 | 2.3 | 0 | 0 | 0 | 0 | 1 |
| Irish Nat | 3 | 7.0 | 0 | 0 | 0 | 3 | 0 |
| Total | 43 | | 0 | 4 | 6[29] | 18 | 19 |

Number of director-M.P.s
elected in 1906 who sat
in the previous Parliament:

| Lib | 11 |
|---|---|
| Con | 17 |
| L.U. | 2 |
| Irish Nat | 2 |
| Total | 32 |

Number of director-M.P.s
elected in January 1910 who sat
in the previous Parliament:

| Lib | 14 |
|---|---|
| Con | 17 |
| L.U. | 1 |
| Irish Nat | 3 |
| Total | 35 |

# Appendix

Table 17
## The railway interest in the House of Commons
## December 1910–14

| | Total | %age | Govt office holders | New members[30] | Foreign rlwys | Local rlwys | National rlwys |
|---|---|---|---|---|---|---|---|
| *December 1910* | | | | | | | |
| Lib | 10 | 26.3 | 0 | 1 | 1 | 7 | 2 |
| Con | 24 | 63.2 | 0 | 1 | 5 | 6 | 13 |
| L.U. | 1 | 2.6 | 0 | 0 | 0 | 0 | 1 |
| Irish Nat | 3 | 7.9 | 0 | 0 | 0 | 3 | 0 |
| Total | 38 | | 0 | 2 | 6 | 16 | 16 |
| *1911* | | | | | | | |
| Lib | 11 | 28.2 | 0 | 1 | 2 | 7 | 2 |
| Con | 24 | 61.5 | 0 | 2 | 6 | 5 | 13 |
| L.U. | 1 | 2.6 | 0 | 0 | 0 | 0 | 1 |
| Irish Nat | 3 | 7.7 | 0 | 0 | 0 | 3 | 0 |
| Total | 39 | | 0 | 3 | 8 | 15 | 16 |
| *1912* | | | | | | | |
| Lib | 15 | 19.4 | 0 | 5 | 3 | 8 | 4 |
| Un[31] | 32 | 62.7 | 0 | 8 | 8 | 8 | 16 |
| Irish Nat | 4 | 7.9 | 0 | 1 | 0 | 4 | 0 |
| Total | 51 | | 0 | 14 | 11 | 20 | 20 |
| *1913* | | | | | | | |
| Lib | 14 | 28.0 | 0 | 1 | 3 | 7 | 4 |
| Un | 32 | 64.0 | 0 | 3 | 8 | 7 | 17 |
| Irish Nat | 4 | 8.0 | 0 | 0 | 0 | 4 | 0 |
| Total | 50 | | 0 | 4 | 11 | 18 | 21 |
| *1914* | | | | | | | |
| Lib | 14 | 30.4 | 0 | 0 | 3 | 7 | 4 |
| Un | 28 | 60.9 | 0 | 0 | 6 | 6 | 16 |
| Irish Nat | 4 | 8.7 | 0 | 0 | 0 | 4 | 0 |
| Total | 46 | | 0 | 0 | 9 | 17 | 20 |

Number of director-M.P.s elected in December
1910 who sat in the previous Parliament:

| | |
|---|---|
| Lib | 9 |
| Con | 21 |
| L.U. | 1 |
| Irish Nat | 3 |
| Total | 34 |

Table 18

# The railway interest in the House of Lords 1906–9

|  | Total | %age | Govt office holders | New members[32] | Foreign rlwys | Local rlwys | National rlwys |
|---|---|---|---|---|---|---|---|
| *1906* | | | | | | | |
| Lib | 6 | 10.7 | 0 | | 2 | 1 | 3 |
| Con | 34 | 60.7 | 0 | | 2 | 14 | 18 |
| L.U. | 16 | 28.6 | 0 | | 3 | 4 | 9 |
| Total | 56 | | 0 | | 7 | 19 | 30 |
| *1907* | | | | | | | |
| Lib | 10 | 14.5 | 1 | 4 | 2 | 2 | 6 |
| Con | 43 | 62.3 | 0 | 8 | 2 | 18 | 23 |
| L.U. | 16 | 23.2 | 0 | 0 | 3 | 4 | 9 |
| Total | 69 | | 1 | 12 | 7 | 24 | 38 |
| *1908* | | | | | | | |
| Lib | 12 | 16.7 | 1 | 2 | 4 | 2 | 6 |
| Con | 44 | 61.1 | 0 | 3 | 2 | 20 | 22 |
| L.U. | 16 | 22.2 | 0 | 1 | 3 | 4 | 9 |
| Total | 72 | | 1 | 6 | 9 | 26 | 37 |
| *1909* | | | | | | | |
| Lib | 11 | 15.9 | 1 | 0 | 4 | 1 | 6 |
| Con | 44 | 63.8 | 0 | 0 | 2 | 20 | 22 |
| L.U. | 14 | 20.3 | 0 | 0 | 3 | 3 | 8 |
| Total | 69 | | 1 | 0 | 9 | 24 | 36 |

Table 19

# The railway interest in the House of Lords 1910–14

| | Total | %age | Govt office holders | New members[33] | Foreign rlwys | Local rlwys | National rlwys |
|---|---|---|---|---|---|---|---|
| *1910* | | | | | | | |
| Lib | 12 | 16.7 | 1 | | 5 | 1 | 6 |
| Con | 46 | 63.9 | 0 | | 2 | 21 | 23 |
| L.U. | 14 | 19.4 | 0 | | 3 | 3 | 8 |
| Total | 72 | | 1 | | 10 | 25 | 37 |
| *1911* | | | | | | | |
| Lib | 12 | 15.6 | 1 | 0 | 5 | 1 | 6 |
| Con | 48 | 62.3 | 0 | 0 | 2 | 22 | 44 |
| L.U. | 16 | 20.9 | 0 | 0 | 3 | 3 | 10 |
| Ind | 1 | 1.2 | 0 | 0 | 0 | 0 | 1 |
| Total | 77 | | 1 | 0 | 10 | 26 | 41 |
| *1912* | | | | | | | |
| Lib | 12 | 16.2 | 1 | 1 | 5 | 2 | 5 |
| Un | 61 | 82.4 | 0 | 1 | 5 | 26 | 30 |
| Ind | 1 | 1.4 | 0 | 0 | 0 | 0 | 1 |
| Total | 74 | | 1 | 2 | 10 | 28 | 36 |
| *1913* | | | | | | | |
| Lib | 12 | 16.7 | 1 | 0 | 5 | 2 | 5 |
| Un | 59 | 81.9 | 0 | 2 | 4 | 26 | 29 |
| Ind | 1 | 1.4 | 0 | 0 | 0 | 0 | 1 |
| Total | 72 | | 1 | 2 | 9 | 28 | 35 |
| *1914* | | | | | | | |
| Lib | 13 | 17.1 | 1 | 0 | 5 | 2 | 6 |
| Un | 62 | 81.6 | 0 | 4 | 5 | 27 | 30 |
| Ind | 1 | 1.3 | 0 | 0 | 0 | 0 | 1 |
| Total | 76 | | 1 | 4 | 10 | 29 | 37 |

# Bibliography

The aim of this bibliography is not to repeat information given in the references to the text, less still to provide a comprehensive guide to books on railway history, for which George Ottley's *A Bibliography of British Railway History* (1965) remains the invaluable work of reference. The bibliography which follows has two limited purposes: first, to form a summary of the main sources upon which the text is based; and second, to indicate those areas of railway history in which scholarly research has been carried out and, by implication, to point to areas where research is still awaited. Unfortunately, of the thousands of books written on railway subjects, only a handful fulfil the criteria of a professional historian. Although during the past two decades historians have turned their attention to railway history, it remains true that the vast majority of railway history books, especially company histories, concentrate excessively on technical and engineering aspects. There are gaps too in the history of railway labour; although the Amalgamated Society of Railway Servants has come under scholarly scrutiny, the history of the footplatemen's union, the Associated Society of Locomotive Engineers and Firemen, has not yet received comprehensive treatment. The history of railway safety also awaits definitive study.

Bibliography

The main subdivision of this bibliography is that between primary and secondary sources, which are further divided into published and unpublished source material. Place of publication of books, unless stated otherwise, is London.

# Primary sources

# Unpublished

1. PUBLIC RECORD OFFICE
   *Board of Trade Railway Department: Correspondence and Papers* (MT 6)
   These papers were transferred to the Ministry of Transport on its formation in 1919. There is no separate list of surviving files, which must therefore be traced through the Department's own Indexes and Registers. The net result of successive waves of official destruction and weeding of the files is that, for the period before 1906, only a fraction of the total correspondence of the Railway Department has survived intact.
   *Board of Trade Establishment Department: Correspondence and Papers* (BT 13)
   *Home Office Correspondence and Papers: Registered Papers* (HO 45)
   *Treasury Board Papers* (T 1)
   *Cabinet Office: Photographic Copies of Cabinet Papers* (CAB 37)
   *Photographic Copies of Cabinet Letters in the Royal Archives* (CAB 41)
   *Papers of G. W. Balfour* (PRO 30/60)

2. BRITISH TRANSPORT HISTORICAL RECORDS
   These records are kept in London, unless otherwise stated in square brackets, or where the class reference itself embodies the letters '(Y)', for York, or '(S)' for Edinburgh, Scotland. The Scottish records have now been transferred to the Scottish Record Office in Edinburgh.

   *Railway Company Records*
   Very little company correspondence has survived, but all important matters concerning relations with the government and with other companies were discussed at meetings of the board of direction, whose minute books have therefore formed the main source of railway company material used.

| | |
|---|---|
| BDC 1/1–2 | Bute Docks Company Minute Books, 1886–95 |
| BDJ 1/2 | Birmingham & Derby Junction Railway Minute Book, 1840–3 |
| BRY 1/4 | Barry Dock & Railway Company Directors Minute Book, 1890–5 |
| CAL 1/19–65 | Caledonian Railway Board & Committee Minutes, 1871–1914 [Edinburgh] |
| CAM 1/3–5 | Cambrian Railways Company Board Minutes, 1868–1917 |
| GCR 1/1–11 | Great Central Railway Proceedings of the Board of Directors, 1898–1917 |
| GE 1/8–32 | Great Eastern Railway Board Minutes, 1872–1916 |
| GN 1/38–64 | Great Northern Railway Minute Books, 1871–1916 |

| | |
|---|---|
| GNS 1/20 | Great North of Scotland Railway Minutes of Meetings of Proprietors, Directors & Committees, 1911–13 [Edinburgh] |
| GW 1/19 and 25–51 | Great Western Railway Minutes of the Board of Directors, 1863 and 1872–1916 |
| HR 1/20–1 | Highland Railway Minute Books, 1909–14 [Edinburgh] |
| LBS 1/83–4 | London, Brighton & South Coast Railway Minutes of Board, 1906–22 |
| LNW 1/26–42 | London & North Western Railway Board Minutes, 1869–1914 |
| LNW 1/121 | London & North Western Railway Minutes of Special Committee, 1894–1902 |
| LNW 4/120 | London & North Western Railway Memoranda Relating to Hours of Duty of Railway Servants on the London & North Western Railway, April 1891 |
| LSW 1/6–11 | London & South Western Railway Minute Books, Court of Directors, 1876–99 |
| LSW 1/26–40 | London & South Western Railway Board Minutes, Extracts, 1899–1918 |
| LVM 1/6 | Liverpool & Manchester Railway Board Minutes, 1842–5 |
| LY 1/350 and 354 | Lancashire & Yorkshire Railway Minutes of Meetings of Committees, 1896–8 |
| LY 1/452, 454, 456 and 458 | Lancashire & Yorkshire Railway Proceedings of Directors' Board, 1899–1908 |
| MID 1/21–9 | Midland Railway Minutes of the Board of Directors, 1873–1916 |
| MSL 1/13–30 | Manchester, Sheffield & Lincolnshire Railway Proceedings of the Board of Directors, 1872–97 |
| MSL 1/31 | Manchester, Sheffield & Lincolnshire Railway Proceedings of Board of Directors, 1897, and Great Central Railway Proceedings of Board of Directors, 1897–8 |
| NBR 1/18–65 | North British Railway Minute Books, 1871–1914 [Edinburgh] |
| NER 1/14–21 | North Eastern Railway Board Minutes, 1872–1921 [York] |
| NER 1/230 | North Eastern Railway Memoranda for Directors [York] |
| NER 1/389 | North Eastern Railway Minutes and Reports, 1885–6 |
| RHY 1/7–8 | Rhymney Railway Minute Books of Board of Directors, 1890–1902 |
| SEC 1/34 | South Eastern & Chatham Railway Companies' Managing Committee Minutes, 1912–13 |
| SER 1/18 and 41–63 | South Eastern Railway Board Minute Books, 1844–5 and 1871–1914 |
| TV 1/10–11 | Taff Vale Railway Directors' Minute Books, 1890–1906 |

*Railway Companies' Association Records*
As the minutes of the association were printed and distributed to the constituent companies, several sets of minutes survive, each containing some material not in the others.

# Bibliography

| | |
|---|---|
| RCA 1/1A | Minutes of Meetings of the Railway Companies' Association, 1858–61 |
| RCA 1/1B | Minutes of Meetings of the United Railway Companies' Committee and of the Railway Companies' Association, 1867–83 |
| RCA 1/2–5 | Minutes of Meetings of the Railway Companies' Association, 1883–1916 |
| RCA 1/44–50 | Minutes of Meetings of the Railway Companies' Association, 1884–1920 |
| RCA(S) 1/1–6 | Minutes of Meetings of the United Railway Companies' Committee and of the Railway Companies' Association, 1867–1919 |
| RCA(S) 1/17–18 | Minutes of Meetings of the Railway Companies' Association, 1892–1907 |
| RCA(Y) 1/2–5 | Minutes of Meetings of the Railway Companies' Association, 1882–1911 |
| RCA(Y) 1/7 | Minutes of Meetings of the Railway Companies' Association, 1911–18 |
| RCA(Y) 1/18–19 | Minutes of Meetings of the Railway Companies' Association, 1874–85 |
| RCA 4/1 | Papers Relating to the History and Constitution of the Railway Companies' Association |
| RCA 4/2 | Papers of the Southern Railway Company relating to the "Square Deal" Campaign, 1932–8 |

*Miscellaneous Records*

| | |
|---|---|
| GEN 3/1A | Papers relating to the Railway Companies' Association and its antecedents |
| HL 1/5 and 9 | Historical Letters and Relevant Documents, Great Western Collection |
| HL 2/14 | Historical Letters and Relevant Documents, London, Midland & Scottish Collection |
| HRP 1/29 | Volume containing various pamphlets, circulars, handbills, etc. |
| HRP(S) 40 | Historical Records, Papers, Notices, Forms and Circulars |
| MT 1/41 | *Railway & Canal Traffic Bill Deputation to The Rt. Hon. James Bryce, M.P. President of the Board of Trade from Members of Parliament 15th June 1894* |
| MT 1/76 | Circulars &C, Re Railway & Canal Traffic Bill 1886 |
| PYB 1/1232 | Railway Companies Rates and Charges Bills, 1885 |
| RC 1/58 | Minutes of Evidence given before the Royal Commission on Railways, 1914 |
| RCH 1/13 | Minutes of Meetings of the Railway Clearing House Committee, 1841–58 |
| SER 4/21 | Notes by Sir Edward Watkin made at meetings of the Select Committee on Railways, March–May 1881 |

3. PRIVATE PAPERS

*Beaverbrook Library*

Private Papers of David, Earl Lloyd George

Private Papers of Andrew Bonar Law
*Birmingham University Library*
Papers of Austen Chamberlain
Papers of Joseph Chamberlain
*Bishopsgate Institute*
Papers of George Jacob Holyoake
*Bodleian Library, Oxford*
Asquith MSS.
*British Museum*
Campbell-Bannerman Papers
Gladstone Papers
Iddesleigh Papers
*Christ Church, Oxford*
Salisbury Papers, Special Correspondence
*Hughenden Manor, Buckinghamshire*
Hughenden (Disraeli) Papers
*Kent Archives Office, Maidstone*
U564 Letters and Papers of Aretas Akers-Douglas, first Viscount Chilston
U951 Knatchbull MSS.
*Sheffield University Library*
Leader Correspondence (typed transcripts, made by A. J. Mundella's daughter, Maria Theresa, of letters written by her father to Robert Leader and his two sons, R. E. and J. D. Leader, proprietors of the Liberal organ the *Sheffield & Rotherham Independent*)
Mundella Correspondence (mostly letters written to Mundella)
*Williamstrip Park, Coln St Aldwyns, Gloucestershire*
Hicks Beach MSS.

# Published

1. DEBATES
   *Parliamentary Debates,* 3rd and 4th series
   *Commons' Debates,* 5th series
   *Lords' Debates,* 5th series

2. JOURNALS OF THE HOUSE OF LORDS

3. DIVISION LISTS OF THE HOUSE OF COMMONS

4. PARLIAMENTARY PAPERS
   *Bills: House of Commons Papers*

| | |
|---|---|
| *1871*, v (5) | Regulation of Railways |
| *1873*, iv (34) | Railway and Canal Traffic |
| *1873*, iv (121) | Railway and Canal Traffic, as amended in Committee |
| *1873*, iv (232) | Regulation of Railways |
| *1874*, v (91) | Workpeople's Compensation |
| *1875*, i (186) | Workpeople's Compensation |
| *1876*, ii (15) | Employers' Liability for Injury |

# Bibliography

| | |
|---|---|
| *1878*, ii (11) | Employers' Liability for Injury |
| *1878–9*, iii (75) | Employers' Liability for Injury |
| *1878–9*, iii (80) | Employers' Liability for Injury |
| *1878–9*, iii (103) | Employers' Liability for Injury |
| *1878–9*, v (270) | Regulation of Railways Acts Continuance |
| *1880*, iii (57) | Employers' Liability (Railway Servants) [not printed] |
| *1880*, iii (118) | Employers' Liability for Injury |
| *1880*, iii (209) | Employers' Liability for Injury |
| *1883*, ix (219) | Railway Passenger Duty |
| *1883*, ix (255) | Railway Passenger Duty, as amended in Committee |
| *1884*, vi (225) | Regulation of Railways Acts Amendment |
| *1886*, v (97) | Railway Regulation |
| *1886*, v (138) | Railway and Canal Traffic |
| *1887*, v (126) | Railway Regulation |
| *1888*, vi (49) | Railway and Canal Companies Charges |
| *1888*, vi (72) | Railway Companies (Carriage of Fish) |
| *1888*, vi (333) | Railway and Canal Traffic [H.L.], as amended by the Standing Committee on Trade |
| *1889*, vii (333) | Regulation of Railways |
| *1889*, vii (360) | Regulation of Railways (No. 2) |
| *1893–94*, iii (53) | Railway Servants (Hours of Labour) |
| *1893–94*, iii (93) | Crown, Municipal, and Railway Servants' Eight Hours |
| *1893–94*, vii (90) | Regulation of Railways Act, 1889, Amendment |
| *1893–94*, vii (165) | Railway Servants (Hours of Labour) |
| *1893–94*, vii (226) | Railway Servants (Hours of Labour) |
| *1893–94*, vii (309) | Railway Companies Charges |
| *1894*, viii (156) | Railway and Canal Traffic Act, 1888, Amendment |
| *1897*, vii (213) | Workmen (Compensation for Accidents) |
| *1899*, vi (99) | Regulation of Railways |
| *1900*, iv (78) | Railway Employment (Prevention of Accidents) |
| *1903*, iv (9) | Railways (Private Sidings) |
| *1904*, iv (4) | Railways (Private Sidings) |
| *1905*, i (17) | Compensation for Damage to Crops |
| *1906*, iv (324) | Railways (Contracts) |
| *1907*, iv (9) | Railways (Contracts) |
| *1910*, v (169) | Railway Companies (Accounts and Returns) |
| *1912–13*, v (124) | Railways |
| *1912–13*, v (331) | Railways (No. 2) |

*Bills: House of Lords Papers*
The set of House of Lords Papers consulted was that in the State Paper Room of the British Museum. Where the arrangement in the British Museum bound volumes differs from that of the official bound set, the British Museum reference is given instead.

| | |
|---|---|
| [*H.L.*] *1873*, vi (12) | Regulation of Railways (Prevention of Accidents [H.L.] |
| [*H.L.*] *1877*, v (46) | Railway Servants (H.L.) |
| [*H.L.*] *1878*, vi (75) | Railway Returns (Continuous Brakes) [H.L.] |

| | |
|---|---|
| [*H.L.*] *1878–9*, vi (7) | Employers' Liability [H.L.] |
| [*H.L.*] *1880*, iii (4) | Employers' Liability [H.L.] |
| [*H.L.*] *1880*, iii (199b) | Employers' Liability Bill. Amendments to be moved in Committee |
| [*H.L.*] *1882* (B.M. bound volume) | Bills, Vol. 4, bill 21: Railways (Continuous Brakes) [H.L.] |
| [*H.L.*] *1887* (B.M. bound volume) | Bills, II, bill 32: Railway and Canal Traffic [H.L.] |
| [*H.L.*] *1888* (B.M. bound volume) | Bills, III, bill 21: Railway and Canal Traffic [H.L.] |

*Reports from Committees: House of Commons Papers*

| | |
|---|---|
| *1841*, viii (354) | Report from the Select Committee on Railways, with the Minutes of Evidence |
| *1872*, xiii parts I and II (364) | Report from the Joint Select Committee on Railway Companies Amalgamation, with the Minutes of Evidence |
| *1873*, xiv (148) | Report from the Select Committee of the House of Lords on the Regulation of Railways (Prevention of Accidents) Bill [H.L.], with the Minutes of Evidence |
| *1876*, xiii (312) | Report from the Select Committee on Railway Passenger Duty, with Minutes of Evidence |
| *1877*, x (285) | Report from the Select Committee on Employers' Liability, with the Minutes of Evidence |
| *1881*, xiii (374) xiv (374–I) | Report from the Select Committee on Railways, with the Minutes of Evidence |
| *1882*, vii (235) | Report from the Select Committee on Artizans' and Labourers' Dwellings Improvement, with the Minutes of Evidence |
| *1882*, xiii (317) | Report from the Select Committee on Railways (Rates and Fares), with the Minutes of Evidence |
| *1888*, xvii (286) | Report from the Standing Committee on Trade on the Railway and Canal Traffic [H.L.] Bill |
| *1890–91*, xiv (394) xv (394) | Report from the Joint Select Committee on the Railway Rates and Charges Provisional Order Bills, with the Minutes of Evidence |
| *1890–91*, xvi (342) | Report from the Select Committee on Railway Servants (Hours of Labour) with the Minutes of Evidence |
| *1892*, xv (187) | Report from the Joint Select Committee on the Railway Rates and Charges Provisional Order Bills, with the Minutes of Evidence |
| *1892*, xvi (125) | Special Report from the Select Committee on Railway Servants (Hours of Labour) with the Minutes of Evidence |
| *1892*, xvi (246) | Report from the Select Committee on Railway Servants (Hours of Labour), with the Minutes of Evidence |
| *1893–94*, xiv (385) | First Report from the Select Committee on Railway Rates and Charges, with the Minutes of Evidence |

*1893–94*, xiv (462)    Second Report from the Select Committee on Railway Rates and Charges, with the Minutes of Evidence

*1893–94*, xv (124)    Report from the Standing Committee on Trade on the Railway Servants (Hours of Labour) Bill

*1900*, viii (175)    Report from the Standing Committee on Trade on the Railways (Prevention of Accidents) Bill

*1904*, vi (133)    Report from the Standing Committee on Trade on the Railways (Private Sidings) Bill

*1905*, vii (97)    Report from the Standing Committee on Trade on the Compensation for Damage to Crops Bill

*1907*, viii (96)    Report from the Standing Committee on Trade on the Railways (Contracts) Bill

*1910*, vi (225)    Report from Standing Committee B on the Railway Companies (Accounts and Returns) Bill

*Reports of Commissions and Departmental Committees: House of Commons Papers*

*1867*, xxxviii part I [3844]  Report of the Royal Commission on Railways

*1877*, xlviii [C–1637]    Report of the Royal Commission on Railway Acci-
[C–1637–I]    dents, with the Minutes of Evidence

*1884–5*, xxx [C–4402–I]    The Royal Commission on the Housing of the Working Classes: Minutes of Evidence as to England and Wales

*1893–94*, xxxiii [C–6894–    The Royal Commission on Labour: Minutes of
VIII]    Evidence taken before Group 'B', Transport and Agriculture

*1894*, xxxv [C–7421–I]    Royal Commission on Labour: Fifth and Final Report Part II: Secretary's Report

*1900*, xxvii [Cd–41]    Report of the Royal Commission appointed to En-
[Cd–42]    quire into the Causes of Accidents, Fatal and Non-Fatal, to Servants of Railway Companies and of Truck Owners, with the Minutes of Evidence

*1905*, lxxv [Cd. 2334]    Minutes of Evidence taken before the Departmental Committee appointed by the Home Office to inquire into the Law relating to Compensation for Injuries to Workmen

*1906*, lv [Cd. 2959]    Report of the Departmental Committee appointed by the Board of Agriculture to inquire into Railway Rates (Preferential Treatment)

*1909*, lxxvi [Cd. 4697]    Report of the Departmental Committee of the Board of Trade on Railway Accounts and Statistical Returns

*1911*, xxix part I    Report of the Royal Commission appointed to investi-
[Cd. 5922]    gate and report on the working of the Railway Conciliation and Arbitration Scheme of 1907

*1911*, xxix part II    Report of the Departmental Committee of the Board
[Cd. 5631]    of Trade on Railway Agreements and Amalgamations,
[Cd. 5927]    with the Minutes of Evidence

*1912–13*, xlv [Cd. 6014]    Minutes of Evidence taken before the Royal Commission appointed to investigate and report on the

working of the Railway Conciliation and Arbitration
Scheme of 1907

*Accounts and Papers: House of Commons Papers*

*1841*, xxv [287]          Report of the Officers of the Railway Department to
                           the President of the Board of Trade

*1874*, lviii (64)         Copy of Board of Trade Circular to Railway Com-
                           panies, 18 November 1873, relative to accidents, with
                           Correspondence

*1877*, lxxii [C–1866]     General Report to the Board of Trade upon railway
                           accidents in the United Kingdom during 1876

*1877*, lxxiii [C–1755]    Continuous Railway Brakes: Copy of Correspondence
                           between the Board of Trade and the Railway Com-
                           panies' Association, and Returns from companies
                           belonging to the association

*1878*, xxv [C–1962]       Fourth Annual Report of the Railway Commissioners

*1878*, lxvi [C–1921]      Copy of Circular issued by the Board of Trade to the
                           Railway Companies of the United Kingdom, with
                           reference to Continuous Brakes, with Correspondence

*1878*, lxvi [C–1963]      Returns of the Several Companies, parties to the
                           Railway Companies' Association, with reference to
                           continuous brakes on passenger trains

*1880*, lxiv [C–1677]      Replies to Circular Letter of the Board of Trade,
                           10 June 1880, with reference to the Adoption of
                           Continuous Brakes

*1881*, lxxxi [C–2857]     Copy of Circular Letter, 20 September 1880, with
                           reference to the Interlocking of Points and Signals,
                           with the replies of the railway companies

*1883*, lxi [C–3535]       Report to the Board of Trade upon the Subject of
                           Workmen's Trains on the Metropolitan Lines

*1886*, lviii [C–4648]     Continuous Brakes: Return by the Railway Com-
                           panies of the United Kingdom

*1890*, lxv [C–5966]       Continuous Brakes: Return by the Railway Com-
                           panies of the United Kingdom

*1890*, lxv [C–6013]       Railway Accidents: Returns of Accidents and Casual-
                           ties during 1889, with Reports of the Inspecting
                           Officers of the Railway Department

*1893–4*, lxxix (502)      Railway Companies (Injuries to Servants). Return
                           showing the Number of Servants killed and injured by
                           Accidents in which the Movement of Vehicles was
                           concerned, during 1870, 1873, 1877, and 1880 to 1892

*1893–4*, lxxix [C–7044]   Railway Rates and Charges: Correspondence between
                           the Board of Trade and the Railway Companies'
                           Association and various railway companies

*1894*, lxxv [C–7542]      Railways (Workmen's Trains on the Metropolitan
                           Lines): Notes of Conference at the Board of Trade,
                           28 June 1893, with representatives of the London
                           County Council and the railway companies having

|  |  |
|---|---|
|  | termini in the Metropolis, with subsequent correspondence |
| *1895*, lxxxvi [C–7567] | Railways (Workwomen's Trains on the Metropolitan Lines): Copy of Correspondence between the Board of Trade and the Railway Companies having termini in the Metropolis |
| *1899*, lxxxv [C–9183] | Memorandum upon the Use of Automatic Couplings on Rolling Stock, with special reference to American Experience |
| *1904*, lxxxiv [Cd. 2045] | Railway Rates and Facilities: Copy of Correspondence between the Board of Agriculture and Fisheries and the Railway Companies in Great Britain |
| *1908*, xcv (312) | Return of Charitable and other Contributions made by the Railway Companies of the United Kingdom during 1907 |
| *1909*, lxxvii (263) | Return of Charitable and other Contributions made by the Railway Companies of the United Kingdom during 1908 |
| *1909*, lxxvii [Cd. 4534] | Report to the Board of Trade upon Matters connected with the Establishment and Working of Railway Conciliation Boards |
| *1909*, lxxvii [Cd. 4677] | Report of the Board of Trade Railway Conference |
| *1909*, lxxvii [Cd. 4695] | Heads of Agreement between the London & North Western and Midland Railway Companies, and between the London & North Western, Midland, and Lancashire & Yorkshire Railway Companies |
| *1910*, lxxx (277) | Return of Charitable and other Contributions made by the Railway Companies of the United Kingdom during 1909 |
| *1911*, lxx (266) | Return of Charitable and other Contributions made by the Railway Companies of the United Kingdom during 1910 |
| *1912–13*, lxxiv (100) | Memorandum explanatory of the Railway Bill |

5. STATUTES

*Public General*

| | |
|---|---|
| 2 & 3 Wm IV, c. 120 | Act for Imposing a Passenger Duty, 1832 |
| 3 & 4 Vict., c. 97 | Act for Regulating Railways, 1840 |
| 5 & 6 Vict., c. 55 | Railway Regulation Act, 1842 |
| 5 & 6 Vict., c. 79 | Railway Passenger Duty Act, 1842 |
| 7 & 8 Vict., c. 85 | Railways Act, 1844 |
| 8 & 9 Vict., c. 20 | Railway Clauses Consolidation Act, 1845 |
| 9 & 10 Vict., c. 93 | Act for Compensating the Families of Persons killed by Accidents (Lord Campbell's Act) 1846 |
| 17 & 18 Vict., c. 31 | Railway and Canal Traffic Act, 1854 |
| 31 & 32 Vict., c. 119 | Regulation of Railways Act, 1868 |
| 34 & 35 Vict., c. 78 | Regulation of Railways Act, 1871 |
| 36 & 37 Vict., c. 48 | Railway and Canal Traffic Act, 1873 |

| | |
|---|---|
| 36 & 37 Vict., c. 76 | Regulation of Railways (Returns) Act, 1873 |
| 41 & 42 Vict., c. 20 | Railway Returns (Continuous Brakes) Act, 1878 |
| 42 & 43 Vict., c. 56 | Regulation of Railways Acts Continuance Act, 1879 |
| 43 & 44 Vict., c. 42 | Employers' Liability Act, 1880 |
| 46 & 47 Vict., c. 34 | Cheap Trains Act, 1883 |
| 51 & 52 Vict., c. 25 | Railway and Canal Traffic Act, 1888 |
| 52 & 53 Vict., c. 57 | Regulation of Railways Act, 1889 |
| 55 & 56 Vict., c. 64 | Witnesses (Public Inquiries) Protection Act, 1892 |
| 56 & 57 Vict., c. 29 | Railway Servants (Hours of Labour) Act, 1893 |
| 57 & 58 Vict., c. 54 | Railway and Canal Traffic Act, 1894 |
| 60 & 61 Vict., c. 37 | Workmen's Compensation Act, 1897 |
| 63 & 64 Vict., c. 27 | Railway Employment (Prevention of Accidents) Act, 1900 |
| 4 Edw VII, c. 19 | Railways (Private Sidings) Act, 1904 |
| 5 Edw VII, c. 11 | Compensation for Damage to Crops Act, 1905 |
| 1 & 2 Geo V, c. 34 | Railway Companies (Accounts and Returns) Act, 1911 |
| 2 & 3 Geo V, c. 29 | Railway and Canal Traffic Act, 1913 |
| 11 & 12 Geo V, c. 32 | Finance Act, 1921 |
| 11 & 12 Geo V, c. 55 | Railways Act, 1921 |
| 19 & 20 Geo V, c. 21 | Finance Act, 1929 |
| *Local and Personal* | |
| 54 & 55 Vict., c. ccxiv–ccxxii | Railway Rates and Charges Provisional Orders Confirmation Acts, 1891 |
| 55 & 56 Vict., c. xxxix–lxiv | Railway Rates and Charges Provisional Orders Confirmation Acts, 1892 |

6. NEWSPAPERS AND PERIODICALS
*Agricultural Economist*
*Birmingham Mail*
*Builders' Journal and Architectural Engineer*
*Carnarvon and Denbigh Herald*
*Chamber of Commerce Journal*
*Commonwealth*
*Crewe and Nantwich Chronicle*
*Daily Chronicle*
*Daily Express*
*Daily Herald*
*Daily News*
*Daily Telegraph*
*Dundee Advertiser*
*Echo*
*Economist*
*Engineer*
*Evening News*
*Evening Standard*
*Fairplay*
*Financial Times*
*Financier and Bullionist*

*Free Labour Gazette*
*Free Labour Press*
*Glasgow Herald*
*Globe*
*Hampshire Advertiser*
*Hampshire Independent*
*Herapath's Railway and Commercial Journal* (from 1894, *Herapath's Railway Journal*)
*Leicester Daily Post*
*Liverpool Daily Post*
*London Catholic Herald*
*Manchester Courier*
*Manchester Examiner & Times*
*Manchester Guardian*
*Mark Lane Express*
*Mirror of the North* (Aberdeen)
*Modern Transport*
*Money*
*Morning Post*
*Nation*
*Newcastle Daily Chronicle*
*North Wales Observer and Express*
*Pall Mall Gazette*
*Produce Markets' Review*
*Railway Clerk*
*Railway Engineer*
*Railway Gazette*
*Railway News*
*Railway Press*
*Railway Record*
*Railway Review*
*Railway Service Gazette*
*Railway Times*
*Salopian and Montgomeryshire Post*
*Sheffield & Rotherham Independent*
*Society*
*South Wales Daily News*
*Standard*
*Statist*
*Stock Exchange Gazette*
*The Times*
*Transport*
*Tribune*
*Western Daily Mercury* (Plymouth)
*Western Mail* (Cardiff)
*Western Times* (Exeter)
*Wilts and Glo'stershire Standard*
*World's Carriers and Carrying Trades' Review*

*Yorkshire Gazette*
*Yorkshire Observer*
*Yorkshire Post*

7. DIRECTORIES AND MANUALS
   *Annual Register*
   *Bradshaw's Railway Almanack, Directory, Shareholders' Guide and Manual,*
      1848 (two editions) and 1849
   *Bradshaw's General Railway Directory,* 1850–2
   *Bradshaw's Shareholders' Guide,* 1853–62
   *Bradshaw's Railway Manual, Shareholders' Guide and Official Directory,* 1863–1923
   *Directory of Directors*
   *Dod's Parliamentary Companion*
   *The New House of Commons* . . ., 1880, 1885, 1892, 1895, 1900, 1910
   *The New Parliament: Ward and Lock's Guide to the House of Commons 1880*
   *The Parliamentary Directory of the Professional, Commercial, And Mercantile*
      *Members of the House of Commons,* 1874
   *The Popular Guide to the House of Commons* (Pall Mall Gazette 'Extra'), 1906 and
      1910
   *The Royal Kalendar*

8. LAW REPORTS

9. BOOKS, ARTICLES AND PAMPHLETS
   *Amalgamations of Railway Companies* . . . *Report of Special Committee* (Liverpool, 1872)
   F. G. Banbury, *Railways Bill: Memorandum by the Chairman of the Great Northern Railway Company* (1921)
   S. Carter, *Railway Legislation: a letter to shareholders* . . . (1874)
   C. D. Collet, *Reasons for the Repeal of the Railway Passenger Duty* (1877)
   E. J. O'B. Croker, *Retrospective Lessons on Railway Strikes* (Cork, 1898)
   C. Edwards, *Railway Nationalisation* (1898)
   W. J. Gordon, *Every-day Life on the Railroad,* 2nd edn, revised (1898)
   C. H. Grinling, *The Ways of Our Railways* (1905)
   F. Harrison, 'The Conservative Reaction', *Fortnightly Review,* New Series, xv (1874), 297–309
   "Hercules", *British Railways and Canals in Relation to British Trade and Government Control* [1884]
   W. A. Hunter, *The Railway & Canal Traders' Association: The New Railway Rates Bills* . . . [1885]
   W. R. Lawson, *British Railways A Financial and Commercial Survey* (1913).
   Liverpool Chamber of Commerce, *Railway Companies' Amalgamation: Report of the Railways, Transit, and Parliamentary Committee* . . . (Liverpool, 1873
   *Lord Bramwell on Liberty and Other Speeches, delivered at the General Meeting of the Liberty and Property Defence League, 1882* (1883)
   A. H. Loring (ed), *Papers and Addresses by Lord Brassey* . . . *Political and Miscellaneous From 1861 to 1894* (1895)

Manchester and Lancashire and Cheshire Corporations, *Railway Rates & Charges . . . Report on the Bills by Sub-Committee on Proposed Alterations in the Law* (Manchester, 1885)

J. B. Maple, *Cheap Trains for London Workers* [1891]

S. A. Pope, 'The Cheap Trains Act, 1883, and its equitable Interpretation . . .', *Great Western Railway (London) Lecture and Debating Society, Session 1905–6*, meeting of 22 February 1906

J. N. Porter, *The Railway Passenger Duty: Its Injustice and its Repeal, considered . . .* (1874)

'Queen Victoria and Railway Accidents', *Railway Magazine*, lxxiii (1933), 164

*Railway Rates and Charges Bills: Three Articles . . . reprinted from the 'Northern Echo'* (Darlington, 1885)

Railway Rates Committee, *Railway Rates: Joint Deputation . . . to the Right Honourable A. J. Mundella, M.P. . . .* [1886]

Railway Shareholders' Association, *Report of the Proceedings at the National Conference of Railway Shareholders, held in the Town Hall, Manchester, on Tuesday & Wednesday, April 14th & 15th, 1868* (Manchester) [1868]

*Regulation of Railways Bill: Automatic Couplings. Deputation to the Rt. Hon. C. T. Ritchie, M.P. . . . from the Mining Association of Great Britain, & C., &C.* (1899)

H. Spencer, *Railway Morals and Railway Policy reprinted from the 'Edinburgh Review' . . .* (1855) [*The Traveller's Library*, vol. 25, 1856]

C. E. Stretton, *A Few Remarks on Railway Accidents, their Cause and Prevention*, 3rd edn (1882)

Travelling Tax Abolition Committee, *Gazette*, 1878–91

10. AUTOBIOGRAPHICAL WORKS

F. A. Channing, *Memories of Midland Politics, 1885–1910* (1918)

W. Collison, *The Apostle of Free Labour* (1913)

Viscount Cross, *A Political History* (privately printed, 1903)

Sir W. B. Forwood, *Recollections of a Busy Life* (Liverpool, 1910)

W. George, *My Brother and I* (1958)

Lord Claud Hamilton, 'Fifty Years a Director of the Great Eastern Railway Company', *London and North Eastern Railway 'Great Eastern' Magazine*, vol. 13 (February 1923), 22–4

G. J. Holyoake, *Bygones Worth Remembering*, two vols (1905)

G. J. Holyoake, *History of the Travelling Tax* (1901)

C. H. D. Howard (ed), *A Political Memoir 1880–92 by Joseph Chamberlain* (1953)

Sir C. W. Macara, *Recollections* (1921)

Sir Herbert Maxwell, *Evening Memories* (1932)

# Secondary sources

## Published

1. RAILWAY SUBJECTS: BOOKS AND ARTICLES

W. M. Acworth, 'Professor Cohn and State Railway Ownership in England', *Economic Journal*, ix (1899)

# Bibliography

W. M. Acworth, *The Elements of Railway Economics* (Oxford, 1905)

W. M. Acworth, 'The State in Relation to Railways in England', in *The State in Relation to Railways Papers read at the Congress of the Royal Economic Society January 11th 1912* (1912), 5–11

G. W. Alcock, *Fifty Years of Railway Trade Unionism* (1922)

D. H. Aldcroft, 'The Efficiency and Enterprise of British Railways, 1870–1914', *Explorations in Entrepreneurial History*, V (1968), 158–74

D. H. Aldcroft, *British Railways in Transition* (1968)

M. Alfassa, *La Crise Ouvrière Récente des Chemins de Fer Anglais Une solution nouvelle des Conflits* (Paris, 1908)

C. J. Allen, *The Great Eastern Railway*, 2nd edn (1956)

W. H. G. Armytage, 'The Railway Rates Question and the Fall of the Third Gladstone Ministry', *English Historical Review*, lxv (1950), 18–51

P. S. Bagwell, *The Railwaymen* (1963)

P. S. Bagwell, 'The Railway Interest: Its Organisation and Influence 1839–1914', *Journal of Transport History*, vii (1965–6), 65–86

P. S. Bagwell, *The Railway Clearing House in the British Economy 1842–1922* (1968)

T. C. Barker and M. Robbins, *A History of London Transport,* Vol I (1963)

'British Railway Progress, 1850–1912', *The Jubilee of The Railway News* [1914], 31–3

C. D. Campbell, *British Railways in Boom and Depression* (1932)

E. Cleveland-Stevens, *English Railways Their Development and their Relation to the State* (1915)

G. Cohn, *Untersuchungen über die Englische Eisenbahnpolitik* (three vols, Leipzig, 1874, 1875, 1883)

G. D. H. Cole and R. P. Arnot, *Trade Unionism on the Railways. Its History and Problems* (1917)

G. Dow, *Great Central*, vol. III ('Fay Sets the Pace 1900–1922') (1965)

H. J. Dyos, 'Workmen's Fares in South London, 1860–1914', *Journal of Transport History*, i (1953–4), 3–19

C. H. Ellis, *British Railway History 1830–1876* (1954)

C. H. Ellis, *British Railway History 1877–1947* (1959)

E. H. Fowkes, 'Sources of History in Railway Records of British Transport Historical Records', *Journal of the Society of Archivists*, iii (1969), 476–88

J. Grierson, *Railway Rates: English and Foreign* (1886)

C. H. Grinling, *The History of the Great Northern Railway 1845–1902* (new issue, 1903)

A. T. Hadley, *Railroad Transportation Its History and its Laws* (New York, 1886)

J. A. B. Hamilton, *Britain's Railways in World War I* (1967)

J. N. Harris, 'Railways and Agricultural Society', *The Jubilee of the Railway News* [1914], 112–14

W. A. Hunter, *The Railway and Canal Traffic Act, 1888. Part I. An Exposition of Section Twenty-Four of the Act* (1889)

W. A. Jepson, 'Railway Companies' Rates', *The Jubilee of the Railway News* [1914], 89–98

R. Kenney, *Men and Rails* (1913)

P. W. Kingsford, 'Labour Relations on the Railways, 1835–75', *Journal of Transport History*, i (1953–4), 65–81

265

# Bibliography

P. W. Kingsford, *Victorian Railwaymen* (1970)

C. E. Lee, *Passenger Class Distinctions* (1946)

S. J. McLean, 'The English Railway and Canal Commission of 1888', *Quarterly Journal of Economics*, xx (1905–6), 1–58

J. Mavor, *The Scottish Railway Strike, 1891: A History and Criticism* (Edinburgh, 1891)

J. Mavor, 'The English Railway Rate Question', *Quarterly Journal of Economics*, viii (1894), 280–318 and 403–15

O. S. Nock, *Historic Railway Disasters* (1966)

H. Parris, *Government and the Railways in Nineteenth Century Britain* (1965)

'The Passing of the Railway Director', *Railway Gazette* (26 December 1947), 719–20

S. Pollard, 'North-West Coast Railway Politics in the Eighteen Sixties', *Transactions of the Cumberland & Westmorland Antiquarian & Archaeological Society*, New Series, lii (1953), 160–77

S. Pollard and J. D. Marshall, 'The Furness Railway and the Growth of Barrow', *Journal of Transport History*, i (1953–54), 109–26

H. Pollins, 'Aspects of Railway Accounting before 1868', in A. C. Littleton and B. S. Yamey (eds), *Studies in the History of Accounting* (1956), 332–55

H. Pollins, *Britain's Railways: An Industrial History* (Newton Abbot, 1971)

F. Potter, *The Government in Relation to the Railways of the Country* [1909]

'Railway Amalgamations and Agreements', *The Jubilee of the Railway News* [1914], 42–5

'The Railway Companies' Association', *Railway Gazette* (26 January 1940), 113–14 (a reprint, with additions, of an article by A. B. Cane which first appeared in *The Jubilee of the Railway News* [1914], 87–8)

M. Riebenack, *Railway Provident Institutions in English-Speaking Countries* (Philadelphia, 1905)

W. Z. Ripley, *Railroads Rates and Regulations* (1913)

M. Robbins, *The Railway Age* (1962)

W. A. Robertson, *Combination Among Railway Companies* (1912)

L. T. C. Rolt, *Red for Danger* (1955)

J. Simmons, *The Railways of Britain: An Historical Introduction* (paperback edn, 1965)

W. E. Simnett, *Railway Amalgamation in Great Britain* (1923)

G. Taylor, *The English Railway Strike and its Revolutionary Bearings* (Chicago, 1911) [*The City Club Bulletin*, Vol. IV, No. 19, 11 October 1911]

W. W. Tomlinson, *The North Eastern Railway Its Rise and Development* (Newcastle-upon-Tyne) [1914]

C. C. Wang, 'Legislative Regulation of Railway Finance in England', *University of Illinois Studies in the Social Sciences*, vii (1918)

P. M. Williams, 'Public Opinion and the Railway Rates Question in 1886', *English Historical Review*, lxvii (1952), 37–73

H. R. Wilson, *The Safety of British Railways or Railway Accidents: How Caused and How Prevented* (1909)

H. R. Wilson, *Railway Accidents: Legislation and Statistics, 1825 to 1924* (1925)

2. OTHER SUBJECTS

G. R. (Lord) Askwith, *Industrial Problems and Disputes* (1920)

W. O. Aydelotte, 'The House of Commons in the 1840's', *History*, New Series, xxxix (1954), 249–62

W. O. Aydelotte, 'The Conservative and Radical Interpretations of Early Victorian Social Legislation', *Victorian Studies*, xi (1967), 225–36

M. J. Barnett, *The Politics of Legislation The Rent Act 1957* (1969)

E. E. Barry, *Nationalisation in British Politics: The Historical Background* (1965)

S. D. Bailey (ed), *The British Party System* (1952)

J. Bateman, *The Great Landowners of Great Britain and Ireland* (4th edn, 1883) (Victorian Library edition, introduced by David Spring, Leicester 1971)

D. E. D. Beales, 'Parliamentary Parties and the "Independent" Member, 1810–1860', in R. Robson (ed), *Ideas and Institutions of Victorian Britain* (1967), 1–19

D. E. D. Beales, *From Castlereagh to Gladstone 1818–1885* (1969)

H. L. Beales, 'The "Great Depression" in Industry and Trade', *Economic History Review*, v (1934–5), 65–75

S. H. Beer, *Modern British Politics* (2nd edn 1969)

A. F. Bentley, *The Process of Government* (Chicago, 1908)

H. Berrington, 'Partisanship and Dissidence in the Nineteenth-Century House of Commons', *Parliamentary Affairs*, xxi (1967–8), 338–74

B. H. Browne, *The Tariff Reform Movement in Great Britain 1881–1895* (New York, 1943)

S. Buxton, *Finance and Politics: An Historical Study 1783–1885* (two vols, 1888)

W. H. Chaloner, *The Social and Economic Development of Crewe 1780–1923* (Manchester, 1950)

*Chambers of Commerce Manual, 1954–1955* (1955)

J. B. Christoph, 'The Study of Voting Behaviour in the British House of Commons', *Western Political Quarterly*, xi (1958), 301–18

H. A. Clegg, A. Fox, and A. F. Thompson, *A History of British Trade Unions since 1889* (vol I, 1889–1910) (Oxford, 1964)

J. Cornford, 'The Transformation of Conservatism in the Late Nineteenth Century', *Victorian Studies,* vii (1963–64), 36–66

R. H. S. Crossman, Introduction to Walter Bagehot, *The English Constitution* (Fontana paperback edn 1963)

S. E. Finer, *Private Industry and Political Power* (1958)

K. Fitzgerald, *Ahead of Their Time: A Short History of the Farmers' Club 1842–1967* (1968)

P. Fraser, 'The Growth of Ministerial Control in the Nineteenth Century House of Commons', *English Historical Review*, lxxv (1960), 444–63

Viscount Gladstone, 'The Chief Whip in the British Parliament', *American Political Science Review,* xxi (1927), 519–28

W. D. Grampp, *The Manchester School of Economics* (1960)

E. Halévy, *The Rule of Democracy 1905–1914* (A History of the English People in the Nineteenth Century, Vol. VI, first paperback edn, 1961)

D. G. Hanes, *The First British Workmen's Compensation Act 1897* (New Haven, 1968)

H. J. Hanham, *Elections and Party Management: Politics in the Time of Disraeli and Gladstone* (1959)

F. J. C. Hearnshaw, *Conservatism in England: An Analytical, Historical, and Political Survey* (1933)

# Bibliography

N. Hunt, 'Early Pressure Groups The Russia Company and the Bank of England', *The Listener* (3 November 1960), 780–2

K. Hutchison, *The Decline & Fall of British Capitalism,* new edn (Connecticut, 1966)

F. E. Hyde, *Mr. Gladstone at the Board of Trade* (1934)

Sir I. Jennings, *Party Politics,* vol. II (Cambridge, 1961)

L. C. A. Knowles, *The Industrial and Commercial Revolutions in Great Britain during the Nineteenth Century* (revised edn 1941)

A. L. Lowell, 'The Influence of Party Upon Legislation in England and America', *Annual Report of the American Historical Association for the Year 1901* (Washington, 1902), vol. I, 319–542

J. M. Ludlow, 'The National Free Labour Association', *The Economic Review,* v (1895), 110–18

J. M. Ludlow, 'The Labour Protection Association', *The Economic Review,* ix (1899), 244–6

R. B. McDowell, *British Conservatism 1832–1914* (1959)

B. McGill, 'Conflict of Interest: English Experience 1782–1914', *Western Political Quarterly,* xii (1959), 808–27

W. C. Mallalieu, 'Joseph Chamberlain and Workmen's Compensation', *Journal of Economic History,* x (1950), 45–57

P. Mantoux and M. Alfassa, *La Crise du Trade-Unionisme* (Paris, 1903)

P. Mathias, 'The Brewing Industry, Temperance and Politics', *Historical Journal,* i (1958), 97–114

P. Mathias, *The First Industrial Nation: An Economic History of Britain 1700–1914* (1969)

A. H. H. Matthews, *Fifty Years of Agricultural Politics, being The History of the Central Chamber of Agriculture, 1865–1915* (1915)

J. H. Munkman, *Employers' Liability at Common Law* (1950)

J. M. Norris, 'Samuel Garbett and the Early Development of Industrial Lobbying in Great Britain', *Economic History Review,* Second Series, x (1957–8), 450–60

M. Ostrogorski, *Democracy and the Organisation of Political Parties* (two vols) (1902)

H. Pelling, *A History of British Trade Unionism* (Penguin Books edn 1965)

L. M. Penson, 'The London West India Interest in the Eighteenth Century', *English Historical Review,* xxxvi (1921), 373–92

J. K. Pollock, 'British Party Organisation', *Political Science Quarterly,* xiv (1930), 161–80

L. H. Powell, *The Shipping Federation: A History of the First Sixty Years 1890–1950* (1950)

R. E. Pumphrey, 'The Introduction of Industrialists into the British Peerage; A Study of Adaptation of a Social Institution', *American Historical Review,* lxv (1959–60), 1–16

D. Read, *The English Provinces c. 1760–1960: A Study in Influence* (1964)

W. W. Rostow, *British Economy of the Nineteenth Century* (Oxford, 1948)

S. B. Saul, *The Myth of the Great Depression, 1873–1896* (1969)

J. Saville, 'Trade Unions and Free Labour: The Background to the Taff Vale Decision' in A. Briggs and J. Saville (ed), *Essays in Labour History* (1960), 317–50

Sir H. L. Smith, *The Board of Trade* (1928)

D. Southgate, *The Passing of the Whigs 1832–1886* (1965)

J. A. Thomas, *The House of Commons, 1832–1901: A Study of its Economic and Functional Character* (Cardiff, 1939)

F. M. L. Thompson, *English Landed Society in the Nineteenth Century* (1963)

A. P. Usher, *An Introduction to the Industrial History of England* (1921)

J. R. Vincent, *Pollbooks: How Victorians Voted* (1967)

S. and B. Webb, *The History of Trade Unionism* (new impression of 1920 edn, 1956)

H. B. Wells, 'Swindon in the 19th and 20th Centuries', in *Studies in the History of Swindon* (Swindon Borough Council 1950)

H. H. Wilson, *Pressure Group: The Campaign for Commercial Television* (1961)

A. J. Wolfe, *Commercial Organizations in the United Kingdom* (U.S.A. Bureau of Foreign and Domestic Commerce Special Agents Series No. 102, Washington, 1915)

G. H. Wright, *Chronicles of the Birmingham Chamber of Commerce A.D. 1813–1913* (Birmingham, 1913)


3. BIOGRAPHICAL WORKS

W. H. G. Armytage, *A. J. Mundella 1825–1897: The Liberal Background to the Labour Movement* (1951)

Lord (G. R.) Askwith, *Lord James of Hereford* (1930)

R. Blake, *Disraeli* (1966)

J. Buchan, 'Charles Beilby Stuart-Wortley', in C. Grosvenor and Lord Stuart of Wortley, *The First Lady Wharncliffe and her Family* (two vols) (1927), Vol. I, ix–xx

W. S. Childe-Pemberton, *Life of Lord Norton* (1909)

R. S. Churchill, *Winston S. Churchill: Volume II Young Statesman 1901–1914* (1967)

P. Fraser, *Joseph Chamberlain: Radicalism and Empire, 1868–1914* (1966)

J. L. Garvin, *Life of Joseph Chamberlain*, vol. I (1836–85), (1935)

M. A. Hamilton, *Arthur Henderson* (1936)

Lady Victoria Hicks Beach, *Life of Sir Michael Hicks Beach (Earl St. Aldwyn)*, (two vols) (1932)

A. Lang, *Life, Letters and Diaries of Sir Stafford Northcote First Earl of Iddesleigh*, new edn (Edinburgh, 1891)

G. G. Lerry, *Henry Robertson, Pioneer of Railways into Wales* (Oswestry, 1949)

J. McCabe, *Life and Letters of George Jacob Holyoake* (two vols) (1908)

L. Masterman, *C. F. G. Masterman* (1939)

J. Morley, *Life of William Ewart Gladstone* (three vols) (1903)

F. Owen, *Tempestuous Journey: Lloyd George, His Life and Times* (1954)


4. WORKS OF REFERENCE

F. Boase, *Modern English Biography* (six vols) (1965)

*Dictionary of National Biography*

*Who Was Who 1897–1916* (1920)

*Who Was Who 1916–1928* (1929)

## Unpublished theses

J. K. Glynn, "The Private Member of Parliament (1833–68)", University of London Ph.D. thesis, 1949

P. J. Cain, "The Railway Rates Problem and Combination amongst the Railway Companies of Great Britain 1893/1913", University of Oxford B.Litt. thesis, 1968

P. S. Gupta, "The History of the Amalgamated Society of Railway Servants, 1871–1913", University of Oxford D.Phil. thesis, 1960

G. K. Roberts, "The Development of a railway interest, and its relation to Parliament, 1830–1868", University of London Ph.D. thesis, 1965

# Notes

## Notes to Chapter 1

9   1. A. F. Bentley, *The Process of Government* (Chicago, 1908), 209 and 403.

10  2. Though it is fair to add that the gap is being filled. Especially important are: W. D. Grampp, *The Manchester School of Economics* (1960); H. H. Wilson, *Pressure Group: The Campaign for Commercial Television* (1961); and M. J. Barnett, *The Politics of Legislation: The Rent Act 1957* (1969).

10  3. Bentley, *op. cit.*, 401.

10  4. S. H. Beer, *Modern British Politics* (2nd edn, 1969).

10  5. B. H. Browne, *The Tariff Reform Movement in Great Britain 1881–1895* (New York, 1943).

11  6. J. K. Glynn, "The Private Member of Parliament (1833–68)", unpublished University of London Ph.D. thesis, 1949; W. O. Aydelotte, 'The House of Commons in the 1840's', *History*, New Series, xxxix (1954), 249–62, and 'The Conservative and Radical Interpretations of Early Victorian Social Legislation', *Victorian Studies*, xi (1967), 225–36.

# Notes

11  7. D. E. D. Beales, 'Parliamentary Parties and the "Independent" Member, 1810–1860', in R. Robson (ed), *Ideas and Institutions of Victorian Britain* (1967), 1–19.

11  8. J. A. Hawgood, in S. D. Bailey (ed), *The British Party System* (1952), 32. So Derek Beales, *From Castlereagh to Gladstone 1815–1885* (1969), 242, speaks of the period 1868–85 as "the classical age of the two-party system."

11  9. J. A. Thomas, *The House of Commons 1832–1901* (Cardiff 1939), 14–15, 158.

12  10. F. Harrison, 'The Conservative Reaction', *Fortnightly Review*, New Series, xv (1874), 297–309.

12  11. S. E. Finer, *Private Industry and Political Power* (1958), 2.

12  12. Hence the term 'railway interest' was used in two senses: to refer, as *Bradshaw* did, for the first time in 1869, to those director-M.P.s who sat in Parliament; and to describe the entire range of railway officials, directors and shareholders, as well as those who sat in Parliament.

12  13. Beer, *op. cit.*, 9–22. N. Hunt, 'Early Pressure Groups The Russia Company and the Bank of England', *Listener* (3 November 1960), 780–782.

12  14. L. M. Penson, 'The London West India Interest in the Eighteenth Century', *E[nglish] H[istorical] R[eview]*, xxxvi (1921), 373–92.

13  15. J. M. Norris, 'Samuel Garbett and the Early Development of Industrial Lobbying in Great Britain', *Economic History Review*, Second Series, x (1957–58), 450. D. Read, *The English Provinces c.1760–1960: A Study in Influence* (1964), 24.

13  16. Beer, *op.cit.*, 29–30.

13  17. A. J. Wolfe, *Commercial Organizations in the United Kingdom* (U.S.A. Bureau of Foreign and Domestic Commerce Special Agents Series No. 102, Washington, 1915), 37.

13  18. P. Mathias, 'The Brewing Industry, Temperance and Politics', *Historical Journal*, i (1958), 97–104; in 1790 the brewers set up a junta in London to attend to parliamentary work.

13  19. On the Farmers' Club see K. Fitzgerald, *Ahead of Their Time: A Short History of the Farmers' Club 1842–1967* (1968).

13  20. Wolfe, *op.cit.*, 46.

13  21. *Ibid.*, 24 and 49.

13  22. The railway companies were not the only exception; the coal interest acquired its own national organization, the Mining Association of Great Britain, in 1854.

13  23. The Midland Railway's headquarters were at Derby, but it had offices in Westminster, as did another important company, the North Eastern Railway.

14  24. B. McGill, 'Conflict of Interest: English Experience 1782–1914', *Western Political Quarterly*, xii (1959), 811–27. In the Lords there was no prohibition on peers with personal or pecuniary interests from voting on public bills.

14  25. G. K. Roberts, "The development of a railway interest, and its relation to Parliament, 1830–1868", unpublished University of London Ph.D. thesis, 1965, 358–9.

# Notes

14  26. Roberts, *op.cit.*, 124–9, gives some early examples, including those of Carlisle, Derby, Durham, Harwich, Southampton and Sunderland. See also chapter 14, note 8.

14  27. *Railway Times* (10 October 1868), 1042.

15  28. P. W. Kingsford, *Victorian Railwaymen* (1970), *passim*.

15  29. *Parl[iamentary] Deb[ates]*, 3rd series (1870), cxcix, 1114: speech of L. L. Dillwyn (1814–92), manager of the Cambrian pottery, Swansea, M.P. for Swansea District and Swansea, 1855–92, and a director of the Great Western Railway.

15  30. H. Parris, *Government and the Railways in Nineteenth-Century Britain* (1965), 149–51, 207–9.

16  31. *Railway Times* (5 May 1838), 222; (30 June), 346.

16  32. *Ibid.* (13 April 1839), 315; (20 April), 330. Some letters and other documents relating to this society, January–July 1839, are in B[ritish] T[ransport] H[istorical] R[ecords] GEN 3/1A, HL1/5, and HL2/14 (File R314). Burke announced the dissolution of the society in a letter to the secretary of the London & Birmingham Railway on 23 December 1839.

16  33. *Railway Times* (22 June 1839), 483.

16  34. B.T.H.R. BDJ 1/2, minutes 1929 and 1966, 2 and 15 July 1840.

16  35. B.T.H.R. HL1/9: J. Eustace Grubb to the secretary of the Great Western Railway, 13 June 1842. This episode is treated at greater length in chapter 3.

16  36. *Railway Times* (26 March 1842), 358.

16  37. F. E. Hyde, *Mr. Gladstone at the Board of Trade* (1934), 170–7.

16  38. *Herapath's Railway and Commercial Journal* (hereafter *Herapath*) (29 June 1844), 763.

16  39. *Railway Chronicle* (29 June 1844), 254–5. B.T.H.R. LVM 1/6, 211.

17  40. *Herapath* (6 July 1844), 791; *Railway Record* (6 July 1844), 295.

17  41. The weakness of railway representation in the House of Commons at this time was a source of worry to the companies. The directors of the Liverpool & Manchester Railway discussed the possibility of the railway interest retaining "a *professional advocate* in the House of Commons, as was the practice with the West India Interest, the Canadian Interest, &C-": B.T.H.R. LVM 1/6, 216, 8 July 1844.

17  42. *Herapath* (13 July 1844), 819. B.T.H.R. LVM 1/6, 225; SER 1/18, 143.

17  43. *Parl. Deb.*, 3rd series (1844), lxxvi, 502–6.

17  44. *Herapath* (20 July 1844), 848–9.

17  45. *Ibid.* (27 July 1844), 868; *Railway Times* (20 July 1844), 801; *Railway Chronicle* (20 July 1844), 326.

17  46. Hyde, *op. cit.*, 177–80, thought that Peel was largely responsible for the government's change of heart; Peel feared the railway interest more than Gladstone, and neither the Prime Minister nor the rest of the Cabinet was convinced that Gladstone's measure was worth a political fight to the death.

17  47. *Railway Times* (14 July 1849), 696–7; (23 February 1850), 185; (2 February 1856), 128–9. *Railway Record* (2 October 1858), 636; (26 March 1859), 198–9; (30 July 1859), 487. On the state of railway accounting see H. Pollins, 'Aspects of Railway Accounting before 1868', in A. C. Littleton and B. S. Yamey (eds), *Studies in the History of Accounting* (1956), 332–55.

# Notes

*Page*

18    48. B.T.H.R. RCH 1/13, min. 176, 11 June 1851.

18    49. *Ibid.*, mins. 188 and 203.

18    50. *Ibid.*, mins. 366 and 386.

18    51. E. Cleveland-Stevens, *English Railways: Their Development and their Relation to the State* (1915), 182–90.

18    52. Roberts, *op. cit.*, 326. 'The Railway Companies' Association', *Railway Gazette* (26 January 1940), 113. An unsigned and undated memorandum headed "Desiderata for the Railway Companies Association", found among London & North Western Railway files of correspondence for 1854, and preserved in B.T.H.R. RCA 4/1, suggests that another factor in the minds of the companies was the need to evolve safe principles of accounting to restore the confidence of the public; this confidence had been badly undermined in the wake of the revelations which had accompanied the fall of George Hudson.

18    53. *Railway Gazette*, *loc.cit.* B.T.H.R. RCA 1/1B, minute nos. 10 and 411.

19    54. This and the following paragraph are based on the Association's minute book, B.T.H.R. RCA 1/1A, *passim*; the extracts in the appendices to *Bradshaw* for 1859, 107–110; 1860, 127; and 1861, 123; *Herapath* (14 September 1861), 951; and P. S. Bagwell, 'The Railway Interest: Its Organization and Influence 1839–1914', *Journal of Transport History*, vii (1965), 67–9. Though Dr Bagwell has supposed that the association of 1858–61 was merely a more formal expression of the committee of 1854, the contents of the minute book make it clear that the two bodies were quite separate; it is of course quite likely that their memberships overlapped.

19    55. Leeman (1809–82), a solicitor in York who was three times Lord Mayor of the city, took a leading part in exposing the activities of Hudson. When Hudson resigned from the board of the York, Newcastle & Berwick Railway, in 1849, Leeman became a director of that company, and in 1855 became deputy chairman of the North Eastern Railway formed by amalgamation the previous year; he was chairman of the North Eastern from 1874 to 1880. He sat as M.P. for York 1865–8 and 1871–80. From 1874 to 1880 he was also chairman of the Railway Companies' Association, and thus virtually head of the railway interest in Parliament. Leeman's deep hostility to any sort of government-inspired centralization was well known: *Yorkshire Gazette* (4 March 1882), 7.

19    56. There are references to its work in 1863 in B.T.H.R. GW 1/19, 107 and 187–8, and RCA 1/1B No. 411.

20    57. *Railway Times* (21 November 1868), 1184.

20    58. Cleveland-Stevens, *op. cit.*, 214–9.

20    59. Railway Shareholders' Association, *Report of the Proceedings at the National Conference of Railway Shareholders, held in the Town Hall, Manchester, on Tuesday & Wednesday, April 14th & 15th, 1868* (Manchester), [1868], 67. C. C. Wang, 'Legislative Regulation of Railway Finance in England', *University of Illinois Studies in the Social Sciences*, vii (1918), 25–6.

20    60. 31 & 32 Vict., c.119.

20    61. B.T.H.R. RCA 1/1B Nos. 1–4, 26 June 1867.

Page
21    62. The first call, authorized in December 1868, produced £2,676 2s. 6d.:
         *ibid.*, No. 237, 18 February 1869.
21    63. The resolutions concerning the constitution of the committee and associa-
         tion make no mention of voting, but it is obvious from the proceedings that
         the voting, like the representation, was by companies.
21    64. *Ibid.*, No. 34.
21    65. Thompson was by then out of Parliament. Brown-Westhead, deputy
         chairman of the London & North Western, sat for Knaresborough 1847–52
         and for York 1857–65; he was re-elected for York in December 1868.
22    66. *Ibid.*, No. 52. Gooch (1816–89), an engineer by profession, was appointed
         locomotive superintendent of the Great Western in 1837. In 1868 he be-
         came the first engineer to receive a baronetcy, in recognition of his services
         in the laying of the Atlantic Cable. He resigned from the Great Western in
         1864, but returned as its chairman in 1866, and held this post till his death.
         He sat as Conservative M.P. for Cricklade 1865–85. Elected deputy chair-
         man of the Railway Companies' Association in 1874, he succeeded Leeman
         as chairman, retiring in 1887. Though he never once spoke in a parlia-
         mentary debate, Gooch performed valuable services for the railway
         companies behind the scenes and in the division lobbies.
22    67. *Ibid.*
22    68. *Ibid.*, No. 225, 18 February 1869.
22    69. *Ibid.*, Nos. 416 and 732.
22    70. *Ibid.*, No. 848, 6 March 1874. The committee will be referred to in the text
         simply as the parliamentary committee.
22    71. *Ibid.*, No. 835, 3 July 1873.
22    72. B.T.H.R. RCA 4/1: typescript memo., headed "Constitution of the
         Association", undated but *circa* 1913; the author was probably A. B.
         Cane, then secretary of the Association.
22    73. C. H. Grinling, *The History of the Great Northern Railway 1845–1902*
         (new issue 1903), gives the date of foundation of the association as 1884;
         so does *The Times* (9 February 1912), 11, in its obituary of Sir Henry
         Oakley. C. H. Ellis, *British Railway History 1877–1947* (1959), 311, gives
         the date as 1897. All the association's minutes were naturally "Private and
         Confidential".
23    74. Gladstone Papers, B[ritish] M[useum] Add. MSS. 44439, fol. 247: memo.
         relating to the claims of Thompson to a peerage, July 1873, almost certainly
         written by Thompson himself.
23    75. 34 & 35 Vict., c.78.
23    76. W. M. Acworth, 'The State in Relation to Railways in England', in *The
         State in Relation to Railways Papers read at the Congress of the Royal
         Economic Society January 11th 1912* (1912), 9.

# Notes to Chapter 2

25   1. H. Spencer, *Railway Morals and Railway Policy reprinted from the 'Edinburgh Review'* . . . (1855), 23–4 [*The Traveller's Library*, vol. 25, 1856].

25   2. "Hercules", *British Railways and Canals in Relation to British Trade and Government Control* [1884], 10–11.

25   3. J. B. Pope, *Railway Rates and Radical Rule* (1884), 282–7.

25   4. Com[mons] Deb[ates], 5th series (1913), xlix, 47, 6 March.

25   5. Parl[iamentary] Papers 1872, xiii, part I (364), qq.4280–1.

25   6. The totals for the House of Commons are based on the tables in J. A. Thomas, *The House of Commons 1832–1901*, 4–6. Thomas' figures must be regarded as minima, as he gives no separate figures of railway representation in the Radical and Irish parties; probably he does not include shareholders, though this is not clear. For purposes of comparison the figures given in *Bradshaw* for total railway representation in the Commons are reproduced in the last column. It is probable that the peak of the numerical representation of the railways in the Commons was not reached till 1866, when it appears from *Bradshaw* that there were 162 railway directors sitting there; in 1867 the figure dropped to 159.

    The totals for the House of Lords are based on Bagwell, *Journal of Transport History*, vii (1965), 83, and the efficient interest on *Bradshaw*. The number of railway directors in the Lords fluctuated a good deal in this period, and the years given are chosen only because, as election years, they enable some comparison to be made with railway representation in the Commons at the same time. In 1864 the number of railway directors in the Lords reached 50 and in 1866, 53.

26   7. W. O. Aydelotte, *History*, New Series, xxxix (1954), 257–9.

26   8. J. A. Thomas, *op. cit.*, 4–7.

26   9. *Herapath* (6 March 1875), 267.

26   10. Lists of shareholders were printed by the companies for their half-yearly meetings, but appear not to have survived. Some Shareholders' Address Books are preserved amongst the British Transport Historical Records. They relate mostly to the early period of railway growth; others exist only for selected years and only for certain companies.

27   11. C. H. Grinling, *The Ways of our Railways* (1905), 13–14.

27   12. H. Spencer, *loc. cit.*

27   13. *Parl. Papers 1872*, xiii, part I (364), q.1675.

27   14. *Ibid.*, q.5104. Joseph Whitwell Pease (1828–1903) entered the Pease banking firm at Darlington in 1845 and joined the boards of several companies, including Robert Stephenson & Co. Ltd. and J. & J. W. Pease, bankers. He was a director of the Stockton & Darlington Railway, 1853–63, and of the North Eastern Railway, 1863–1902, becoming chairman of the North Eastern in 1895. Pease sat as a Liberal M.P. for South Durham 1865–85, and for the Barnard Castle division 1885–1903; he remained a strong Gladstonian throughout his political career.

# Notes

27    15. A director, by virtue of his being on the board of a large company, might also have sat on the boards of several smaller subsidiary companies. This does not, however, affect the argument.

28    16. See W. W. Tomlinson, *The North Eastern Railway: its rise and development* (Newcastle-upon-Tyne) [1914], 703–7, for the case of the Hull & Barnsley line, built as a rival to the North Eastern.

28    17. *Herapath* (18 September 1875), 984.

28    18. P. M. Williams, 'Public Opinion and the Railway Rates Question in 1886', *E.H.R.*, lxvii (1952), 53–4.

28    19. This point was recognized by W. M. Acworth, 'Professor Cohn and State Railway Ownership in England', *Economic Journal*, ix (1899), 92–3.

28    20. Appendix, tables 1–3.

29    21. Appendix, tables 1–3, "New members".

29    22. Appendix, tables 4–6; J. Bateman, *The Great Landowners of Great Britain and Ireland*, 4th edn (1883), (Victorian Library edition, introduced by David Spring, Leicester 1971), *passim*.

29    23. To these should perhaps be added the Liberal-Conservative Lord Wharncliffe, of the Manchester, Sheffield & Lincolnshire Railway, who received an earldom in 1876.

30    24. F. M. L. Thompson, *English Landed Society in the Nineteenth Century* (1963), 263 and 306, gives evidence on the general preoccupation of landed society with secondary and branch lines, though he does not distinguish between the political parties.

31    25. Sir Edward Watkin (1819–1901) entered his father's business as a cotton-broker in Manchester, but left the cotton trade in 1845 to become secretary of the Trent Valley Railway; when this was sold to the London & North Western he joined that company as secretary to its famous general manager, Captain Mark Huish. Eight years later he moved to the Manchester, Sheffield & Lincolnshire Railway as general manager. In the early 1860s he resigned from the Sheffield company and spent some time in Canada. He rejoined the company in 1863 as a director and was its chairman from 1864 to 1894; he was chairman of the South Eastern Railway 1866–94, and of the Metropolitan Railway from 1872. Watkin was elected Liberal M.P. for Great Yarmouth in 1857 but was unseated on petition; he sat as M.P. for Stockport 1864–8 and for Hythe 1874–95. In 1885 Watkin became a Unionist [see *Dod's Parliamentary Companion*, 1885 and 1886 (two editions)]; but for him the break with Liberalism had really come much earlier, and from the time of his knighthood in 1868 he fought successive administrations over every step to increase government control of railways.

        Richard Monckton Milnes, Lord Houghton (1809–85) entered Parliament as Conservative M.P. for Pontefract in 1837, but voted for the repeal of the Corn Laws in 1846 and joined the Liberals. He received a peerage in 1863. As a director of the Lancashire & Yorkshire Railway he was active on behalf of the railway interest throughout the 1870s; when the Railway Association elected its Parliamentary Committee in 1873, Houghton was the only member of the Lords to be given a place on it.

31    26. B.T.H.R. RCA 1/1B No. 34, 5 November 1867.

# Notes

*Page*

31    27. *Parl. Papers 1867*, xxxviii part I [3844], pp. lxxxvii–xc.

31    28. 31 & 32 Vict., c. 119. Wang, *op. cit.*, 167–9 and 182–7, discusses the scope and effect of the Act.

32    29. Cleveland-Stevens, *op. cit.*, 316–24.

32    30. *Ibid.*, 233–8.

32    31. Sir W. B. Forwood, *Recollections of a Busy Life* (Liverpool 1910), 81–2. *Amalgamations of Railway Companies . . . Report of Special Committee* (Liverpool 1872), *passim*.

33    32. J. Mavor, 'The English Railway Rate Question', *Quarterly Journal of Economics*, viii (1894), 282–4. P. J. Cain, "The Railway Rates Problem and Combination amongst the Railway Companies of Great Britain 1893/1913", unpublished University of Oxford B.Litt. thesis, 1968, 9. See also H. Pollins, *Britain's Railways: An Industrial History* (Newton Abbot 1971), 108.

33    33. 17 & 18 Vict., c.31.

33    34. *Parl. Papers 1872*, xiii part I (364), pp. xxii–xiii.

33    35. B.T.H.R. RCA 1/1B No. 648.

34    36. *Parl. Papers 1872*, xiii part I (364), qq.148–9.

34    37. *Ibid.*, q.420; running powers were powers granted to one company to use the tracks of another.

34    38. *Ibid.*, qq.689–90.

34    39. *Ibid.*, q.1425, 2085–6, 2624–5, 3255, 3263.

34    40. *Ibid.*, q.4492.

34    41. *Ibid.*, qq.5169–80, 6613.

34    42. *Ibid.*, p. xxv.

35    43. *Ibid.*, q.7179. Tyler (1827–1908) later became Conservative M.P. for Harwich, 1880–85, and for Great Yarmouth, 1885–92, and rose to become deputy chairman of the Great Eastern Railway.

35    44. *Ibid.*, pp. xiii–xxiv, xxxix, xliv. Terminal charges, which covered charges both for accommodation of goods and for handling services incidental to actual carriage, formed a subject of bitter dispute between the railways and the traders; the railways claimed the right to make such charges over and above the maximum rates laid down in their Acts of Parliament.

35    45. *Ibid.*, pp. xlviii–xlix. The Railway and Canal Traffic Act of 1873 gave this body the title of the Railway Commission; the Railway and Canal Traffic Act of 1888, which made the Commission permanent, changed its title to that of the Railway and Canal Commission.

35    46. Sir H. L. Smith, *The Board of Trade* (1928), 135.

35    47. Liverpool Chamber of Commerce, *Railway Companies' Amalgamation: Report of the Railways, Transit, and Parliamentary Committee . . .* (Liverpool 1873), 19.

35    48. *Parl. Deb.*, 3rd series (1873), ccxiv, 241.

35    49. *Parl. Papers 1873*, iv (34).

36    50. B.T.H.R. RCA 1/1B No. 747.

36    51. *Ibid.*, No. 748.

36    52. *Parl. Deb.*, 3rd series (1873), ccxiv, 1050, 27 February.

36    53. *Railway Times* (8 March 1873), 257.

*Page*

36  54. Only six Liberals who were railway directors voted against the second reading of the Irish Universities bill on 11 March; all sat on the boards of very minor Irish and English lines: *House of Commons' Divisions* (1873), Numb. 20. Defeated on the bill, Gladstone resigned on 13 March but resumed office three days later. This episode is treated in John Morley, *Life of William Ewart Gladstone* vol. II (1903), 434–56.

36  55. B.T.H.R. RCA 1/1B Nos. 749 and 754.

36  56. *Ibid.*, No. 767.

37  57. P[ublic] R[ecord] O[ffice], CAB 41/5/16: Gladstone to the Queen, 22 March 1873.

37  58. B.T.H.R. RCA 1/1B No. 769, 19 March 1873.

37  59. *Ibid.*, No. 771.

37  60. *Ibid.*, Nos. 775 and 779; there is a copy of the circular in the Gladstone Papers, B.M. Add. MSS. 44641, fols. 90–91.

37  61. *Parl Deb.*, 3rd series (1873), ccxv, 350, 31 March.

37  62. *Ibid.*, 376–81.

38  63. *Ibid.*, 381–3.

38  64. B.T.H.R. RCA 1/1B Nos. 780 and 781; extracts from the London & North Western circular appeared in the *Railway Times* (5 April 1873), 374.

38  65. *Parl. Deb.*, 3rd series (1873), ccxv, 591–3, 3 April.

38  66. *Ibid.*, 597–8; the voting on Gregory's clause was 81 to 51, figures which reveal much, in a negative way, about the supposed colossal strength of the railway interest in the Commons.

38  67. *Railway Times* (5 April 1873), 374.

38  68. *Parl. Deb.*, 3rd series (1873), ccxv, 1027, 1105–8. The first three Commissioners were Sir Frederick Peel, Mr MacNamara, Q.C., and W. P. Price, chairman of the Midland Railway.

38  69. B.T.H.R. RCA 1/1B No. 792; the bill as amended in committee in the Commons is in *Parl. Papers 1873*, iv (121).

39  70. Contacts between Salisbury, Richmond and the Railway Association are confirmed in the Salisbury Papers, Christ Church, Oxford, Class K: Special Correspondence, Great Eastern Railway Series: Samuel Swarbrick (general manager of the Great Eastern) to Salisbury, 8 May 1873.

39  71. B.T.H.R. RCA 1/1B No. 799, 13 May 1873.

39  72. *Parl. Deb.*, 3rd series (1873), ccxv, 1844–9.

39  73. B.T.H.R. RCA 1/1B No. 804.

39  74. *Parl. Deb.*, 3rd series (1873), ccxvi, 1305–6.

39  75. Moon (1814–99) became a director of the London & North Western in 1851 and was chairman from 1861 to 1891; he was created a baronet in 1887. He never entered Parliament, though he was once asked to stand as a Conservative candidate for Liverpool. Moon had a not undeserved reputation as the hardest of Victorian businessmen.

39  76. B.T.H.R. RCA 1/1B Nos. 830 and 837.

39  77. *Parl. Deb.*, 3rd series (1873), ccxvii, 9–10, 8 July.

39  78. B.T.H.R. RCA 1/1B No. 837. Oakley (1823–1912) worked as a clerk in the Library of the House of Commons. There he acquired a thorough knowledge of parliamentary procedure, and came into contact with E. B. Denison,

first chairman of the Great Northern. In 1851 Oakley became assistant secretary of that company, secretary in 1858, and general manager in 1870; when he retired, in 1898, he was taken on to the Great Northern board. He held the post of Honorary Secretary of the Railway Companies' Association from 1867 to 1900. An expert parliamentary witness, Oakley was eminently suited to acting as intermediary between the companies and the Board of Trade. His knighthood, in 1891, reflected the esteem in which he was held by Whitehall.

40   79. *Parl. Deb.*, 3rd series (1873), ccxvii, 383; 36 & 37 Vict., c.48.

40   80. *Railway Times* (24 May 1873), 542.

40   81. *Parl. Deb.*, 3rd series (1873), ccxv, 1553–4; Bagwell, *Journal of Transport History*, vii (1965), 86, note 50; *Railway Times* (28 March 1874), 329: advertisement by the Railway Commissioners.

40   82. J. A. Thomas, *op. cit.*, 15. Brewers, for instance, had increased since 1868 from 7 to 14, merchants from 10 to 19, textile manufacturers from 3 to 6. The number of Conservative landowners increased from 185 to 232, and many of these, like the traders, would have wanted through rates for their produce.

40   83. *Parl. Deb.*, 3rd series (1874), ccxxix, 454; B.T.H.R. RCA 1/1B Nos. 885–6, 890; and see S. Carter, *Railway Legislation: a letter to shareholders . . .* (1874), *passim*.

40   84. B.T.H.R. RCA 1/1B Nos. 900 and 910; *Parl. Papers 1881*, xiv (374–I), 1.

40   85. *Lords' Journals*, cv (1873), 347–8.

41   86. *Ibid.*, 558.

41   87. In the analysis which follows, references to the interest and to directors always refer to the efficient interest, unless the contrary is stated.

41   88. *House of Commons' Divisions* (1873), Numb. 28; W. P. Adam, the Liberal Chief Whip, was himself a director of the North British Railway.

41   89. *Ibid.*, Numb. 29.

41   90. *Ibid.*, Numb. 36.

41   91. *Ibid.*, Numb. 173.

41   92. *House of Commons' Divisions* (1874), Numb. 32.

41   93. *House of Commons' Divisions* (1873), Numb. 40.

41   94. *Ibid.*, Numb. 51. The motion was defeated by 197 votes to 65; its originator was Lord Claud Hamilton (not to be confused with Lord Claud John Hamilton) who was Conservative M.P. for Tyrone and a director of the Porto Alegre & New Hamburg line in Brazil.

41   95. *House of Commons' Divisions* (1874), Numb. 15. On an amendment definitely rejecting such a policy, eighteen of the efficient interest voted in favour of the amendment (eight Conservatives, one Liberal-Conservative and nine Liberals) and none against it: *ibid.*, Numb. 16.

42   96. B.T.H.R. RCA 1/1B Nos. 736, 752–3, 791, 817.

42   97. Cleveland-Stevens, *op. cit.*, 274, fails to make the point that the speeches of men like C. B. Denison (Conservative, Great North Railway) and Pease were speeches of railway directors with interests of their own to preserve.

# Notes to Chapter 3

Page
45    1. Parris, *op. cit.*, 30–33.
45    2. 3 & 4 Vict., c. 97.
45    3. *Parl. Papers 1841*, xxv [287], 3.
45    4. *Ibid.*, 12.
45    5. *Ibid.*, 14.
45    6. Parris, *op. cit.*, 50–2, deals with the passage of this bill at some length.
45    7. *Herapath* (9 January 1841), 40.
45    8. B.T.H.R. HRP 1/29/50: *Resolutions & C. Passed at a Numerous Meeting of Railway Directors held at Birmingham, June 19 1841*, v–15; the date is obviously a misprint; see *Herapath* (30 January 1841), 99–100, where the resolutions are reprinted.
45    9. E. H. Fowkes, 'Sources of History in Railway Records of British Transport Historical Records', *Journal of the Society of Archivists*, iii (1969), 483. In fact, though a set of rules was again drafted in 1867, no standard rule book ·was adopted till March 1876: H. R. Wilson, *Railway Accidents: Legislation and Statistics, 1825 to 1924* (1925), 7; P. S. Bagwell, *The Railway Clearing House in the British Economy 1842–1922* (1968), 224–6.
46   10. *Herapath* (13 February 1841), 154; (6 March), 221–2.
46   11. *Ibid.* (13 March), 245.
46   12. *Parl. Papers 1841*, viii (354), p.v.
46   13. Parris, *op. cit.*, 53.
46   14. 5 & 6 Vict., c. 55.
46   15. Parris, *op. cit.*, 34, 45–6.
46   16. *Ibid.*, 182. P.R.O. MT6/217/9660/1878, file 4497 of 1878: William Yolland, Chief Inspecting Officer, to H. G. Calcraft, the Assistant Secretary of the Railway Department, 1 June 1878.
47   17. *Parl. Papers 1867*, xxxviii part I [3844], pp. lxxviii, xc. Lord Campbell's Act, 9 & 10 Vict., c.93, gave a right of compensation to near relatives of persons killed by the wrongful acts or neglect of others.
47   18. 31 & 32 Vict., c.119, clause 22.
47   19. B.T.H.R. RCA 1/1B No. 75, 27 February 1868.
47   20. *Ibid.*, No. 262, 4 March 1869.
47   21. *Ibid.*, No. 720, 30 July 1872. H. R. Wilson, *The Safety of British Railways or Railway Accidents: How Caused and How Prevented* (1909), 50.
47   22. *Railway Times* (28 March 1874), 341.
47   23. G. Cohn, *Untersuchungen über die Englische Eisenbahnpolitik*, vol. II (Leipzig 1875), 227.
48   24. P.R.O. MT6/114/2358/1874, file 313 of 1874: memo. by Malcolm, 23 March 1874.
48   25. *Parl. Papers 1871*, v (5). B.T.H.R. RCA 1/1B Nos. 562 and 565, 7 and 14 March 1871; the bill was withdrawn.
48   26. 34 & 35 Vict., c.78.
48   27. L. T. C. Rolt, *Red for Danger* (1955), 223–4, prints a chronological list of the major accidents; for the railways this was a period of boom, the growing volume of traffic itself increasing accident risks.

# Notes

Page
48  28. B.T.H.R. RCA 1/1B No. 593, 8 June 1871. Edward Tyer did not perfect his instruments for block working till 1874: Rolt, *op. cit.*, 33. Parris, *op. cit.*, 199, states that interlocking, invented in 1859: "became within eight years universal in theory, and general in practice, on new lines." The logical sequel, the mechanical combination of the two systems, was not effected till 1877: *The Times* (23 November 1877), 4. For some account of the different brakes in use see C. H. Ellis, *British Railway History 1830–1876* (1954), 376–7, and O. S. Nock, *Historic Railway Disasters* (1966), 33–5; Nock ignores the fierce technical controversies, and those within the Board of Trade, above all on the question of the advisability of government interference.

49  29. *Parl. Papers [H.L.] 1873*, vi (12). Gladstone Papers, B.M. Add. MSS. 44123, fols. 39–41: Fortescue to Gladstone, 21 March 1873.

49  30. B.T.H.R. RCA 1/1B No. 755, 4 March 1873.

49  31. *Parl. Papers 1873*, xiv (148), qq. 498, 555, 986, 997, 1031, 1057.

49  32. *Ibid.*, q. 1528.

49  33. *Ibid.*, v–vi.

49  34. *Parl. Papers 1873*, iv (232).

49  35. B.T.H.R. RCA 1/1B No. 842, 21 July 1873. 36 & 37 Vict., c.76.

49  36. *Annual Register* (1873), part I, 92.

50  37. This letter is printed in the *Railway Magazine*, lxxiii (1933), 164.

50  38. P.R.O. CAB 41/5/37 and 38: Gladstone to the Queen, 12 and 15 November 1873.

50  39. *Parl. Papers 1874*, lviii (64), 1–2.

50  40. *Ibid.*, 17–18, 28–30.

50  41. Wilson, *The Safety of British Railways*, 42.

50  42. Viscount Cross, *A Political History* (privately printed 1903), 25.

50  43. W. S. Childe-Pemberton, *Life of Lord Norton* (1909), 141.

50  44. Iddesleigh Papers, B.M. Add. MSS. 50052, fol. 3: Northcote to Adderley, 7 March 1874.

51  45. Childe-Pemberton, *op. cit.*, 220, 224–8, 238.

51  46. R. Blake, *Disraeli* (1966), 553–4. Northcote, however, clearly favoured a tougher line in dealing with railway accidents: P.R.O. MT6/126/8684/1874, file 7492 of 1874: Northcote to Adderley, 13 November 1874.

51  47. *Annual Register* (1874), part I, 6.

51  48. Hughenden Manor, Hughenden Papers, box 116, B/XXI/A/105: Adderley to Montagu Corry; this letter is undated, but appears to have been written in 1874, prior to the appointment of the Royal Commission on Railway Accidents.

51  49. *Parl. Deb.*, 3rd series (1874), ccxviii, 1150–65, 27 April.

51  50. *Railway Times* (9 May 1874), 485.

51  51. *Railway Review* (19 May 1899), 10.

52  52. P. S. Gupta, "The History of the Amalgamated Society of Railway Servants, 1871–1913", unpublished University of Oxford D.Phil. thesis, 1960, 62.

52  53. *Railway Service Gazette* (19 February 1875) 9.

52  54. Gupta, *op. cit.*, 63.

52  55. The protracted deliberations of the commission were due in part to the

technical complexities with which it had to deal, but also to the fact that when the report was about to be prepared its chairman, the Duke of Buckingham, was sent out to India as Governor of Madras (May 1875), and took the draft report and the secretary with him as far as Egypt: *Parl. Deb.*, 3rd series (1874), ccxxix, 1098–9; Hughenden Papers, box 116, B/XXI/A/117: Adderley to Disraeli, 21 February 1876.

52    56. *Parl. Papers 1877*, xlviii [C–1637–I], qq. 168, 399.

52    57. *Ibid.*, q. 831.

52    58. *Ibid.*, qq. 1481–3, 1501.

52    59. *Ibid.*, qq. 2178, 2255.

52    60. Against intemperance, for instance: *ibid.*, qq. 6425–7, 11350.

52    61. *Ibid.*, qq. 7237, 9262.

53    62. *Ibid.*, qq. 16544, 20522.

53    63. *Ibid.*, q. 30420.

53    64. B.T.H.R. RCA 1/1B No. 913, 4 March 1875, and meeting of general managers, 12 April 1875.

53    65. *Parl. Papers 1877*, xlviii [C–1637], 97–8. In the early years of railway development, hand brakes on engine tenders and guards' vans only were considered sufficient. Continuous brakes did not appear till the 1850s. Automatic continuous brakes, which were immediately self-acting in case of accident, did not appear until much later; the Westinghouse continuous brake was not made automatic till 1874: C. E. Stretton, *A Few Remarks on Railway Accidents, their Cause and Prevention* (3rd edn 1882), 7; Parris, *op. cit.*, 171; Nock, *op. cit.*, 33. For a description of the Westinghouse brake and the automatic vacuum brake, also continuous, see Stretton, *op. cit.*, 13–14.

53    66. *Parl. Papers 1877*, xlviii [C–1637], 115.

53    67. *Ibid.*, [C–1637–I], qq. 30727, 31198, 31770.

53    68. *Parl. Deb.*, 3rd series (1874), ccxxix, 1098.

53    69. *Parl. Papers 1877*, xlviii [C–1637–I], qq. 33453–4.

53    70. P. S. Bagwell, *The Railway Clearing House*, 226–30.

53    71. B.T.H.R. RCA 1/1B Nos. 971 and 979.

54    72. *Ibid.*, Nos. 1003, 1008 and 1014; see also *Parl. Papers 1877*, xlviii [C–1637], 129. There is no evidence to indicate whether this agreement was ever acted upon.

54    73. *Parl. Papers 1877*, xlviii [C–1637], 11, 21, 35–6.

54    74. *Ibid.*, 37–9.

54    75. *Ibid.*, 79–82.

55    76. Hughenden Papers, box 116, B/XXI/A/117: Adderley to Disraeli, 21 February 1876.

55    77. Iddesleigh Papers, B.M. Add. MSS. 50018, fols. 3–4: Northcote to Lord Beaconsfield, 10 February 1877; although Disraeli went to the Lords in August 1876, he will continue to be referred to in the text by his former name.

55    78. *Parl. Deb.*, 3rd series (1877), ccxxxii, 255, 13 February.

55    79. This correspondence, which lasted during most of February 1877, is in the Hughenden Papers, box 161; Northcote sided with Disraeli: *ibid.*, box 161, C/VI/39: memo. by Northcote, 10 February.

*Page*
55    80. B.T.H.R. RCA 1/1B No. 1033, 21 February 1877; *Parl. Papers 1877*, lxxiii [C–1755], 3–4: Farrer to Oakley, 13 January 1877.

55    81. B.T.H.R. RCA 1/1B No. 1042, 21 March 1877.

55    82. *Parl. Deb.*, 3rd series (1877), ccxxxiii, 769–70, 9 April.

56    83. B.T.H.R. RCA 1/1B Nos. 1051, 1056, and 1066, 14, 18, and 23 April 1877.

56    84. *Parl. Deb.*, 3rd series (1877), ccxxxiv, 10, 27 April; B.T.H.R. RCA 1/1B No. 1075, 8 May 1877.

56    85. *Parl. Deb.*, 3rd series (1877), ccxxxiv, 25; Bury withdrew his motion.

56    86. B.T.H.R. RCA 1/1B No. 1091, 4 June 1877. The returns were printed in *Parl. Papers 1877*, lxxiii [C–1755].

56    87. *Herapath* (17 February 1877), 181.

56    88. *Parl. Papers 1877*, lxxiii [C–1755], 14 and 18. B.T.H.R. MSL 1/16, min. 5796.

56    89. *Parl. Papers 1877*, lxxii [C–1866], 27.

57    90. *Parl. Papers 1878*, lxvi [C–1912], 3–4. The most important of the conditions were that the brake should be "instantaneously self-acting" in case of accident, and applied to every vehicle of the train (i.e., continuous).

57    91. B.T.H.R. RCA 1/1B No. 1125, 5 December 1877. Perhaps, too, Adderley had in mind the barrenness of the last session, the Irish Judicature bill being one of its "few accomplished facts": *Annual Register* (1877), part I, 53.

57    92. *Parl. Papers 1878*, lxvi [C–1963].

57    93. B.T.H.R. RCA 1/1B No. 1134, 26 February 1878.

57    94. O. S. Nock, *op. cit.*, 33–4.

57    95. *Ibid.*, 33–5; J. Simmons, *The Railways of Britain: An Historical Introduction* (paperback edn 1965), 165. Nock's judgment suffers from being wise after the event; even the Westinghouse brake was not without its faults: *Railway Times* (23 March 1878), 265.

57    96. *Parl. Deb.*, 3rd series (1878), ccxxxviii, 1282, 14 March.

58    97. *Parl. Papers [H.L.] 1878*, vi (75).

58    98. *Parl. Deb.*, 3rd series (1878), ccxxxix, 1086, 11 April.

58    99. 41 & 42 Vict., c. 20; *Railway Times* (20 April 1878), 341.

58    100. *Ibid.* (7 September 1878), 764; Stretton, *op. cit.*, 9, 11, 32–3.

## Notes to Chapter 4

60    1. B.T.H.R. RCA 1/1B No. 630, 2 November 1871.

60    2. P. W. Kingsford, 'Labour Relations on the Railways, 1835–1875', *Journal of Transport History*, i (1953–4), 76. P. S. Bagwell, *The Railwaymen* (1963), 27.

60    3. M. Robbins, *The Railway Age* (1962), 83.

60    4. P. W. Kingsford, *Journal of Transport History*, i (1953–4), 66–9.

60    5. *Ibid.*, 70. W. H. Chaloner, *The Social and Economic Development of Crewe 1780–1923* (Manchester 1950), 53–62. H. B. Wells, 'Swindon in the 19th and 20th Centuries', *Studies in the History of Swindon* (Swindon Borough Council 1950), 111–16.

60    6. W. J. Gordon, *Every-day Life on the Railroad* (2nd edn, revised, 1898), 186.

*Page*
60    7. Gupta, *op. cit.*, 17–18, 25, 30.

61    8. J. H. Munkman, *Employer's Liability at Common Law* (1950), 5–10.

61    9. Bagwell, *The Railwaymen*, 47–53.

61    10. *Parl. Deb.*, 3rd series (1871), ccv, 34–6, 15 March. *The Times* (25 August 1871), 9; (15 September), 6; (29 September), 3; (2 October), 6. The Amalgamated Society was formed at the beginning of December.

61    11. *Parl. Deb.*, 3rd series (1873), ccxvi, 831, 12 June.

61    12. *The Times* (20 December 1873), 3; (22 December), 9. The prosecution was withdrawn and it was decided instead to lay the correspondence before Parliament: see P.R.O. MT6/114/2358/1874.

61    13. *The Times* (16 September 1874), 6 and 9. The Great Western also came under fire: *ibid.* (9 October 1874), 4 and 7. The enquiries were made for Bass by his 'agent', E. Phillips, editor of the *Railway Service Gazette*, the organ of the Amalgamated Society.

62    14. Gupta, *op. cit.*, 66–8, gives some account of the circumstances.

62    15. *Western Times* (17 November 1873), 3; (18 November), 3; (19 November), 2; (22 November), 4. *Railway Service Gazette* (22 November 1873), 9; (29 November), 6; (6 December), 8.

62    16. *Parl. Papers 1874*, v (91).

62    17. P.R.O. HO 45/9458/72731A: "Mining Association of Great Britain . . . Workpeoples' Compensation Bill Reasons against" (19 May 1874), 2. B.T.H.R. RCA 1/1B No. 875, 30 April 1874.

62    18. *Railway Service Gazette* (26 February 1875), 5.

62    19. *Ibid.* (22 January 1875), 4.

63    20. *Parl. Papers 1875*, i (186); *Parl. Deb.*, 3rd series (1875), ccxxiv, 916–7, 25 May.

63    21. Gupta, *op. cit.*, 67–8.

63    22. P.R.O. HO 45/9458/72731A: memo. by Lushington, entitled "Compensation for accidents to Workmen Bill", 5 June 1875.

63    23. B.T.H.R. RCA 1/1B No. 940, 22 June 1875.

63    24. G. W. Alcock, *Fifty Years of Railway Trade Unionism* (1922), 145.

63    25. The two other M.P.s who put their names on the back of the 1874 bill were both directors of Watkin companies: the Liberal Charles Gilpin, a director of the South Eastern Railway, and the Conservative J. Chapman, a director of the Manchester, Sheffield & Lincolnshire. In 1875 the two other M.P.s who backed the bill were the Liberals A. Laverton, of the Sheffield company, and A. F. Kinnaird of the Buckinghamshire Railway, a line with which Watkin's Aylesbury & Buckingham Railway had a working arrangement.

63    26. *Parl. Papers 1876*, ii (15).

64    27. B.T.H.R. RCA 1/1B No. 992, 22 May 1876.

64    28. *Parl. Deb.*, 3rd series (1876), ccxxix, 1170–9, 24 May.

64    29. P.R.O. HO 45/9458/72731A: memo. by Lushington entitled "Employers Liability for Injury Bill", 1876.

64    30. *Parl. Deb.*, 3rd series (1876), ccxxix, 1177–8, 1181, 24 May. Rodwell, M.P. for Cambridgeshire, was a director of a small East Anglian line, the Bury St Edmunds & Thetford; on 7 March he had spoken on behalf of the railways against the passenger duty: *ibid.*, ccxxvii, 1590.

# Notes

*Page*
64    31. B.T.H.R. RCA 1/1B No. 1005, 25 June 1876.
64    32. *Ibid.*, No. 1006, 17 July 1876; *Parl. Deb.*, 3rd series (1876), ccxxx, 324–5.
65    33. B.T.H.R. RCA 1/1B No. 1032, 21 February 1877; *Parl. Papers 1877*, xlviii [C–1637], 27. But the report also pointed out that in the case of railway servants "the relationship of master is, as regards liability for negligence, a mere fiction."
65    34. B.T.H.R. RCA 1/1B Nos. 1059, 1068 and 1073. Findlay held the post of Chief Traffic Manager; Grierson and Oakley were both general managers.
65    35. *Parl. Papers 1877*, x (285), qq. 1297, 1305–8, 1333–5, 1353, 1368.
65    36. *Ibid.*, viii–xviii. Lowe's draft report was a slightly more radical document, recommending compensation by employers to all employees injured by reason of the negligence of any person "excercising authority mediately or immediately derived" from the employer. On 19 June Lowe's draft was rejected by four votes to eight, Jackson, Tennant, Gooch and Knowles voting against it; Jackson's draft was then read a second time without a division.
65    37. *Ibid.*, v.
65    38. *Parl. Papers [H.L.] 1877*, v (46); *Parl. Deb.*, 3rd series (1877), ccxxxiv, 709–23, 11 May; B.T.H.R. RCA 1/1B No. 1079.
65    39. *Railway Times* (12 January 1878), 37–8.
66    40. Gupta, *op. cit.*, 70–71; *Parl. Papers 1878*, ii (11); *Parl. Deb.*, 3rd series (1878), ccxxxvii, 224, 18 January.
66    41. *The Times* (31 January 1878), 7. Brassey boasted "that he owed everything to the railways, and was only too glad to recognise the obligation."
66    42. *Railway Times* (30 March 1878), 280. A. H. Loring (ed), *Papers and Addresses by Lord Brassey . . . Political and Miscellaneous From 1861 to 1894* (1895), 119–120.
66    43. *Parl. Deb.*, 3rd series (1878), ccxxxix, 1042–71, 10 April.
66    44. P.R.O. HO 45/9458/72731A: Holker to Cross, 8 June 1878; manuscript draft of a bill "to amend the law relating to the liability of employers for injury occasioned by the negligence of their servants."
67    45. Ridley (1842–1904), "a typical country squire", succeeded Sir J. W. Pease as chairman of the North Eastern in 1902. He was Home Secretary 1895–1900, and went to the Lords as Viscount Ridley in February 1901: *Railway Times* (3 December 1904), 808–9.
67    46. P.R.O. HO 45/9458/72731A: memo. by Ridley, 22 July 1878.
67    47. *Ibid.*, memo. by Lushington, 30 July 1878.
67    48. *Ibid.*, memo. by Thring entitled "Employers Liability for Injuries to their Servants", 13 November 1878.
67    49. The *Railway Times* (10 May 1879), 397, declared: "We do not propose to take up the gauntlet . . . in defence of the existing law of compensation."
68    50. C. D. Campbell, *British Railways in Boom and Depression* (1932), 44.
68    51. B.T.H.R. RCA 1/1B No. 1206, 14 January 1879.
68    52. Gupta, *op. cit.*, 72. *Railway Times* (7 December 1878), 1036–7. *Parl. Papers 1878–9*, iii (75); *Parl. Papers [H.L.] 1878–9*, vi (7).
68    53. *Parl. Papers 1878–9*, iii (80); clause 2 set a time limit of six months, from the date of accident, within which proceedings could be brought.

*Page*

68    54. P.R.O. HO 45/9458/72731A: "Employers' Liability for Injuries to Work-men", a paper by Holker printed for the use of the Cabinet, 27 Nov. 1878.

69    55. *Parl. Papers 1878-9*, iii (103); *Parl. Deb.*, 3rd series (1879), ccxliv, 1135–43, 17 March.

69    56. B.T.H.R. RCA 1/1B No. 1215, 24 March 1879.

69    57. *Ibid.*, No. 1228, 28 March 1879.

69    58. *Ibid.*

69    59. *Ibid.*, No. 1245, 25 April 1879.

70    60. *Ibid.*, No. 1246, 9 May 1879, 2–3.

70    61. *Ibid.*, 3–4; *The Times* (10 May 1879), 14. The combined deputation, about 100 strong, contained a powerful railway contingent; *The Times* mentioned ten M.P.s, of whom five were railway directors, and Conservatives, and the Railway Association's minutes mention another four, of whom the only Liberal was Leeman. The deputation thus had a strong political flavour at a time when the government's stature was none too high.

70    62. *Railway Times* (17 May 1879), 416; *Parl. Deb.*, 3rd series, ccxlviii, 1632.

70    63. *Parl. Papers [H.L.] 1880*, iii (4). *Parl. Deb.*, 3rd series (1880), ccl, 260–3, 9 February; 486–7, 12 February. B.T.H.R. RCA 1/1B No. 1293, 2 March 1880. Bass, Brassey and S. Morley sponsored a bill, unfortunately not printed, dealing exclusively with railway servants: *Parl. Papers 1880*, iii (57).

71    64. *Parl. Deb.*, 3rd series (1880), ccli, 732–7, 9 March. D. Davies, the Welsh Liberal M.P. and coalowner, supported the motion: *ibid.*, 739–40; he was on the boards of the Brecon & Merthyr Tydfil Junction, Van, and Great Western of Brazil Ltd. railways. According to *Dod's Parliamentary Companion* Davies was also a director of the Cambrian Railways, but he is not listed as such in *Bradshaw* or the *Directory of Directors*. The mover of the motion was the Conservative H. C. Raikes, supported by A. W. Hall, another Conservative; so Watkin may have had in mind tactics by both parties.

71    65. *Railway Times* (3 April 1880), 290–1; (29 May), 448–9.

71    66. Gladstone Papers, B.M. Add. MSS. 44544, fol. 5: Gladstone to Dodson, 9 May 1880.

71    67. Gladstone Papers, B.M. Add. MSS. 44252, fol. 74: Dodson to Gladstone, 8 May 1880.

71    68. *Ibid.*, fols. 76–7: Dodson to Gladstone, 15 May 1880.

71    69. *Parl. Papers 1880*, iii (118).

71    70. B.T.H.R. RCA 1/1B No. 1296, 27 May 1880; *Parl. Deb.*, 3rd series (1880), cclii, 638–9. Whitworth was also on the boards of several coal and iron companies.

72    71. B.T.H.R. RCA 1/1B, special meeting of the association, 1 June 1880, 1–3. The meeting was a very large one; amongst those representing the railways were Gooch, Lords Colville and Houghton, Dillwyn, Knowles, Moon, Joseph Pease, Watkin and T. F. Fremantle, the Conservative M.P. and a director of the London, Brighton & South Coast Railway. Two non-railway M.P.s were also present, Barnes and Charles Morgan Norwood, also a Liberal, a steamship owner of London and Hull and first chairman of the Associated Chambers of Commerce of the United Kingdom. There were

# Notes

also present representatives of the Mining Association, the National Federation of Employers of Labour, the London Builders Association, the London and St Katherine's Dock Company, and "other Associations connected with the trading interests of the country."

72    72. *Parl. Deb.*, 3rd series (1880), cclii, 114–15, 20 May. *Railway Times* (5 June 1880), 468.

72    73. *Ibid.*, 471–2. This deputation included, besides the industries specifically represented at the Railway Association's special meeting, representatives of the factory occupiers, the iron manufacturing trades, the dock companies, the shipbuilders and shipowners, and the gas companies.

72    74. B.T.H.R. RCA 1/1B, special meeting of the Association, 1 June 1880, 4–5.

72    75. Sheffield University Library, Leader Correspondence, blue box marked "Letters of Mundella to R. Leader 1880–85" (typed transcripts): Mundella to Robert Leader, 3 June 1880.

72    76. *Railway Times* (5 June 1880), 472.

72    77. *Parl. Deb.*, 3rd series (1880), cclii, 1135, 3 June.

72    78. *Ibid.*, 1282, 4 June 1880; *Parl. Papers 1880*, iii (209).

73    79. *House of Commons' Divisions*, 1880 (Session 2), Numbs. 92 and 93, 5 August 1880.

73    80. B.T.H.R. RCA 1/1B No. 1305, 10 June 1880; *Parl. Deb.*, 3rd series (1880), ccliii, 1756–64, 1786–7.

74    81. *Annual Register*, 1880, part I, 87–9.

74    82. B.T.H.R. RCA 1/1B No. 1309, 9 July 1880.

74    83. *Railway Times* (7 August 1880), 657.

74    84. *Ibid.*, 31 July 1880, 642; *Parl. Papers 1893–4*, xxxiii [C–6894–VIII], q. 27426.

74    85. *Parl. Deb.*, 3rd series (1880), cclv, 211–19, 3 August.

74    86. *Ibid.*, 237, 257, 275–8, 4 August; the amendment was defeated by 65 votes to 175.

75    87. *Ibid.*, 278–81; this amendment was in contemplation of a clause moved on 6 August by Pease, whereby employers contributing to a mutual assurance society or fund were not to be liable for compensation under the Act. Jackson supported the clause, which was defeated by 28 votes to 68: *ibid.*, 574–94. Lord Randolph Churchill also moved a clause providing for amounts obtained from mutual insurance schemes to be deducted from the compensation awarded under the Act; his supporters were mostly Liberals.

75    88. *Ibid.*, 342–50, 5 August 1880.

75    89. B.T.H.R. RCA 1/1B No. 1311.

75    90. *Parl. Deb.*, 3rd series (1880), cclv, 1113–20, 1158, 1183, 13 August.

75    91. B.T.H.R. RCA 1/1B No. 1311, 10 August 1880; *Parl. Papers [H.L.] 1880*, iii (199b), 1–2.

75    92. *Parl. Deb.*, 3rd series (1880), cclv, 1981; cclvi, 62–73.

75    93. *Ibid.*, cclvi, 1110; Hughenden Papers, box 120, B/XXI/B/791: Brabourne to Rowton, 2 September 1880.

75    94. *Parl. Deb.*, 3rd series (1880), cclvi, 1172–3; 43 & 44 Vict., c. 42.

76    95. B.T.H.R. RCA 1/1B No. 1321, 13 January 1881.

76    96. *Parl. Papers 1894*, xxxv [C–7421–I], 216–17, 559; *Railway Review* (25 February 1881), 5.

*Page*
76     97. Gibbs and others v. The Great Western Railway Company (1883–84): 11
       Q[*ueen's*] B[*ench*] D[*ivision*], 22; 12 *Q.B.D.*, 208. This case is noted by Gupta,
       *op. cit.*, 80.
76     98. Bagwell, *The Railwaymen*, 120–1.
76     99. Gladstone Papers, B.M. Add. MSS. 44252, fols. 80–81: Dodson to Glad-
       stone, 20 July 1880.
77    100. B.T.H.R. RCA 1/1B Nos. 1271–2 and 1314–15.
77    101. *House of Commons' Divisions*, 1880 (Session 2), Numb. 43.
77    102. *Ibid.*, Numb. 90.
77    103. *Ibid.*, Numbs. 91 and 95. Beach sat on the London & South Western
       board, and Bruce on the boards of the Highland and London & North
       Western companies.
78    104. *Lord's Journals*, cxii (1880), 376.
78    105. *Ibid.*, 377; the motion was carried by 72 votes to 40. In the Commons this
       provision was altered to extend the measure to the end of 1887; thereafter
       it was re-enacted from year to year: *Parl. Deb.*, 3rd series, cclvi, 1115–19.
78    106. B.T.H.R. RCA 1/1B No. 1338; the proposal was negatived.
78    107. *House of Commons' Divisions*, 1880 (Session 2), Numb. 98; the two were
       Lord F. C. Cavendish of the Furness Railway, and Sir Sydney Waterlow of
       the London, Chatham & Dover.
78    108. *Ibid.*, Numb. 114.
78    109. *Ibid.*, Numb. 115.
78    110. *Ibid.*, Numb. 165; the Liberal chief whip, Lord Richard Grosvenor, was a
       director of the London & North Western.
79    111. In the division on Giffard's clause, *House of Commons' Divisions*, 1880
       (Session 2), Numb. 113, no Conservative member of the efficient interest
       voted for the clause; only two, Makins and Tyler, voted against it, together
       with four Liberal members. This, taken together with division Numb. 114,
       might suggest that the companies were apathetic towards the questions of
       special treatment for railways and mutual insurance. But the history of
       their campaign in the employers' liability question makes this most un-
       likely.
79    112. Salisbury Papers, Class K, Special Correspondence, Great Eastern Railway
       Series: Watkin to Salisbury, 21 February 1874; Watkin did not say he would
       join a purely Conservative government.
79    113. The *Annual Register* (1880), part I, 91 and 94, noted that both the Em-
       ployers' Liability Act and the Ground Game Act were blows at the concept
       of freedom of contract.
79    114. *Ibid.* (1877), part I, 3–4.
80    115. Salisbury Papers, Special Correspondence, Class E, Main Series: Brabourne
       to Salisbury, 24 February 1882 (filed under "Hugessen").
80    116. See *Dod's Parliamentary Companion* and the division on the second reading
       of the Home Rule bill, *House of Commons' Divisions*, 1886, Numb. 124, 7
       June 1886. In 1880 MacPherson-Grant was on the board of the Highland
       Railway.
80    117. G. G. Lerry, *Henry Robertson* (Oswestry 1949), 38–9.

# Notes to Chapter 5

Page

81    1. Birmingham University Library, Joseph Chamberlain Papers, JC2/9/21: Chamberlain to Farrer, 27 October 1880.

82    2. S. Buxton, *Finance and Politics: an Historical Study 1873–1885*, vol. II (1888), 309. *Railway Gazette* (19 April 1929), 558. 2 & 3 Wm IV, c. 120; 5 & 6 Vict., c. 79.

82    3. H. Parris, *op. cit.*, 77; C. E. Lee, *Passenger Class Distinctions* (1946), 13–16.

82    4. 7 & 8 Vict., c. 85.

82    5. Lee, *op. cit.*, 45.

82    6. Buxton, *op. cit.*, 309.

82    7. *Parl. Deb.*, 3rd series (1877), ccxxxiii, 1275–6: speech by Knatchbull-Hugessen, 17 April. The railways, by driving the stage-coaches out of business, hastened the repeal of the duties upon them. Buxton, *loc. cit.*, states that in 1868, the year before their repeal, they yielded only £50,000. The horse tax, which replaced the mileage tax on stage-coaches, was repealed in 1874: *Parl. Papers 1876*, xiii (312), vi.

82    8. "British Railway Progress, 1850–1912", *The Jubilee of the Railway News* [1914], 33; the percentage of working expenses to gross receipts rose from 48% in 1870 to 53% in 1883.

83    9. B.T.H.R. RCA 1/1B No. 411, 27 January 1870.

83    10. *Ibid.*, No. 722, 30 July 1872; *Parl. Deb.*, 3rd series (1877), ccxxxiii, 1277; *Parl. Papers 1876*, xiii (312), iv.

83    11. *Ibid.*, qq. 194, 2266; P.R.O. T1/7584A/3598/1877, file 14379 of 1876: Farrer to the Treasury, 29 August 1876.

83    12. B.T.H.R. RCA 1/1B Nos. 281 and 354; J. N. Porter, *The Railway Passenger Duty: Its Injustice and its Repeal, considered* . . . (1874), 5.

84    13. B.T.H.R. RCA 1/1B Nos. 411, 421, 432 and 469.

84    14. *Ibid.*, Nos. 458 and 469; *Parl. Papers 1876*, xiii (312), q. 737.

84    15. *Ibid.*, iv.

84    16. *Parl. Deb.*, 3rd series (1872), ccxii, 1369–70, 18 July.

84    17. B.T.H.R. RCA 1/1B Nos. 719 and 726; *Railway Times* (14 December 1872), 1267–8.

84    18. *The Times* (14 December 1872), 7.

85    19. B.T.H.R. RCA 1/1B No. 766, 11 March 1873.

85    20. *Railway Times* (29 March 1873), 345.

85    21. *Ibid.* (19 April 1873), 421.

85    22. B.T.H.R. RCA 1/1B Nos. 805, 820, 824 and 829.

85    23. Northcote had formerly been chairman of the South Devon Railway.

85    24. *Railway Times* (14 February 1874), 172; (7 March), 267. The companies also gave the Repeal Association financial support; see for example B.T.H.R. GE 1/10, 214 and 235, and GW 1/26, 20.

85    25. B.T.H.R. RCA 1/1B No. 865, 17 March 1874.

85    26. Iddesleigh Papers, B.M. Add. MSS. 50052, fol. 4: Northcote to Adderley, 10 March 1874.

85    27. *Ibid.*, Add. MSS. 50016, fols. 177–8: Northcote to Disraeli, 20 and 22 March 1874; P.R.O. CAB 41/6/5: Disraeli to the Queen, 21 March.

Page
85   28. A. Lang, *Life, Letters and Diaries of Sir Stafford Northcote First Earl of Iddesleigh*, new edn (Edinburgh 1891), 259.
86   29. B.T.H.R. RCA 1/1B No. 865, 17 March 1874.
86   30. *Ibid*: letter from John Stirling, chairman of the North British Railway.
86   31. Law Reports, Court of Exchequer: 9 *Ex*, 330–8.
86   32. B.T.H.R. RCA 1/1B No. 894, 14 July 1874.
86   33. *Ibid.,* Nos. 895 and 898, 23 September and 14 October 1874. Only the Midland Railway, then making strenuous efforts to attract the third-class passenger, refused to adopt these resolutions: Lee, *op. cit.,* 43.
86   34. *Railway Times* (7 November 1874), 1119.
86   35. *Herapath* (6 March 1875), 267; (20 March), 300–2.
86   36. *Ibid.* (27 March 1875), 324.
86   37. Lang, *op. cit.,* 261. Iddesleigh Papers, B.M. Add.MSS. 50052, fol. 78: Northcote to Sir William Stephenson, 13 January 1875.
87   38. H. J. Dyos, 'Workmen's Fares in South London, 1860–1914', *Journal of Transport History*, i (1953–4), 5–6.
87   39. Lee, *op. cit.,* 51–5; C. J. Allen, *The Great Eastern Railway* (2nd edn 1956), 63; T. C. Barker and M. Robbins, *A History of London Transport*, Vol. I (1963), 116, 173–4.
87   40. Law Reports, Appeal Cases: I *App Cas*, 148, 22 February 1876.
87   41. *Parl. Deb.,* 3rd series, (1876), ccxxvii, 1586.
87   42. *Ibid.,* 1590; *Herapath* (19 February 1876), 223. Privately to Northcote in 1879, Spinks rejected any suggestion that either he or Rodwell was acting as a representative of the railway interest: Iddesleigh Papers, B.M. Add. MSS. 50053, fol. 173: Northcote to Spinks, 9 July 1879.
87   43. B.T.H.R. RCA 1/1B No. 949, 7 March 1876; *Parl. Deb.,* 3rd series (1876), ccxxvii, 1590.
87   44. *Ibid.,* 1591–3, 1601–2.
87   45. B.T.H.R. RCA 1/1B Nos. 970, 974 and 981.
88   46. *Parl. Papers 1876*, xiii (312), qq. 615, 1307, 1830, 1991, 2859, and 3607. This argument had particular force in regard to companies such as the Metropolitan and Metropolitan District, which had to contend with stiff road and river competition: *ibid.,* qq. 728, 760 and 1181.
88   47. *Ibid.,* q. 3262.
88   48. *Ibid.,* q. 885.
88   49. *Ibid.,* vii, xxii–xxiii.
88   50. Iddesleigh Papers, B.M. Add. MSS. 50053, fol. 54: Northcote to Sir William Stephenson, 28 February 1877.
88   51. *Herapath* (24 February 1877), 215; B.T.H.R. RCA 1/1B No. 1027, 21 February.
89   52. *Ibid.,* Nos. 1045 and 1049, 21 March and 14 April; *Parl. Deb.,* 3rd series (1877), ccxxxiii, 1273–1365, 17 April.
89   53. Iddesleigh Papers, BM. Add. MSS. 50053, fol. 54: Northcote to Stephenson, 28 February 1877.
89   54. *The Times* (9 September 1876), 4.
89   55. *Railway News* (19 August 1882), 276.

# Notes

89    56. Knatchbull MSS., Kent Archives Office, U951 F27/5; Political Journal kept by Sir Edward Knatchbull-Hugessen, 1874–8, 63.

89    57. B.T.H.R. RCA 1/1B No. 1082, 8 May 1877. On 22 April 1879 a move by Watkin to re-open negotiations with the government was defeated on a show of hands: *ibid.*, No. 1237.

89    58. J. McCabe, *Life and Letters of George Jacob Holyoake*, 2 vols (1908), *passim*; G. J. Holyoake, *Bygones Worth Remembering*, vol. II (1905), 267–70; Travelling Tax Abolition Committee, *Gazette*, No. 1 (April 1878), 1.

89    59. G. J. Holyoake, *History of the Travelling Tax* (1901), 9–11; B.T.H.R. GN 1/41, 228, 29 September 1876.

89    60. *Herapath* (3 March 1877), 234. The text of the paper is in C. D. Collet, *Reasons for the Repeal of the Railway Passenger Duty* (1877).

90    61. *Railway Times* (27 April 1878), 363. Further evidence of contacts between the committee and Houghton, Rodwell and Spinks is provided in the minutes of the committee, now amongst the George Jacob Holyoake papers in the Bishopsgate Institute, especially in the volume for 1877–85, 35, 107 and 171.

90    62. Holyoake, *History of the Travelling Tax*, 11.

90    63. Travelling Tax Abolition Committee, *Gazette,* Nos. 1–13, April 1878–September 1883.

90    64. *Railway Times* (7 December 1878), 1032.

90    65. Holyoake, *Bygones Worth Remembering*, vol. I (1905), 43. Lee, *op. cit.*, 47, relying on Holyoake, has also exaggerated the importance of the committee's work.

90    66. P.R.O. MT6/439/3616/1887, file 8463 of 1878: minute by Farrer, 27 October 1878, and by Sandon, 28 October.

90    67. *Ibid.*, file 4601 of 1880: minute of 29 May.

90    68. *Ibid.*, file 5499 of 1880: minute by Chamberlain, 30 June.

90    69. B.T.H.R. RCA 1/1B No. 1370, 21 March 1882: speech by Chamberlain in reply to a deputation from the association.

90    70. J. L. Garvin, *Life of Joseph Chamberlain*, vol. I (1836–85), (1935), 408–37, deals only with the Bankruptcy and Patent Acts of 1883, and the abortive Merchant Shipping bill of 1884. The equally abortive Railway Regulation bill of 1884 receives a bare mention; the Cheap Trains Act of 1883 is not mentioned at all.

91    71. P. Fraser, *Joseph Chamberlain* (1966), 22.

91    72. *Parl. Papers 1882*, vii (235), x.

91    73. P.R.O. MT6/337/6866/1883, file 4104 of 1882: copy letter from Watkin to Plumstead Board of Works, 9 March 1882.

91    74. *Evening News* (27 June 1883), 1.

91    75. P.R.O. MT6/337/6866/1883, file 5330 of 1882: Farrer to Redesdale, 19 June 1882; file 8159 of 1882: minute by Chamberlain, 14 August.

91    76. *Ibid.*, file 11218 of 1882; Joseph Chamberlain Papers, JC2/17/2: memorandum, apparently by his private secretary, I. B. Walker, 19 December 1882; *Parl. Deb.*, 3rd series (1882), cclxxiv, 949–50, 7 November.

91    77. *Ibid.*, 1542, 16 November; P.R.O. MT6/337/6866/1883, file 11326 of 1882.

91    78. *Ibid.*, file 3307 of 1883; *Parl. Papers 1883*, lxi [C–3535], 23.

Notes

*Page*
91  79. P.R.O. MT6/337/6866/1883, file 5587 of 1883: Henry Calcraft to Plumstead Board of Works, 23 April.

92  80. Gladstone Papers, BM. Add.MSS. 44130, fol. 253: Childers to Gladstone, 11 June 1883.

92  81. *Parl. Deb.*, 3rd series (1883), cclxxvii, 1534.

92  82. This information was 'leaked' by the *Pall Mall Gazette* (18 April 1883), 5, which pointed out what "very large tracts of country" would be included "in some given district of the Midlands, or Lancashire, or Yorkshire". At the Railway Association, Ralph Dutton, chairman of the London & South Western, spoke strongly against the scheme: B.T.H.R. RCA 1/2 No. 1499, 23 April.

92  83. B.T.H.R. RCA 1/2 Nos. 1484, 1486 and 1488, 21 and 28 June, and 3 July 1883. *Parl. Papers 1883*, ix (219); the bill did not extend to Ireland.

92  84. B.T.H.R. RCA 1/2 No. 1489, 4 July; *The Times* (5 July 1883), 9.

92  85. *Parl. Papers 1883*, ix (255).

93  86. *Parl. Deb.*, 3rd series (1883), cclxxxii, 674, 26 July; B.T.H.R. RCA 1/2 No. 1503, 27 July.

93  87. *Parl. Deb.*, 3rd series (1883), cclxxxii, 1095, 30 July; 46 & 47 Vict., c. 34.

93  88. *The Times* (1 August 1883), 11; (9 August), 11. *Herapath* (4 August), 946; (11 August), 967, 976. B.T.H.R. RCA 1/2 No. 1499, 23 July.

93  89. *Railway Times* (5 January 1884), 7, 9 and 21. Wemyss' organization attracted some railway support at its foundation, mainly from directors and officers of Watkin's companies. The Railway Association ignored approaches from it, in 1883, and from an earlier State Resistance Union in 1882: *Lord Bramwell on Liberty and Other Speeches, delivered at the General Meeting of the Liberty and Property Defence League, 1882* (1883), 2–5, 34–9; B.T.H.R. RCA 1/1B No. 1378; RCA 1/2 No. 1415.

93  90. Knatchbull MSS., U951 F27/9: Political Journal kept by Sir Edward Knatchbull-Hugessen, 1882–5, 50–1; B.T.H.R. RCA 1/2 Nos. 1509 and 1511, 22 November 1883 and 16 January 1884.

93  91. *Parl. Papers 1884–5*, xxx [C–4402–I], q. 12426.

93  92. *Ibid.*, qq. 9968–70.

93  93. B.T.H.R. MSL 1/19, min. 8789, 19 October 1883.

94  94. P.R.O. T1/8109A/12974/1884: Treasury minute, 21 July 1884; MT6/409/3375/1886, file 2982 of 1886; the complaints concerned the delineation of urban districts.

94  95. Dyos, *op. cit.*, 10–13; P.R.O. MT6/387/3324/1885, file 4067 of 1884: memo. by Farrer, undated, advocating "a general pressure on the Companies to provide accommodation". The railway case and experience is well summarized in S. A. Pope, 'The Cheap Trains Act, 1883, and its equitable Interpretation . . .', *Great Western Railway (London) Lecture and Debating Society, Session 1905–6*, meeting of 22 February 1906, 5–10. In 1921 (11 & 12 Geo V, c.32) fares not exceeding minimum fares were exempted from duty. The duty was eventually abolished by Winston Churchill in 1929, but only on condition that the capital equivalent of the whole of the relief from taxation should be used for the development and modernization of railway transport: *Railway Gazette* (19 April 1929), 558; 19 & 20 Geo V, c.21.

## Notes to Chapter 6

*Page*

95  1. S. B. Saul, *The Myth of the Great Depression, 1873–1896* (1969), 12–13, 32, 36, 41–2, 54.

95  2. P. Mathias, *The First Industrial Nation: An Economic History of Britain 1700–1914* (1969), 397.

96  3. See generally D. H. Aldcroft, 'The Efficiency and Enterprise of British Railways, 1870–1914', *Explorations in Entrepreneurial History*, V (1968), 158–74, and the same author's *British Railways in Transition*, (1968), 1–26.

96  4. J. Mavor, 'The English Railway Rate Question', *Quarterly Journal of Economics*, iii (1894), 288.

96  5. C. D. Campbell, *op. cit.*, 44.

96  6. P. J. Cain, *op. cit.*, 12.

96  7. An article in the agricultural journal *Mark Lane Express* (1 November 1880), 554, by W. A. Hunter, announced: "The severe pressure of foreign competition has obliged farmers to examine a variety of charges, which were submitted to without inquiry in more prosperous times".

96  8. J. Grierson, *Railway Rates: English and Foreign* (1886), 25–35. Section 2 of the Railway and Canal Traffic Act of 1854 prohibited a company from giving any "undue or unreasonable Preference or Advantage to or in favour of any particular Person or Company, or any particular Description of traffic, in any respect whatsoever". About 1880 the question of differential rates between one locality and another came before the Railway Commission and the law courts; the decisions reached made such rates illegal: Mavor, *op. cit.*, 286.

96  9. These were known as "station terminals", to distinguish them from "service terminals" – charges for cartage, loading, unloading, and covering of wagons – the legality of which was generally not in dispute. On this subject see W. A. Hunter, *The Railway and Canal Traffic Act, 1888. Part I: An Exposition of Section Twenty-Four of the Act* (1889), 55–9.

97  10. Grierson, *op. cit.*, 68–76; L. C. A. Knowles, *The Industrial and Commercial Revolutions in Great Britain during the Nineteenth Century*, (revised edn 1941), 277–8; W. M. Acworth, *The Elements of Railway Economics* (Oxford 1905), 20, 49–52; W. Z. Ripley, *Railroads Rates and Regulations* (1913), 55; A. T. Hadley, *Railroad Transportation Its History and its Laws* (New York 1886), 113, 123–4. Section 90 of the 1845 Act, 8 & 9 Vict., c.20, whilst prohibiting a railway from varying its tolls in favour of or against any individual or company using the railway, affirmed the right of a railway "to vary the Tolls upon the Railway so as to accommodate them to the circumstances of the Traffic".

97  11. A. P. Usher, *An Introduction to the Industrial History of England* (1921), 469–70.

97  12. Knowles, *op. cit.*, 277; Hadley, *op. cit.*, 173–4.

97  13. *Parl. Papers 1878*, xxv [C–1962], pp. 6–7; the report is dated 10 November 1877. Under the 1873 Act through rates could be demanded by railway companies, but not by traders.

97  14. B.T.H.R. RCA 1/1B Nos. 1088 and 1122.

*Page*

97    15. Iddesleigh Papers, B.M. Add. MSS. 50052, fol. 88: Northcote to W. H. Smith, 13 November 1877.

97    16. *Ibid.,* Add. MSS. 50018, fol. 132: Northcote to Beaconsfield, 9 January 1879; B.T.H.R. RCA 1/1B No. 1205; *Railway Times* (6 April 1878), 305.

98    17. B.T.H.R. RCA 1/1B No. 1208, 12 February 1879.

98    18. *Parl. Papers 1878–9,* v (270); 42 & 43 Vict., c. 56; B.T.H.R. RCA 1/1B No. 1268. In 1878, and from 1882 to 1887 inclusive, the Act of 1873 was incorporated in the annual Expiring Laws Continuance Act.

98    19. *Mark Lane Express* (5 May 1879), 8; (6 February 1882), 180; *The Mirror of the North* (Aberdeen, 8 March 1881), 97. William Alexander Hunter, of Aberdeen and London universities, and an expert in Roman Law, became Liberal M.P. for Aberdeen North in November 1885.

98    20. A. H. H. Matthews, *Fifty Years of Agricultural Politics, being the History of the Central Chamber of Agriculture, 1865–1915* (1915), 219.

98    21. *Railway Times* (12 June 1880), 491; the deputation was led by a number of Liberal M.P.s, including Samuel Morley and the spokesman, John Whitwell. See also the thirty memorials to the Board of Trade from chambers of commerce, ranging in date from 12 October 1879 to 29 December 1880, cited in *Parl. Papers 1881*, xiv (374–I), 3–4.

98    22. B.T.H.R. RCA 1/2 No. 1557, 28 March 1884.

98    23. G. H. Wright, *Chronicles of the Birmingham Chamber of Commerce A.D. 1813–1913* [Birmingham], 1913, 278–9.

99    24. Joseph Chamberlain Papers, JC2/9/21: Chamberlain to Farrer, 27 October 1880; the "stormy time" referred, no doubt, to Irish affairs.

99    25. *Parl. Deb.,* 3rd series (1881), cclviii, 999; B.T.H.R. RCA 1/1B No. 1331, 15 February 1881.

99    26. *Herapath* (26 February 1881), 261. The analogy with the Liberal government's policy of attacks upon "all vested property of any sort" in Ireland was made again in 1884 by Lord Brabourne at a meeting of Watkin's Association of Railway Shareholders: *Railway Times* (7 June 1884), 731.

99    27. *Parl. Deb.,* 3rd series (1881), cclix, 226, 3 March; 1038, 14 March. The same seven were reappointed to the Select Committee the following session: *ibid.,* cclxvi, 474–5, 10 February 1882.

99    28. B.T.H.R. RCA 1/1B No. 1341, 9 March 1881; meeting of general managers and consulting solicitors, 10 March; MSL 1/17, min. 7403, 11 March.

100    29. Matthews, *op. cit.,* 219–20; A. J. Wolfe, *op. cit.,* 9–11. *The Times* (11 February 1882), 10; *Mark Lane Express* (13 February 1882), 217; (12 June), 747; *Chamber of Commerce Journal* (1 July 1882), 91; (1 September 1882), 147; *The Chambers of Commerce Manual* (1954–5), 1 and 4. P. M. Williams, 'Public Opinion and the Railway Rates Question in 1886', *E.H.R.,* lxvii (1952), 41, states that in 1886 65 chambers were affiliated to the Associated Chambers.

100    30. *Parl. Papers 1881*, xiii (374), qq. 2494, 5806, 8707, 10109.

100    31. P.R.O. BT 13/13/E5326/1882.

100    32. *Parl. Papers 1881*, xiii (374), qq. 1819, 2464, 2723, 4221, 8755. In q. 11559 one manufacturer advocated protective rates in favour of Birmingham.

# Notes

100    33. B.T.H.R. RCA 1/1B No. 1344, 24 June 1881. Watkin's notes taken during the proceedings of the Select Committee, March–May 1881, show great attention to the details of the traders' evidence: *ibid.*, SER 4/21.

100    34. *Parl. Papers 1881*, xiii (374), qq. 12276, 12524, 12671, 12700–5, 12721.

100    35. B.T.H.R. RCA 1/1B Nos. 1353 and 1362; *Parl. Papers 1882*, xiii (317), qq. 12–13, 23–132.

101    36. B.T.H.R. RCA 1/1B Nos. 1383, 1392, 1399. For the draft reports of Ashley and Barclay see *Parl. Papers 1882*, xiii (317), xxiii–xlii.

101    37. *Ibid.*, 1, lxvii, lxix, lxxxi, lxxxv.

101    38. *Ibid.*, v, xi, xiv–xv; the report is dated 12 July 1882.

102    39. B.T.H.R. RCA 1/1B No. 1402, 8 August 1882.

102    40. *Annual Register* (1883), part i, 102.

102    41. *Parl. Deb.*, 3rd series (1883), cclxxvii, 188, 12 March; B.T.H.R. RCA 1/2 No. 1430, 3 April 1883.

102    42. *Parl. Deb.*, 3rd series (1883), cclxxviii, 1881.

102    43. *Ibid.*, 1899–1901, 1914; Samuelson had, in fact, altered the terms of his motion to meet Chamberlain's wishes: Gladstone Papers, B.M. Add. MSS. 44125, fol. 184: Chamberlain to Gladstone, 3 May 1883.

103    44. P.R.O. MT6/356/691/1884: memo. by Farrer on the negotiation, 15 January 1884. B.T.H.R. RCA 1/2 No. 1509. The general managers and solicitors of the companies took much trouble in working out a new classification of goods and scale of terminal charges: B.T.H.R. RCA (Y) 1/19: meetings of managers and solicitors, 29 November (wrongly dated 29 September), 12 and 18 December 1883; 9 January, 12 and 19 February 1884.

103    45. P.R.O. MT6/356/691/1884: minute by Chamberlain on Farrer's memo., 21 January 1884.

103    46. B.T.H.R. RCA 1/2 No. 1515, 7 February 1884: speech by Chamberlain in reply to a deputation from the association, same day. In December 1880 the Amalgamated Society of Railway Servants had urged on Chamberlain the necessity of acting on the problem of railway brakes: *Railway Times* (4 December 1880), 1017–8. In 1882 Earl De La Warr introduced a bill making it obligatory on railway companies to provide continuous brakes on passenger trains; it was given a second reading in the Lords on 20 March: *Parl. Deb.*, 3rd series (1882), cclxvi, 1495–6; cclxvii, 1254–60; *Parl. Papers [H.L.] 1882* (B.M. bound volumes), Bills, vol. 4, bill 21. On 10 June 1880 the Board of Trade had circularized the companies urging the adoption of continuous brakes on passenger trains, and a circular of 20 September 1880 referred to interlocking: *Parl. Papers 1880*, lxiv [C–1677], 3–4; *Parl. Papers 1881*, lxxxi [C–2857], 3.

103    47. B.T.H.R. RCA (Y) 1/19, deputation of railway officers to Board of Trade, 26 February 1884; RCA 1/2 No. 1545, meeting of Parliamentary Committee, 4 March, when a resolution was passed "That . . . the question of Terminals ought to be dealt with without conditions".

103    48. *Ibid.*, No. 1547, 12 March 1884: deputation of officers to Chamberlain on 4 March; RCA (Y) 1/19, meeting of officers' committee, 14 March.

103    49. *Ibid.*, meeting of officers' committee, 21 March 1884, deputation to Board of Trade.

*Page*

103    50. B.T.H.R. RCA 1/2 No. 1557, 28 March 1884.

104    51. B.T.H.R. RCA (Y) 1/19, meeting of officers' committee, 4 and 8 April 1884; RCA 1/2 No. 1558, 8 April.

104    52. *Ibid.*, No. 1567, 8 May; RCA (Y) 1/19, meeting of officers' committee, 7 May.

104    53. *Parl. Papers 1884*, vi (225): clause 21 made the legality of station terminals dependent upon a company having its revised classification of rates and schedule of maximum rates approved by Parliament.

104    54. B.T.H.R. RCA 1/2 No. 1573, interview between a special committee of the association and Chamberlain, 20 June 1884.

104    55. *Railway Times* (31 May 1884), 688, 700; (14 June), 755; (21 June), 785, 792, 795–6; (28 June), 825. Matthews, *op. cit.*, 221.

104    56. The shipowners were roused, not merely by the contents of the Merchant Shipping bill, "but by the manner in which the Minister was conducting the campaign" against them: *Annual Register* (1884), part i, 168; the bill was never given a second reading.

104    57. B.T.H.R. RCA 1/44, meeting of officers' committee, 21 May 1884. *Parl. Deb.*, 3rd series (1884), cclxxxviii, 914–35; ccxc, 578–634. This was not a government division. No member of the efficient interest voted for the standing order, but 24 (fifteen Liberals and nine Conservatives) voted against, with the Liberal Joseph Pease and the Conservative Colonel Makins acting as tellers: *House of Commons' Divisions*, 1884, Numb. 155, 9 July. On 22 July a similar standing order was passed in the Lords on the motion of Lord Henniker: *Parl. Deb.*, 3rd series (1884), ccxci, 8–18; B.T.H.R. RCA 1/2 No. 1583.

104    58. *Parl. Deb.*, 3rd series (1884), ccxc, 666.

105    59. B.T.H.R. RCA (Y) 1/19, meeting of officers' committee, 21 March 1884.

105    60. *Ibid.*, meeting of general managers and solicitors, 3 and 14 November 1884. RCA 1/2 Nos. 1584 and 1586, 4 November and 9 December. RCA 1/44 Nos. 1584B, 1584C, 1584D, 1854E, 25 November to 9 December. Other companies were of course brought into the discussions. A set of the bills is in B.T.H.R. PYB 1/1232; the terminals clause—section 7 of the Midland bill—gave legal recognition both to station and service terminals, with power to the Railway Commissioners to hear and determine any dispute as to their amount.

105    61. *The Times* (15 January 1885), 10; *Railway Times* (17 January 1885), 88; those present also included the Liberals Barclay, Samuelson and Hunter, and the Conservative C. T. Ritchie. The main complaints of the traders were to the legalization of station terminals and the increased rates proposed for lots under two tons and small parcels: *Railway Rates and Charges Bills: Three Articles . . . reprinted from the 'Northern Echo'* (Darlington 1885), *passim.;* W. A. Hunter, *The Railway & Canal Traders' Association: The New Railway Rates Bills . . .* [1885], 3–7, 37; Manchester and Lancashire and Cheshire Corporations, *Railway Rates & Charges . . . Report on the Bills by Sub-Committee on Proposed Alterations in the Law* (Manchester 1885), *passim.*

105    62. *The Times* (31 January 1885), 6; B.T.H.R. RCA 1/2 No. 1589, 29 January.

105    63. *Ibid.*, No. 1591, 16 February 1885.

# Notes

*Page*

106    64. Joseph Chamberlain Papers, JC2/17/4: Farrer to Chamberlain, 3 March 1885. Farrer's obsession was with the reputation of the Board of Trade. As a staunch free-trader he deprecated the raising of railway rates on imported goods simply to protect home industries, and years before had written in defence of shareholders' profits: P.R.O. MT6/280/6698/1881, memo. by Farrer, 3 July 1881.

106    65. C. H. D. Howard (ed), *A Political Memoir 1880–92 by Joseph Chamberlain* (1953), 108–111.

106    66. Wright, *op. cit.*, 307; *Railway Times* (24 January 1885), 121; (31 January), 154.

106    67. *Railway Times* (21 February 1885), 251. In all, 280 petitions were presented against the bills: *ibid.* (14 February), 218; (21 February), 250–1; (7 March), 308; (14 March), 342. Matthews, *op. cit.*, 222. The traders took a further step in parliamentary organization at this time, when a committee of peers and M.P.s was formed, with Lord Henniker as chairman, to combat the bills; the committee was not formally constituted till 8 July: *Parl. Deb.*, 3rd series (1885), ccxcv, 226, 6 March; *Railway Times* (11 July 1885), 887; P. M. Williams, *op. cit.*, 40.

106    68. *Parl. Deb.*, 3rd series (1885), ccxcvi, 1853, 16 April.

106    69. *Ibid.*, ccxcvii, 652–3; *Railway Times* (2 May 1885), 568; B.T.H.R. RCA 1/2 No. 1609.

107    70. *Ibid.*, No. 1611, 24 April 1885. W. A. Hunter, *The Railway and Cana Traffic Act, 1888*, 41, 58–9. 15 *Q.B.D.*, 505–48.

107    71. *Railway Times* (24 October 1885), 1367; this statement is all the more remarkable as Chamberlain was facing an election at this time.

107    72. "Hercules", *British Railways and Canals in Relation to British Trade and Government Control* [1884], 228–9.

107    73. Grierson, *op. cit.*, 79–80.

# Notes to Chapter 7

108    1. Appendix, table 7.

108    2. Appendix, table 11.

109    3. B.T.H.R. GE 1/19, 292; GN 1/48, 220–2; GN 1/49, 71 and 81; MSL 1/20, mins. 10434, 10449; MSL 1/21, min. 10527.

109    4. C. D. Campbell, *op. cit.*, 21, 44.

109    5. *Morning Post* (13 January 1886), 5. *Daily Telegraph* (27 March 1886), 5.

109    6. *Morning Post* (4 February 1886), 4.

109    7. W. H. G. Armytage, 'The Railway Rates Question and the fall of the Third Gladstone Ministry', *E.H.R.*, lxv (1950), 23. *Railway Times* (16 January 1886), 81. B.T.H.R. RCA 1/2 No. 1630, 1 February; LNW 1/28, min. 5418.

109    8. P. M. Williams, *op. cit.*, 40. S. H. Beer, *Modern British Politics*. 67–8.

110    9. Kent Archives Office, Chilston Papers, U564 6306/8: Iddesleigh to Akers-Douglas, 18 August 1885.

# Notes

*Page*

110    10. P.R.O. CAB 37/17/10, p. 2 and clauses 4, 9, 11, 19 and 21.

110    11. *Parl. Deb.*, 3rd series (1886), cccv, 388–93, 455, 6 May.

110    12. B.T.H.R. RCA 1/2 No. 1631, 1 February 1886.

111    13. *Parl. Deb.*, 3rd series (1886), cccv, 455. Sheffield University Library, Mundella Correspondence, brown box marked "Folio III F-G"; Farrer to Mundella, 7 May 1886.

111    14. *Railway Times* (27 February 1886), 283.

111    15. The Railway Rates Committee, *Railway Rates: Joint Deputation . . . to the Right Honourable A. J. Mundella, M.P.* . . . [1886], 3–10, 22–3, 25–6.

111    16. *Parl. Deb.*, 3rd series (1886), ccciii, 555–63, 587–9, 592–3.

111    17. *Railway Times* (3 April 1886), 445.

112    18. *Parl. Papers 1886.*, v (138). B.T.H.R. RCA 1/2 No. 1641, 7.

112    19. P. M. Williams, *op. cit.*, 41–4. G. H. Wright, *op. cit.*, 320. *Railway Times* (20 March 1886), 380; (3 April), 444–5.

112    20. *Ibid.* (27 March 1886), 401.

112    21. B.T.H.R. RCA 1/2 No. 1641, 23 March, 7–8.

112    22. *Ibid.*, 9–10; some of the views expressed at this meeting suggest that an additional reason for bringing in the shareholders was to establish a sort of collective responsibility as protection for directors in case the bill became law. For further details of the individual meetings see *Railway Times* (27 March 1886), 401, and B.T.H.R. CAL 1/30, mins. 982 and 1043; GE 1/19, 184–6; GN 1/49, 6–9; GW 1/36, 449–50; LNW 1/28, min. 5595; NBR 1/32, 647–8; NER 1/17, mins. 9289–91. Many of the circulars sent to shareholders by their companies, and reports of the meetings, are in B.T.H.R. MT 1/76; the North Eastern Railway's circular is in NER 1/389.

112    23. *Standard* (27 March 1886), 5. *Railway Times* (27 March), 401. *Money* (28 April), 278.

113    24. *Money* (31 March 1886), 213.

113    25. B.T.H.R. RCA 1/2 Nos. 1643 and 1648, 23 and 30 March 1886.

113    26. *The Times* (5 May 1886), 5: letter from James Grierson.

113    27. P. M. Williams, *op. cit.*, 57–9. *Parl. Deb.*, 3rd series (1888), cccxxv, 1841: speech by Mundella, 10 May. *Railway Times* (3 April 1886), 432–3, 443–4; (10 April), 475; (17 April), 501.

113    28. *Globe* (6 April 1886), 1.

113    29. *Daily Telegraph* (26 March 1886), 5: letter to Gladstone from 74 Liberal county members on 18 March. *Railway Times* (3 April 1886), 445.

113    30. *Bradshaw.*

113    31. *Railway Times, loc. cit.*

113    32. B.T.H.R. RCA 1/2 No. 1653, 7 April 1886, 3.

114    33. Salisbury Papers, Special Correspondence, Class E, Main Series: Cross to Salisbury, 9 and 26 April 1886.

114    34. *Railway Times* (3 April 1886), 444–5; (10 April), 474–5. *Standard* (6 April 1886), 3. A. H. H. Matthews, *op. cit.*, 223. P. M. Williams, *op. cit.*, 41–4, 48–9.

114    35. *Ibid.*, 49.

114    36. Appendix, tables 7 and 8.

114    37. B.T.H.R. RCA 1/2 No. 1656, 4 May 1886.

# Notes

*Page*

115    38. *Ibid. Parl. Deb.*, 3rd series (1886), cccv, 380–8.

115    39. *Ibid.*, 466.

115    40. *Ibid.*, (1886), cccvi, 1290.

115    41. W. H. G. Armytage, *E.H.R.*, lxv (1950), 18–51, reproduced with minor corrections in the same author's *A. J. Mundella 1825–1897* (1951), 237–66; P. M. Williams, *E.H.R.*, lxvii (1952), 37–73. Armytage argued that Mundella's measure materially contributed to the defeat of Home Rule by enabling opponents of the Ministry to use the railway bill to prepare the ground for the condemnation of the Home Rule bill as an attack on the principle of private property; Williams, whose concern was more with industrial and agricultural opinion than with the views of the railway interest *per se*, contended that as the vast body of traders and agriculturists who used the railways supported Mundella's proposals, his bill could only have played a minor part in the fall of the government.

115    42. Barclay's amendment, calling in general terms for further land reform, and especially for fair rents, was defeated by 211 votes to 183; other Liberals who voted against it included Leonard Courtney, G. J. Goschen, the Marquis of Hartington and Sir Henry James, all of whom (but not Pease) subsequently left the Liberal party: *House of Commons' Divisions*, 1886 Session I, Numb. 1, 25 January 1886; *Parl. Deb.*, 3rd series, cccii, 352. The incident is referred to in A. D. Eliot, *The Life of George Joachim Goschen*, vol. II (1911), 12, and Lord (G. R.) Askwith, *Lord James of Hereford* (1930), 153.

115    43. Gladstone Papers, B.M. Add. MSS. 44497, fol. 223: Pease to Gladstone, 14 May 1886. B.T.H.R. RCA 1/2 No. 1656.

115    44. *Ibid.*, No. 1666, 13 May.

115    45. *House of Commons' Divisions*, 1886 Session I, Numb. 124, 7 June; the total of 17 does not include Lord Richard Grosvenor who, having taken a peerage, did not vote.

115    46. P. M. Williams, *op. cit.*, 49.

116    47. Corbett was on the board of the Bishop's Castle & Montgomery Railway; Vivian was on the board of the Rhondda & Swansea Bay company.

116    48. The eleven were: Sir A. Fairbairn (Great Northern); Lord Edward Cavendish (Furness); A. H. G. Grey (North Eastern); Lord R. Grosvenor, who became Lord Stalbridge the same year, (London & North Western); Sir G. MacPherson-Grant (Highland); Sir H. M. Meysey-Thompson (North Eastern); H. Robertson (various Welsh lines, see introduction to the appendix); Marquis of Stafford (London & North Western); C. R. M. Talbot (Great Western); H. Wiggin (Midland); Sir E. Watkin (Manchester, Sheffield & Lincolnshire, South Eastern, etc.). Of these, only Grey had voted with the Conservatives against Collings' amendment on 28 January, when Salisbury's Ministry was turned out: *House of Commons' Divisions*, 1886 Session I, Numb. 3.

116    49. Salisbury Papers, Special Correspondence, Class E, Main Series: Stalbridge to Salisbury, 6 December 1890, recommending Findlay for a knighthood.

116    50. Chilston Papers, U564 C206/1: Fenton to Akers-Douglas, 7 January 1889.

*Page*

Fenton was given a knighthood by the Salisbury government in 1888, and
Findlay in 1892.

116  51. Salisbury Papers, Special Correspondence, Class E, Main Series: Lord C.
Hamilton to Salisbury, 12 December 1886.

116  52. *Railway Times* (16 October 1886), 508.

116  53. Appendix, tables 7–10.

117  54. Excluding Lord Richard Grosvenor.

118  55. Appendix, tables 11–13.

118  56. Cross, on the board of the Manchester, Sheffield & Lincolnshire, was elevated to the peerage in 1886; Muncaster, elevated 1898, was on the Furness
board; Newlands, elevated 1898, was on the Caledonian board; Rathmore,
elevated 1895, sat on the North London and London & North Western
boards.

119  57. Lord Richard Grosvenor (1837–1912) entered Parliament as a Liberal in
1861, and was elected on to the London & North Western board in 1870.
Gladstone's chief whip, 1880–5, he broke with the Liberal leader in 1886,
and went to the Lords as Lord Stalbridge. In 1891 he succeeded Moon as
chairman of the London & North Western; in the same year he became
deputy chairman of the Railway Companies' Association, and was its
chairman 1894–1900.

W. L. Jackson (1840–1917) made his fortune in the Leeds worsted trade.
He entered the Leeds City Council in 1869, and became M.P. in 1880; in
1883 he became a director of the Great Northern Railway. His ready grasp
of financial details was recognized by Salisbury, who in January 1886, and
again in August, appointed him Financial Secretary to the Treasury. In
November 1891 he entered the Cabinet as Chief Secretary for Ireland, and
in 1902 went to the Lords as Baron Allerton. In the spring of 1895 he
succeeded Lord Colville of Culross as chairman of the Great Northern.
He was elected deputy chairman of the Railway Companies' Association in
1896, and succeeded Stalbridge as chairman in 1900.

119  58. R. E. Pumphrey, 'The Introduction of Industrialists into the British
Peerage: A Study of Adaptation of a Social Institution', *American Historical
Review*, lxv (1959–60), 8–9.

119  59. J. A. Thomas, *The House of Commons 1832–1901*, 14–16.

119  60. D. Southgate, *The Passing of the Whigs 1832–1886* (1965), 336, 365–7,
390. Sir I. Jennings, *Party Politics*, vol. II (Cambridge 1961), 128 .

119  61. Quoted in F. J. C. Hearnshaw, *Conservatism in England: An Analytical,
Historical, and Political Survey* (1933), 225.

119  62. F. Harrison, 'The Conservative Reaction', *Fortnightly Review*, New Series,
xv (1874), 304.

120  63. M. Ostrogorski, *Democracy and the Organisation of Political Parties*, vol. I
(1902), 324. R. B. McDowell, *British Conservatism 1832–1914* (1959), 116
and 145. J. Cornford, 'The Transformation of Conservatism in the Late
Nineteenth Century', *Victorian Studies*, vii (1963–4), 42. K. Hutchison,
*The Decline & Fall of British Capitalism*, new edn (Connecticut 1966),
70–1, 121.

120  64. McDowell, *op. cit.*, 139. *Annual Register* (1886), part I, 286.

# Notes

*Page*

120    65. *Morning Post* (3 March 1887), 5. P. M. Williams, *op. cit.*, 43, is probably right in ascribing the determination of Salisbury's government to revive Mundella's bill mainly to its sensitivity to agricultural feeling on the subject.

120    66. B.T.H.R. RCA 1/2 No. 1671, 7 December 1886.

120    67. *Ibid.*, No. 1674, 20 December 1886; Stanley later became the 16th Earl of Derby.

120    68. *Herapath* (22 January 1887), 87–8. *Parl. Deb.*, 3rd series (1887), cccxi, 689, 28 February. W. H. G. Armytage, *E.H.R.*, lxv (1950), 43–4.

120    69. *Parl. Papers* [*H.L.*] *1887* [B.M. bound volume], Bills. 1887. II (32). Mundella thought it "a very good Bill": Leader Correspondence, blue box marked "Mundella-Leader Letters 1871–96" (types transcripts): Mundella to Leader, 4 March 1887.

121    70. *Parl. Deb.*, 3rd series (1887), cccxii, 149–55, 14 March.

121    71. B.T.H.R. MSL 1/21, min. 10727, 4 March 1887.

121    72. *Ibid.*, RCA 1/2 No. 1707, 10 March 1887.

121    73. *Parl. Deb.*, 3rd series (1887), cccxii, 139–47, 165–6. Knatchbull MSS., Political Journal kept by Lord Brabourne 1886–7. U951 F27/11, p. 31. Tweeddale was chairman of the North British Railway.

122    74. *Herapath* (26 March 1887), 326, 333. P. M. Williams, *op. cit.*, 69–70.

122    75. B.T.H.R. RCA 1/2 No. 1709, 24 March 1887.

122    76. *Parl. Deb.*, 3rd series (1887), cccxii, 1755; cccxiii, 188–208.

122    77. *Ibid.*, (1887), cccxiv, 335.

122    78. B.T.H.R. RCA 1/2 No. 1715, 4 May 1887.

122    79. *Herapath* (9 April 1887), 389; (23 April), 433. A. H. H. Matthews, *op. cit.*, 224.

122    80. *Herapath* (7 May 1887), 487.

123    81. *Parl. Deb.*, 3rd series (1887), cccxiv, 931; cccxv, 50.

123    82. B.T.H.R. RCA 1/2 No. 1726, 8 June 1887.

123    83. *Ibid.*, No. 1733, 28 June. *Parl. Deb.*, 3rd series (1887), cccxviii, 694; cccxxii, 1793.

123    84. B.T.H.R. RCA 1/2 No. 1736, 5–6; Watkin to Oakley, 29 November 1887; MSL 1/21, min. 11065.

123    85. *Herapath* (21 January 1888), 55. *Parl. Deb.*, 3rd series (1888), cccxxii, 238. *Parl. Papers 1888*, vi (72).

123    86. *Sheffield & Rotherham Independent* (24 January 1888), 3. *Parl. Deb.*, 3rd series (1888), cccxxii, 235. *Parl. Papers 1888*, vi (49).

123    87. B.T.H.R. RCA 1/2 Nos. 1748, 1765, 1767, 22 February, 11 April 1888.

123    88. *Ibid.*, No. 1745.

124    89. Hicks Beach MSS., Williamstrip Park: BR/1. *Bradshaw.*

124    90. *Herapath* (5 May 1888), 514: speech of Hicks Beach in reply to a traders' deputation. Hicks Beach MSS., PCC/69: Salisbury to Hicks Beach, 11 February 1888. Salisbury Papers, Special Correspondence, Class E, Main Series: Hicks Beach to Salisbury, 14 February 1888.

124    91. *Parl. Deb.*, 3rd series (1888), cccxxii, 370. *Parl. Papers* [*H.L.*] *1888* [B.M. bound volume], Bills. 1888. II (12).

124    92. *Parl. Deb.*, 3rd series (1888), cccxxii, 1796–1806, 1 March 1888.

124    93. A. H. H. Matthews, *op. cit.*, 224–5. G. H. Wright, *op. cit.*, 332–3.

*Page*
124  94. B.T.H.R. RCA 1/2 No. 1758, 12 March 1888. *Parl. Deb.*, 3rd series (1888) cccxxiii, 1039–1052, 13 March. *Lords' Journals*, cxx (1888), 76: only nine members of the efficient railway interest in the Lords voted here, all against the amendment; the total efficient interest in the Upper House at this time was 24.

124  95. *Herapath* (17 March 1888), 306.

124  96. B.T.H.R. RCA 1/2 No. 1764, 11 April 1888.

124  97. *Ibid.*, Nos. 1775, 1777, 1784.

125  98. *Hampshire Advertiser* (2 May 1888), 2–3.

125  99. *Herapath* (14 April 1888), 431; (28 April), 491; (5 May), 514.

125  100. Leader Correspondence, blue box marked "Mundella-Leader Letters 1871–96" (typed transcripts): Mundella to Leader brothers, 16 July 1888.

125  101. *Herapath* (12 May 1888), 551; (23 June), 716.

125  102. *Ibid.* (30 June), 744; (21 July), 822. G. H. Wright, *op. cit.*, 332–3.

125  103. *Parl. Papers 1888*, xvii, (286), 3–4: the eight were William Lowther, T. H. Sidebottom, Sir M. W. Ridley and W. L. Jackson (Conservatives), J. C. Bolton, Sir Joseph Pease and Lewis Dillwyn (Liberals), and the Marquis of Hartington (Liberal Unionist).

125  104. B.T.H.R. RCA 1/2 No. 1791, 31 May 1888.

125  105. *Ibid.*, Nos. 1799 and 1800.

125  106. *Parl. Papers 1888*, xvii (286), 12–19. B.T.H.R. RCA 1/2 Nos. 1807–9. The companies acquiesced in the clause, but were by no means satisfied that it gave them adequate protection.

125  107. *Parl. Papers 1888*, xvii (286), 19–22, 25. B.T.H.R. RCA 1/2 Nos. 1810–11.

126  108. *Parl. Papers 1888*, vi (333), 11.

126  109. *Ibid.*, xvii (286), 25–7. B.T.H.R. RCA 1/2 Nos. 1813–4.

126  110. *Ibid.*, Nos. 1816–7. 51 & 52 Vict., c. 25.

126  111. F. Potter, *The Government in Relation to the Railways of the Country* [1909], 34. Lady Victoria Hicks Beach, *Life of Sir Michael Hicks Beach (Earl St. Aldwyn)*, vol. I (1932), 333.

126  112. B.T.H.R. RCA 1/2 Nos. 1835–6.

126  113. W. A. Jepson, 'Railway Companies' Rates', *The Jubilee of the Railway News* [1914], 89–90.

126  114. *Standard* (20 March 1889), 5. *Herapath* (1 June 1889), 615. G. H. Wright, *op. cit.*, 339–40.

127  115. *Herapath* (29 June 1889), 733–4; but according to the same journal for 8 February 1890, 146, the conference was originally formed in 1885 to combat the companies' bills for that year.

127  116. *Ibid.* (27 July 1889), 816–7. *Times* (27 July), 5. The Lancashire and Cheshire Conference did not formally merge with the Mansion House Association till 1897 (*Railway Times*, 29 May 1897, 693). At its formation the association was known as the Mansion House Committee. In 1892, after the Railway and Canal Traders' Association had amalgamated with it, it became known as the Mansion House Association on Railway and Canal Traffic, and in the text will be referred to throughout as the Mansion House Association. Lord Henniker's committee was absorbed about the same time, though a formal merger did not take place till 1902. The Mansion House Association

*Page*

　　　　thus became, after 1891, the premier negotiating body acting on behalf of
　　　　the traders on the subject of railway rates: P. M. Williams, *op. cit.*, 45,
　　　　footnote 7. A. H. H. Matthews, *op. cit.*, 228.

127　117. *Herapath* (13 July 1889), 762–3; (27 July), 817, B.T.H.R. RCA 1/2 Nos.
　　　　1852 and 1860. Detailed accounts of many of the meetings, 7 August to 10
　　　　December 1890, are in B.T.H.R. RCA (Y) 1/2, sets of minutes numbered
　　　　312f–g, 313d–j, 313L–p, 314a–c.

127　118. *Herapath* (10 August 1889), 893; (24 May 1890), 604. B.T.H.R. RCA 1/2
　　　　No. 1893, 20 March 1890.

127　119. J. Mavor, 'The English Railway Rate Question', *Quarterly Journal of
　　　　Economics,* viii (1893–4), 293–315.

127　120. *Herapath* (24 May 1890), 610.

127　121. *Parl. Deb.*, 3rd series (1890), cccxlvii, 338–9, 21 July. P.R.O. MT6/521/
　　　　8141/1890: minute by Lord Balfour, 3 July.

127　122. P.R.O. MT6/528/10240/1890: speech by Findlay introducing a deputation
　　　　to Hicks Beach on 28 October 1890. B.T.H.R. RCA 1/2 No. 1907, 24 July.
　　　　*Herapath* (26 July 1980), 839, 850–1.

128　123. P.R.O. MT6/528/10240/1890. The Lancashire and Cheshire Conference
　　　　complained in December that the maximum rates proposed by the Board of
　　　　Trade were still too high; the Birmingham Chamber of Commerce thought
　　　　likewise: *Herapath* (13 December 1890), 1401–2; G. H. Wright, *op. cit.*,
　　　　345.

## Notes to Chapter 8

130　1. P. S. Bagwell, *The Railwaymen,* 88–90, 102–4, P. S. Gupta, *op. cit.*, 32–4,
　　　　83–4.

130　2. Channing was elevated to the peerage in 1912.

130　3. F. A. Channing, *Memories of Midland Politics, 1885–1910* (1918), 2, 53, 117.

130　4. *Ibid.*, 37, 42.

130　5. *Parl. Papers 1886*, v (97).

131　6. *Parl. Deb.*, 3rd series (1886), cccii, 704, 1192; cccv, 1455–65. B.T.H.R.
　　　　RCA 1/2 No. 1667, 13 May 1886.

131　7. *Ibid.*, Nos. 1686, 1720, 1749, 1769. *Parl. Deb.*, 3rd series, (1887), cccx, 245;
　　　　(1888), cccxxii, 240. *Parl. Papers 1887*, v (126); the 1888 bill was not printed.

131　8. *Parl. Deb.*, 3rd series (1888), cccxxv, 1686–8. B.T.H.R. RCA 1/2 No. 1788,
　　　　10 May 1888. The motion was withdrawn.

132　9. *Parl. Deb.*, 3rd series (1888), cccxxxi, 1760, 11 December. B.T.H.R. RCA
　　　　1/2 No. 1842, 6 March 1889. *Herapath* (8 March 1890), 298. P.R.O. MT6/
　　　　507/3177/1890, file 4289 of 1889: Channing to the Board of Trade, 17
　　　　March 1889.

132　10. H. R. Wilson, *The Safety of British Railways,* 102–3. In May 1886 Mundella
　　　　told the Commons that the number of railway passengers killed had dropped

from 29 in 1880 to six in 1885. In conversation with the author, Dr Bagwell has suggested that Channing's bill of 1886 did have a distinctive effect in spurring the companies to more rapid progress in the matter of the adoption of continuous brakes conforming to Board of Trade requirements. Some evidence in support of this view is provided by the Board's own statistics, which show that on 30 June 1886 only 52 per cent of the engines and 52 per cent of the carriages were fitted with such brakes, so that in the following three-year period another 23 per cent of engines and 20 per cent of carriages were so fitted. On the other hand, during the period 30 June 1879 to 30 June 1882 no less than 26 per cent of the engines and 25 per cent of the carriages were so fitted, which supports the view that the Act of 1878 did make an appreciable contribution to the settlement of this question. Throughout the decade after 1878 the railway companies lived with the threat of legislation on this issue; but there does not appear to be any evidence to show that they felt the threat to be more imminent after 1886 than before. For details of the statistics, see *Parl. Papers 1886* lviii [C–4648], 3 and *Parl. Papers 1890*, lxv [C–5966], 3. For the Board of Trade's requirements of 1877 as to continuous brakes, see chapter 3, note 90.

132   11. H. R. Wilson, *The Safety of British Railways*, 94–6. L. T. C. Rolt. *Red for Danger* (1955), 159-62. O. S. Nock, *Historic Railway Disasters* (1966), 42–51.

132   12. *Parl. Papers 1890*, lxv [C–6013], 55; the report is dated 8 July 1889.

132   13. The phrase was Channing's: *Railway Press* (12 June 1889), 2.

132   14. *Parl. Deb.*, 3rd series (1889), cccxxxviii, 116–7, 409. *Parl. Papers 1889*, vii (333).

133   15. B.T.H.R. LNW 1/31, min. 9370, 19 July 1889; RCA 1/2 No. 1867, 25 July.

133   16. *Railway Review* (2 August 1889), 366. *Parl. Deb.*, 3rd series (1889), cccxxxix, 228, 2 August. P.R.O. MT6/494/11484/1889, files 10063,10064, 10139 and 10373 of 1889.

133   17. B.T.H.R. RCA 1/2 No. 1861, 17 July. On 23 July the second reading was postponed after objection, apparently by James Craig, a Liberal M.P. who was not, however, a railway director: *Parl. Deb.*, 3rd series (1889), cccxxxviii, 1174–5. *Railway Times* (27 July 1889), 119.

133   18. *Herapath* (27 July 1889), 831. *Railway Review* (26 July 1889), 352. *Railway Times* (27 July 1889), 122. P.R.O. MT6/494/11484/1889, file 10260 of 1889: Executive of the Amalgamated Society to Hicks Beach, 25 July 1889; file 10369 of 1889: Channing to Hicks Beach, 29 July.

133   19. *Parl. Deb.*, 3rd series (1889), cccxxxviii, 1684–5; 1792. *Parl. Papers 1889*, vii (360).

133   20. *Parl. Deb.*, 3rd series (1889), cccxxxix, 226, 421–2, 639–42.

133   21. 52 & 53 Vict., c. 57. B.T.H.R. RCA (Y) 1/2, meeting of managers and solicitors, 4 December 1889; meeting of managers, 14 October 1890; RCA 1/2, Nos. 1872, 1882 and 1911. P.R.O. MT6/709/19052/1895.

134   22. *Railway Review* (25 January 1889), 37; (1 March), 97. Gupta, *op. cit.*, 41 and 47.

134   23. *Herapath* (26 October 1889), 1176; (17 May 1890), 578–9.

# Notes

*Page*

134    24. B.T.H.R. GW 1/39, 325, 9 January 1890.

134    25. *Ibid.*, NER 1/17, mins. 9732 and 9807. *Railway Review* (25 October 1889), 506. In December 1890 the company made some concessions, including a six-day guaranteed week and a 48-hour week for shunters: B.T.H.R. NER 1/17, mins. 9913 and 9917; P. S. Bagwell, *The Railwaymen*, 136, H. A. Clegg, A. Fox, and A. F. Thompson, *A History of British Trade Unions since 1889*, vol. I (Oxford 1964), 231–2, are probably right in ascribing the relatively rapid growth of collective bargaining on the North Eastern to the prevalence of local industrialists on its board; many of these were skilled and experienced conciliators, and a significant proportion were Quakers. The North Eastern was unique amongst the companies in having a virtual monopoly of traffic within an area of the country already distinguished by the prevalence of trade union activity there.

134    26. *Western Mail* (28 July 1890), 5; (5 August), 5; (15 August), 5. *Herapath* (23 August 1890), 978. B.T.H.R. BDC 1/1, 370–2; BDC 1/2, 9–10; BRY 1/4, 32–3, 43, 48–9, 53, 196; RHY 1/7, 39–40.

134    27. *Western Mail* (1 August 1890), 5.

134    28. B.T.H.R. RHY 1/7, 32.

134    29. *Railway Review* (6 November 1891), 5.

134    30. B.T.H.R. LNW 1/31, mins. 4849–50, 9770. *Crewe and Nantwich Chronicle* (30 November 1889), 8; (21 December), 8. W. H. Chaloner, *The Social and Economic Development of Crewe 1780–1923* (Manchester, 1950), 153–66, 308–10. By August 1891, when the Liberals regained control of the Council, the alliance between Conservatives and railway nominees was about to break up; by November the railway nominees had disappeared from the Council.

135    31. J. Mavor, *The Scottish Railway Strike, 1891: A History and Criticism* (Edinburgh 1891), 63 *et passim*.

135    32. *Parl. Deb.*, 3rd series (1891), cccxlix, 525, 656. Lady Victoria Hicks Beach, *op. cit.*, vol. I, 335.

135    33. B.T.H.R. RCA 1/2 No. 1912, 1 December 1890.

135    34. H. R. Wilson, *The Safety of British Railways*, 166.

135    35. H. L. Beales, 'The "Great Depression" in Industry and Trade', *Economic History Review*, v, No. 1 (October 1934), 70. W. W. Rostow, *British Economy of the Nineteenth Century* (Oxford 1948), 33.

135    36. 'British Railway Progress, 1850–1912', *The Jubilee of the Railway News* [1914], 33.

135    37. *Railway Times* (10 August 1889), 176.

135    38. *Herapath* (23 August 1890), 980.

136    39. *Parl. Papers 1890–91*, xvi (342), 506–7.

136    40. P. S. Gupta, *op. cit.*, 143.

136    41. *Parl. Deb.*, 3rd series (1891), cccxlix, 904–16, 23 January.

136    42. B.T.H.R. RCA 1/2 No. 1915, 23 January 1891.

136    43. *Parl. Deb.*, 3rd series (1891), cccxlix, 932, 949–51, 966–9, 1000–2.

136    44. *Ibid.*, 920–2, 951–3, 957–9, 974–5, 980.

136    45. *Ibid.*, 979; and see Baumann's letter to *The Times* (28 January 1891), 13–14. Baumann chided Conservative M.P.s who wished for an inquiry, for want-

*Page*

ing "anything to save them from voting for the regulation of adult male labour."

136   46. *Parl. Deb.*, 3rd series (1891), cccxlix, 1008. *House of Commons' Divisions* 1890–1, Numb. 13, 23 January 1891.

136   47. *Railway Review* (30 January 1891), Supplement 1–14. Gupta, *op. cit.*, 145.

136   48. B.T.H.R. RCA 1/2 No. 1926. *Parl. Deb.*, 3rd series (1891), cccxlix, 1727.

137   49. *Ibid.*, (1891), cccl, 1504–10, 1948; (1891), cccli, 860.

137   50. *Parl. Papers 1890–91*, xvi (342), qq. 2317–2623.

137   51. B.T.H.R. RCA 1/44, meeting of managers and solicitors, 28 April 1891: speeches by Findlay, Oakley, and Henry Tennant, director and former general manager of the North Eastern Railway; meeting of Parliamentary Sub-Committee, 30 April 1891. See also *ibid.*, LNW 4/120, *Memoranda Relating to Hours of Duty of Railway Servants on the London & North Western Railway: April 1891*, 20.

137   52. *Parl. Papers 1890–91*, xvi (342), qq. 5250, 5257.

137   53. *Ibid.*, q. 8166.

138   54. *Ibid.*, qq. 5359, 5818, 6169–71, 6332, 6511, 7055, 7095, 7249–50, 8271, 9013–14. *Railway Review* (21 August 1891), 1.

138   55. *Parl. Papers 1890–91*, xvi (342), qq. 4743, 8466. B.T.H.R. GE 1/21, 360–1, 5 May 1891.

138   56. *Parl. Papers 1892*, xvi (125), qq. 6, 581–2. B.T.H.R. CAM 1/3, min. 4388, 31 March 1892. *Railway Review* (21 August 1891), 4.

138   57. *Salopian & Montgomeryshire Post* (26 March 1892), 4. 55 & 56 Vict., c. 64.

138   58. *Parl. Deb.*, 4th series (1892), iii, 883–964, 7 April.

138   59. *Western Daily Mercury* (8 April 1892), 4.

138   60. *Pall Mall Gazette* (8 April 1892), 1; and see the comments of the less discreet *Society* (16 April 1892), 346.

138   61. B.T.H.R. RCA 1/2 Nos. 1938 and 1996.

138   62. *Railway Review*, 15 April–15 July 1892.

138   63. *Parl. Papers 1892*, xvi (246), xxii–xxxv; l–li.

139   64. *Ibid.*, li; the voting was twelve to six; the only Liberals to vote for Hicks Beach's draft were the railway directors Pease and MacInnes.

139   65. *Ibid.*, iii–x; lii–lvii.

140   66. *Railway Review* (24 June 1892), 4; (8 July), 5–6; (15 July), 5–6. Gupta, *op. cit.*, 154.

140   67. Gladstone Papers, B.M. Add. MSS. 44514, fols. 309–10: Channing to Gladstone, 28 May 1892.

140   68. *Manchester Examiner & Times* (12 July 1892), 5.

140   69. Gupta, *op. cit.*, 156–7. P. S. Bagwell, *The Railwaymen*, 168.

140   70. Gladstone Papers, B.M. Add. MSS. 44648, fol. 36: a list, undated but *circa* 19–23 November 1892, headed "Bills to be prepared."

140   71. *Parl. Deb.*, 4th series (1893), viii, 171. *Parl. Papers 1893–94*, iii (53).

140   72. *Ibid.*, (93).

140   73. *Parl. Deb.*, 4th series (1893), ix, 401–2. *Parl. Papers 1893–94*, vii (226).

140   74. *Parl. Deb.*, 4th series (1893), viii, 650; ix, 155. *Parl. Papers 1893–94*, vii (165).

140   75. B.T.H.R. RCA 1/2 No. 2027, 20 February 1893; LNW 1/33, min. 12542, 17 March.

*Page*
140   76. *The Times* (28 February 1893), 8. Gupta, *op. cit.*, 161.
141   77. *Parl. Papers 1893–94*, xv (124), 6–7; Mundella's amendment was accepted without a division; see Channing's letter to the *Railway Review* (24 March 1893), 5, and F. A. Channing, *op. cit.*, 142.
141   78. Even the officers of the Railway Department were hostile to Channing's proposals; see Major Marindin's memorandum of 26 April 1893, arguing against his plan to limit the hours of signalmen to a maximum of ten per day: P.R.O. BT 13/35/E16054/1903, file E10709 of 1893.
141   79. *The Times* (24 April 1893), 10: deputation of drivers and firemen to Mundella on 22 April, introduced by C. T. Murdoch.
141   80. *Railway Review* (28 April 1893), 5; *Herapath* (29 April), 450.
141   81. *Parl. Deb.*, 4th series (1893), xi, 1089–1106, 24 April. *House of Commons' Divisions*, 1893–94, Numb. 60. Walter Long, a director of the Great Western, voted with Gorst. He was the only director of a large company to do so; ten such directors, including four Liberals, voted against.
141   82. *Parl. Deb.*, 4th series (1893), xii, 438; xiii, 1167, 1173–4, 1176; xiv, 1245–6. 56 & 57 Vict., c. 29.
142   83. B.T.H.R. RCA 1/2 Nos. 2050 and 2058; MSL 1/27, min. 15659. Courtenay Boyle's letter was reprinted in *The Times* (22 September 1893), 9.
142   84. *Herapath* (28 October 1894), 1058. *Railway Review* (15 November 1895), 4.
142   85. On Hopwood (1860–1947), see *Herapath* (31 May 1901), 542; in 1900 he succeeded Courtenay Boyle as Permanent Secretary.
142   86. Amalgamated Society of Railway Servants, *Annual Report 1894*, 2, and *1895*, 2, quoted by Gupta, *op. cit.*, 163. *Railway Review* (2 November 1894), 4. G. W. Alcock, *Fifty Years of Railway Trade Unionism* (1922), 256.
142   87. Gupta, *op. cit.*, 166, 169–71. R. Kenney, *Men and Rails* (1913), 38, 42–3.
142   88. *Parl. Papers 1890–91*, xvi (342), q. 9445.
142   89. *Parl. Papers 1892*, xvi (246), p. xix. *The Times* (10 May 1892), 9.

## Notes to Chapter 9

144   1. See chapter 7.
145   2. *Herapath* (28 February 1891), 239. B.T.H.R. RCA 1/44, meeting of general managers, solicitors and goods managers, 16 February 1891, 3.
145   3. The report from the Select Committee on Railway Rates and Charges, *Parl. Papers 1893–94*, xiv (462), iv, recognized that "These Orders, as finally settled, reduced the maximum rates in many cases to a point below the actual rates then charged by the companies, and entailed upon them an immediate loss of income."
145   4. B.T.H.R. RCA 1/2 Nos. 1941 and 1946.
145   5. *Economist* (7 March 1891), 305.
145   6. B.T.H.R. RCA 1/44, meetings of general managers, solicitors and goods managers, 8, 10, 13 and 14 April 1891, and 8 June; RCA 1/2, meeting of 8 May. *Parl. Deb.*, 3rd series (1891), cccli, 423, 1042; 4th series (1892), 1331.

*Page*

145    7. B.T.H.R. RCA 1/2, No. 1948, 10 April 1891; RCA 1/44, meetings of general managers, solicitors and goods managers, 13 April and 25 May.

145    8. *Parl. Papers 1890–91*, xiv (394), xii–lxviii; *Parl. Papers 1892*, xv (187), xiv–lvi.

145    9. These were the bills of the London & North Western, Great Western, Midland, Great Northern, Great Eastern, London & South Western, London, Brighton & South Coast, South Eastern, and London, Chatham & Dover companies: 54 & 55 Vict., c. ccxiv–ccxxii (Local and Personal). The 1892 Acts are 55 & 56 Vict., c. xxxix–lxiv (Local and Personal).

146   10. B.T.H.R. RCA 1/2 No. 1960, 31 July 1891.

146   11. *Herapath* (25 July 1891), 815. W. W. Rostow, *op. cit.*, 86–8.

146   12. *Herapath* (1 August 1891), 844. C. D. Campbell, *op. cit.*, 21 and 44.

146   13. B.T.H.R. RCA 1/44, meeting of general managers, solicitors and goods managers, 13 July 1891.

146   14. *Ibid.*, meeting of general managers, solicitors and goods managers of the nine companies, 28 October 1891, 3. In 1889 Oakley had written: "The fallacy . . . which appears to be somewhat popular is that when the revision takes effect the Companies will seek to charge the new maximum rates. This is altogether a mistaken view": *Herapath* (6 April 1889), 376.

146   15. B.T.H.R. NER 1/230, North Eastern Railway Memoranda for Directors, 16 November 1892: "Memorandum as to Revision of Rates on Merchandise Traffic", 10.

146   16. B.T.H.R. RCA 1/2 No. 2004, 13 May 1892; meetings of managers and honorary solicitors, 17 and 23 June. P.R.O. MT6/591/7750/1892, file 5987 of 1892: undated memo. by Boyle, probably 13 June. In July the operation of the nine Acts was postponed till 1 January 1893: *ibid.*, file 6509 of 1892: order signed by Calcraft on 21 July; and Oakley to Boyle, 29 June, agreeing on behalf of the companies that, as a condition of the postponement, all special rates in force at that time would continue until the new schedules were adopted.

146   17. B.T.H.R. RCA 1/2, meeting of October 1892.

147   18. *Parl. Papers 1893–94*, xiv (385), qq. 135, 139–40.

147   19. *Wilts and Glo'stershire Standard* (17 December 1892), 5; this newspaper pointed out that for grain from Cirencester to London, the present rate of 10s. per ton was to be raised to 11s. 3d., an increase of 12½ per cent.

147   20. *Western Mail* (20 December 1892), 4; (23 December), 4; (30 December), 6. *South Wales Daily News* (29 December), 5.

147   21. *Leicester Daily Post* (26 December 1892), 2.

147   22. B.T.H.R. RCA(S) 1/17, account of deputation from London Chamber of Commerce to Mundella, 17 December 1893, 6.

147   23. *Morning Post* (26 December 1892), 4.

147   24. *Wilts and Glo'stershire Standard* (31 December 1892), 4; *The Times* (5 January 1893), 9; (19 January), 6.

147   25. *The Times* (16 January 1893), 7; (20 January), 11; (2 February), 11.

147   26. *Leicester Daily Post* (27 December 1892), 4.

147   27. *The Times* (25 January 1893), 12.

148   28. *Ibid.* (26 January), 10.

# Notes

148     29. *Ibid.* (31 January), 7. Whitehead was M.P. for Leicester, 1892–4.

148     30. *Parl. Deb.*, 4th series (1893), viii, 168–9, 172. *Herapath* (28 January 1893), 90.

148     31. *The Times* (8 February 1893), 10.

148     32. *Ibid.* (16 February 1893), 7; *Herapath* (18 February), 175. Channing, *op. cit.*, 140.

148     33. B.T.H.R. RCA 1/2 No. 2017, 4 January 1893.

148     34. *Ibid.*, 10–12. An account of a deputation from various firms of brewers in Burton to the general managers at Euston station on 24 January is in RCA(S) 1/17. See also P.R.O. MT6/615/5638/1893, file 1944 of 1893: Oakley to Boyle, 7 February.

149     35. B.T.H.R. RCA 1/2 No. 2025, 20 February 1893, 3–5.

150     36. *Parl. Deb.*, 4th series (1893), ix, 46–7, 21 February; the reductions were back-dated to 1 January.

150     37. B.T.H.R. RCA 1/2 No. 2037, 24 February.

150     38. *The Times* (3 March 1893), 10.

150     39. B.T.H.R. RCA 1/2 No. 2038, 28 February 1893, 6: speeches of William Birt and Oakley.

151     40. *Ibid.*, 6–7; GW 1/41, 152–4.

151     41. B.T.H.R. RCA 1/2 No. 2038, 9. *The Times* (3 March 1893), 10; subsequently the companies, with the exception of the London & North Western and Great Western, informed Mundella that no increases would exceed 5 per cent: *Parl. Deb.*, 4th series (1893), ix, 1059–60.

151     42. *Ibid.*, 1024–41.

151     43. *Ibid.*, 973, 1061–6.

151     44. *The Times* (20 March 1893), 10. B.T.H.R. MSL 1/26, min. 14890. *Parl. Papers 1893–94*, xiv (462), x. See the correspondence between the Board of Trade and individual companies in March and April 1893 in *ibid.*, lxxix [C–7044], especially 34–7, 40–3, 46.

151     45. B.T.H.R. RCA 1/2, printed copy of letter from Oakley to Boyle, 12 April.

151     46. J. Mavor, 'The English Railway Rate Question', *Quarterly Journal of Economics*, viii (1893–4), 409.

151     47. *Parl. Deb.*, 4th series (1893), xi, 540. *Parl. Papers 1893–94*, vii (309).

151     48. *The Times* (25 April 1893), 10.

152     49. *Parl. Deb.*, 4th series (1893), xii, 426–7, 1005–7, 1151–3.

152     50. B.T.H.R. LNW 1/33, min. 12612, 21 April 1893.

152     51. Chilston Papers, Kent Archives Office U564 C40/20: Jackson to Akers-Douglas, 29 April 1893.

152     52. B.T.H.R. RCA 1/2 No. 2040, 29 May 1893.

152     53. *Parl. Papers 1893–94*, xiv (385), qq. 1819, 2007, 2177, 2288–90, 2657, 2671, 2806, 4407.

152     54. *Ibid.*, qq. 5080, 5096, 5417–9, 5430, 5437–8, 5905, 6354, 6703; see also q. 7231, where J. S. Beale, the Midland Railway solicitor, asserted that "the bargain that Parliament made with the railway companies . . . [is] . . . to charge what they please within their maximum rates, and provided that they do not offend against the law of undue preference."

153     55. *Ibid.*, qq. 5021, 5025, 5047, 5110.

153     56. *Ibid.*, qq. 5115–7, 7542.

*Page*
153    57. *Ibid.*, qq. 5173, 7550, 7553. B.T.H.R. RCA 1/2, meeting of general managers, solicitors and goods managers, 9 June 1893, to discuss the evidence to be given.

153    58. *Parl. Papers 1893–94*, xiv (462), vii.

153    59. *Ibid.*, xvii–xxii.

154    60. *Ibid.*, xxvi.

154    61. *Ibid.*, iii–xiii.

154    62. *Produce Markets' Review* (24 February 1894), 139. A. H. H. Matthews, *op. cit.*, 230.

154    63. B.T.H.R. RCA 1/2 No. 2057, 28 February 1894, 3–5. P.R.O. MT6/663/7286/1894, file 796 of 1894: Edwin Clements (Secretary, Mansion House Association) to Courtenay Boyle, 18 January 1894.

154    64. B.T.H.R. RCA 1/2 No. 2057, 2–3: Hopwood to Oakley, 25 January 1894.

154    65. *Ibid.*, 6–8: Oakley to Hopwood, 6 March.

154    66. *Herapath* (6 April 1894), 334.

155    67. P.R.O. MT6/663/7286/1894, file 2658 of 1894: minute by Hopwood, 6 March.

155    68. B.T.H.R. RCA 1/2 No. 2069, 9–11: Boyle to Oakley, 14 March.

155    69. *Parl. Papers 1894*, viii (156).

155    70. B.T.H.R. RCA 1/2 No. 2083, 18 April 1894. *Herapath* (20 April 1894), 385–6: deputation from the railway companies, led by Stalbridge, to Mundella on 19 April.

155    71. W. H. G. Armytage, *A. J. Mundella*, 303–4.

155    72. *Herapath* (18 May 1894), 485–6.

155    73. *Ibid.* (25 May 1894), 509–10.

156    74. *The Times* (16 June 1894), 15; a much fuller account is in B.T.H.R. MT 1/41: *Railway & Canal Traffic Bill: Deputation to the Rt. Hon. James Bryce, M.P. . . . 15th June 1894*, 2, 5, 8–13.

156    75. *Herapath* (29 June 1894), 634, 636. *The Times* (26 June), 9. B.T.H.R. RCA 1/2 No. 2086, 26 June.

156    76. *Ibid.*, No. 2087, 28 June, 3–4.

156    77. *Ibid.*, No. 2090, 6 July, 2–4: Oakley to Boyle, 30 June, and Boyle to Oakley, 4 July.

156    78. *Ibid.*, No. 2090, 4.

156    79. *Ibid.*, No. 2091, 10 July, 3.

156    80. Not least because they were still having to pay the companies increased rates in many cases: *Parl. Deb.*, 4th series (1894), xxvii, 1660–1; xxviii, 639–40.

156    81. B.T.H.R. RCA 1/2 Nos. 2096–7. *The Times* (13 July), 10.

156    82. *The Times* (17 July), 5; (20 July), 5; (3 August), 8. *Herapath* (20 July), 708. B.T.H.R. RCA 1/2 No. 2098. P.R.O. BT 13/22/E11364/1894: Whitehead to Bryce, 30 July and 1 August 1894.

157    83. 57 & 58 Vict., c. 54.

157    84. In 1892 the average earnings on goods and mineral traffic carried over the railways of the United Kingdom was 2s. 8d. per ton; in 1895 it fell to 2s. 6½d. per ton, and in 1902 to 2s. 5d. per ton: W. A. Jepson, 'Railway Companies' Rates', *The Jubilee of the Railway News* [1914], 90.

157    85. C. Edwards, *Railway Nationalisation* (1898), 213.

# Notes

157    86. See, for instance, B.T.H.R. MSL 1/27, min. 15659, relating to porters and goods guards on the Manchester, Sheffield & Lincolnshire Railway.

157    87. E. E. Barry, *Nationalisation in British Politics: The Historical Background* (1965), 96; the Trades Union Congress became committed in 1896: *ibid.*, 97.

157    88. B.T.H.R. LNW 4/120, *Memoranda Relating to Hours of Duty of Railway Servants on the London & North Western Railway: April 1891*, 20.

158    89. The contracting-out clause was moved in the Commons by the radical M.P. for Crewe, W. S. B. McLaren, on 8 November. On 10 November its second reading was rejected by a small majority, 236 votes to 218; 19 members of the efficient railway interest voted in favour of the amendment, including two Liberals, Sir James Kitson and Miles MacInnes; only two members of the efficient interest, both Liberals, voted against: Sir James Joicey and David Thomas. The London & North Western, London, Brighton & South Coast, and other organizations, then turned for help to Lord Salisbury and the Duke of Devonshire, and the upper House obliged by inserting a contracting-out clause. The bill was dropped in February 1894: *Parl. Deb.*, 4th series (1893), xiv, 346, 543; xviii, 483–94, 756. *House of Commons' Divisions*, 1893–4, Numb. 311, 10 November 1893. B.T.H.R. RCA 1/2 No. 2059; GE 1/22, 259–60; LNW 1/33, min. 12541; LNW 1/34, min. 12935. *The Times* (1 June 1893), 11. *Herapath* (23 September 1893), 1011; (30 September), 1045; (4 November), 1172; (2 December), 1267; (2 February 1894), 110. *Railway Review* (23 February 1894), 1. See also D. G. Hanes, *The First British Workmen's Compensation Act 1897* (New Haven, 1968), 57–86.

158    90. Chamberlain and the *Annual Register* believed that Asquith's bill lost the Liberals the by-election at Hereford in August 1893: Joseph Chamberlain Papers, JC6/3/3/1: Chamberlain to the Editor of the *Birmingham Mail* (17 August 1893); *Annual Register* (1893), part I, 209.

158    91. *North Wales Observer* (2 February 1894), 5.

158    92. For the Liberal abstentions on Channing's motion, see chapter 8, 208. In the debate on Hood's case, an amendment calling for compensation or reinstatement for him was defeated by 274 votes to 159, two Liberal members of the efficient railway interest, Dillwyn and D. A. Thomas, voting in the minority, with 16 members of the efficient interest, including the Liberals Robert Allison (Midland), Bolton, MacInnes and Pease, voting in the majority: *House of Commons' Divisions*, 1892, Numb. 74. For the voting on the question of contracting-out, see note 89 above.

158    93. Though Hicks Beach had expressed approval of both bills: *Parl. Deb.*, 4th series, viii, 1973; xxvi, 101.

158    94. *Annual Register* (1892), part I, 170.

158    95. J. N. Harris, 'Railways and Agricultural Society', *The Jubilee of the Railway News* [1914], 112. *The Times* (9 December 1892), 7; (14 December), 5.

159    96. The judgment was only partially in favour of the traders: B.T.H.R. RCA 1/2 No. 2122. P.R.O. MT6/731/2160/1896, file 12730 of 1895. *Hampshire Independent* (13 April 1895), 6. *Agricultural Economist* (1 May 1895), 104. A. H. H. Matthews, *op. cit.*, 230–1. S. J. McLean, 'The English Railway and Canal Commission of 1888', *Quarterly Journal of Economics*, xx (1905–6), 20–3.

*Page*

159   97. *Liverpool Daily Post* (18 April 1895), 5.

159   98. *Railway Times* (20 July 1895), 80.

159   99. P.R.O. BT 13/18/E9451/1890, file E9443 of 1890: draft letter, Board of Trade to Treasury, July 1890.

159  100. P.R.O. MT6/549/5779/1891: manuscript draft circular dated June 1891.

159  101. *Railway News* (6 June 1891), 1009–10.

159  102. B.T.H.R. RCA 1/2 No. 2119, 26 April 1895. P.R.O. MT6/650/2509/1894: memo. by E. Stoneham, 17 January 1894. *Herapath* (30 March 1894), 308, commented: "There is a growing disposition on both sides to accept the advice of the Board of Trade officials."

160  103. B.T.H.R. RCA 1/2 Nos. 1927 and 1945, 27 January and 25 February 1891; meetings of managers and solicitors, 3 March and 17 June 1892. On 26 November 1890 the Conservative M.P.s James Theobald and John Blundell Maple had introduced a Cheap Trains (London) bill, to fix a maximum return fare of $\frac{1}{2}d$. per mile. Its second reading was defeated on 24 February 1891 by 73 votes to 54. The efficient railway interest could claim here one of its rare victories on the floor of the House, for the slender majority against the second reading included 16 of its members, with Pease acting as teller for the Noes: *Parl. Deb.*, 3rd series (1891), cccxlix, 110; cccl, 1510–34. *House of Commons' Divisions*, 1890–1, Numb. 66. See J. B. Maple, *Cheap Trains for London Workers* [1891], *passim*.

160  104. *Parl. Papers 1894*, lxxv [C–7542], 3–31; and see *ibid.*, 32–3: Oakley to Hopwood, 18 January 1894. Between May and December 1894 a long correspondence took place between Hopwood, Oakley, and the managers of the London companies, with respect to the adequacy of cheap trains for work-women: *Parl. Papers 1895*, lxxxvi [C–7567], 5–15.

160  105. B.T.H.R. RCA 1/2 No. 2066, 11 April 1894.

160  106. *Ibid.*, Nos. 1963, 1972, 2047, 2105, 2133.

## Notes to Chapter 10

162   1. G. W. Alcock, *op. cit.*, 302–3.

162   2. Chilston Papers, U564 C255/6: Lord Claud Hamilton to Akers-Douglas, 29 June 1892, threatening, if Ritchie were put forward in the South Kensington constituency, to stand against him himself—"and I shall be supported by the great bulk of the Party."

162   3. B.T.H.R. RCA 1/2 Nos. 2148 and 2158. P.R.O. MT6/742/12049/1896, file 1406 of 1896: memo. by Hopwood, 30 January 1896.

162   4. *Railway Times* (1 February 1896), 151; (4 April), 446; (13 June), 764–5. *Produce Markets' Review* (14 November 1896), 1767. *The Times* (2 May 1904), 3. P.R.O. MT6/742/12049/1896, file 4399 of 1896: Stalbridge to Ritchie, February 1896; Ritchie to Stalbridge, 11 April 1896.

163   5. W. C. Mallalieu, 'Joseph Chamberlain and Workmen's Compensation', *Journal of Economic History*, x (1950), 50.

# Notes

Page

163   6. Joseph Chamberlain Papers, JC6/3/3/17c: Cabinet papers circulated by Chamberlain, February 1897, headed "Workmen's Accidents Compensation", 9.

163   7. *Ibid.*, JC6/3/3/3: Webster to Ridley (typed copy), 18 December 1895; JC6/3/3/12: Ridley to Chamberlain, 11 February 1897.

163   8. *Ibid.*, JC6/3/3/13: Chamberlain to Ridley (typed copy), 11 February 1897; JC6/3/3/23: memo. by Chamberlain, 15 March 1897.

163   9. *Parl. Papers 1897*, vii (213). *Railway Times* (8 May 1897), 604–5.

163   10. See chapter 4.

164   11. B.T.H.R. RCA 1/44, meeting of general managers and solicitors, 28 May 1897. *Parl. Deb.*, 4th series (1897), 1, 123–33, 2 June.

164   12. B.T.H.R. RCA 1/2 Nos. 2204, 2210 and 2212.

164   13. 60 & 61 Vict., c. 37.

164   14. M. Riebenack, *Railway Provident Institutions in English-Speaking Countries* (Philadelphia 1905), 101–6.

164   15. *Ibid.*, 92–3. *Parl. Papers 1905*, lxxv [Cd. 2334], qq. 1711–13.

164   16. P. S. Bagwell, *The Railwaymen*, 177.

164   17. B.T.H.R. MSL 1/30, min. 16920; the North Eastern Railway refused to abide by this decision.

164   18. B.T.H.R. LNW 1/35, mins. 14849 and 14851, 10 and 18 December 1896. *Daily Telegraph* (10 December), 8; (11 December), 7; (12 December), 7. *Railway Times* (12 December), 779.

165   19. L. H. Powell, *The Shipping Federation: A History of the First Sixty Years 1890–1950* (1950), 1–8. *Fairplay* (17 December 1896), 1041.

165   20. B.T.H.R. MSL 1/30, min. 17175, 26 March 1897; MSL 1/31, min. 23, 27 August 1897.

165   21. *Railway News* (3 April 1897), 535. Gupta, *op. cit.*, 207–10.

165   22. B.T.H.R. MSL 1/31, min. 24, 27 August 1897. *Railway News* (9 October 1897), 527. *Railway Times* (16 October), 516–17; (30 October), 580.

165   23. B.T.H.R. MSL 1/31, mins. 145–6, 5 November 1897; GN 1/56, 325, 5 November 1897.

165   24. *Newcastle Daily Chronicle* (5 November 1897), 8.

165   25. B.T.H.R. LY 1/354, 356, 10 November 1897.

166   26. *Manchester Guardian* (5 November 1897), 6. *Railway Times* (6 November), 620.

166   27. B.T.H.R. MSL 1/31, min. 168, 19 November 1897; GW 1/43, 466–7, 18 November. The companies represented were the London & North Western, Great Northern, Great Western, Midland, Lancashire & Yorkshire, and Great Central.

166   28. *Ibid.*, MSL 1/31, min. 194, 3 December 1897. *Newcastle Daily Chronicle* (3 December), 5.

166   29. B.T.H.R. MSL 1/31, mins. 194 and 224; LNW 1/121, min. 6588; LSW 1/10, min. 847; MID 1/26, min. 6938; NBR 1/44, 426. *Railway Times* (11 December 1897), 797.

166   30. P.R.O. MT6/808/13907/1897, file 13764 of 1897. *Manchester Guardian* (4 December 1897), 10; (6 December), 6.

166   31. *Ibid.* (8 December 1897), 9.

*Page*

167  32. The first occasion on which it came into use was during the Taff Vale strike in 1900: B.T.H.R. RHY 1/8, 316, 4 October 1901.

167  33. B.T.H.R. LNW 1/36, min. 15522, 17 December 1897. *Newcastle Daily Chronicle* (24 December), 4.

167  34. B.T.H.R. LNW 1/36, min. 15576, 21 January 1898; MID 1/26, mins. 6965, 6966a and 6978.

167  35. B.T.H.R. RCA 1/2 No. 2232, 30 June 1898. E. J. O'B. Croker, *Retrospective Lessons on Railway Strikes* (Cork 1898), 78–165.

167  36. Croker, *op. cit.*, 166. J. M. Ludlow, 'The Labour Protection Association', *The Economic Review*, ix (1899), 244–6.

167  37. P. Mantoux and M. Alfassa, *La Crise du Trade-Unionisme* (Paris 1903), 213 and 320: statements by a railway director and a general manager.

167  38. *Parl. Papers 1908*, xcv (312); *1909*, lxxvii (263); *1910*, lxxx (277); *1911*, lxx (266). The figure for the National Free Labour Association does not include the £105 given by the London & South Western Railway in 1907, increased to £120 from 1908 to 1910, to the Southampton Free Labour Association.

168  39. *Railway News* (8 January 1898), 69; (30 April), 668.

168  40. W. Collison, *The Apostle of Free Labour* (1913), 93–5. J. M. Ludlow, 'The National Free Labour Association', *The Economic Review*, v (1895), 110–11.

168  41. *Free Labour Gazette* (7 November 1894), 1 and 3. Ludlow, *The Economic Review*, v (1895), 112–13. J. Saville, 'Trade Unions and Free Labour. The Background to the Taff Vale Decision', in A. Briggs and J. Saville (ed), *Essays in Labour History* (1960), 338.

168  42. Mantoux and Alfassa, *op. cit.*, 185–6, 214, 325–6; the railways were not represented on the Employers' Parliamentary Council.

168  43. J. Saville, *op. cit.*, 337.

168  44. W. Collison, *op. cit.*, 141, B.T.H.R. TV 1/11, min. 321, 21 August 1900.

168  45. *Railway Times* (1 September 1900), 250; (6 October), 639.

168  46. In 1907 the Lib-Lab M.P. Clement Edwards accused the London & North Western of having contributed £25 to the Free Labour Association in 1893. This was a charge which Collison and the company's director Amelius Lockwood, a Conservative M.P., both publicly denied: *Parl. Deb.*, 4th series (1907), clxxi, 763; clxxiii, 352. *Free Labour Press* (30 March 1907), 5–6.

168  47. B.T.H.R. NBR 1/64, 430, 16 April 1914.

169  48. *Railway Times* (13 October 1900), 407.

169  49. *Ibid.* (1 September 1900), 251. B.T.H.R. GCR 1/3, min. 1501, 7 September 1900.

169  50. B.T.H.R. RCA 1/2 No. 2251; RCA 1/3 Nos. 2437, 2446, 2759 and 2778.

169  51. J. Saville, *op. cit.*, 339.

169  52. B.T.H.R. RCA 1/3 Nos. 2531 and 2537; RHY 1/8, 294.

169  53. *Ibid.*, RCA 1/2, No. 2260, 2 March 1899. P.R.O. MT6/911/13535/1899, files 6411, 7131, 8128 of 1898, and file 1454 of 1899. P. S. Bagwell, *The Railwaymen*, 193–5.

169  54. P.R.O. MT6/1116/13235/1902, files 9074 of 1900 and 13235 of 1902; minutes attached to these files make it clear that papers dating at least from the beginning of 1899 have been destroyed.

# Notes

*Page*

170    55. *Parl. Papers 1900*, xxvii [Cd–42], qq. 2571–2605: evidence of Bell before the Royal Commission, 1899. Gupta, *op. cit.*, 303.

170    56. *Parl. Papers 1893–94*, vii (90). There is an illustration of an automatic coupling in the *Railway Times* (28 April 1899), 5.

170    57. See chapter 8.

170    58. *Parl. Papers 1893–94*, lxxix (502), 8–10.

170    59. *Parl. Papers 1900*, xxvii [Cd–42], 18.

170    60. *Parl. Deb.* (1898), 4th series, lxiii, 563–4, 29 July.

170    61. *Parl. Papers 1899*, lxxxv [C–9183], 10.

171    62. *Transport* (2 December 1898), 470; (16 December), 512–13. *Railway Engineer* (January 1899), 5–6.

171    63. *Echo* (9 January 1899), 1; (24 January), 1; (13 February), 1.

171    64. *Railway Review* (3 February 1899), 1. Gupta, *op. cit.*, 305.

171    65. *Parl. Deb.*, 4th series (1899), lxvi, 343, 1118, 1561–79.

171    66. *The Commonwealth* (organ of the Christian Socialist Union) (January 1899), 20; I owe this reference to Mr N. C. Masterman.

171    67. *Parl. Deb.*, 4th series (1899), lxvi, 1587.

171    68. *Ibid.* (1899), lxvii, 645–8, 27 February. *Parl. Papers 1899*, vi (99).

171    69. See chapter 8.

172    70. This was a point which Hopwood admitted in private, putting the proportion of accidents caused by shunting operations at one-fifth of all shunting accidents: B.T.H.R. RCA 1/2 No. 2247, 7.

172    71. *Ibid.*, No. 2257, 2 March 1899, 2.

172    72. *Ibid.*, 3; for the formation of the Council, see chapter 11.

172    73. B.T.H.R. RCA 1/2 No. 2263, 1–2.

172    74. Salisbury Papers, Special Correspondence, Class E, Main Series: Hamilton to Salisbury, 3 March 1899.

172    75. *The Times* (7 March 1899), 11; Hamilton was not at this time an M.P.

173    76. *Ibid.* (16 March 1899), 12. B.T.H.R. RCA 1/2 Nos. 2263 and 2267.

173    77. *Railway Times* (4 March 1899), 307; (18 March), 366.

173    78. *Regulation of Railways Bill: Automatic Couplings. Deputation to the Rt. Hon. C. T. Ritchie, M.P. . . . from the Mining Association of Great Britain, &C., &C., &C.* (1899), 6–13, 19; this is a 48-page booklet inserted in B.T.H.R. RCA 1/2.

173    79. *The Times* (23 March 1899), 10.

173    80. B.T.H.R. RCA 1/2 No. 2268, 17 March 1899.

173    81. *Ibid.*, 2–3.

173    82. *Railway Times* (1 April 1899), 435–6: Mining Association to Ritchie, 20 March 1899.

173    83. *Parl. Deb.*, 4th series (1899), lxix, 505–6, 663.

173    84. *Railway Review* (31 March 1899), 8: article by F. W. Evans.

174    85. *Ibid.* (7 April 1899), 5. *Transport* (11 November 1898), 405.

174    86. *Railway Review* (21 April 1899), 1.

174    87. *Ibid.* (28 April 1899), 5. *Parl. Deb.*, 4th series (1899), lxx, 366, 512, 603, 690, 819, 949, 1224.

174    88. *Ibid.*, 696.

174    89. *Railway Review* (28 April 1899), 4.

*Page*
174    90. B.T.H.R. RCA 1/2 No. 2268, 17 March 1899, 2: statement by Stalbridge.
174    91. *Parl. Papers 1900*, xxvii [Cd–42], q. 2935.
174    92. *Railway Times* (28 April 1900), 530.
174    93. B.T.H.R. RCA 1/2 No. 2269, 20 April 1899. Ritchie was undoubtedly made aware of this plan, but rejected it, owing probably to the opposition of the private owners: *Parl. Deb.*, 4th series (1899), lxx, 696.
174    94. *The Times* (17 April 1899), 10. B.T.H.R. RCA 1/2 No. 2269.
174    95. *Parl. Papers 1900*, xxvii [Cd–41], 3–4. Gupta, *op. cit.*, 3–4.
175    96. B.T.H.R. RCA 1/2 Nos. 2278, 2283 and 2290; RCA 1/3 No. 2329, 3.
175    97. *Parl. Papers 1900*, xxvii [Cd–42], 20, 60: remarks by Scotter and Paget; qq. 3473, 6039–43, 6228.
175    98. *Ibid.*, qq. 487, 508, 3755, 4899, 4900, 4908, 4980–5.
175    99. B.T.H.R. RCA 1/2 No. 2299, 5 July 1899.
175    100. *Parl. Papers 1900*, xxvii [Cd–42], qq. 6307, 6681, 7362, 7431, 7558, 7612.
175    101. *Ibid.* [Cd–41], 8–10, 13.
176    102. *Ibid.*, 11–13.
176    103. *Parl. Papers 1900*, iv (78).
176    104. B.T.H.R. RCA 1/3 Nos. 2356, 2360 and 2372. *Parl. Deb.*, 4th series, lxxxi, 1300–4, 5 April 1900.
176    105. *Parl. Papers 1900*, viii (175), 3–4. *Railway Review* (11 May 1900), 1. The other six railway M.P.s on the committee were Sir William Houldsworth (London & North Western), Walter Long (Great Western), Sir Herbert Maxwell (Glasgow & South Western), Charles Bine Renshaw (Caledonian), James Round (London, Tilbury & Southend) and Sir Barrington Simeon (London & South Western); Simeon was a Liberal Unionist, the other five were Conservatives.
176    106. *Parl. Papers 1900*, viii (175), 6–7. B.T.H.R. RCA 1/3 No. 2380, 2 May 1900.
176    107. *Parl. Deb.*, 4th series, lxxxiii, 1608–23, 28 May 1900. B.T.H.R. RCA 1/3 Nos. 2381, 2392, 3. *Railway Times* (26 May 1900), 648. Whips were sent out in support of this alteration.
177    108. B.T.H.R. RCA 1/3 No. 2396, 6–7. 63 & 64 Vict., c. 27.
177    109. *Parl. Deb.*, 4th series (1900), lxxxi, 1283, 5 April: speech of Alfred Lyttelton, M.P. for Warwick and Leamington.
178    110. *Ibid.* (1900), lxxxiv, 1277, 28 June.

## Notes to Chapter 11

179    1. P. J. Cain, *op. cit.*, 94.
179    2. 'British Railway Progress, 1850–1912', *The Jubilee of the Railway News* [1914], 33.
179    3. *Statist* (13 July 1901), 64; (12 October 1901), 650. *Herapath* (26 December 1902), 1186. *Railway News* (18 February 1905), 283–7. W. A. Robertson, *Combination Among Railway Companies* (1912), 22.

# Notes

*Page*

180    4. B.T.H.R. RCA 1/3 No. 2761, 17 March 1903, and committee meeting of 2 April 1903; GE 1/26, min. 1537; GCR 1/4, min. 2488.

180    5. *Railway News* (10 August 1901), 246–8. E. Cleveland-Stevens, *op. cit.*, 297–311.

180    6. W. A. Robertson, *op. cit.*, 23. 'Railway Amalgamations And Agreements', *The Jubilee of the Railway News* [1914], 42.

180    7. Appendix, table 14.

180    8. Appendix, table 15.

180    9. Gupta, *op. cit.*, 368.

181    10. *Parl. Deb.*, 4th series (1902), ciii, 1083–1148. *House of Commons' Divisions*, 1902, Numb. 50; nine Unionists voted for the motion.

181    11. Of the 56 Unionist M.P.s who held railway directorships in 1904 and 1905, only five (of whom only two were members of the efficient interest) were listed by Asquith as being Free Traders: Bodleian Library, Oxford, Asquith MSS., 92, fols. 3–6: a four-page typescript list headed "Conservative or Liberal Unionist M.P. Free Traders", dating from late 1903 or early 1904.

181    12. G. W. Alcock, *op. cit.*, 345.

181    13. Salisbury Papers, Special Correspondence, Class E, Main Series: Hamilton to Salisbury's secretary, S. K. McDonnell, 9 January 1901.

181    14. P.R.O. MT6/1053/1309/1902, file 14885 of 1900: memo. by Hopwood, 15 November 1900, with concurring minute by G. W. Balfour, 16 November.

181    15. *Ibid.*, file 14885 of 1900. B.T.H.R. RCA 1/3 Nos. 2472 and 2477.

181    16. *Herapath* (15 February 1901), 182. *Parl. Deb.*, 4th series (1901), xc, 50; xcv, 341–2.

182    17. *Herapath* (26 April 1901), 422; (13 May 1901), 542. *Parl. Deb.*, 4th series (1901), xcii, 548–9; xcv, 559–60. B.T.H.R. RCA 1/3 No. 2540, 14 May 1901.

182    18. B.T.H.R. RCA 1/3 Nos. 2549, 2555 and 2560.

182    19. *Ibid.*, No. 2591, 3 December 1901; meeting of 4 December 1901.

182    20. *Ibid.*, meeting of 15 May 1902, 1. P.R.O. MT6/1053/1309/1902, file 421 of 1902. *Parl. Deb.*, 4th series (1902), cvii, 1355–6.

182    21. *The Times* (6 December 1911), 23.

182    22. *Herapath* (27 September 1901), 988. P.R.O. MT6/2032/10004 part 1/1911, files 9876 of 1902; minute by Colonel Yorke, 22 July 1902; 6825 of 1903: memo. by Yorke, 10 June 1903.

182    23. B.T.H.R. RCA 1/3, meetings of 11 February, 12 March and 19 June 1902.

182    24. *Herapath* (1 August 1902), 685. P.R.O. MT6/2032/10004 part 1/1911, file 11687 of 1902. H. R. Wilson, *The Safety of British Railways*, 185–8. The rules confirmed by the Railway Commissioners came into force in August 1902: P.R.O. MT6/2032/10004 part 1/1911, files 10997 and 11160 of 1902. *Herapath* (22 August 1902), 766.

182    25. B.T.H.R. RCA 1/3, meetings of 26 November 1902, 12 and 19 January 1903, and 25 June 1903. P.R.O. MT6/2032/10004 part 1/1911, file 13620: a list of objectors and objections, printed by the Railway Association; file 2585 of 1903: typescript memo. by Board of Trade officers, probably February 1903.

182    26. *Ibid.*, file 8565 of 1903: minute by J. G. Willis, 12 November 1903; file

*Page*

13707 of 1903: Granet to Sir H. Jekyll, 17 November 1903; file 5491 of 1904.

182   27. *Ibid.*, file 5680 of 1904: minute by Jekyll, 10 May 1904.

183   28. *Ibid.*, file 8703 of 1904: memo. by Yorke, 25 June 1904, and minute by Hopwood, 4 July.

183   29. *Ibid.*, file 12727 of 1904: Granet to Jekyll, 9 November 1904; file 4635 of 1905: typescript report by Yorke, 15 April 1905. B.T.H.R. RCA 1/3 Nos. 2891, 2897 and 2909.

183   30. P.R.O. MT6/2033/10004 part 2/1911, file 7267 of 1905: Bell to Railway Department, 20 June 1905; file 823 of 1906: minute by Jekyll, 1 March 1906. B.T.H.R. RCA 1/4 No. 3010.

183   31. P.R.O. MT6/2033/10004 part 2/1911, files 9023 of 1907 to 13757 of 1908 inclusive.

183   32. *Ibid.*, file 14284 of 1908. *The Times* (19 December 1908), 4; (23 December), 3.

183   33. P.R.O. MT6/2033/10004 part 2/1911, files 2886, 4174 and 10203 of 1910; file 10004 of 1911. *The Times* (6 December 1911), 23.

183   34. B.T.H.R. RCA 1/3, meeting of 22 July 1903.

183   35. *Parl. Deb.*, 4th series (1903), cxxvi, 1587–8. *Parl. Papers 1904*, lxxxiv [Cd.–2045], 9–15. B.T.H.R. LNW 1/38, min. 19386, 14 August 1903. P.R.O. MT6/1231/3609/1904, file 9304 of 1903: memo. by Sir H. Jekyll, 30 July 1903.

183   36. *Railway Times* (25 July 1903), 86.

184   37. *Ibid. Parl. Papers 1904*, lxxxiv [Cd.–2045], 15–7. B.T.H.R. RCA 1/3 No. 2873.

184   38. *Ibid.*, No. 2913, 7. *Parl. Papers 1904*, lxxxiv [Cd.–2045], 17–8. In 1905 Alfred Baldwin became chairman of the Great Western in succession to Earl Cawdor; he resigned from the Departmental Committee and was replaced by the general manager of the Great Eastern Railway, J. F. S. Gooday: B.T.H.R. RCA 1/4 Nos. 2971 and 2975.

184   39. *Ibid.*, No. 3011, 1 August 1905. *Parl. Deb.*, 4th series (1905), cxli, 1247–8, 24 February. P.R.O. Gerald Balfour Papers, P.R.O. 30/60/44: six-page typescript list, undated, headed "Departmental Committee on Railway Rates".

184   30. A. H. H. Matthews, *op. cit.*, 235–6.

184   41. *Herapath* (21 February 1902), 190. P.R.O. BT 13/37/E16668, file E16034: typescript memo. prepared by the Railway Association, 1903. B.T.H.R. RCA 1/3 No. 2669, 8 May 1902; meeting of solicitors, 5 May 1903.

184   42. *Parl. Deb.*, 4th series (1903), cxviii, 401–2. *Parl. Papers 1903*, iv (9).

184   43. P.R.O. BT 13/37/E16668: minute by Hopwood, 23 October 1903, between files E16034 and E16541.

184   44. *Parl. Deb.*, 4th series (1904), cxxix, 480–1; cxxxii, 55–61. *Parl. Papers 1904*, iv (4).

184   45. *Ibid.*, vi (133), 6–8. P.R.O. BT 13/37/E16668: letters to Granet and Sir William Tomlinson (a Conservative supporter of the bill), 5 January 1904, and copy letter from Hopwood to Granet, 13 April 1904, between files E16034 and E16541; file E16548 of 1904: Granet to Hopwood, 14 April 1904; file E16668 of 1904; Granet to Hopwood, 26 May 1904; Jekyll to Granet, 11 April, approved by Balfour.

# Notes

*Page*

184  46. B.T.H.R. RCA 1/3 No. 2875, 21 April 1904.

184  47. *Ibid.*, No. 2890, 20 June 1904. *Parl. Deb.*, 4th series (1904), cxxxvi, 362–71, 17 June. P.R.O. BT 13/37/E16668, file E16548 of 1904: Granet to Hopwood, 14 and 16 June 1904; undated memo. by W. F. Marwood; minute by Hopwood, 22 June 1904. 4 Edw. 7, c. 19.

185  48. B.T.H.R. RCA 1/3 No. 2510, 5 March 1901; the second reading was carried in 1901 by 301 votes to 80; Lockwood and Maxwell abstained: *Parl. Deb.*, 4th series (1901), xc, 759–64, 6 March.

185  49. B.T.H.R. RCA 1/3 Nos. 2529, 2550 and 2562.

185  50. *Parl. Deb.*, 4th series (1905), cxli, 476. *Parl. Papers 1905*, i (17).

185  51. *Parl. Deb.*, 4th series (1905), cxlii, 360–2.

185  52. *Parl. Papers 1905*, vii (97), 9–10. B.T.H.R. RCA 1/4 No. 2997, 5 July 1905; report on parliamentary legislation during 1905 session (this report occurs immediately after the Council minutes of 7 November).

185  53. 5 Edw. 7, c. 11.

185  54. B.T.H.R. RCA 1/3, RCA 1/4 and RCA 1/5, *passim*.

185  55. B.T.H.R. RCA 1/3 No. 2725, 22 January 1903; RCA 1/45 *passim*., and especially meeting of accountants' committee, 19 December 1905, 124; RCA 1/46, *passim*.

186  56. P. Fraser, 'The Growth of Ministerial Control in the Nineteenth Century House of Commons', *E.H.R.*, lxxv (1960), 462.

186  57. See chapter 9.

186  58. B.T.H.R. RCA 1/2 No. 2176, 4 March 1897.

186  59. *Ibid.*, No. 2217, 15 March 1898; the minutes of the committee are in loose sheets at the end of RCA 1/2.

186  60. See Chapter 1.

187  61. B.T.H.R. RCA 1/2 No. 2230, 30 June 1898, 3–5.

187  62. C. H. Ellis, *British Railway History 1877–1947* (1959), 81.

188  63. *House of Commons' Divisions*, 1900, Numb. 125; 27 director-M.P.s of the efficient railway interest voted against the second reading: two were Liberals, the rest Unionists. Jackson and Lockwood acted as tellers for the Noes.

188  64. B.T.H.R. RCA 1/3 No. 2391, 21 May 1900.

188  65. *Ibid.*, No. 2393: at this meeting, on 24 May, there were exactly 22 director-M.P.s present, besides Jackson; five of them were Liberals, the rest Unionists.

189  66. *Ibid.*, No. 2396, 21 June 1900, 6–11.

189  67. *Ibid.*, No. 2421, 24 July 1900; No. 2441, 12 October, 8.

189  68. *Ibid.*, Nos. 2436, 2441, 6–8, 2443. The North Eastern's proposals, with a memo., are inserted after the minutes of the association's meeting on 12 October 1900, in RCA 1/3; identical copies are in B.T.H.R. GEN 3/1A.

189  69. B.T.H.R. RCA 1/3 Nos. 2458, 7 November 1900; 2474–5, 4 December 1900; CAM 1/4, min. 5570, 14 November 1900.

189  70. *Ibid.*, RCA 1/3 No. 2491, 22 January 1901, 6–7.

189  71. *Ibid.*, No. 2492, 26 February 1901.

189  72. *Ibid.*, No. 2491, 4–5.

189  73. *Ibid.*, No. 2501, 26 February 1901.

*Page*
189   74. *Ibid.*, Nos. 2514, 2525–7.
190   75. *Ibid.*, RCA 1/4 No. 2993, 5 July 1905.
190   76. *Ibid.*, RCA (S) 1/3, printed letter of 8 January 1901.
191   77. *Ibid.*, GEN 3/1A: *Memorandum as to the Constitution and Procedure of the Railway Association*, 4.
191   78. B.T.H.R. RCA 1/3 Nos. 2702, 2713, 2737, 6.
191   79. *Ibid.*, Nos. 2442, 2452 and 2487.
191   80. *Ibid.*, Nos. 2442 and 2459, 12 October and 7 November 1900. The preference for men with a legal training persisted. Granet, who left in 1905 to become assistant general manager, and in 1906 general manager, of the Midland Railway, was succeeded as the association's secretary by W. Temple Franks, also a barrister and at that time Assistant Librarian in the House of Commons. In 1909 Temple Franks became Controller-General of Patents; in his place the association chose another barrister, Arthur Beresford Cane, who remained with the association till 1929: B.T.H.R. RCA 1/4 Nos. 2993 and 3336. *Railway Gazette* (9 July 1926), 53; (5 January 1940), 22.
191   81. B.T.H.R. RCA 1/2 No. 2231, 30 June 1898; RCA 1/3 No. 2924, 13 December 1904, 8–9: copy of a memorandum as to the constitution and functions of the Railway Companies' Association, submitted to the Royal Commission on Trade Disputes.

## Notes to Chapter 12

192   1. *Parl. Deb.*, 4th series (1907), clxxi, 765–8, 19 March.
192   2. Appendix, table 16.
192   3. Appendix, table 17.
193   4. Appendix, tables 18 and 19.
193   5. *Railway News* (3 February 1906), 177.
193   6. B.T.H.R. RCA 1/4 No. 3047, 7 February 1906.
193   7. Stuart-Wortley sat as M.P. for Sheffield 1880–5, and for the Hallam division 1885–1916, when he became Lord Stuart of Wortley. He was a director of the Manchester, Sheffield & Lincolnshire and Great Central railways from 1894 to 1922.
193   8. John Buchan, 'Charles Beilby Stuart-Wortley', in C. Grosvenor and Lord Stuart of Wortley, *The First Lady Wharncliffe and her Family*, vol. I (1927), ix–xx.
193   9. F. G. Banbury, *Railways Bill: Memorandum by the Chairman of the Great Northern Railway Company* (1921), *passim*.
194   10. *Parl. Papers 1912–13*, xlv [Cd. 6014], q. 10,229. B.T.H.R. RCA 1/4 Nos. 3056 and 3191. Salisbury Papers, Special Correspondence, Class E, Main Series: Hamilton to Salisbury, 26 December 1871. Lord Claud Hamilton, 'Fifty Years a Director of the Great Eastern Railway Company', *London and*

# Notes

Page

*North Eastern Railway 'Great Eastern' Magazine*, vol. 13 (February 1923), 22–4.

195   11. *Railway News* (29 February 1908), 392; (14 February 1914), 369. See also *Railway Times* (1 February 1913), 123–4 (Liberal support for nationalization) and *London Catholic Herald* (2 September 1911), 5 (article by the Labour M.P. G. N. Barnes.).

195   12. For Lloyd George's support of nationalization see *Com. Deb.*, 5th series (1912), xxxviii, 528, 8 May; and for Churchill's, see *The Times* (4 October 1911), 7. Herbert Gladstone's view was that railway nationalization was a possibility only "in the dim socialistic future wh[ich] we cannot now practically consider": Campbell-Bannerman Papers, B.M. Add. MSS. 41217, fol. 172: Herbert Gladstone to Campbell-Bannerman, 4 January 1905. On this subject, as on much else, Asquith was non-committal: *The Times* (14 March 1908), 12; *Morning Post* (21 May 1912), 9–10.

195   13. *Railway Times* (16 December 1905), 659.

195   14. *North Wales Observer and Express* (29 January 1892), 6. *Carnarvon and Denbigh Herald* (24 June 1892), 7; (26 October 1894), 5; (23 November 1894), 7.

195   15. *The Times* (17 February 1906), 10; Cheap trains legislation was proposed in the 1907 session, but never introduced: P.R.O. CAB 37/85/91, 3 December 1906.

195   16. *Parl. Deb.*, 4th series (1907), clxx, 770, 6 March; clxxi, 756–76, 19 March; clxxiii, 349–71, 25 April. P.R.O. CAB 37/90/116. The controversy had been sparked off by the support given by the London & North Western Railway to the London Municipal Society, a Conservative organization, at the London County Council elections in 1906. At least three companies— the London & North Western, Great Eastern and London & South Western —had subscribed to the society in that year; but there was never any suggestion that railway companies had given financial support to candidates at parliamentary elections: B.T.H.R. LNW 1/40, min. 21737; GE 1/28, 63; LSW 1/33, typescript extract No. 80 from Board meeting of 12 July 1906. *Economist*, 2 March 1907, 369. See also the papers in P.R.O. MT6/ 2069/2215/1912, files 2893, 3716, 4787, 5490 and 5539 of 1907.

196   17. B.T.H.R. RCA 1/4 No. 3146, 4 December 1906.

196   18. *Railway Times* (23 June 1906), 797.

196   19. *Parl. Papers 1906*, lv [Cd. 2959], 36. B.T.H.R. RCA 1/4 No. 3114, 3 July 1906. The report is dated 6 April 1906.

196   20. *Parl. Deb.*, 4th series (1906), clx, 1212–35; clxi, 1221. *Parl. Papers 1906*, iv (324).

196   21. *Railway Times* (15 December 1906), 601; (29 December), 665. A. H. H. Matthews, *op. cit.*, 236–7.

196   22. *Parl. Deb.*, 4th series (1907), clxix, 417. *Parl. Papers 1907*, iv (9). P.R.O. BT 13/41/E18832/1907.

197   23. B.T.H.R. RCA 1/4, report on "Owners' Risk Rates and Railway Contracts Bill", 2 March 1907, following Council minutes of 5 March. P.R.O. MT6/ 1786/2859/1909, file 13859 of 1908.

197   24. *Railway Gazette* (8 March 1907), 226.

*Page*

197    25. B.T.H.R. RCA 1/47, meeting of general managers and solicitors, 12 March 1907.

197    26. *Parl. Deb.*, 4th series (1907), clxxi, 344–81. *Parl. Papers 1907*, viii (96), 4–5. B.T.H.R. RCA 1/47 No. 3208, 24 April 1907.

197    27. B.T.H.R. GE 1/27, 273–5, 6 December 1905. P.R.O. MT6/1592/6907/ 1907, file 727 of 1907: memo. by W. F. Marwood, 11 January 1907. P. J. Cain, *op. cit.*, 125.

197    28. *Western Daily Mercury* (1 January 1907), 5.

197    29. *Ibid.* (2 January 1907), 5; (5 January), 5. *Parl. Deb.* 4th series (1907), clxx, 26–7, 27 February.

197    30. *The Times* (20 March 1907), 12: meetings of the Caledonian and Glasgow & South Western railways on 19 March.

197    31. *Ibid.* (25 April 1907), 5: speech in reply to a deputation from the Silk Association.

198    32. Gupta, *op. cit.*, 277–82, 348–52.

198    33. *The Times* (31 July 1907), 14; (10 August), 13; (25 August), 8.

198    34. *Railway Review* (28 June 1907), 2.

198    35. The best account, in spite of minor inaccuracies, remains that of E. Halévy, *The Rule of Democracy 1905–1914* (A History of the English People in the Nineteenth Century, Vol. VI, first paperback edition 1961), 108–14.

198    36. *The Times* (17 October 1907), 4; (18 October), 8; (19 October), 10. *Railway News* (12 October 1907), 635; (19 October), 670–3.

199    37. *Ibid.* (19 October 1907), 673.

199    38. M. Alfassa, *La Crise Ouvrière Récente des Chemins De Fer Anglais Une solution nouvelle des conflits* (Paris 1908), 40–1, 48.

199    39. B.T.H.R. LNW 1/39, min. 21239; LNW 1/40, min. 21452; LY 1/458, 88 and 174. *The Times* (30 October 1907), 9. *Railway Gazette* (1 November 1907), 415.

199    40. *The Times* (7 November 1907), 4. Alfassa, *op. cit.*, 6.

199    41. *Parl. Papers 1909*, lxxvii [Cd. 4534], 17–19.

199    42. P.R.O. CAB 41/31/35: Campbell-Bannerman to Edward VII, 5 November 1907. See also S. and B. Webb, *The History of Trade Unionism* (new impression of 1920 edn, 1956), 527.

199    43. F. Owen, *Tempestuous Journey: Lloyd George, His Life and Times* (1954), 155: Lloyd George to Campbell-Bannerman, 25 October 1907. B.T.H.R. LY 1/458, 406–9, 5 November 1907.

200    44. W. George, *My Brother and I* (1958), 212: Lloyd George to William George, 21 October 1907. Lord (Sir G. R.) Askwith, *Industrial Problems and Disputes* (1920), 121.

200    45. W. George, *op. cit.*, 212: Lloyd George to William George, 29 and 31 October 1907. Alfassa, *op. cit.*, 46–7.

200    46. W. George, *op. cit.*, 212: Lloyd George to William George, 25 October and 1 November 1907. Beaverbrook Library, Lloyd George Papers, B/1/1/6: Maxwell to Lloyd George, 25 October 1907.

200    47. Sir H. Maxwell, *Evening Memories* (1932), 105–6.

200    48. *The Times* (24 October 1907), 5. *Railway News* (26 October 1907), 712–13.

Notes

*Page*

200   49. On Fay (1856–1953), see *Railway Times* (27 July 1912), 85, and G. Dow, *Great Central*, vol. III (1965), *passim*. Fay, who was Claud Hamilton's junior by more than ten years, had an illegitimate son in 1908, was knighted in 1912, and played an important part in the running of the railways during the First World War.

200   50. B.T.H.R. GCR 1/6, min. 3887, 8 November 1907; GW 1/48, 431. 21 November 1907. W. George, *op. cit.*, 212: Lloyd George to William George, 1 and 4 November 1907.

200   51. Birmingham University Library, Austen Chamberlain Papers, AC8/2/7: A. J. Balfour to Austen Chamberlain, 3 January 1908, passing on information supplied to his brother, Gerald Balfour, by Lord Allerton, chairman of the Great Northern Railway and a member of the negotiating committee. This is supported by the evidence of Guy Granet, general manager of the Midland Railway, before the Royal Commission of 1911: *Parl. Papers 1912–13*, xlv [Cd. 6014], q. 12,912; and the extract in B.T.H.R. LY 1/458, 409–10, 5 November 1907.

200   52. P. S. Bagwell, *The Railwaymen*, 269. Dow, *op. cit.*, 85. For the text of the scheme see *Parl. Papers 1911*, xxix part I [Cd. 5922], 21–4.

200   53. *The Times* (8 November 1907), 9.

200   54. The official view, given only some years after, was that the scheme had emanated from Sir H. L. Smith, Permanent Secretary at the Board of Trade: Askwith, *Industrial Problems and Disputes*, 122.

201   55. 'British Railway Progress, 1850–1912', *Jubilee of the Railway News* [1914], 33; the percentage of working expenses to gross receipts stood at 62 per cent in 1906, rose to 63 per cent in 1907, and reached 64 per cent in 1908.

201   56. *Railway Gazette* (8 November 1907), 439.

201   57. *Railway Gazette, loc. cit. Financial Times* (7 December 1907), 3. *Daily Chronicle* (9 December), 6. *Financier and Bullionist* (24 September 1910), 4. *Yorkshire Post* (6 July 1911), 6. B.T.H.R. RCA(S) 1/4, Minutes of Conference between the President of the Board of Trade and Members of the Railway Companies' Association, 19 December 1907, 1–2, 5, 7. P.R.O. MT6/1786/2859/1909, file 15924 of 1907: typescript memo., 21 December 1907. *Parl. Papers 1911*, xxix part I [Cd. 5927], q. 18,215: evidence of Guy Granet.

201   58. B.T.H.R. RCA 1/4 No. 3243, 3 December 1907. P.R.O. MT6/1786/2859/1909, file 15924 of 1907.

201   59. *The Times* (14 December 1907), 15. *Railway Gazette* (16 August 1907), 145; (20 December), 583 and 597.

201   60. Dow, *op. cit.*, 116. *Daily Telegraph* (30 November 1907), 11. *Daily Chronicle* (9 December 1907), 6; (14 December), 5. *Tribune* (14 December 1907), 6–7.

201   61. B.T.H.R. RCA 1/4 No. 3251, 17 December 1907.

202   62. B.T.H.R. RCA(S) 1/4, Minutes of Conference between the President of the Board of Trade and Members of the Railway Companies' Association, 19 December 1907, 5.

202   63. B.T.H.R. RCA 1/47, meeting of general managers and honorary solicitors, 29 January and 5 February 1908.

Page
202    64. *Produce Markets' Review* (22 February 1908), 151. *Builders' Journal and Architectural Engineer* (26 February 1908), 176; (18 March), 249; (1 April), 296.

202    65. B.T.H.R. RCA 1/4 No. 3317, 3 December 1908.

202    66. *Builders' Journal and Architectural Engineer* (4 March 1908), 211. *Evening Standard* (3 January 1908), 1.

202    67. P.R.O. MT6/1770/550/1909, file 549 of 1909: typescript memo. by A. R. Thomson headed "Railway Agreements", 18 December 1908, 1 and 10. *Manchester Courier* (28 January 1908), 6–7. *Pall Mall Gazette* (28 January 1908), 5.

202    68. *The Times* (3 March 1908), 3.

202    69. *Railway News* (8 August 1908), 276. *The Times* (13 August 1908), 10; (15 August), 4. *Parl. Papers 1909*, lxxvii [Cd. 4695], 3–4.

202    70. *Daily Express* (15 September 1908), 1; (19 September), 5.

202    71. *Ibid.* (21 September 1908), 5; (23 September), 1.

202    72. *Standard* (18 December 1908), 2.

202    73. *Daily Express* (22 September 1908), 1; and see *ibid.* (26 September), 5. The September 1908 articles in the *Daily Express* were later used as anti-railway propaganda by the Amalgamated Society of Railway Servants: *Parl. Papers 1911*, xxix part II [Cd. 5927], qq. 16,581, 16,600, 16,612.

203    74. *Daily Express* (25 September 1908), 1.

203    75. *Yorkshire Post* (6 June 1908), 9. P.R.O. MT6/1799/4635/1909, file 46 of 1909.

203    76. Bodleian Library, Oxford, Asquith MSS. 11, fol. 241: Churchill to Asquith, 26 December 1908.

203    77. R. S. Churchill, *Winston S. Churchill Volume II Young Statesman 1901–1914* (1967), 276–8, 281.

203    78. Asquith MSS. 11, fols. 251–3: Churchill to Asquith, 29 December 1908.

203    79. P.R.O. MT6/1770/550/1909, file 549 of 1909: minute by Churchill, 26 December 1908.

203    80. *The Times* (4 March 1909), 9. *Railway Times* (6 March 1909), 237.

203    81. Asquith MSS. 5, fol. 90: Asquith to Edward VII, 10 March 1909.

203    82. *Com. Deb.*, 5th series (1909), iii, 846–8, 5 April. The minority of 111 against the bill was composed of eight Unionists, 66 Liberals, six Irish Nationalists, 24 Labour M.P.s, and seven Lib-Labs: *House of Commons' Divisions*, 1909, Numb. 50.

204    83. *Com. Deb.*, 5th series (1909), iii, 841, 5 April.

204    84. *Ibid.*, 996–7, 1014–40, 6 April 1909.

204    85. *Ibid.*, 1039; iv, 179, 27 April. See also P.R.O. MT6/1799/4635/1909, file 2761 of 1909: draft letter, not sent, Churchill to Lord Allerton, April 1909.

204    86. *Com. Deb.*, 5th series (1909), vi, 711, 14 June.

# Notes to Chapter 13

*Page*

205    1. *Com. Deb.*, 5th series (1909), viii, 1647, 2 August.

205    2. *Parl. Papers 1911*, xxix part II [Cd. 5631], 3.

205    3. B.T.H.R. RCA 1/4 No. 3360, 25 May 1909; RCA 1/47, meeting of committee, 24 June.

206    4. *Ibid.*, RCA 1/4 No. 3368, 26 July 1909, 5.

206    5. *Ibid.*, RCA 1/47, meeting of committee, 21 July 1909, 2. *Parl. Papers 1911*, xxix part II [Cd. 5927], qq. 11,697, 12,146–7.

206    6. *Ibid.*, qq. 893–4, 4736, 5934, 8739–47, 9417.

206    7. *Ibid.*, qq. 2301, 3197, 3253, 3990.

206    8. *Ibid.*, [Cd. 5631], 18, 29, 33–4.

206    9. *Parl. Papers 1909*, lxxvi [Cd. 4697], iv. P.R.O. BT 13/43/E20806/[1909].

206    10. *Parl. Papers 1909*, lxxvi [Cd. 4697], 1. *Financial Times* (20 June 1910), 3.

206    11. *Parl. Papers 1909*, lxxvi [Cd. 4697], 22.

206    12. *Parl. Papers 1910*, v (169); vi (225), 5–6. B.T.H.R. RCA 1/5 No. 3416, 5 July 1910.

206    13. *Railway Gazette* (15 July 1910), 84.

207    14. *Com. Deb.*, 5th series (1910), xx, 235. The bill was passed with hardly any debate in 1911, but the reference to the Railway Companies' Association was omitted: 1 and 2 Geo. 5, c. 34.

207    15. *Parl. Papers 1911*, xxix part II [Cd. 5927], q. 18, 180: evidence of Guy Granet.

207    16. *Ibid.*, q. 18,195.

207    17. *Railway Times* (2 October 1909), 341.

207    18. *Ibid.* (20 November 1909), 514.

208    19. *Ibid.* (23 April 1910), 432; (8 October), 380.

208    20. *Railway Review* (10 June 1910), 6; (14 October), 1. *Daily Express* (20 August 1910), 1.

208    21. *Parl. Papers 1912–13*, xlv [Cd. 6014], qq. 105, 1175, 1878, 2867–73, 4826. On the working of the Conciliation Scheme, see P. S. Bagwell, *The Railwaymen*, 275–84.

208    22. P.R.O. MT6/1931/10397/1910, file 10397 of 1910.

208    23. *The Times* (15 August 1911), 7. *Daily News* (17 August 1911), 1.

208    24. *Daily News* (17 August 1911), 1 and 5.

208    25. *The Times* (17 August 1911), 6–7. Asquith MSS. 92, fol. 184: memo. by Buxton, 23 August 1911.

208    26. *Daily News* (18 August 1911), 1.

208    27. M. A. Hamilton, *Arthur Henderson* (1938), 87–8.

208    28. *Daily News* (19 August 1911), 1. L. Masterman, *C. F. G. Masterman* (1939), 204.

208    29. *Daily News* (21 August 1911), 1. G. Taylor, *The English Railway Strike and its Revolutionary Bearings* (Chicago 1911), 15. [*The City Club Bulletin*, vol. IV, no. 19 (11 October 1911)].

208    30. In Liverpool, where the trouble began, free labour was non-existent: P.R.O. HO 45/10654/212470 (1–140), file la of 1911: Head Constable of

*Page*

Liverpool to Home Office, 7 August 1911. It is noteworthy that Collison, in his autobiography, made no mention of the National Free Labour Association having played a part in the 1911 railway strike: W. Collison, *The Apostle of Free Labour* (1913), 288–93.

208    31. Masterman, *op. cit.*, 205–6, 208.

209    32. *Ibid.*, 207. P.R.O. HO 45/10655/212470 (141–250), file 161 of 1911: memo. by Gibb, 19 August 1911 (typescript copy).

209    33. Asquith MSS. 92, fol. 186: memo. by Buxton, 23 August 1911. Askwith, *Industrial Problems and Disputes*, 165.

209    34. *Railway Gazette* (1 July 1921), 24. *Modern Transport* (28 August 1920), 11. When Buxton set up the Industrial Council in October 1911, Claughton was an automatic choice for membership of it: *Railway Times* (14 October 1911), 367. It is worth noting that by 1911 the North Eastern had been joined by the North Staffordshire and Barry companies in recognizing the Amalgamated Society: Clegg, Fox and Thompson, *op. cit.*, 427.

209    35. *Modern Transport* (23 July 1921), 9.

209    36. *Railway Review* (8 September 1911), 5. Asquith MSS. 92, fol. 187: memo. by Buxton, 23 August 1911.

209    37. Asquith MSS. 92, fol. 187. *Daily News* (21 August 1911), 1. Masterman, *op. cit.*, 207.

209    38. Halévy, *op. cit.*, 460.

209    39. H. Pelling, *A History of British Trade Unionism* (Penguin Books edn. 1965), 137.

210    40. B.T.H.R. RCA 1/48, meeting of chairmen, 8 September 1911, 3: speech by Claughton.

210    41. B.T.H.R. RCA 1/5 No. 3536, 4. P.R.O. MT6/2022/8739/1911, file 8739 of 1911. *Daily News* (21 August 1911), 1. *The Times* (21 August 1911), 6.

210    42. *Parl. Papers 1912–13*, xlv [Cd. 6014], q. 10,356.

210    43. Technically this was a meeting at the Railway Companies' Association's offices, but not a meeting of the association.

210    44. B.T.H.R. RCA 1/48, meeting of chairmen, 8 September 1911, 2: speech by Allerton.

211    45. *Ibid.*, 3.

211    46. *Ibid.*, 4: speech by Cosmo Bonsor.

211    47. *Ibid.*, 6. Renshaw did not vote: presumably Claughton did, but evidently without much sincerity.

211    48. *Parl. Papers 1912–13*, xlv [Cd. 6014], q. 9080: evidence of Herbert Walker, Assistant General Manager of the London & North Western Railway; see also q. 10,448: evidence of W. H. Hyde, General Manager of the Great Eastern Railway. The companies were fortified in their fears of the consequences of recognition by events on the North Eastern Railway, which had suffered in 1911 along with the other companies, and which had been plagued for more than a year by labour troubles, many of them traceable to friction between unionists and non-unionists: P.R.O. MT6/2029/9717/1911, file 6674 of 1910, and files 1326 and 5299 of 1911.

212    49. *Parl. Papers 1912–13*, xlv [Cd. 6014], qq. 9650, 9879.

212    50. *Parl. Papers 1911*, xxix part I [Cd. 5922], 11, para. 54; 15–21.

# Notes

*Page*

212   51. *The Times* (24 October 1911), 8 and 15; (26 October), 6; (30 October), 8.

212   52. *Railway Times* (11 November 1911), 472–3. *The Times* (4 November 1911), 8; (6 November), 9.

212   53. B.T.H.R. RCA 1/48, meeting of 17 November 1911.

212   54. *Com. Deb.*, 5th series (1911), xxxi, 1218–9.

212   55. *Ibid.*, 1265–6, 1323–7.

212   56. B.T.H.R. RCA 1/5 No. 3479. *Railway Times* (2 December 1911), 552.

212   57. B.T.H.R. RCA 1/5 Nos. 3482–4, 3486, meeting of committee, 8 December 1911. *The Times* (9 December 1911), 8; (12 December), 9–10. *Railway Times* (16 December 1911), 603. G. D. H. Cole and R. P. Arnot, *Trade Unionism on the Railways: Its History and Problems* (1917), 23–4, 116–24.

212   58. B.T.H.R. RCA 1/5 No. 3482, 7.

212   59. *Ibid.*, No. 3479, 4.

213   60. *Ibid.*, 5; GNS 1/20, 232–3, 5 December 1911; HR 1/21, 47–8, 29 November 1911. *The Times* (2 December 1911), 8.

213   61. B.T.H.R. RCA 1/5 No. 3482, 4.

213   62. *Ibid.*, 5–6.

213   63. P.R.O. MT6/2144/12216 part 1/1912, file 5495 of 1912: account of deputation from Railway Association to Buxton, 20 May 1912, 22: speech by Buxton.

213   64. *Parl. Papers 1912–13*, lxxiv (100): Memorandum explanatory of the Railways Bill. P.R.O. MT6/2144/12216 part 1/1912, file 10480 of 1911: Marwood to Arthur Thring (Parliamentary Counsel), 9 November 1911.

214   65. *Com. Deb.*, 5th series (1912), xxxvi, 883, 1 April. *Parl. Papers 1912–13*, v (124).

214   66. *Stock Exchange Gazette* (11 April 1912), 570. *Nation* (12 April 1912), 43. *Engineer* (19 April 1912), 398. *Glasgow Herald* (30 April 1912), 12. *World's Carriers and Carrying Trades' Review* (15 May 1912), 220–1. *The Times* (12 June 1912), 7. A. H. H. Matthews, *op. cit.*, 244.

214   67. *Manchester Guardian* (23 April 1912), 6. P.R.O. MT6/2144/12216 part 1/1912, files 2011, 2867 and 4990 of 1912; the papers concerning objections and deputations to the Board of Trade, in regard to the bill, from a variety of trading manufacturing and farming organizations are in P.R.O. MT6/2144/12216 part 1/1912 and MT6/2145/12216 part 2/1912. For the origins of Macara's association, see Sir C. W. Macara, *Recollections* (1921), 217–28.

214   68. Churchill was embarrassed by a request from the Dundee Chamber of Commerce to oppose the bill: *Dundee Advertiser* (3 May 1912), 3.

214   69. *Railway Review* (12 April 1912), 8. *Railway Clerk* (15 April 1912), 91.

214   70. *Daily Herald* (17 April 1912), 12.

214   71. *Railway Times* (20 April 1912), 414.

214   72. B.T.H.R. RCA 1/5 No. 3514, 3, 16 April 1912.

214   73. *Ibid.*, meeting of 22 April 1912, Nos. 3521 and 3526. P.R.O. MT6/2144/12216 part 1/1912, file 5495 of 1912: account of deputation from Railway Association to Buxton, 20 May 1912.

214   74. B.T.H.R. RCA 1/5 Nos. 3532 and 3536. P.R.O. MT6/2144/12216 part

Page

1/1912, file 4990 of 1912: Buxton to Sir Alfred Mond, 10 July 1912 (type-script copy).

215    75. *Railway Times* (24 August 1912), 209; (7 September), 255–6; (23 November), 529.

215    76. B.T.H.R. RCA 1/5 No. 3544, 1 November 1912. P.R.O. MT6/2145/12216 part 2/1912, file 10970 of 1912: G. J. Armytage (chairman of the Railway Association) to Buxton, 1 November 1912.

215    77. *Com. Deb.*, 5th series (1912), xliii, 1432, 7 November.

215    78. B.T.H.R. RCA 1/5 No. 3548, 13 November 1912.

215    79. Halévy, *op. cit.*, 546. *Com. Deb.*, 5th series (1912), xliii, 1765–78; the amendment was moved by Banbury.

215    80. B.T.H.R. RCA 1/5 No. 3553, 25 November 1912, 2.

215    81. *Ibid.*, 3–4.

215    82. *Com. Deb.*, 5th series (1912), xliv, 2065, 2263. *Parl. Papers 1912–13*, v (331).

215    83. *The Times* (12 December 1912), 8; (28 December), 11. *Manchester Guardian* (19 December 1912), 8. P.R.O. MT6/2192/6047 part 1/1913, files 12257, 12504, 12634 of 1912.

215    84. *Com. Deb.*, 5th series (1913), xlvii, 1571–80; 1588–91; 1599–1606; 1620–22; 1634–5, 30 January.

215    85. *Ibid.*, 1606–20; 1628–30.

216    86. *Ibid.*, 1591–5; 1631–4.

216    87. The voting was 229 to 52; seven members of the efficient railway interest voted for the second reading: only one was a Liberal. No member of the efficient interest voted with the minority, made up of an assortment of Conservative, Liberal and Labour M.P.s: *Com. Deb.*, 5th series (1913), xlvii, 1653; *House of Commons' Divisions*, 1912–13, Numb. 556, 30 January 1913.

216    88. B.T.H.R. RCA 1/5 No. 3557, 7 February 1913. P.R.O. MT6/2193/6047 part 2/1913, unnumbered file containing typescript letter from A. B. Cane to Buxton, 7 February 1913.

216    89. *Com. Deb.*, 5th series (1913), xlviii, 1140–2, 12 February.

216    90. *Ibid.*, 1130–8; the voting was 139 to 42.

216    91. *Ibid.*, 1333–4; 1345–6; 1353–4; 1357–9; 1363–4; 1381–92.

216    92. B.T.H.R. RCA 1/5 Nos. 3560 and 3561.

217    93. Beaverbrook Library, Bonar Law Papers 19/1/26: Lansdowne to Bonar Law, 20 February 1913. *Lord's Deb.*, 5th series (1913), xiii, 1449–73, 19 February.

217    94. Bonar Law Papers 29/1/29: Hamilton to Bonar Law, 24 February 1913.

217    95. *Com. Deb.*, 5th series (1913), xlix, 77. 2 and 3 Geo. 5, c. 29.

217    96. *Railway Times* (10 May 1913), 471; the increases were of course within the statutory maxima.

217    97. *Daily Telegraph* (1 March 1913), 4. *Yorkshire Observer* (12 April 1913), 10. *The Times* (8 May 1913), 17; (21 June), 19. *Railway Times* (2 August 1913), 112–3. A. H. H. Matthews, *op. cit.*, 245.

217    98. B.T.H.R. RCA 1/5 No. 3595, 11 June 1913. P.R.O. MT6/2193/6047 part 2/1913, file 6047 of 1913: Cane to Buxton, 12 June 1913.

# Notes

Page

217 99. P.R.O. CAB 37/116/51: Cabinet paper by Buxton, "Enquiry into Railway Companies of Great Britain", 23 July 1913.

217 100. Asquith MSS. 7, fols. 61–2: Asquith to George V, 31 July 1913.

217 101. *Railway Times* (25 October 1913), 389 and 404.

217 102. *Ibid.* (8 November 1913), 442.

218 103. B.T.H.R. RC 1/58, Minutes of Evidence given before the Royal Commission on Railways, 1914, q. 7659: evidence of Owens, 11 June 1914.

218 104. *The Times* (11 November 1913), 17. *Daily News* (13 November 1913), 9; (15 November) 9.

218 105. *Railway News* (4 April 1914), 732.

218 106. *Ibid.* (8 August 1914), 267; (15 August), 298. The Irish companies remained under private control till the end of 1916, when the 1871 Act was applied to them also, and an Irish Railway Executive formed: W. E. Simnett, *Railway Amalgamation in Great Britain* (1923), 20.

218 107. B.T.H.R. RCA 1/5 No. 3665, 25 November 1914.

218 108. *Morning Post* (2 October 1914), 4. *Railway Review* (9 October 1914), 9. P.R.O. MT6/2323/11230/1914, file 11230 of 1914: Sir Guy Granet to Sir H. L. Smith, 2 October 1914.

218 109. Simnett, *op. cit.*, 19. In 1896 the Army Railway Council had been formed; known from 1903 as the War Railway Council, it was dissolved when the Railway Executive Committee came into being. A voluntary organization of railway officers, to study the movement of troops by train, and known as the Engineers and Railway Staff Corps, had been formed as early as 1865: *ibid.*, 18; and see J. A. B. Hamilton, *Britain's Railways in World War I* (1967), 18–24.

219 110. Bonar Law Papers 24/3/38: memo. by Lord Balcarres for Bonar Law, 15 November 1911.

219 111. B.T.H.R. RCA 1/5 No. 3568, 5 March 1913; LBS 1/84, 55, 19 February 1913; SEC 1/34, mins. 6923 and 6953; SER 1/63, pp. 196–8.

219 112. *Ibid.*, RCA 1/5, meeting of committee, 16 April 1913; No. 3590, 6 May 1913.

219 113. *Ibid.*, RCA 1/4 Nos. 3048, 3082, 3135, 3206, 3215.

219 114. *Ibid.*, RCA 1/5 No. 3615, 28 January 1914, 5: speech by Claude de Jamineau Andrewes, honorary solicitor and solicitor of the London & North Western Railway.

219 115. *The Times* (30 October 1907), 4. *Financial Times* (28 July 1913), 4.

219 116. B.T.H.R. RCA 4/2: Papers of the Southern Railway Company relating to the "Square Deal" Campaign 1932–8.

220 117. B.T.H.R. RCA 1/5 Nos. 3550 and 3581; HRP(S) 40, 17: extract from minutes of meeting of General Managers, held at the Railway Clearing House, 5 November 1912 (minute 829).

220 118. B.T.H.R. RCA 4/1: typescript memo. by A. B. Cane, 25 July 1929, headed "The Railway Companies' Association", 1.

220 119. *Ibid.*, typescript memo. headed "Constitution of the Association", undated but probably *circa* 1913, 7–8; the author was probably A. B. Cane.

220 120. 11 and 12 Geo. 5, c. 55. The Act also did away with the maximum rate system and the Act of 1894. In place of the Railway and Canal Commission a Railway Rate Tribunal was established to fix standard rates cal-

culated to bring the railways a net revenue equivalent to the revenue they
enjoyed in 1913; the tribunal did not complete its task until 1928; see
P. J. Cain, *op. cit.*, 235.

221  121. B.T.H.R. RCA 4/1: typescript memo. by A. B. Cane, 25 July 1929, headed
"The Railway Companies' Association", 2–7. As a result of the general
election of 1922 the number of railway directors in the Commons was reduced to 17; at the time of nationalization the number had fallen to six:
*Bradshaw* (1923); P. S. Bagwell, *Journal of Transport History*, vii (1965), 82.

# Notes to Chapter 14

223  1. Viscount Gladstone, 'The Chief Whip in the British Parliament', *American
Political Science Review*, xxi (1927), 519–23. J. K. Pollock, Jr, 'British
Party Organization', *Political Science Quarterly*, xlc (1930), 165–6. M.
Ostrogorski, *Democracy and the Organisation of Political Parties*, vol I.
(1902), 137.

223  2. Introduction by R. H. S. Crossman to Walter Bagehot's *The English
Constitution* (Fontana Library paperback edn) (1963), 42. In view of his
important position in the Labour hierarchy, Mr Crossman's reference to the
party's acceptance of "the semi-military discipline of democratic centra-
lism" is revealing, though not wholly accurate.

223  3. A. L. Lowell, 'The Influence of Party upon Legislation in England and
America', *Annual Report of the American Historical Association for the Year
1901* (Washington 1902), vol. I, 326–7.

223  4. Lowell, *op. cit.*, 542; for a later use of Lowell's arguments see J. B. Christoph, 'The Study of Voting Behaviour in the British House of Commons',
*Western Political Quarterly*, xi (1958), 306.

223  5. This is a crucial qualification, which Hugh Berrington, in his important
article 'Partisanship and Dissidence in the Nineteenth-Century House of
Commons', *Parliamentary Affairs*, xxi (1967–8), 338–74, appears to have
ignored. Division lists have never been the be-all and end-all of parliamentary party cohesion.

224  6. S. H. Beer, *op. cit.*, 9–28, 33–43.

226  7. The Railway and Canal Traffic Act, 1888; Regulation of Railways Act,
1889; Railway Servants (Hours of Labour) Act, 1893; Railway and Canal
Traffic Act, 1894; and Railway Employment (Prevention of Accidents)
Act, 1900.

226  8. See J. R. Vincent, *Pollbooks: How Victorians Voted* (Cambridge 1967), 94,
for the Carlisle elections of 1865 and 1868, and H. J. Hanham, *Elections
and Party Management: Politics in the Time of Disraeli and Gladstone* (1959),
51, for the hold of Swindon over Sir Daniel Gooch's constituency, Crick-
lade. See also chapter I, note 26.

226  9. A case in point is the example of the Furness Railway, the Duke of Devonshire, and the development of Barrow-in-Furness: S. Pollard, 'North-West

Coast Railway Politics in the Eighteen Sixties', *Transactions of the Cumberland & Westmorland Antiquarian & Archaeological Society*, New Series, lii (1953), 160–77; S. Pollard and J. D. Marshall, 'The Furness Railway and the Growth of Barrow', *Journal of Transport History*, i (1953–4), 109–26.

226   10. For some discussion of the part played by railways in American politics see Ostrogorski, *op. cit.*, vol. II (1902), 181–5.

227   11. W. R. Lawson, *British Railways: A Financial and Commercial Survey* (1913), 218–23; Lawson was chairman of the Railway Shareholders' Association. See also 'The Passing of the Railway Director', *Railway Gazette* (26 December 1947), 719–20.

227   12. *Railway News* (18 February 1905), 287.

227   13. C. H. Grinling, *The Ways of Our Railways* (1905), 12–14.

# Notes to Appendix

229   1. By then *Bradshaw* had changed its title. Of the 1848 volume there were two editions, both 1847; between then and 1863 the work underwent several changes of title. From the edition of that year (vol. xv) to 1923 (vol. lxxv) it appeared as *Bradshaw's Railway Manual, Shareholders' Guide and Official Directory*. Details of the various editions can be found in G. Ottley, *A Bibliography of British Railway History* (1965), p. [468], item 7949.

230   2. Previous estimates of the size of the railway interest in Parliament, as given in P. M. Williams, *E.H.R.*, lxvii, 1952, 37–73, and P. S. Bagwell, *Journal of Transport History*, vii (1965), 65–86, appear not to have taken this point into account.

230   3. G. G. Lerry, *Henry Robertson* (Oswestry 1949), *passim*.

232   4. For 1868 this figure refers to the number of director-M.P.s first elected in that year.

232   5. Includes two Liberal-Conservatives.

232   6. Includes three Liberal-Conservatives.

232   7. Includes four Liberal-Conservatives.

232, 234 8. Includes one Liberal-Conservative.

233   9. For 1874 this figure refers to the number of director-M.P.s first elected in that year.

233, 234, 238 10. Includes Henry Robertson.

233, 239, 243 11. For the period February 1874 to January 1876.

234   12. For 1880 this figure refers to the number of director-M.P.s first elected in that year.

235   13. For the House of Lords, the figures under "New members" refer in all years to those peers who first held directorships in those years. No figures have been given for 1868.

236   14. No figures have been given for 1874.

237   15. No figures have been given for 1880.

*Page*

238    16. For 1885 and 1886 these figures refer to the number of director-M.P.s first elected in those years.

238    17. Includes Sir M. A. Bass, who was returned in 1886 but went to the Lords in the same year as Lord Burton; he is also included in the House of Lords' figures.

238    18. Includes Sir R. A. Cross, who was returned in 1886 but went to the Lords in the same year as Viscount Cross; he is also included in the House of Lords' figures.

239    19. Includes Lord Richard Grosvenor, who went to the Lords in 1886 as Lord Stalbridge.

239    20. These figures include those who did not stand for election, and those who stood but were defeated.

240    21. For 1892 this figure refers to the number of director-M.P.s first elected in that year.

241    22. For 1895 this figure refers to the number of director-M.P.s first elected in that year.

242    23. No figures have been given for 1885.

243    24. No figures have been given for 1892.

244    25. No figures have been given for 1895.

245    26. For 1900 this figure refers to the number of director-M.P.s first elected in that year.

246    27. No figures have been given for 1900.

247    28. For 1906 this figure refers to the number of director-M.P.s first elected in that year.

247    29. For January 1910 this figure refers to the number of director-M.P.s first elected then.

248    30. For December 1910 this figure refers to the number of director-M.P.s first elected then.

248    31. The Conservative and Liberal Unionist parties were formally merged in 1912; thus for the years 1912–14 a total "Unionist" figure has been given.

249    32. No figures have been given for 1906.

250    33. No figures have been given for 1910.

# Index

# Index

# Index

# Index

# Index

# Index